FAIRY TAIL

フェアリーテイル

Chapter 336: I'll Give Today All I've Got

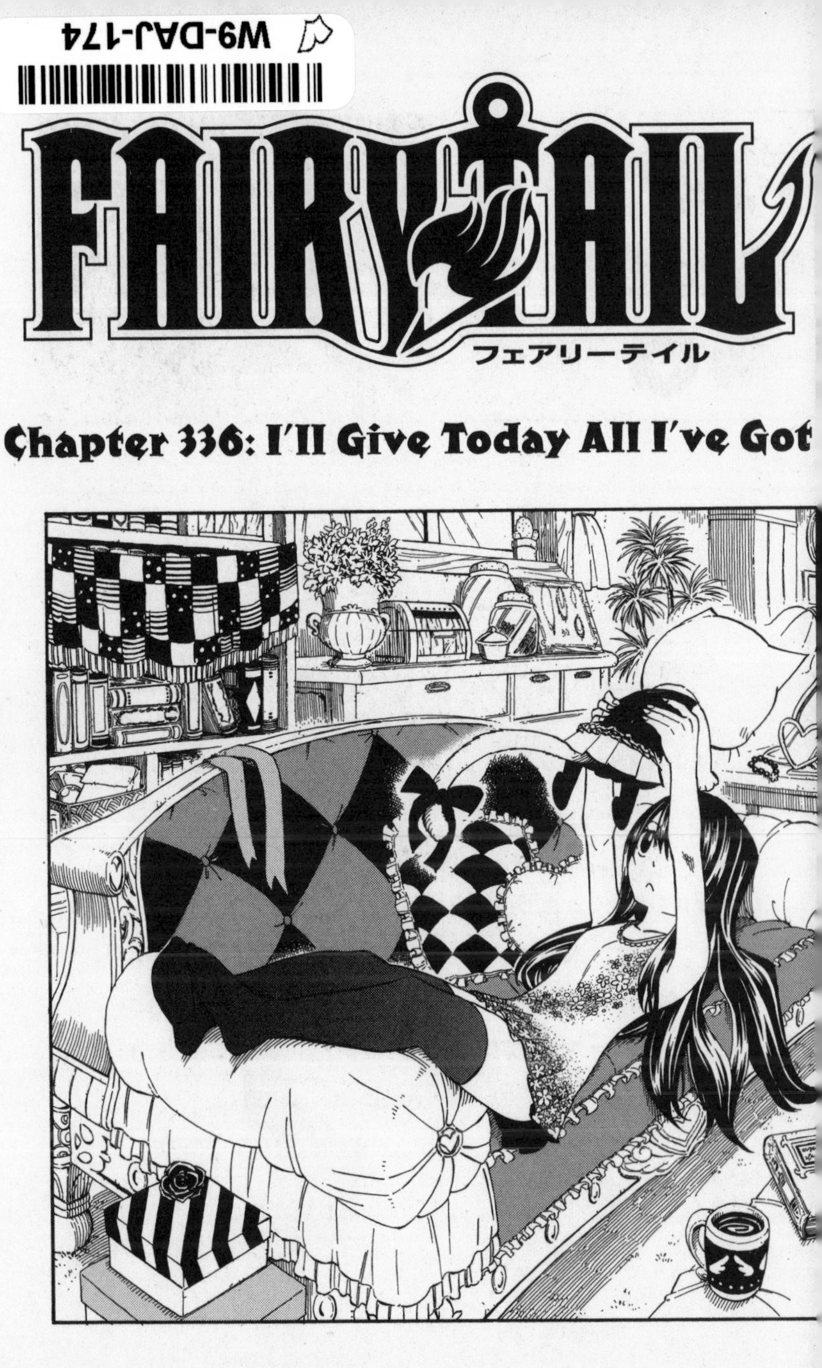

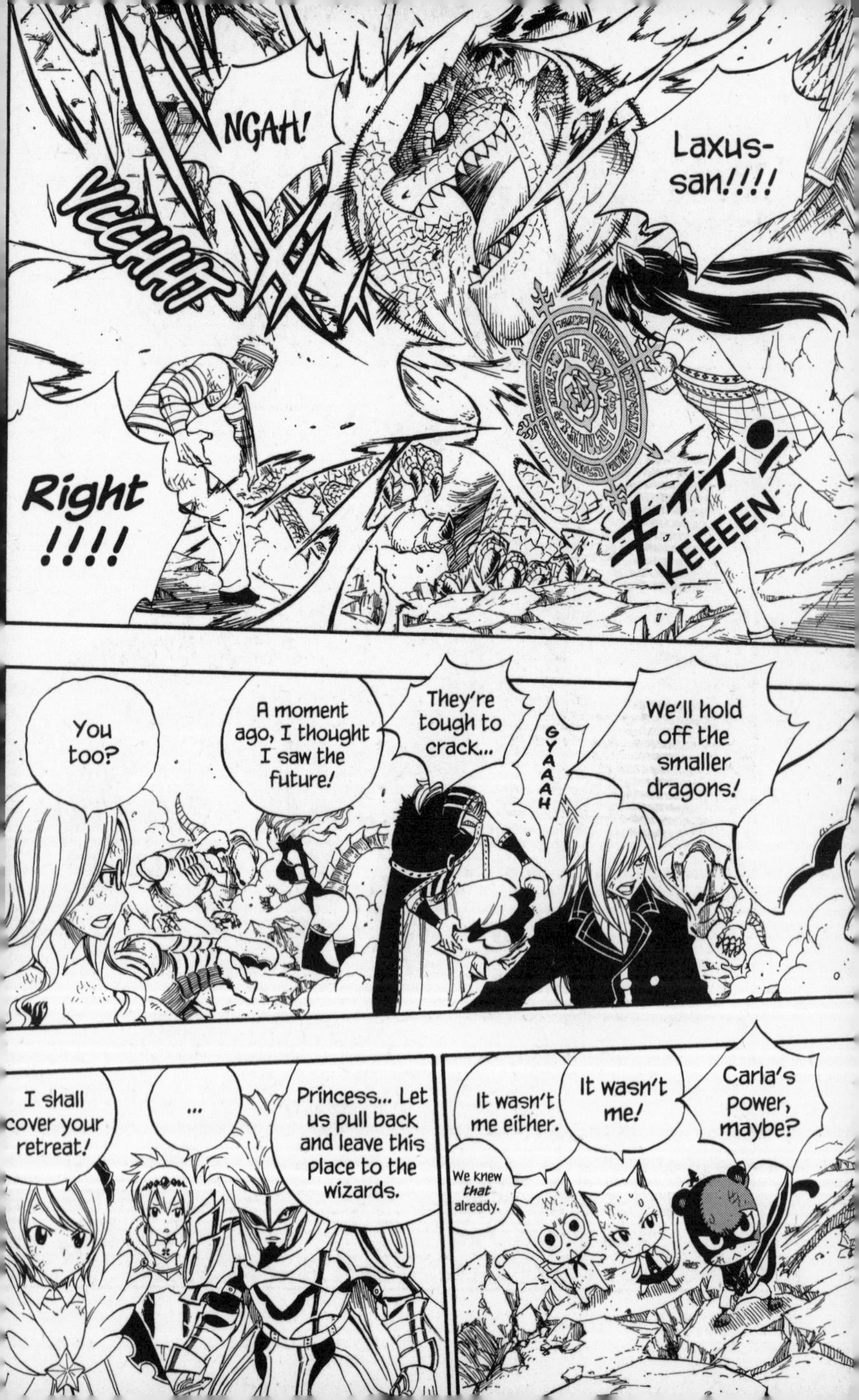
Laxus-san!!!!
NGAH!
VCCHHT
KEEEEN
Right!!!!
We'll hold off the smaller dragons!
GYAAAH
They're tough to crack...
A moment ago, I thought I saw the future!
You too?
Carla's power, maybe?
It wasn't me!
It wasn't me either.
We knew *that* already.
Princess... Let us pull back and leave this place to the wizards.
...
I shall cover your retreat!

FAIRY TAIL

40

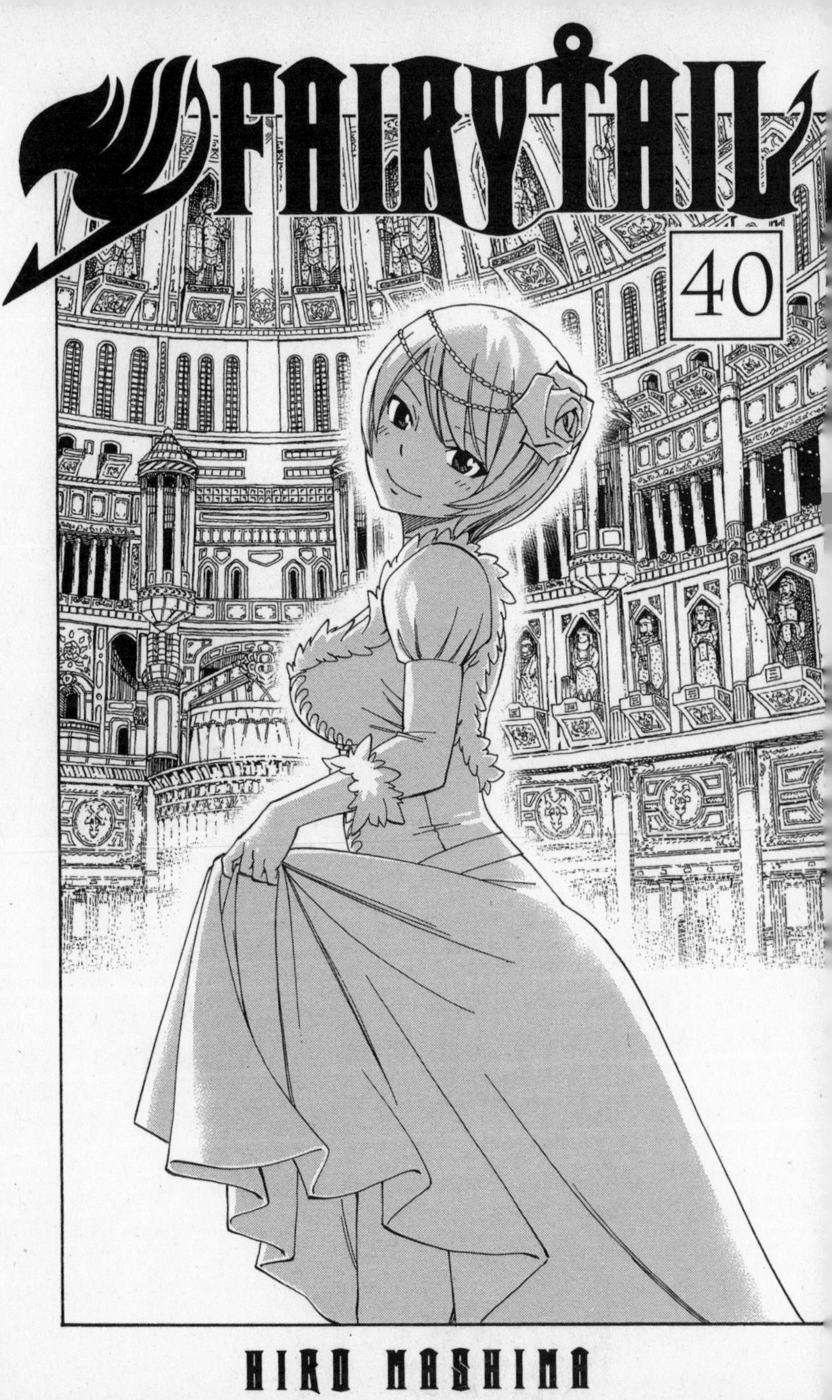

HIRO MASHIMA

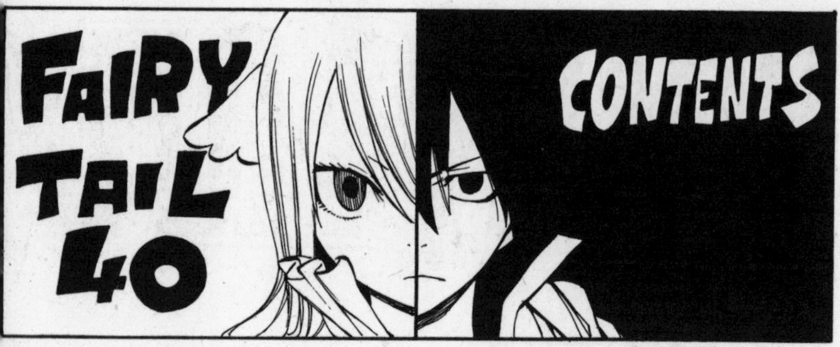
FAIRY TAIL 40
CONTENTS

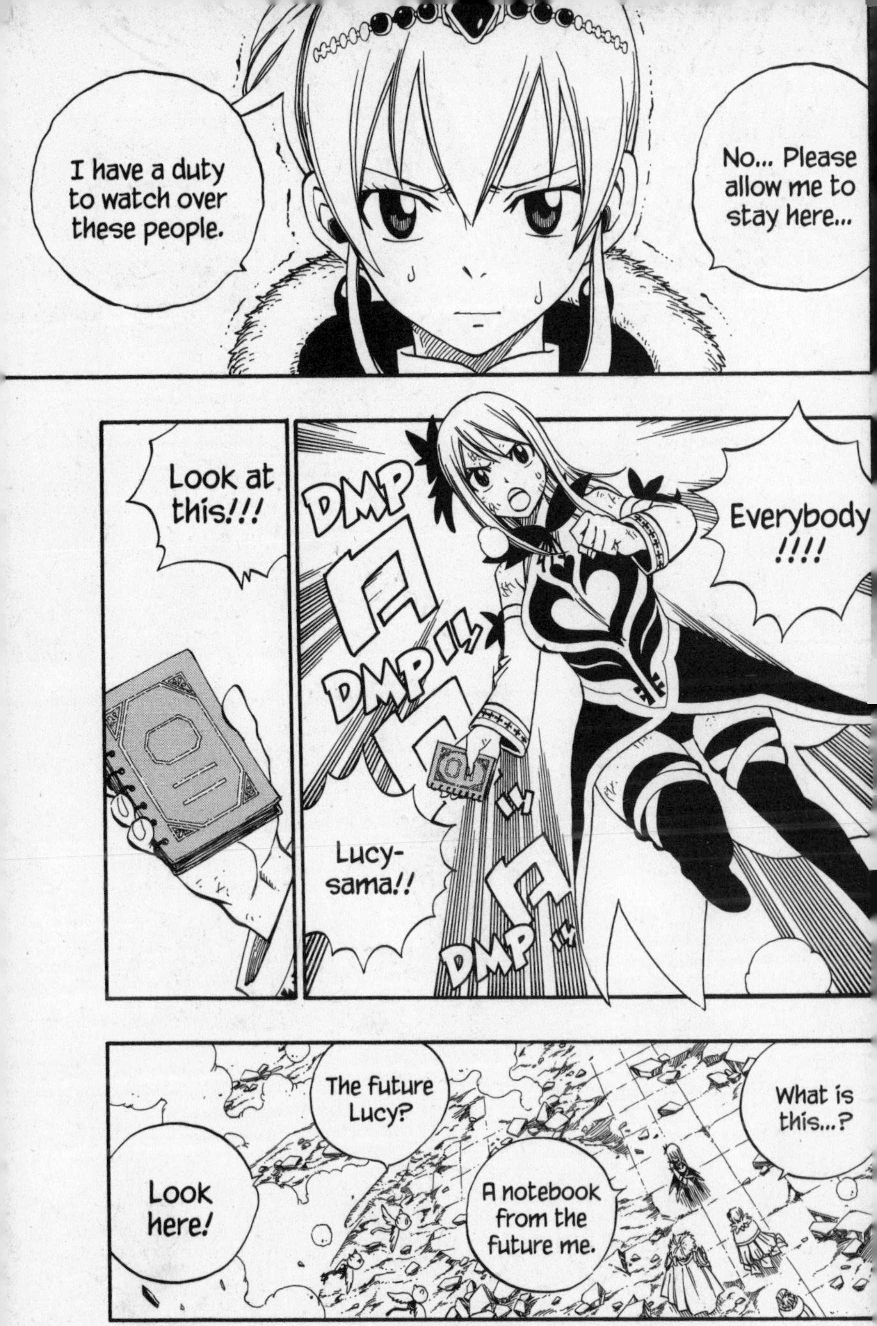
No... Please allow me to stay here...
I have a duty to watch over these people.
Everybody!!!!
DMP
DMP
DMP
Lucy-sama!!
Look at this!!!
What is this...?
The future Lucy?
A notebook from the future me.
Look here!

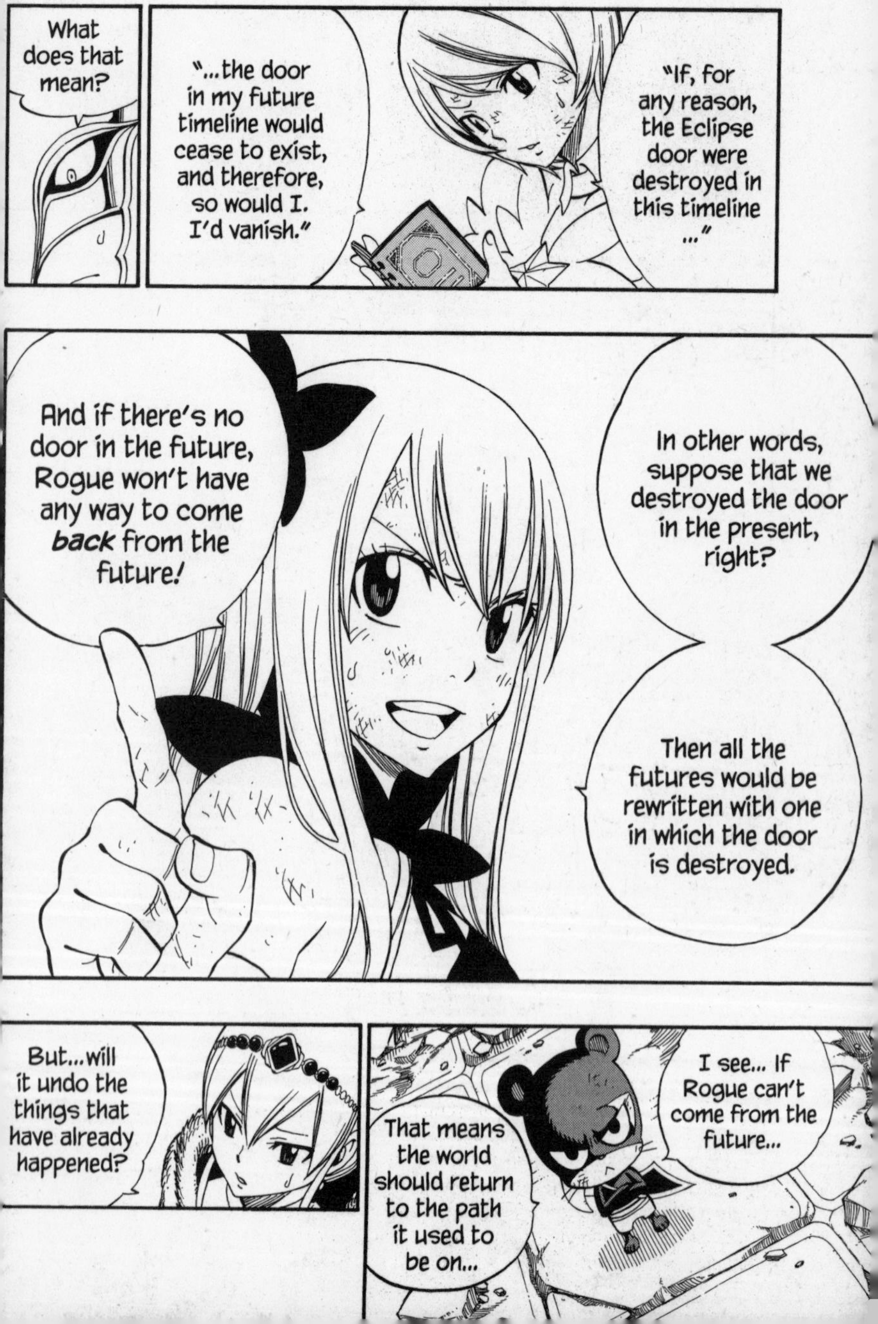
"If, for any reason, the Eclipse door were destroyed in this timeline ..."
"...the door in my future timeline would cease to exist, and therefore, so would I. I'd vanish."
What does that mean?
In other words, suppose that we destroyed the door in the present, right?
Then all the futures would be rewritten with one in which the door is destroyed.
And if there's no door in the future, Rogue won't have any way to come *back* from the future!
I see... If Rogue can't come from the future...
That means the world should return to the path it used to be on...
But...will it undo the things that have already happened?

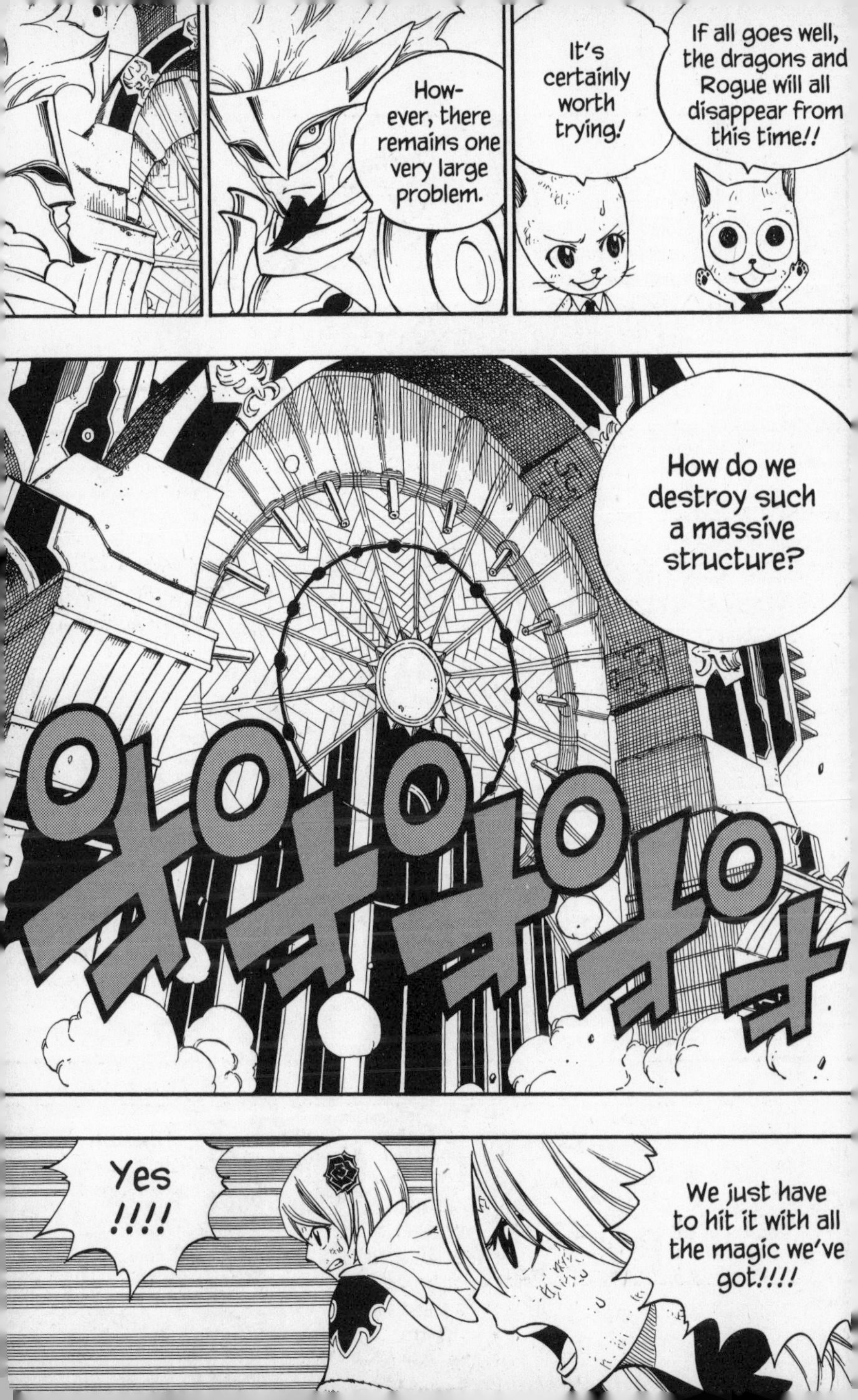
If all goes well, the dragons and Rogue will all disappear from this time!!
It's certainly worth trying!
How-ever, there remains one very large problem.
How do we destroy such a massive structure?
We just have to hit it with all the magic we've got!!!!
Yes!!!!

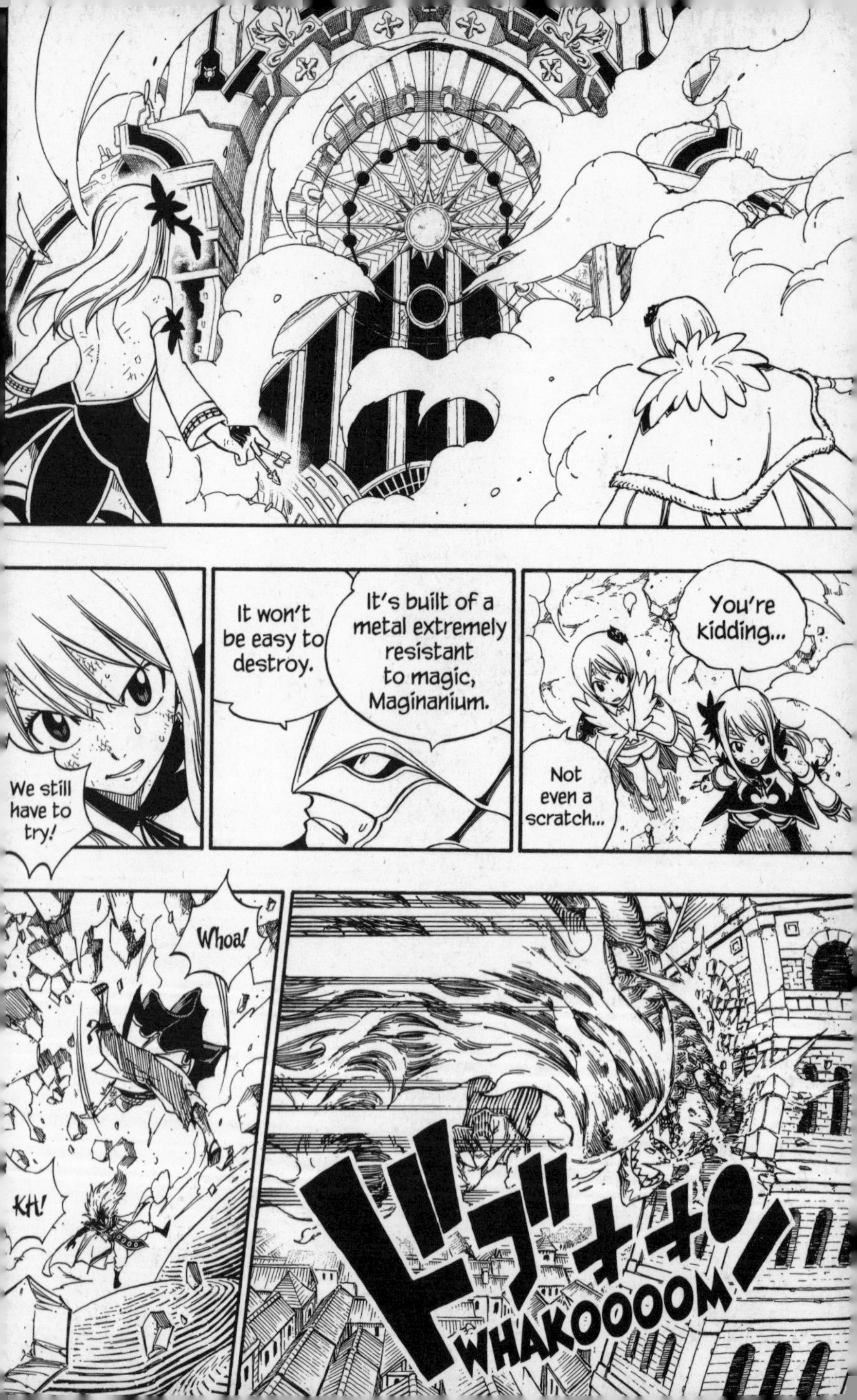
You're kidding...
Not even a scratch...
It's built of a metal extremely resistant to magic, Maginanium.
It won't be easy to destroy.
We still have to try!
WHAKOOOOM
Whoa!
Kh!

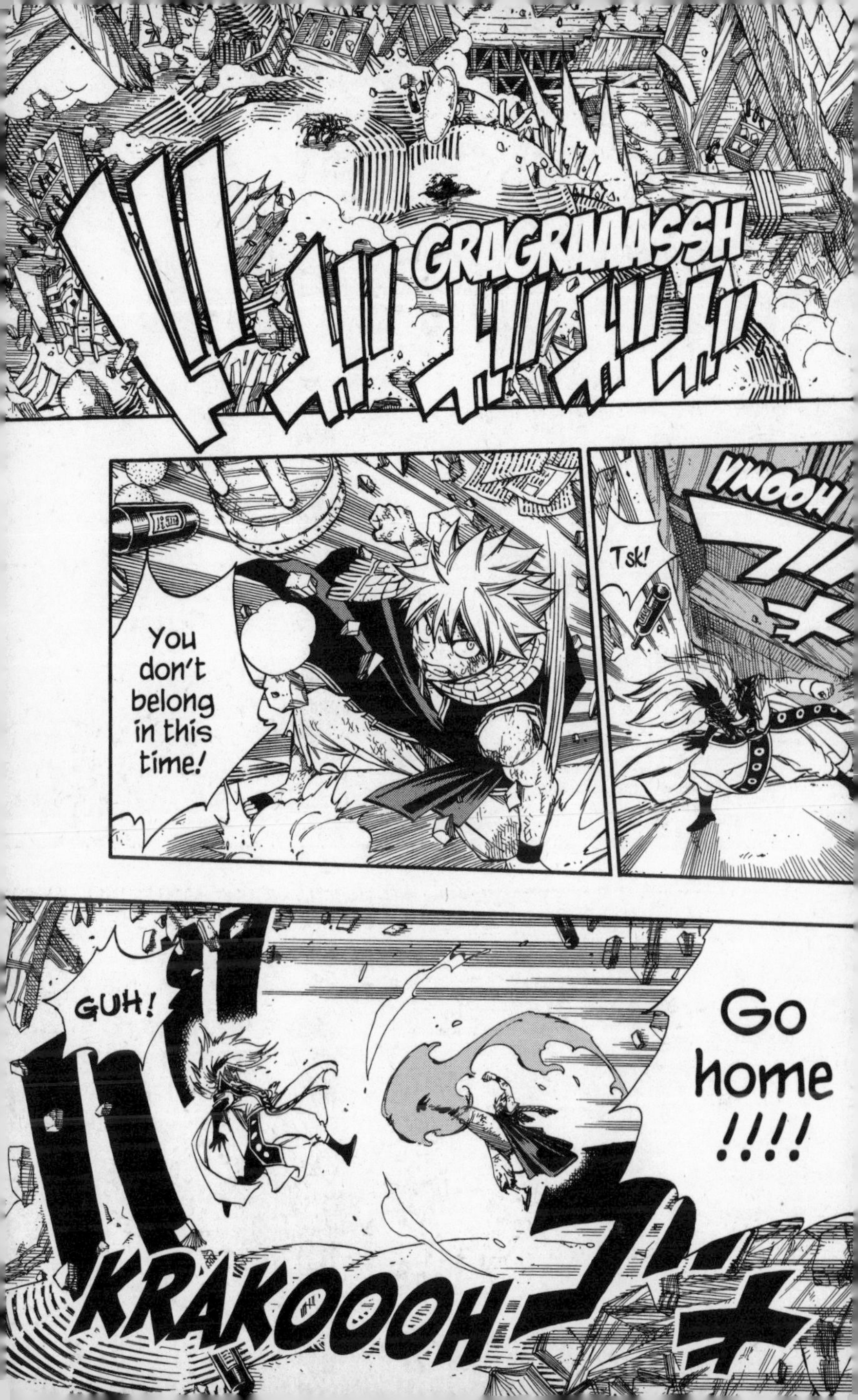
GRAGRAAASSH
VWOOH
Tsk!
You don't belong in this time!
Go home !!!!
GUH!
KRAKOOOH

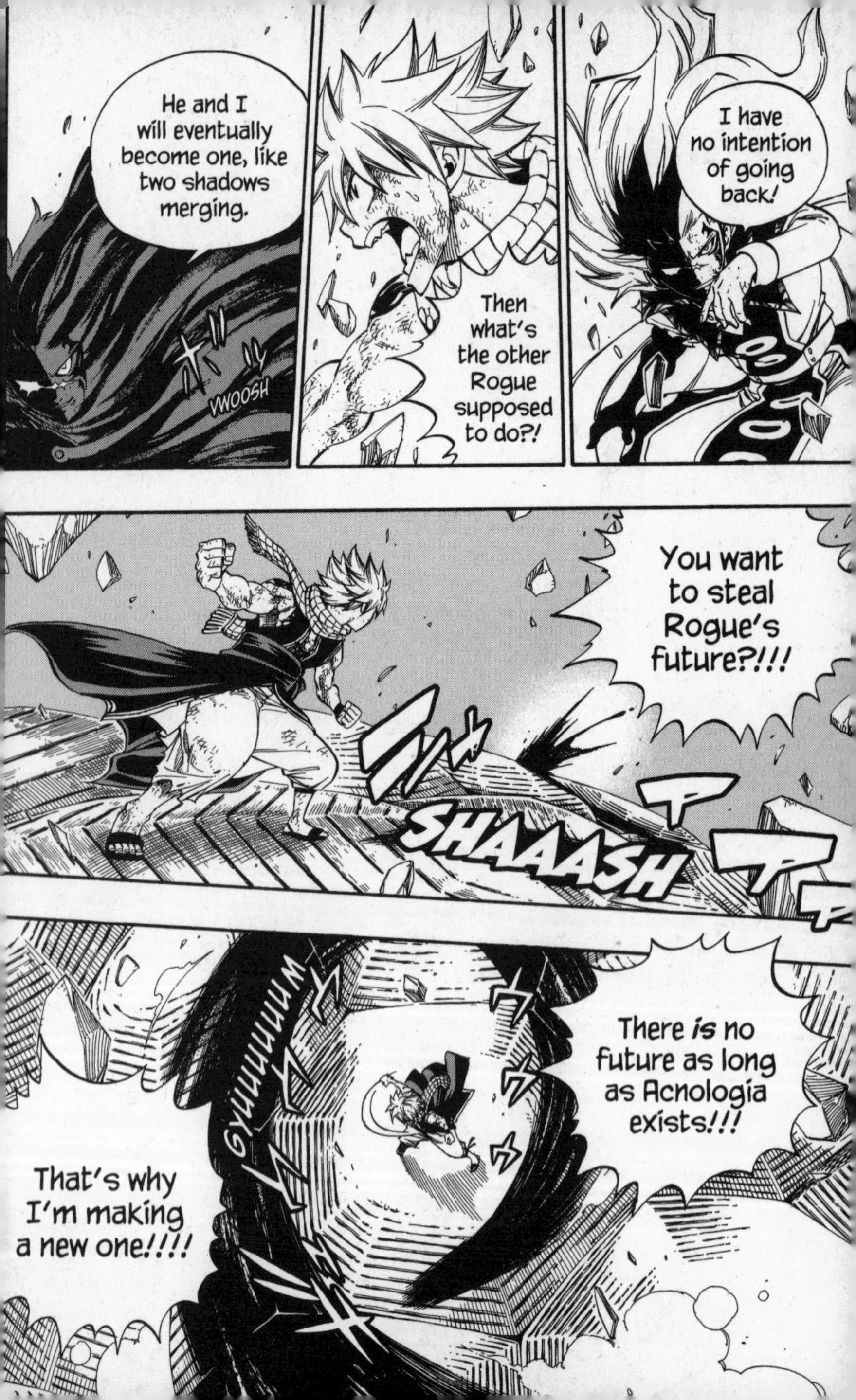
I have no intention of going back!
Then what's the other Rogue supposed to do?!
He and I will eventually become one, like two shadows merging.
VWOOSH
You want to steal Rogue's future?!!!
SHAAASH
There *is* no future as long as Acnologia exists!!!
GYuuuuuuM
That's why I'm making a new one!!!!

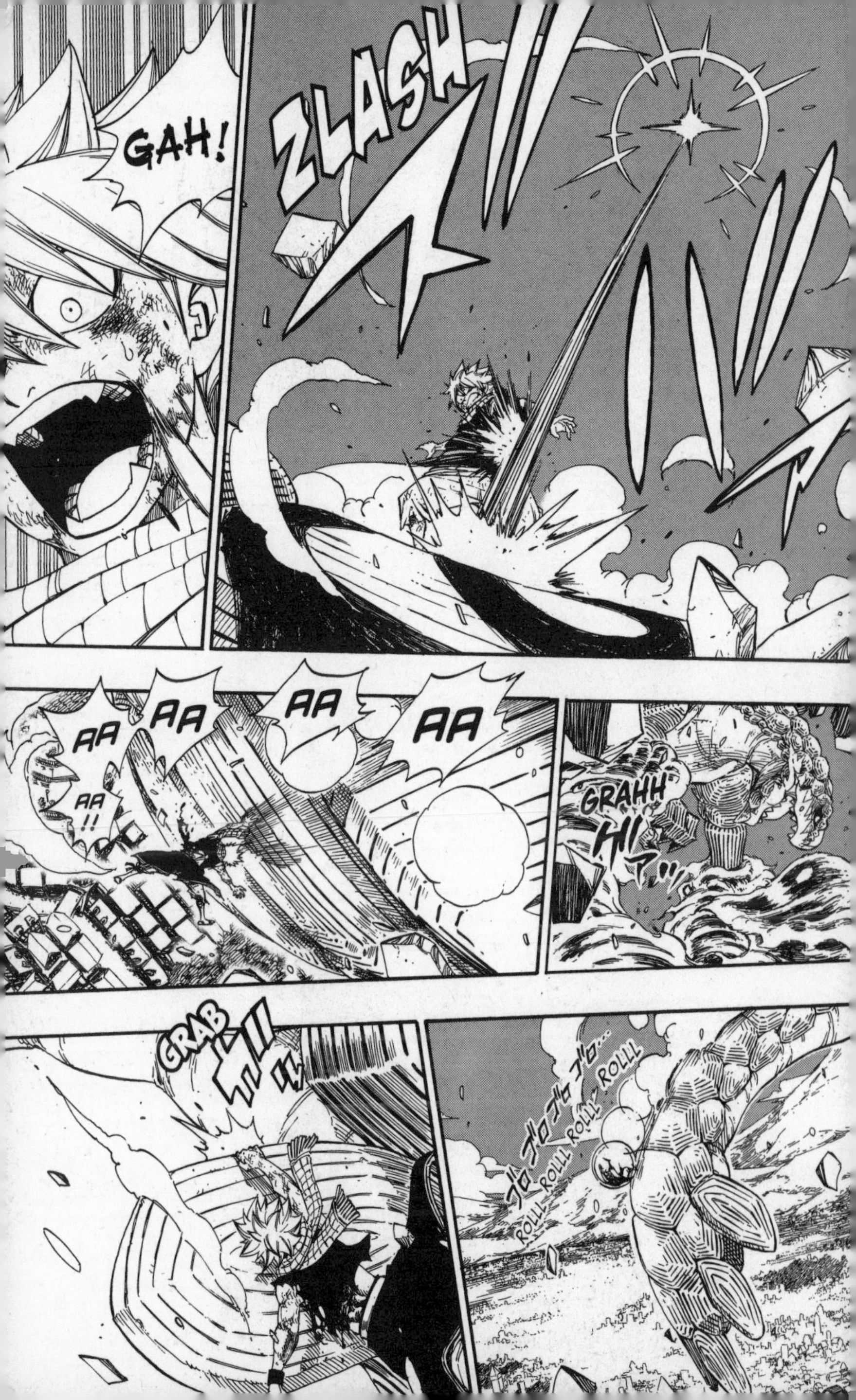
ZLASH
GAH!
GRAHH
AA
AA
AA
AA
AA !!
ROLLL ROLLL ROLLL
GRAB

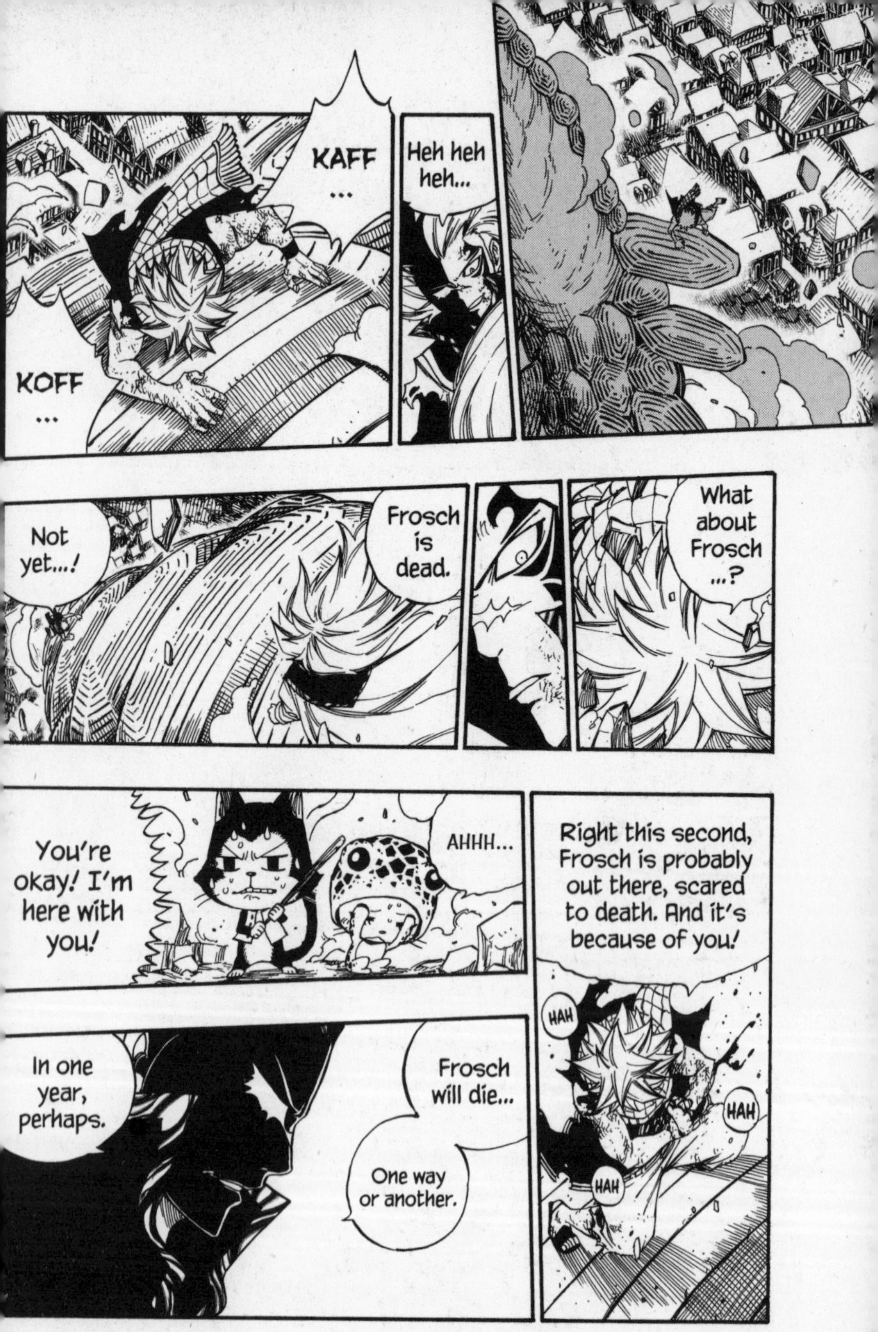
Heh heh heh...
KAFF ...
KOFF ...
What about Frosch ...?
Frosch is dead.
Not yet...!
Right this second, Frosch is probably out there, scared to death. And it's because of you!
HAH
HAH
HAH
AHHH...
You're okay! I'm here with you!
Frosch will die...
One way or another.
In one year, perhaps.

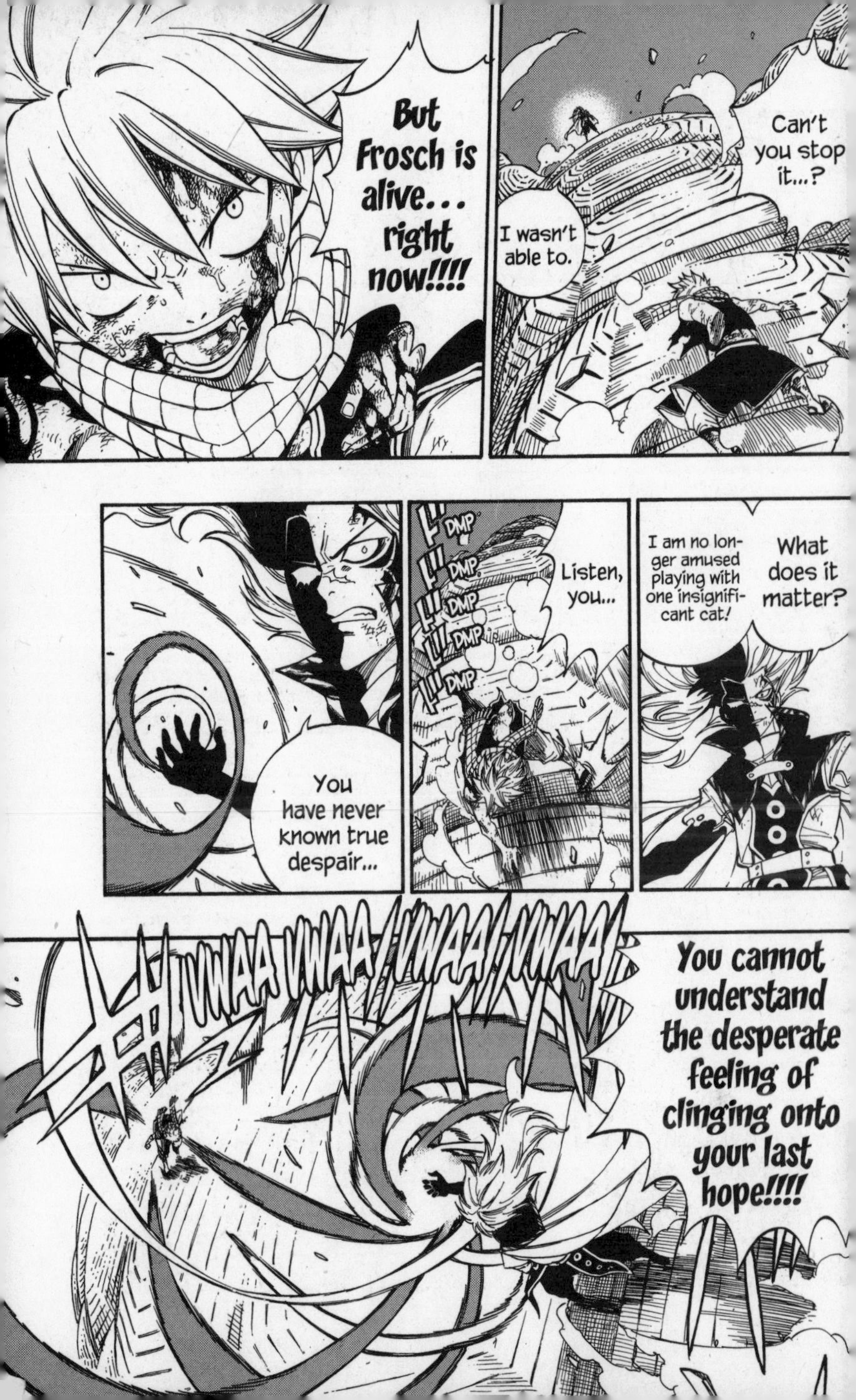

Can't you stop it...?
I wasn't able to.
But Frosch is alive... right now!!!!
What does it matter?
I am no longer amused playing with one insignificant cat!
DMP
DMP
DMP
DMP
DMP
Listen, you...
You have never known true despair...
You cannot understand the desperate feeling of clinging onto your last hope!!!!
VWAA VWAA VWAA VWAA

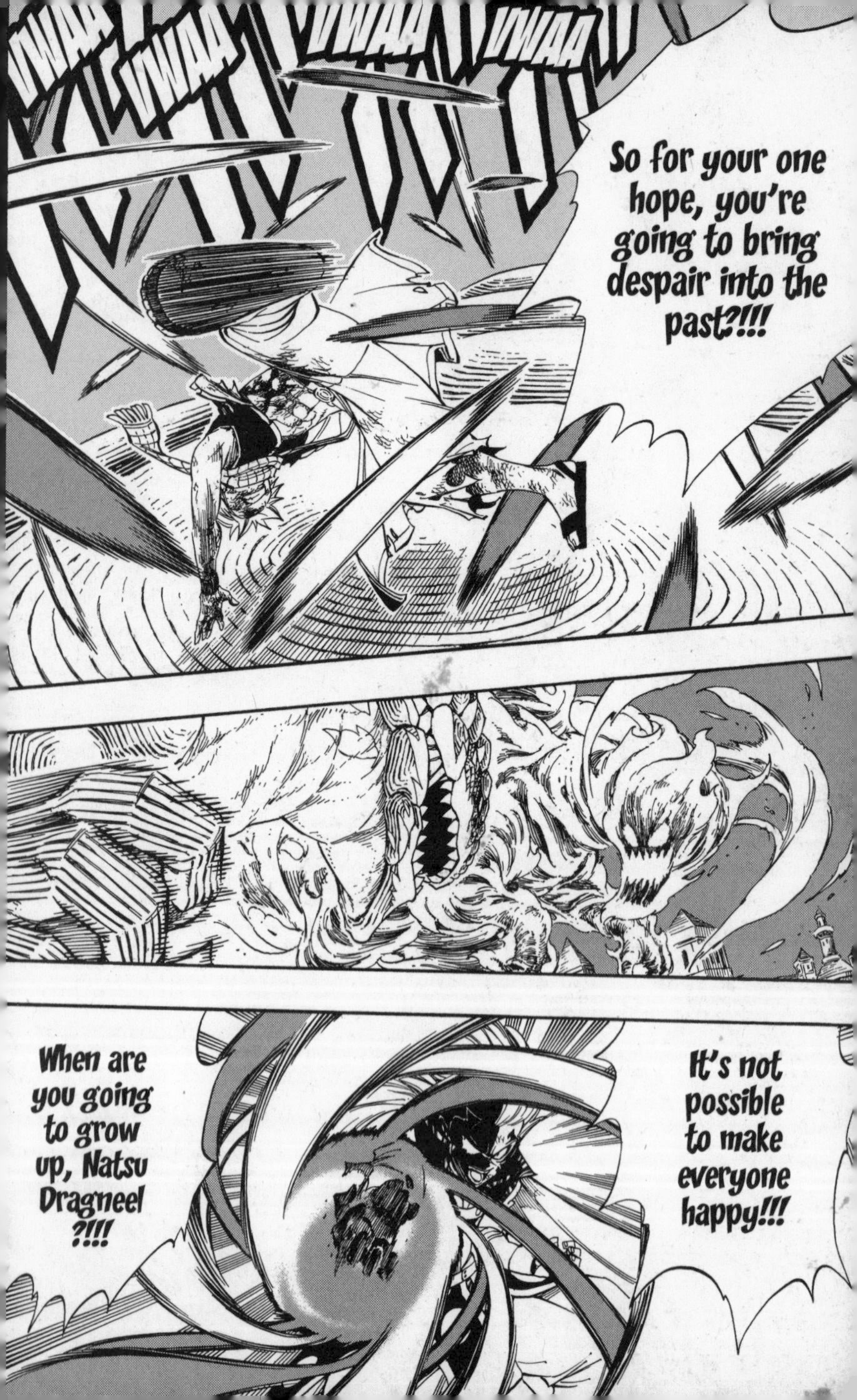
VWAA
VWAA
VWAA
VWAA
So for your one hope, you're going to bring despair into the past?!!!
It's not possible to make everyone happy!!!
When are you going to grow up, Natsu Dragneel?!!!

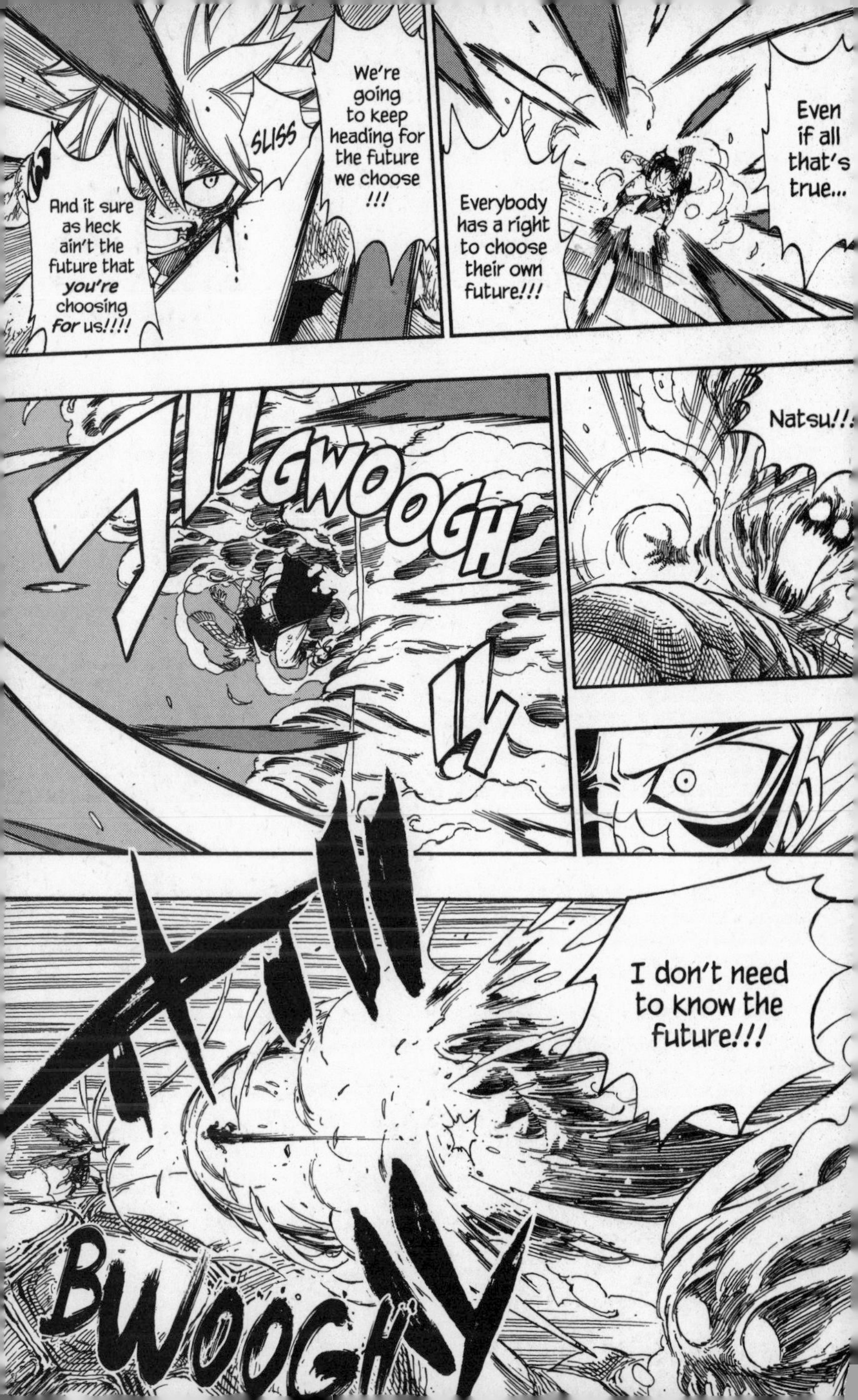
Even if all that's true...
Everybody has a right to choose their own future!!!
We're going to keep heading for the future we choose!!!
SLISS
And it sure as heck ain't the future that *you're* choosing *for* us!!!!
Natsu!!
GWOOGH
I don't need to know the future!!!
BWOOGHY

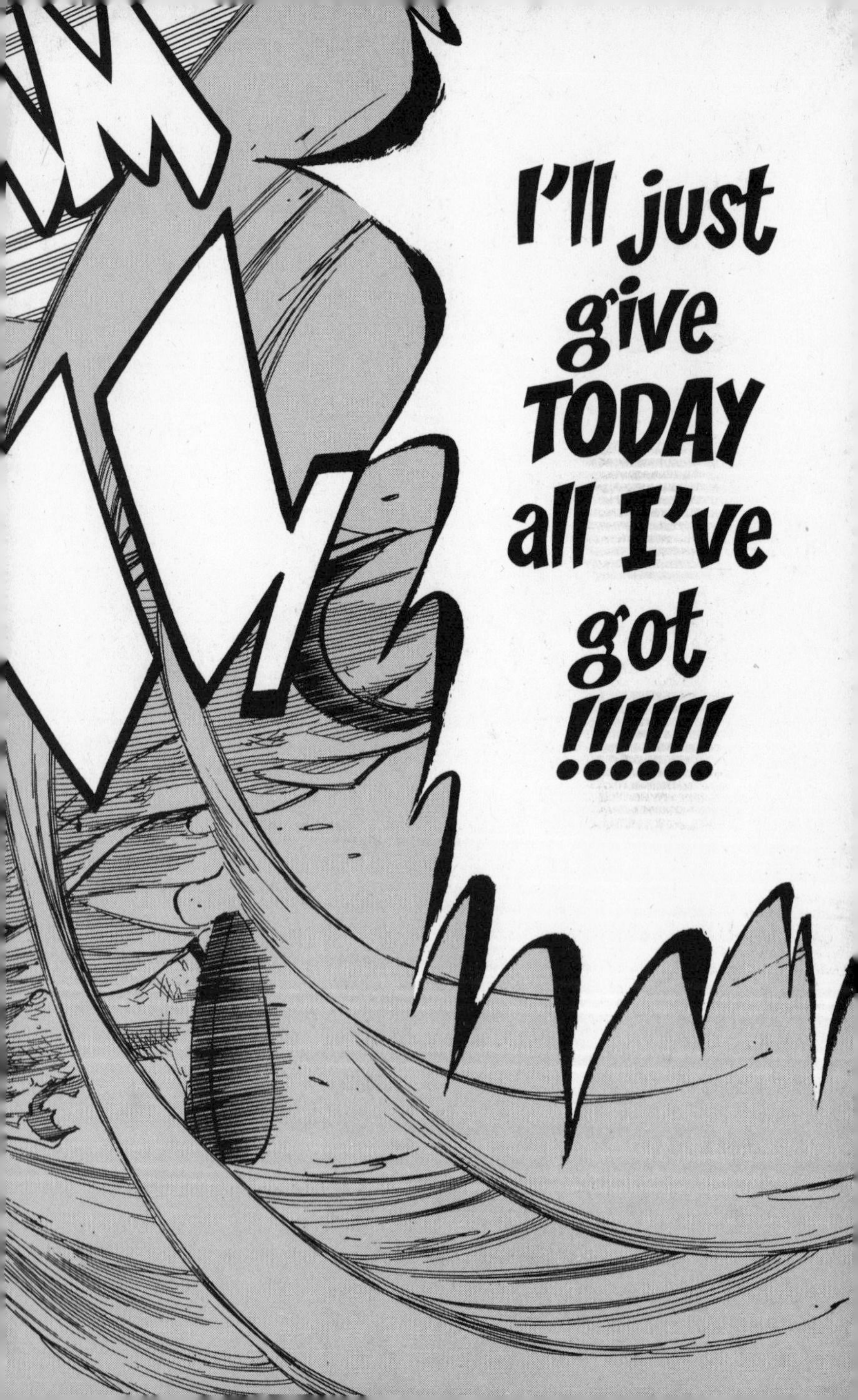
I'll just give TODAY all I've got!!!!!!

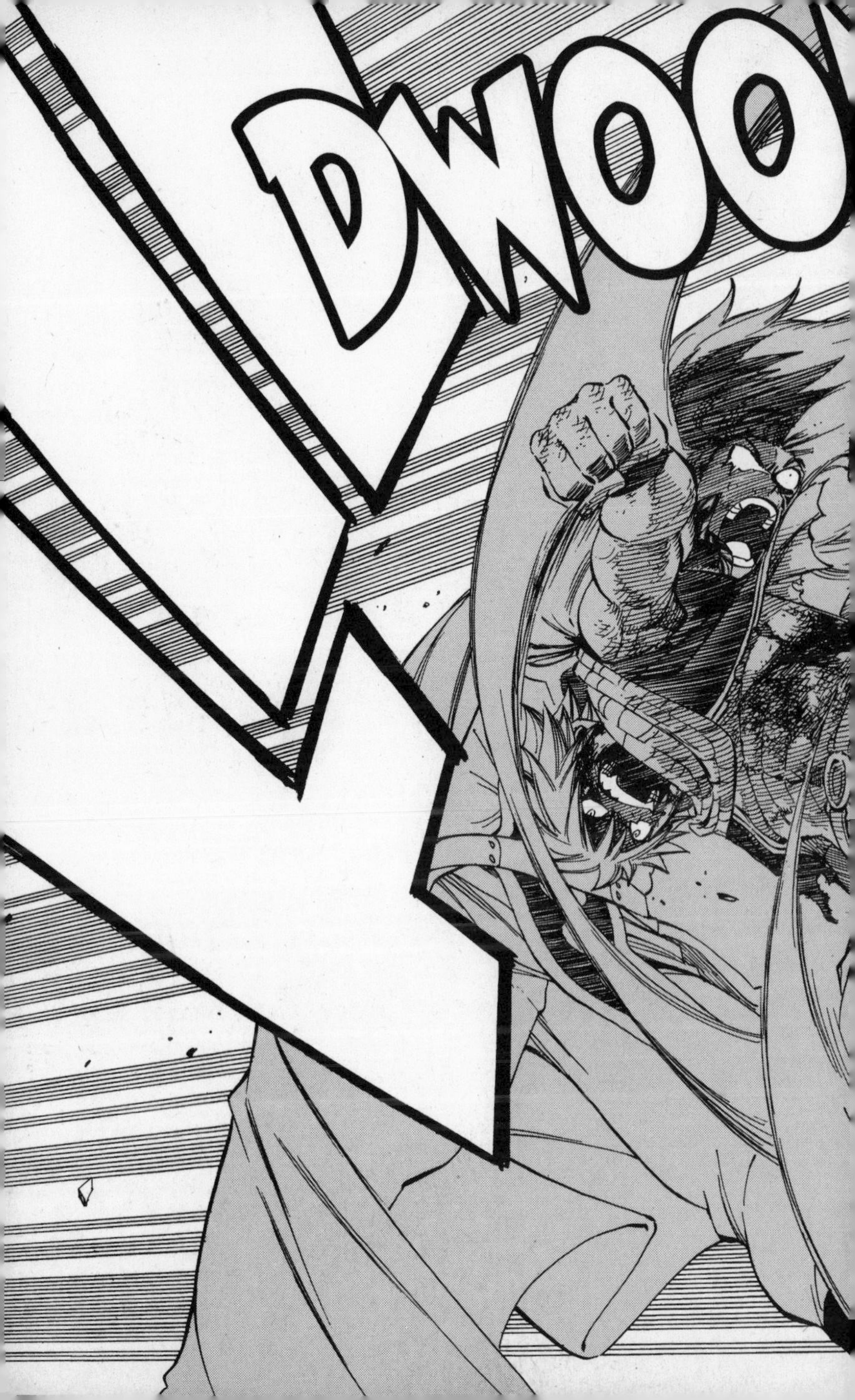
DWOO

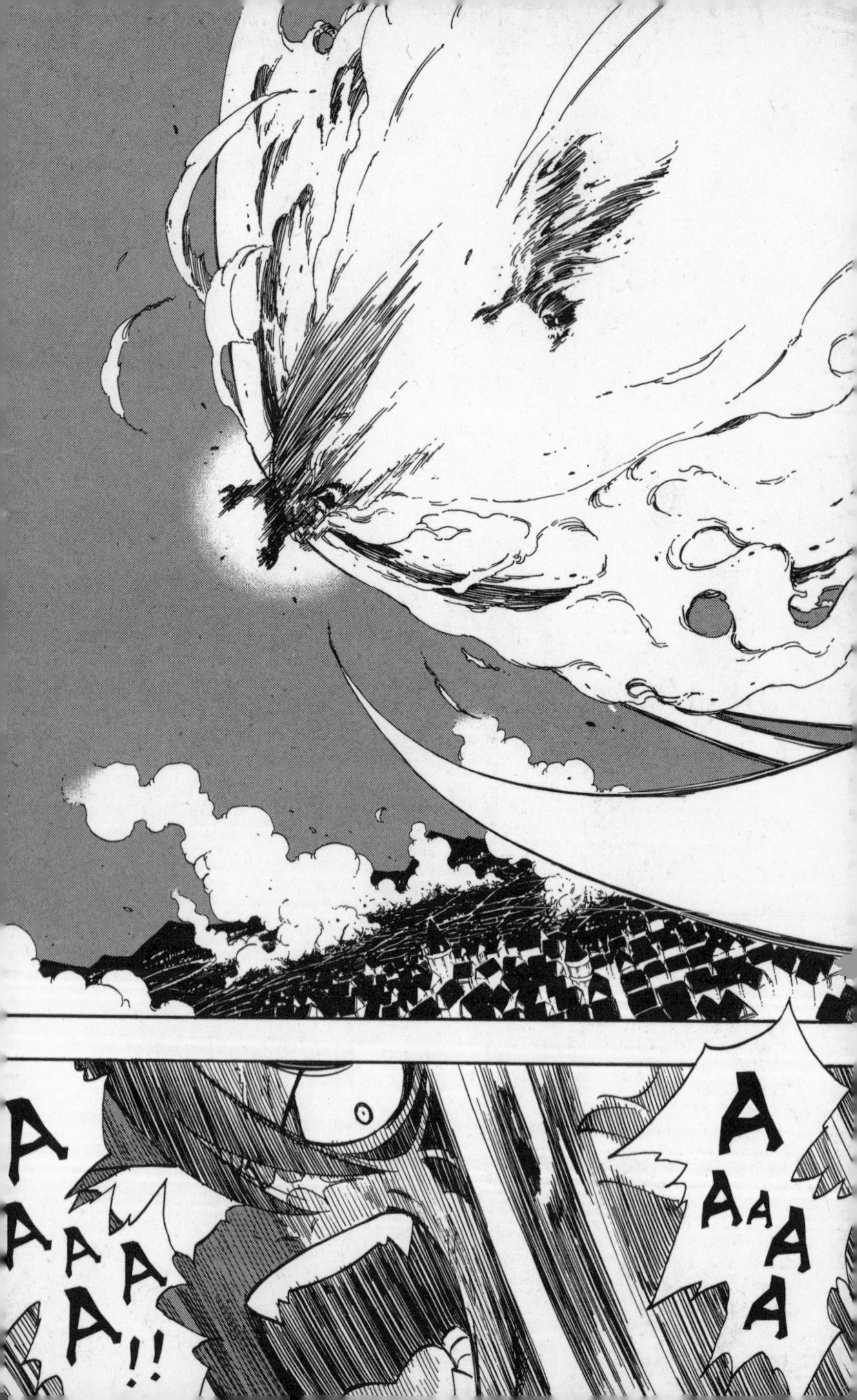
AAAAAA
AAAAA!!

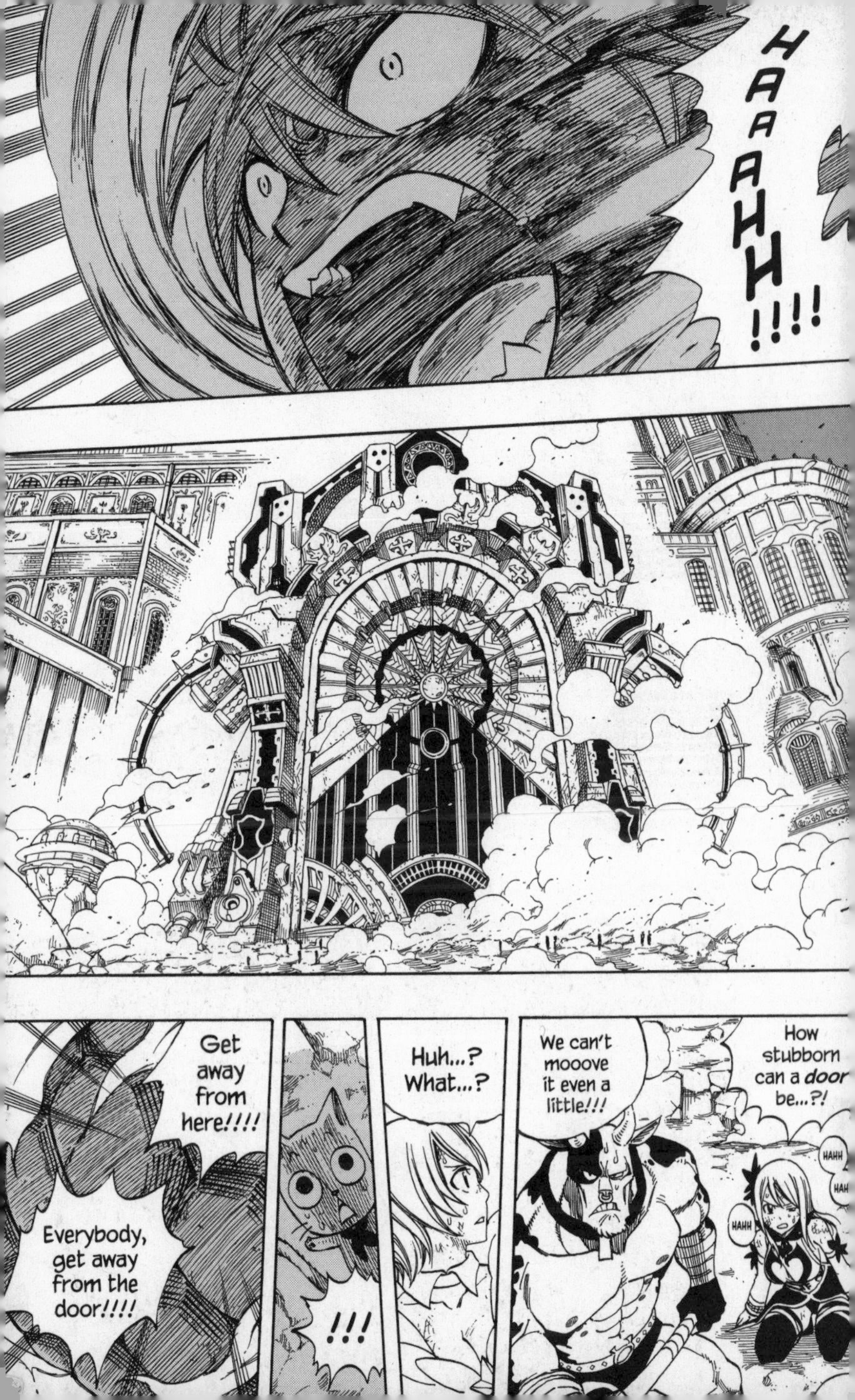
HAAAAHH!!!!
How stubborn can a *door* be...?!
HAHH
HAH
HAHH
We can't mooove it even a little!!!
Huh...? What...?
!!!
Get away from here!!!!
Everybody, get away from the door!!!!

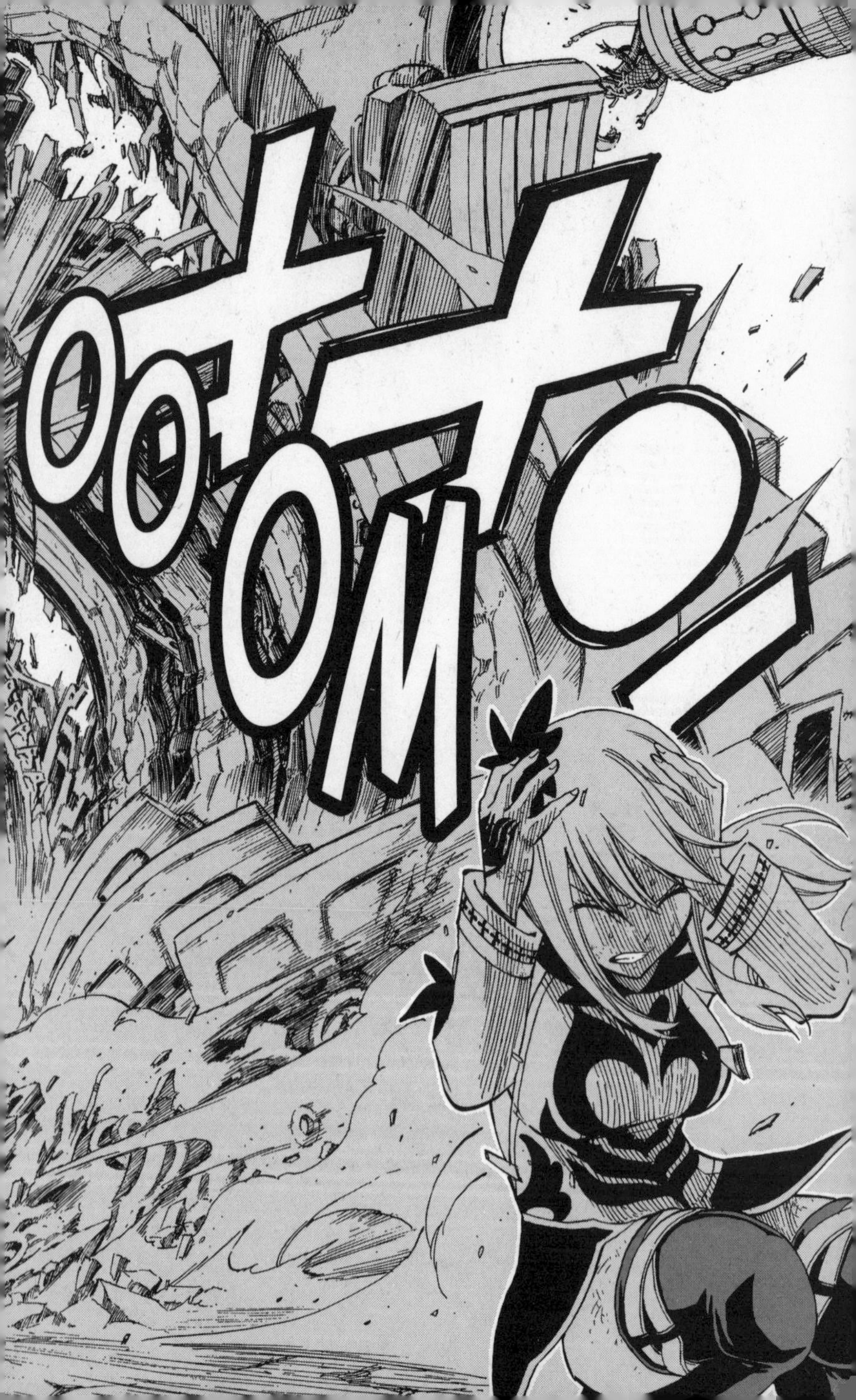

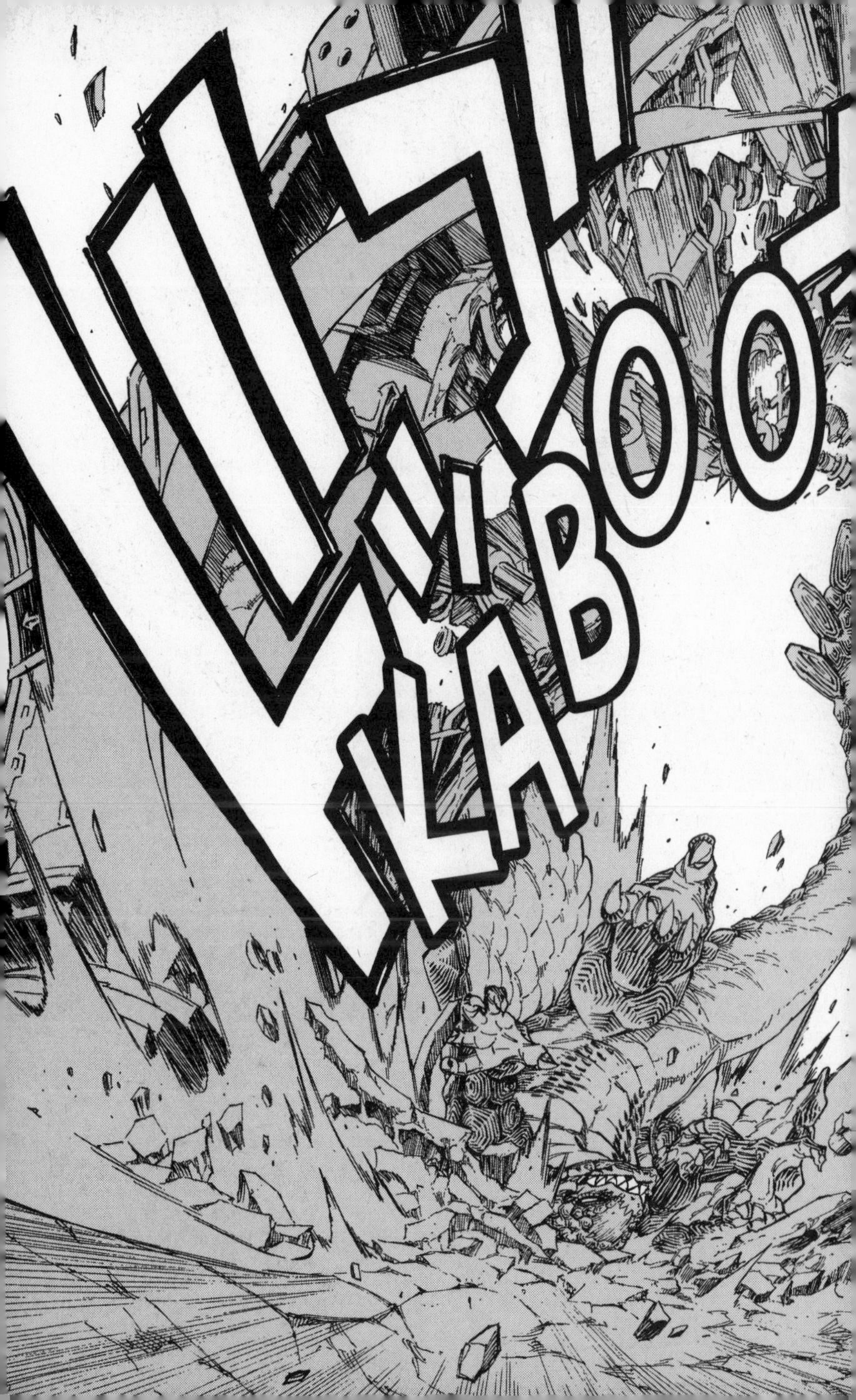
KABOO

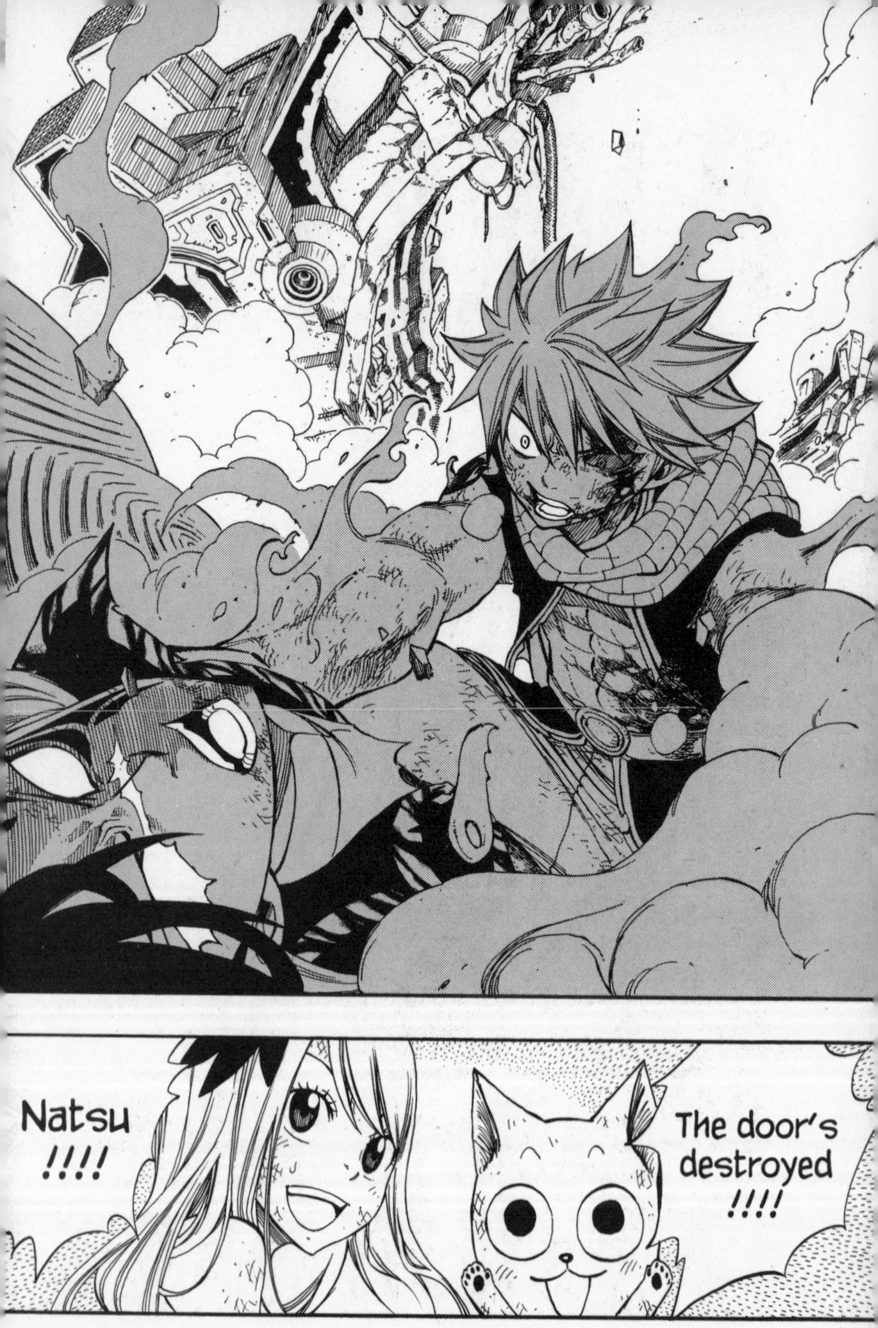
The door's destroyed !!!!
Natsu !!!!

FAIRY TAIL
フェアリーテイル

Chapter 337: The Golden Grasslands

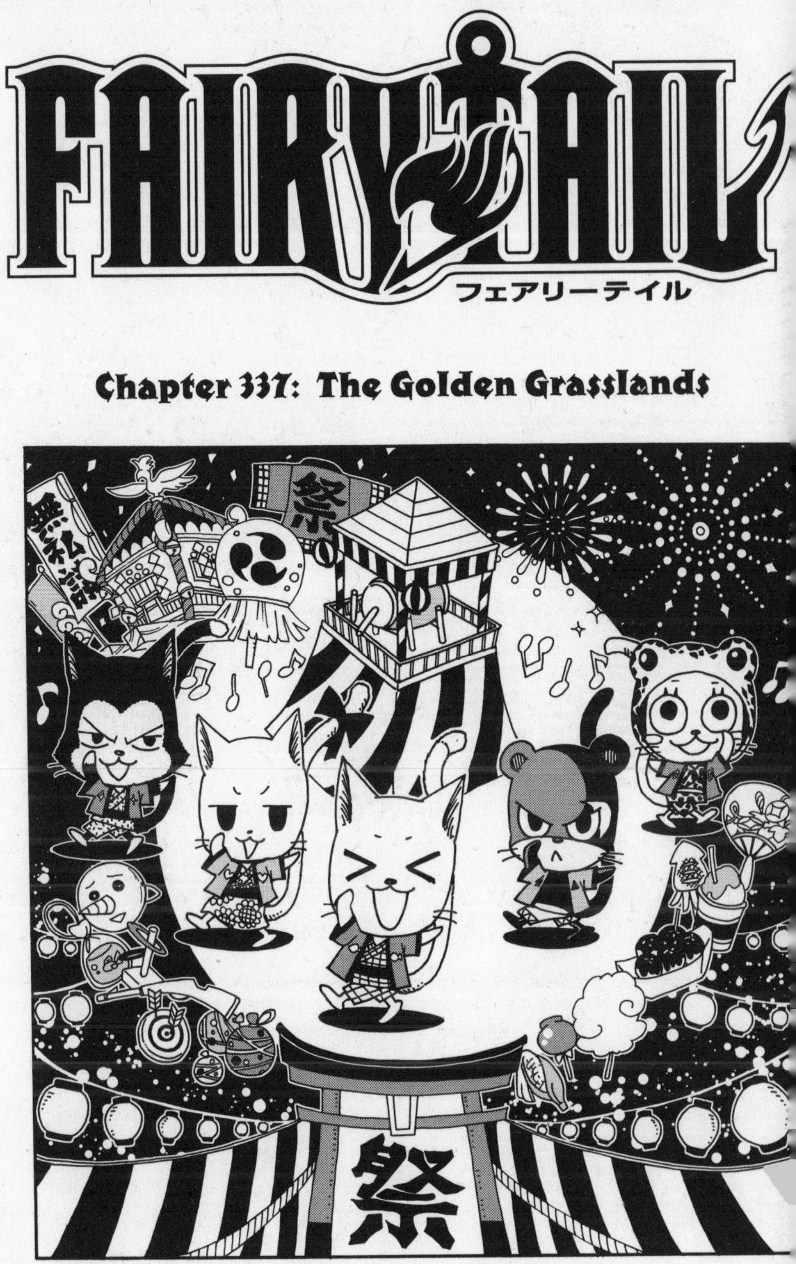
祭
祭
祭

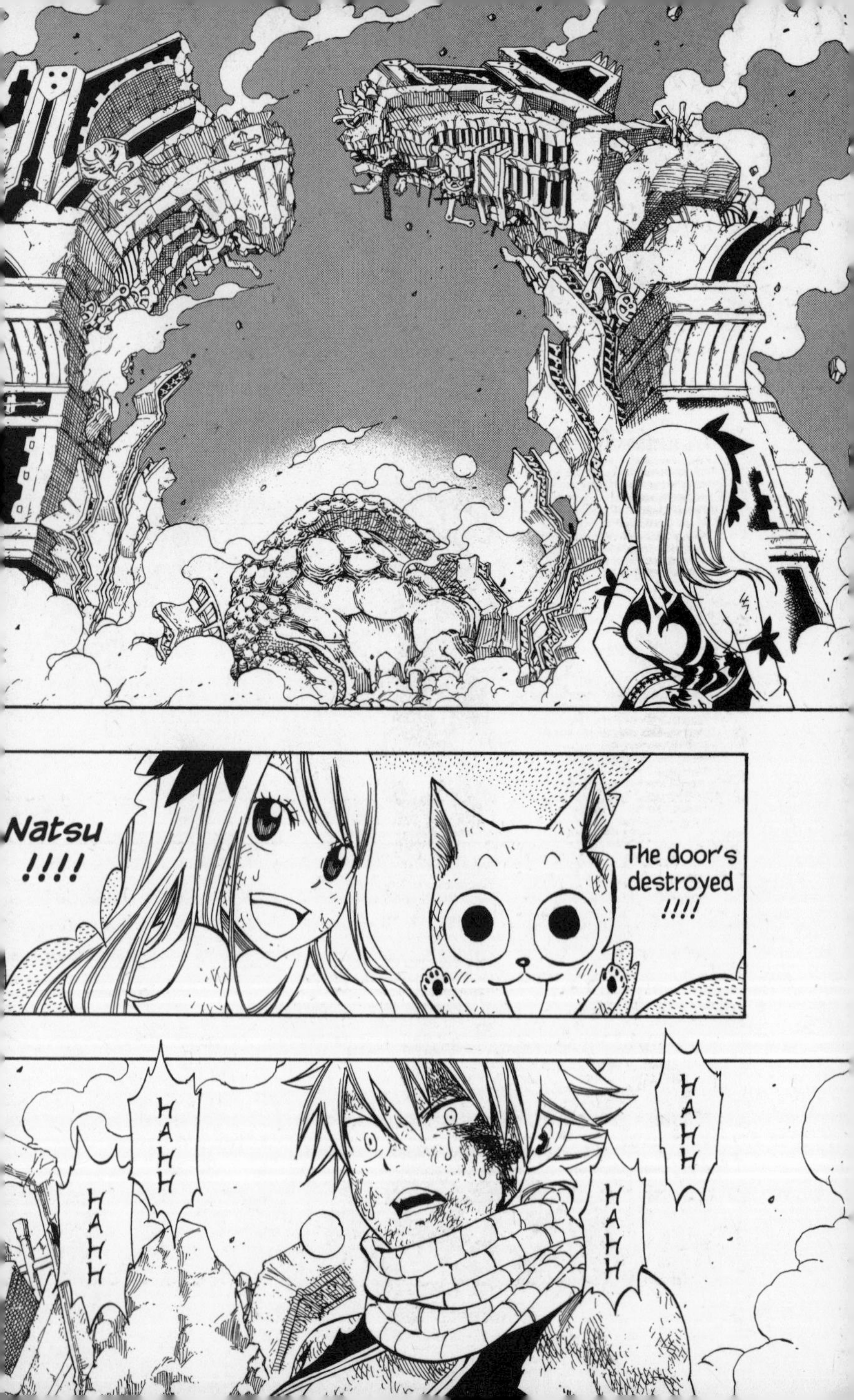
The door's destroyed !!!!
Natsu !!!!
HAHH
HAHH
HAHH
HAHH

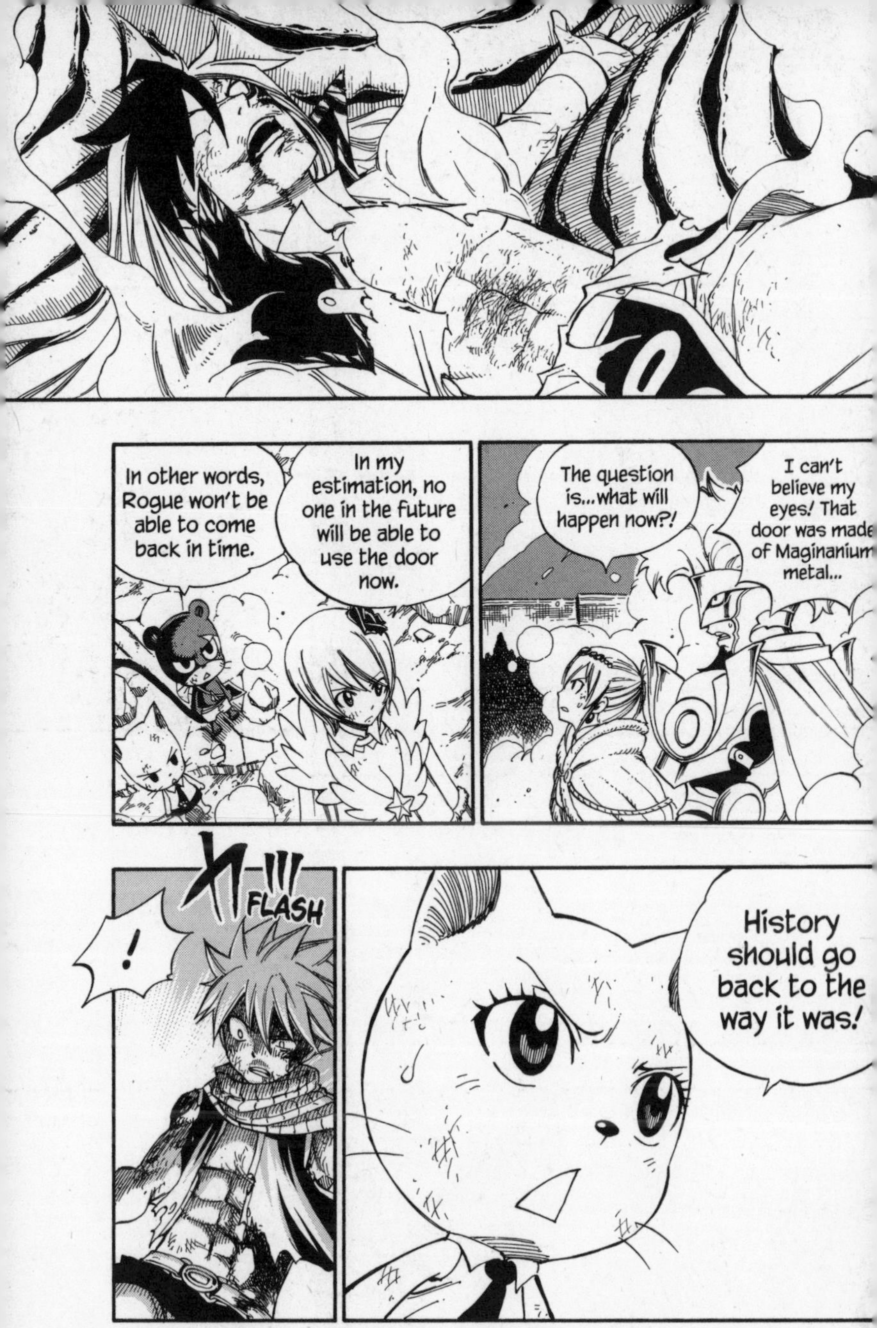
I can't believe my eyes! That door was made of Maginanium metal...
The question is...what will happen now?!
In my estimation, no one in the future will be able to use the door now.
In other words, Rogue won't be able to come back in time.
History should go back to the way it was!
FLASH
!

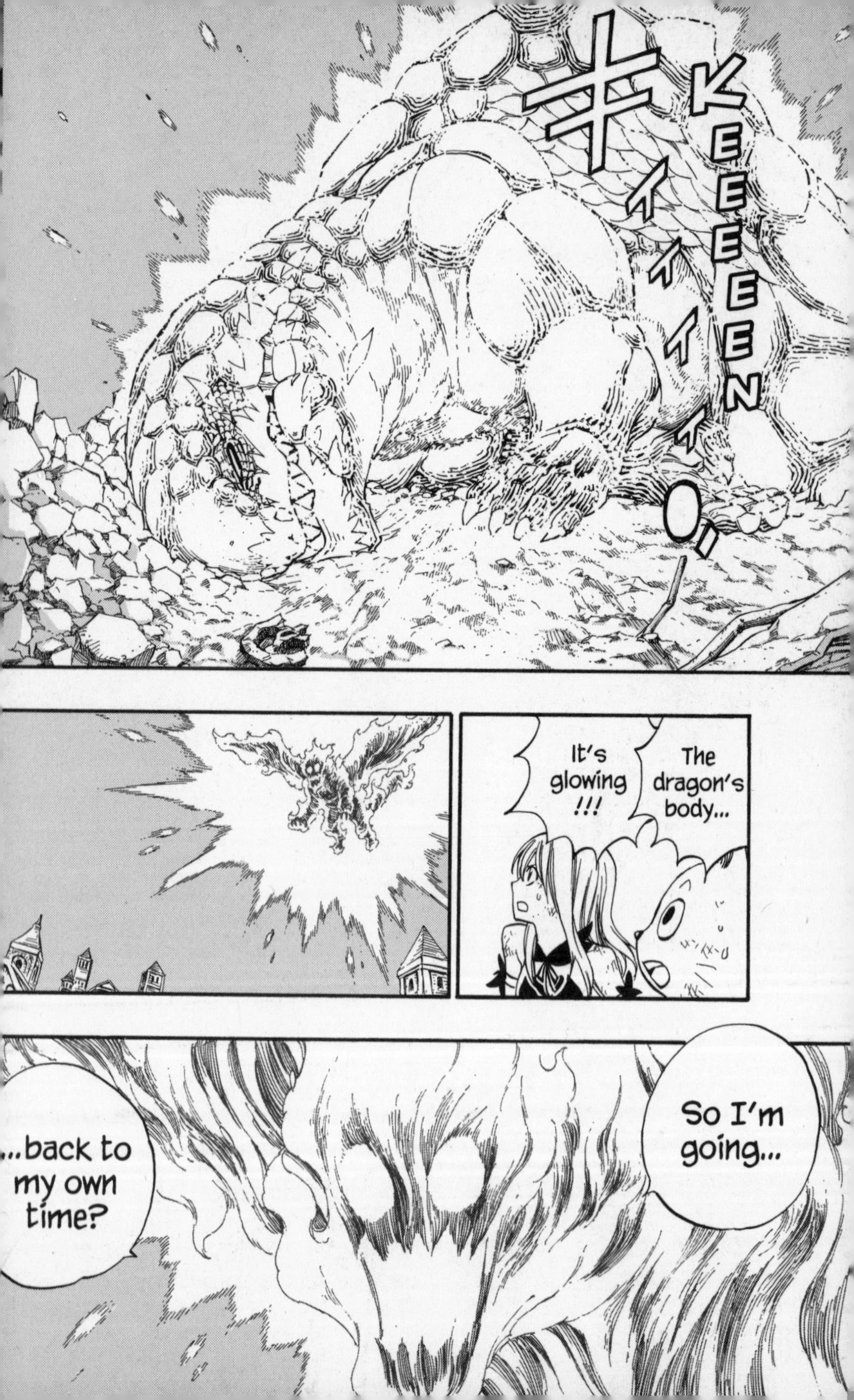
KEEEEEN
The dragon's body...
It's glowing!!!
So I'm going...
...back to my own time?

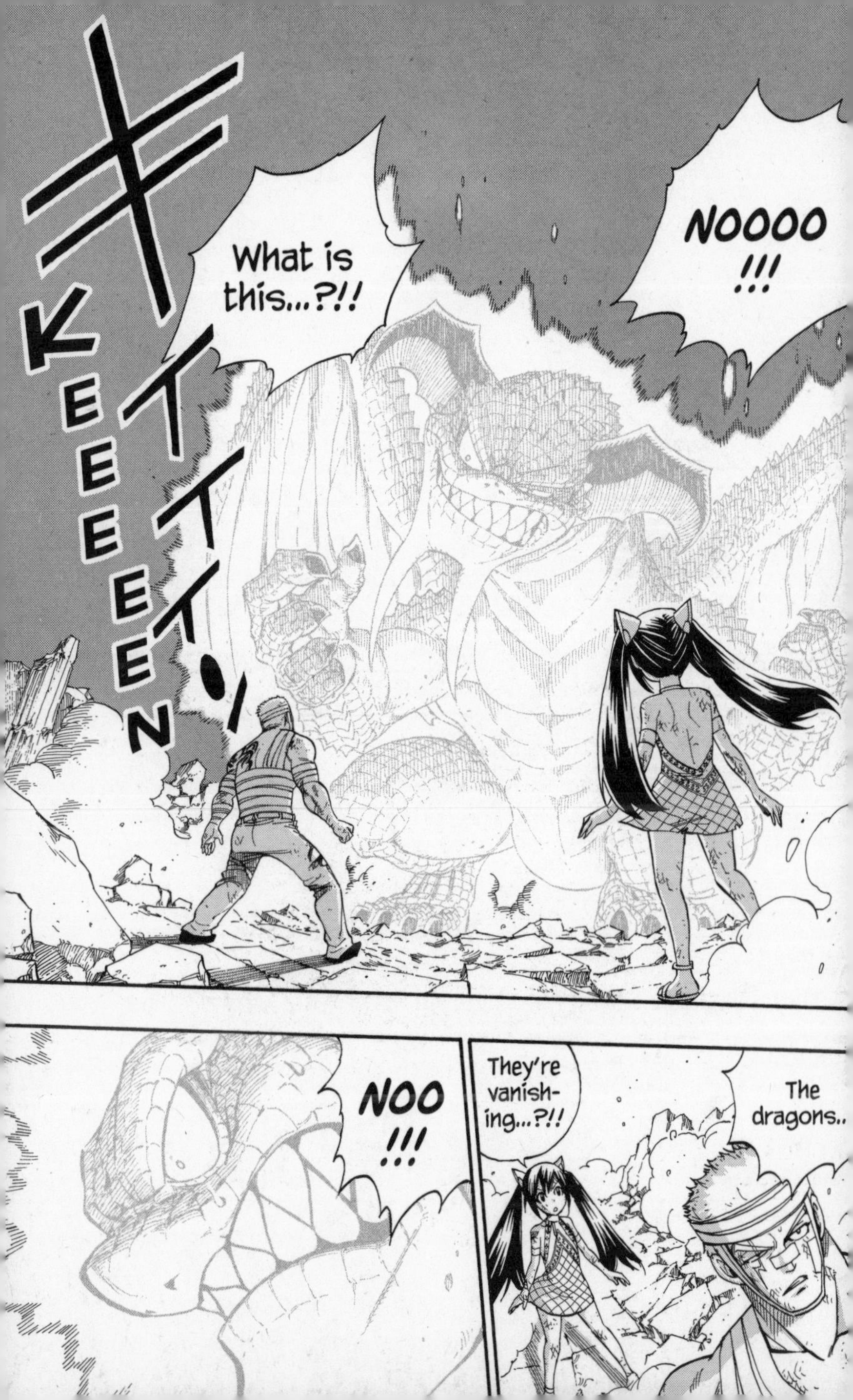
NOOOO !!!
What is this...?!!
KEEEEEEN
The dragons..
They're vanish-ing...?!!
NOO !!!

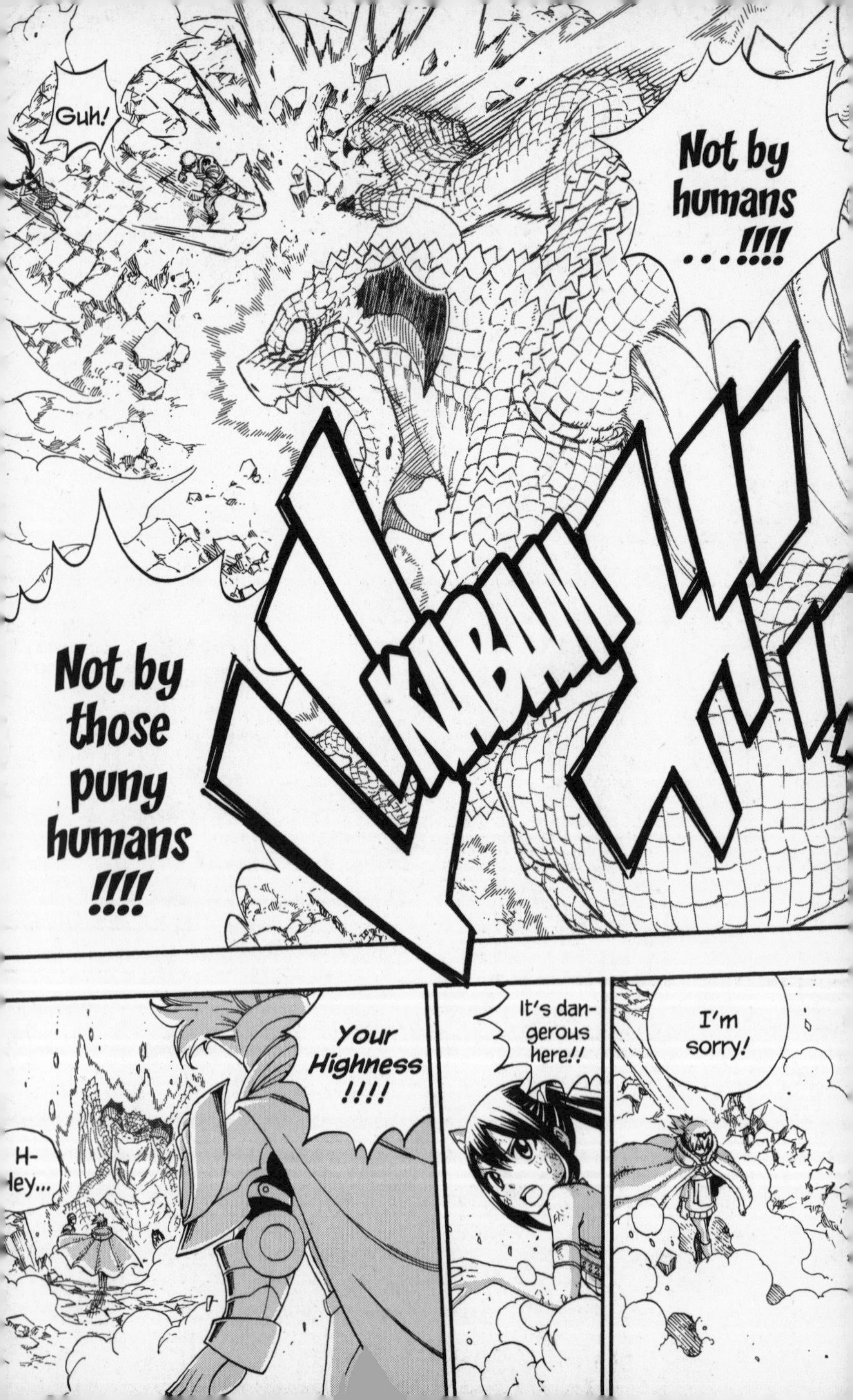
Not by humans ....!!!!
Guh!
KABAMM!!
Not by those puny humans !!!!
I'm sorry!
It's dangerous here!!
Your Highness !!!!
H- ey...

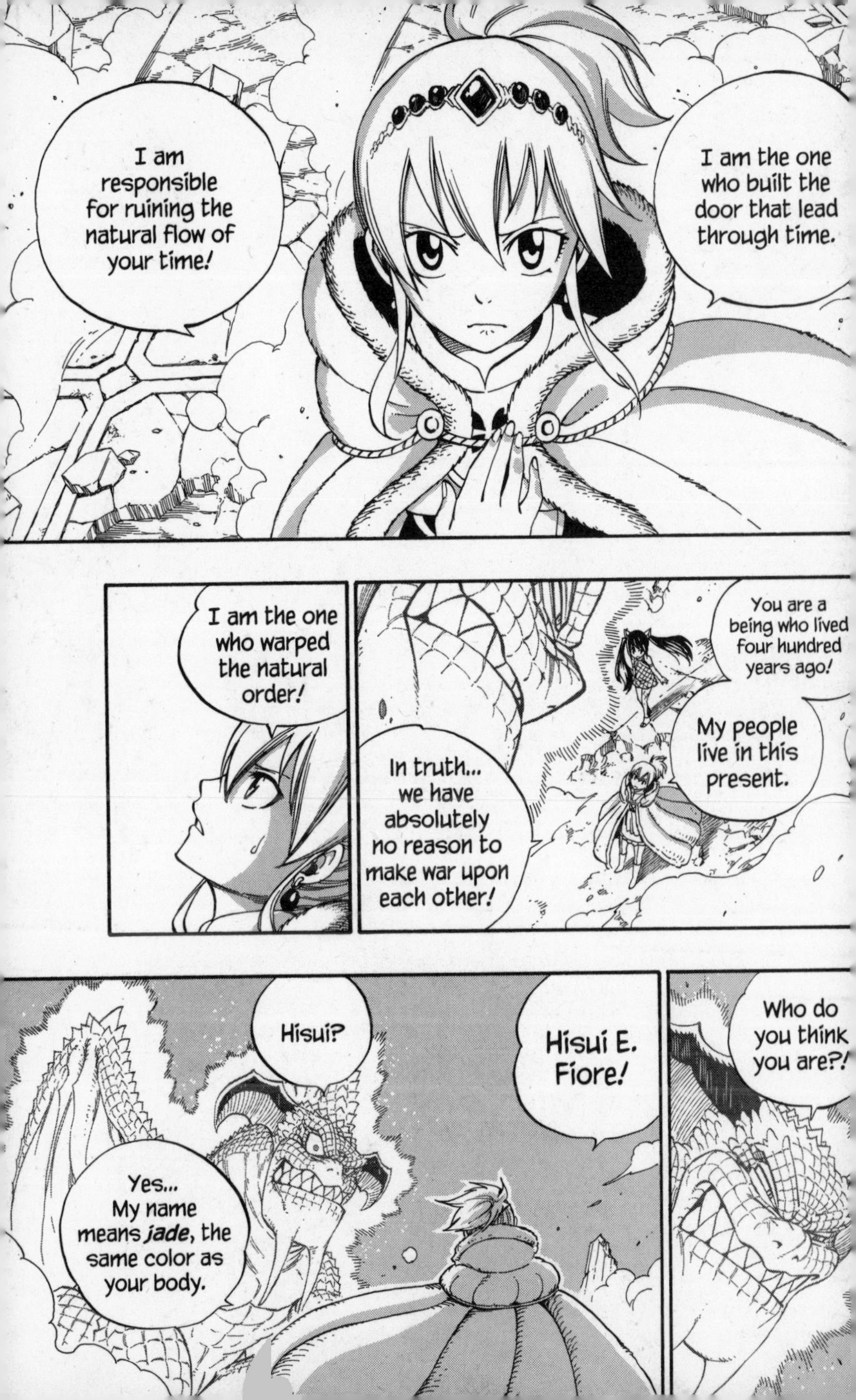
I am the one who built the door that lead through time.
I am responsible for ruining the natural flow of your time!
You are a being who lived four hundred years ago!
My people live in this present.
In truth... we have absolutely no reason to make war upon each other!
I am the one who warped the natural order!
Who do you think you are?!
Hisui E. Fiore!
Hisui?
Yes... My name means *jade*, the same color as your body.

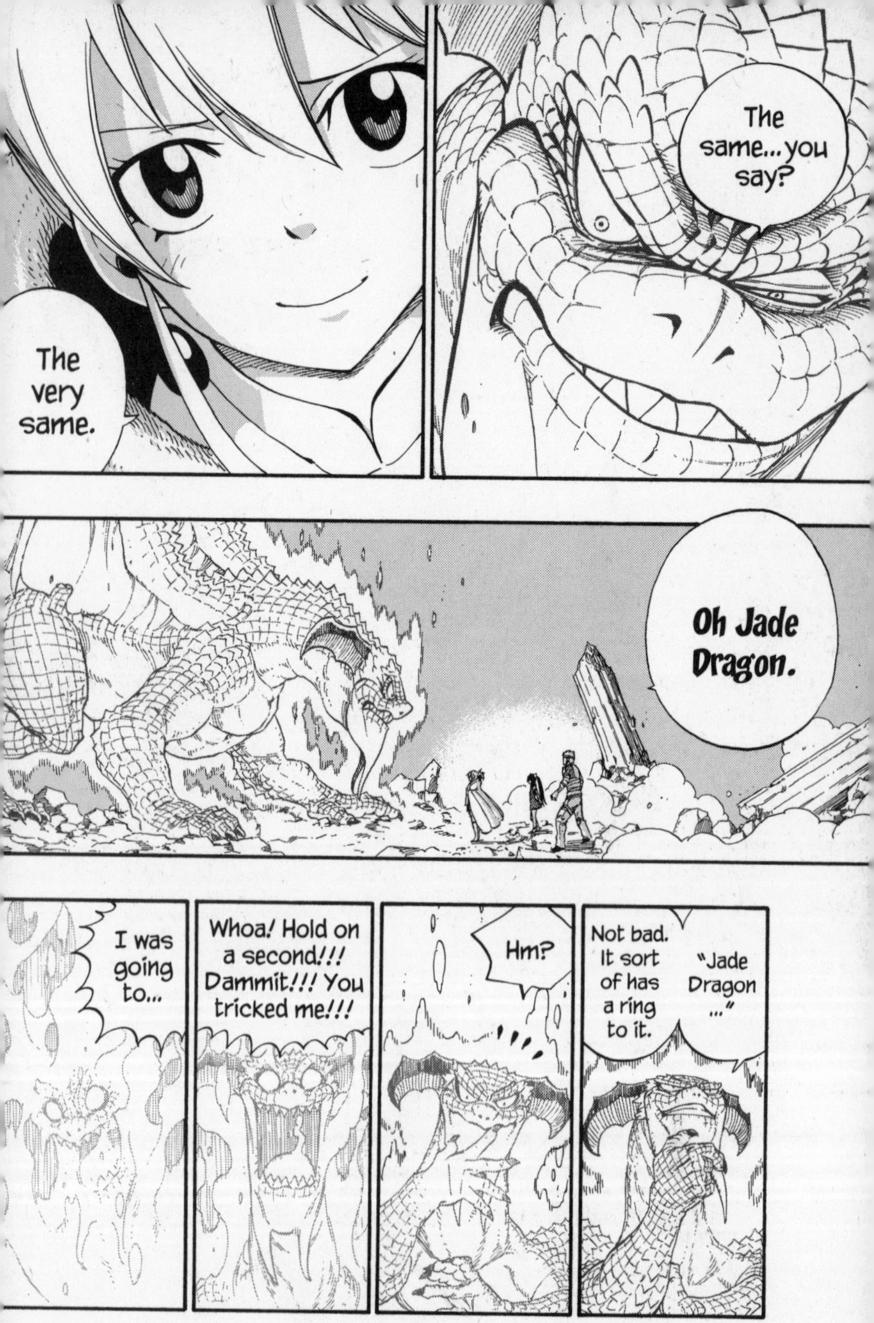

The same...you say?
The very same.
Oh Jade Dragon.
"Jade Dragon..."
Not bad. It sort of has a ring to it.
Hm?
Whoa! Hold on a second!!! Dammit!!! You tricked me!!!
I was going to...

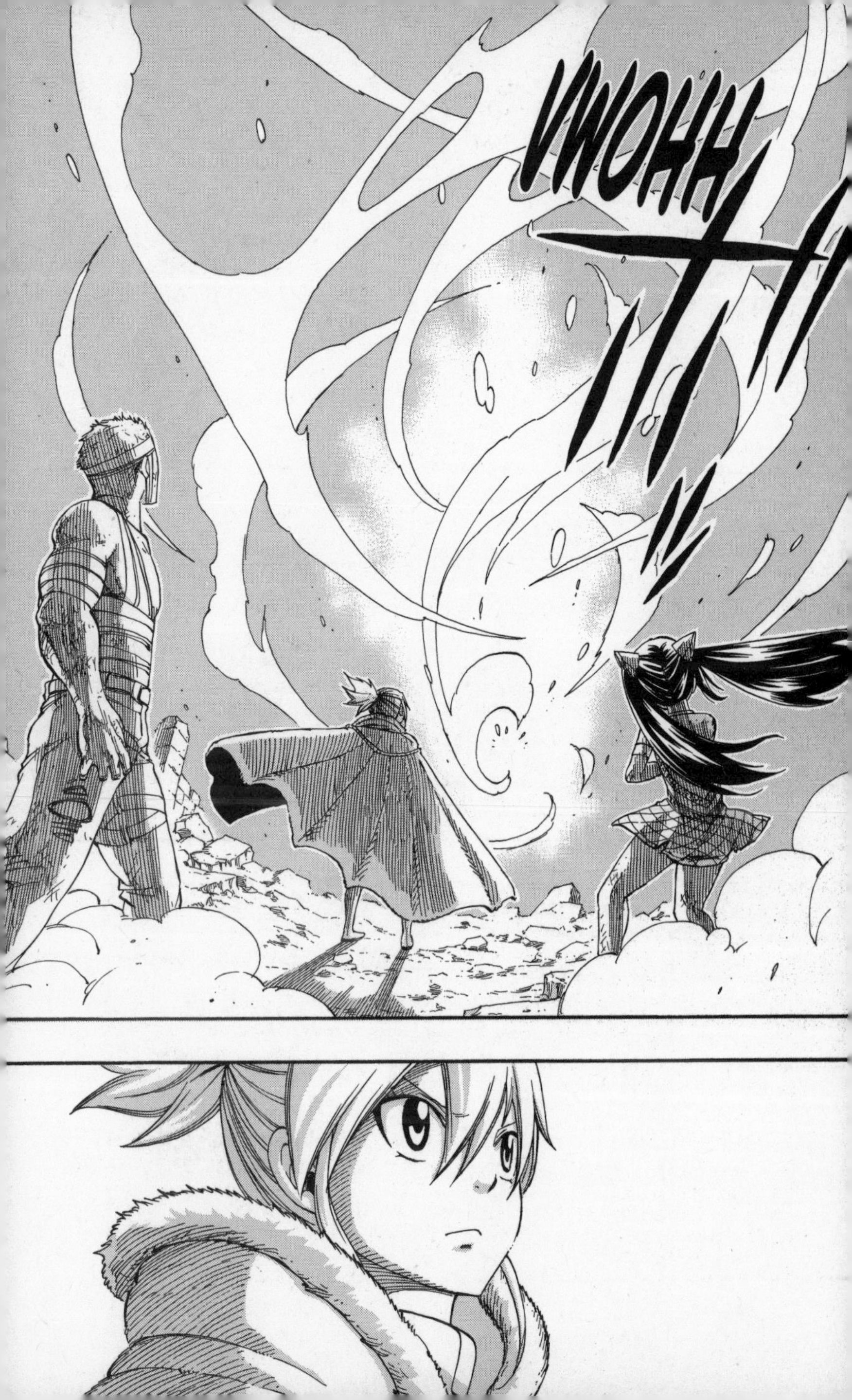
VWOHH

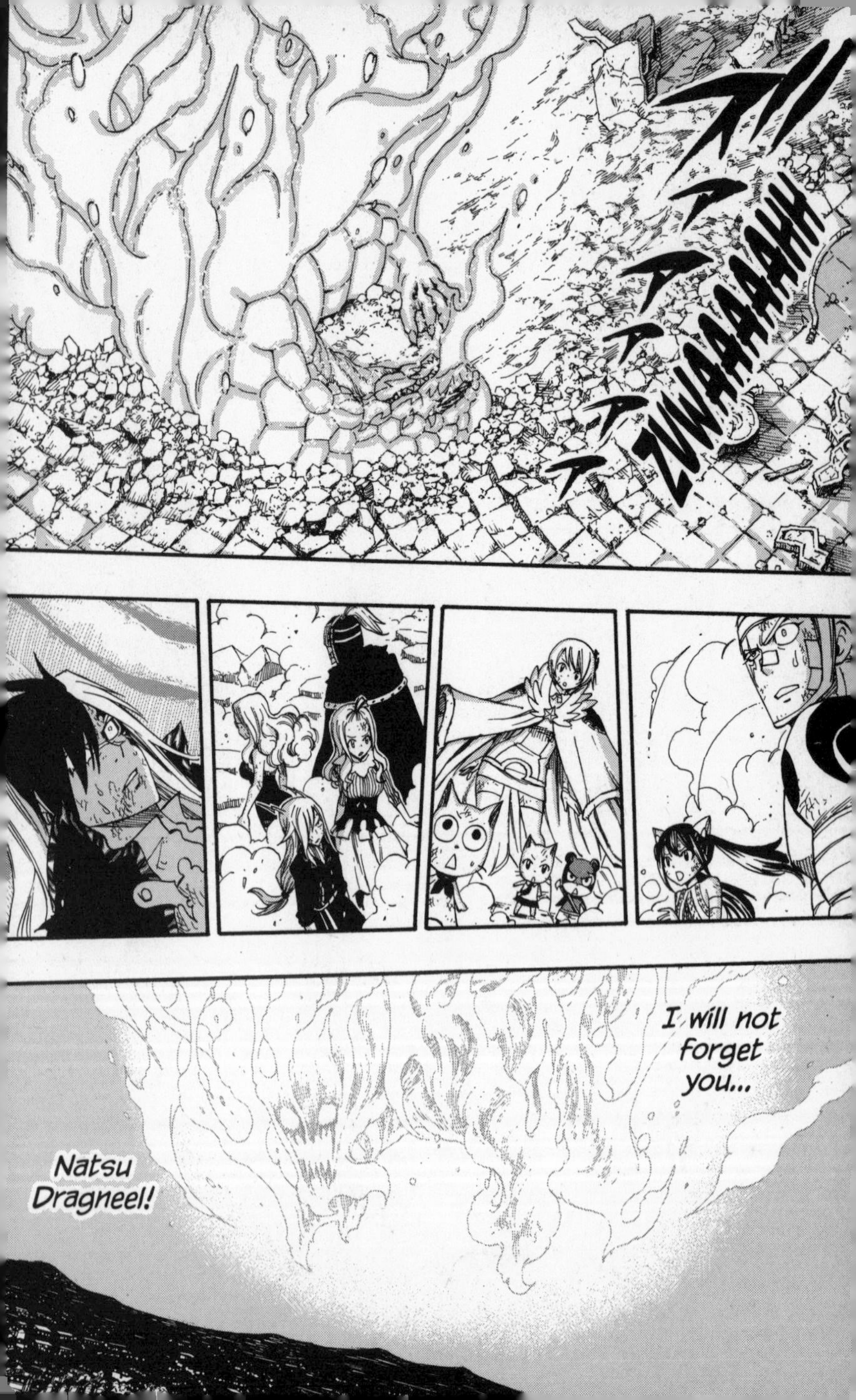
ZWAAAAHH
I will not forget you...
Natsu Dragneel!

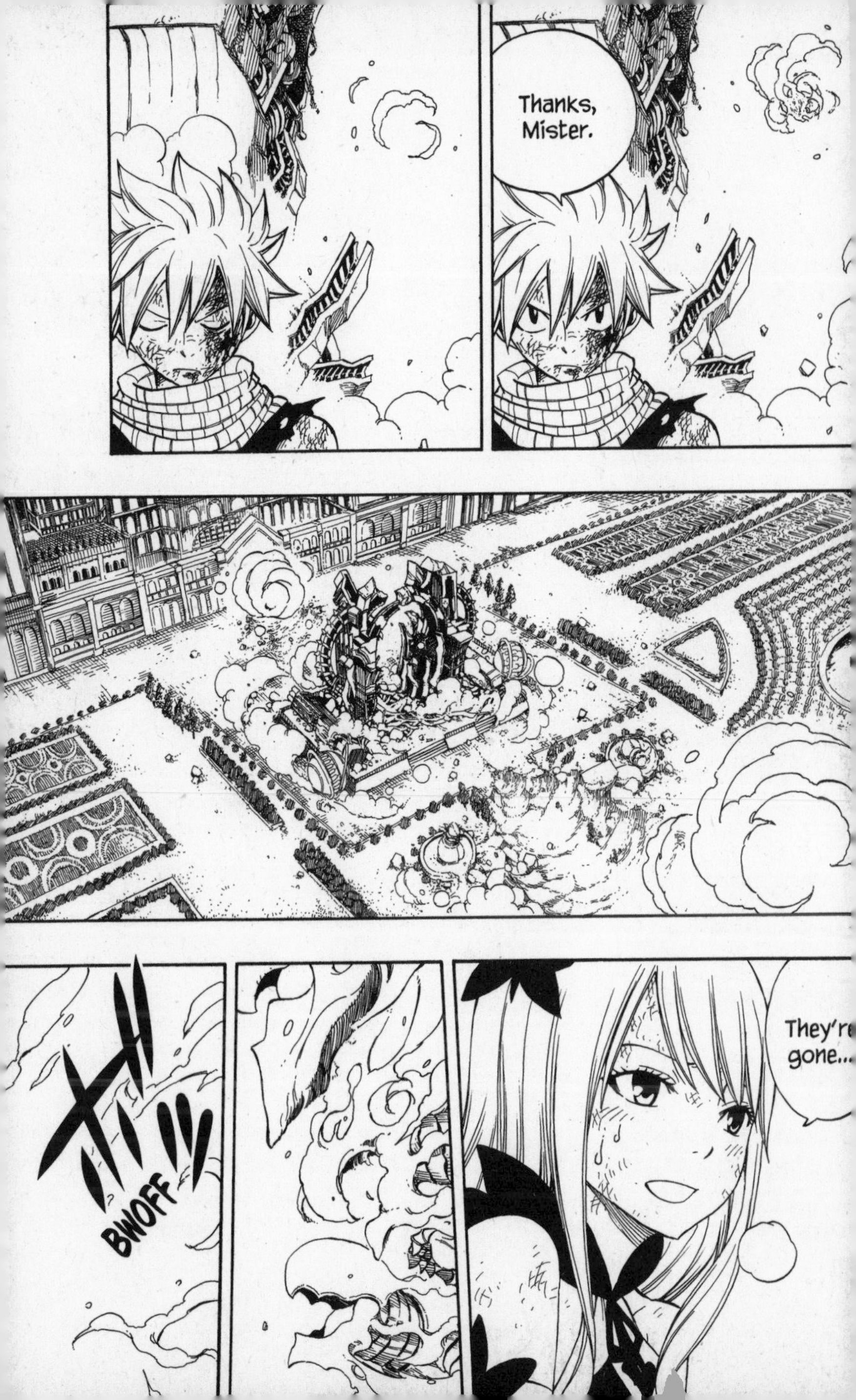
Thanks, Mister.
They're gone...
BWOFF

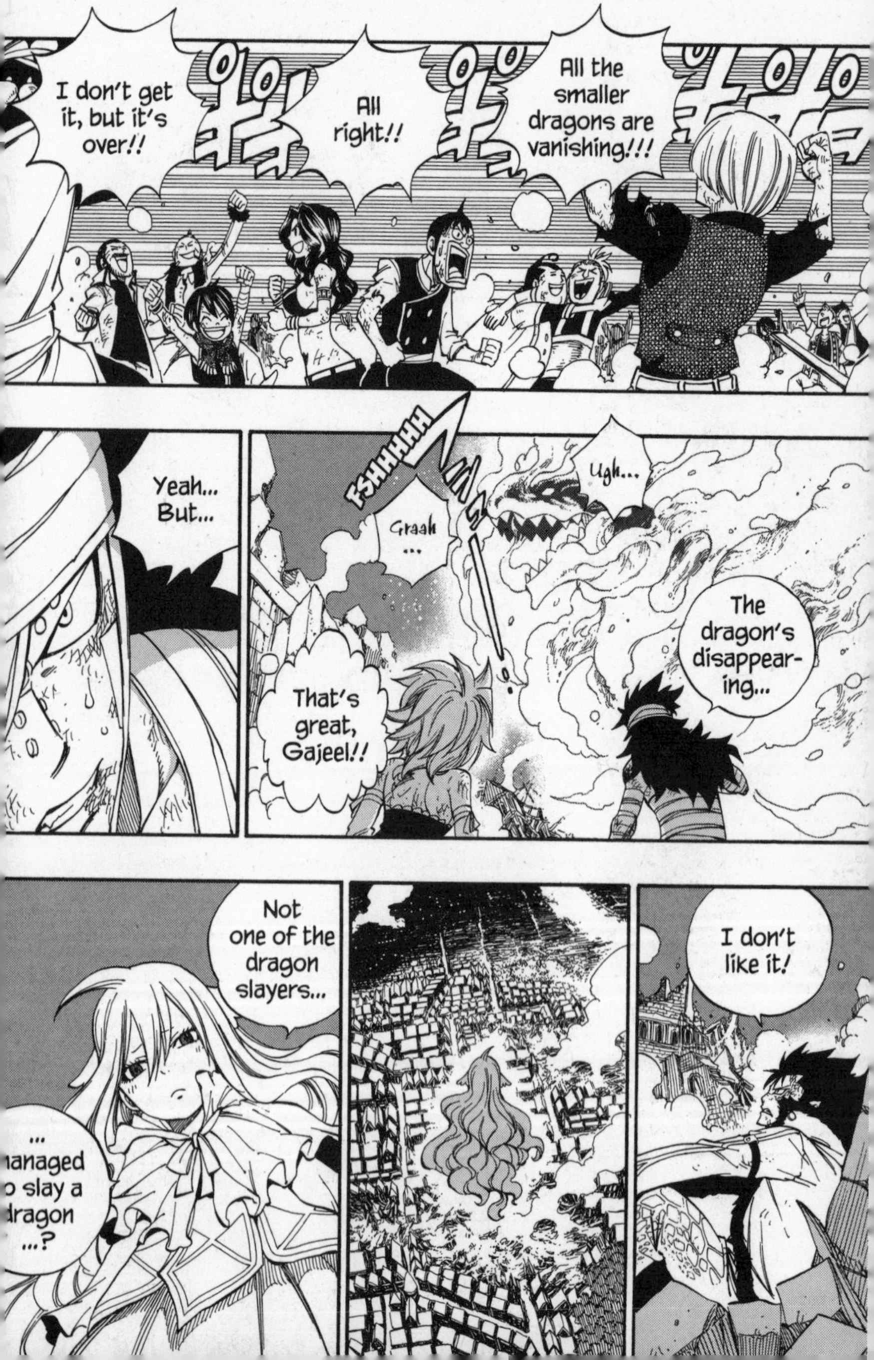
All the smaller dragons are vanishing!!!
All right!!
I don't get it, but it's over!!
Ugh...
The dragon's disappearing...
FSHHHH
Graah ...
That's great, Gajeel!!
Yeah... But...
I don't like it!
Not one of the dragon slayers...
... anaged o slay a dragon ...?

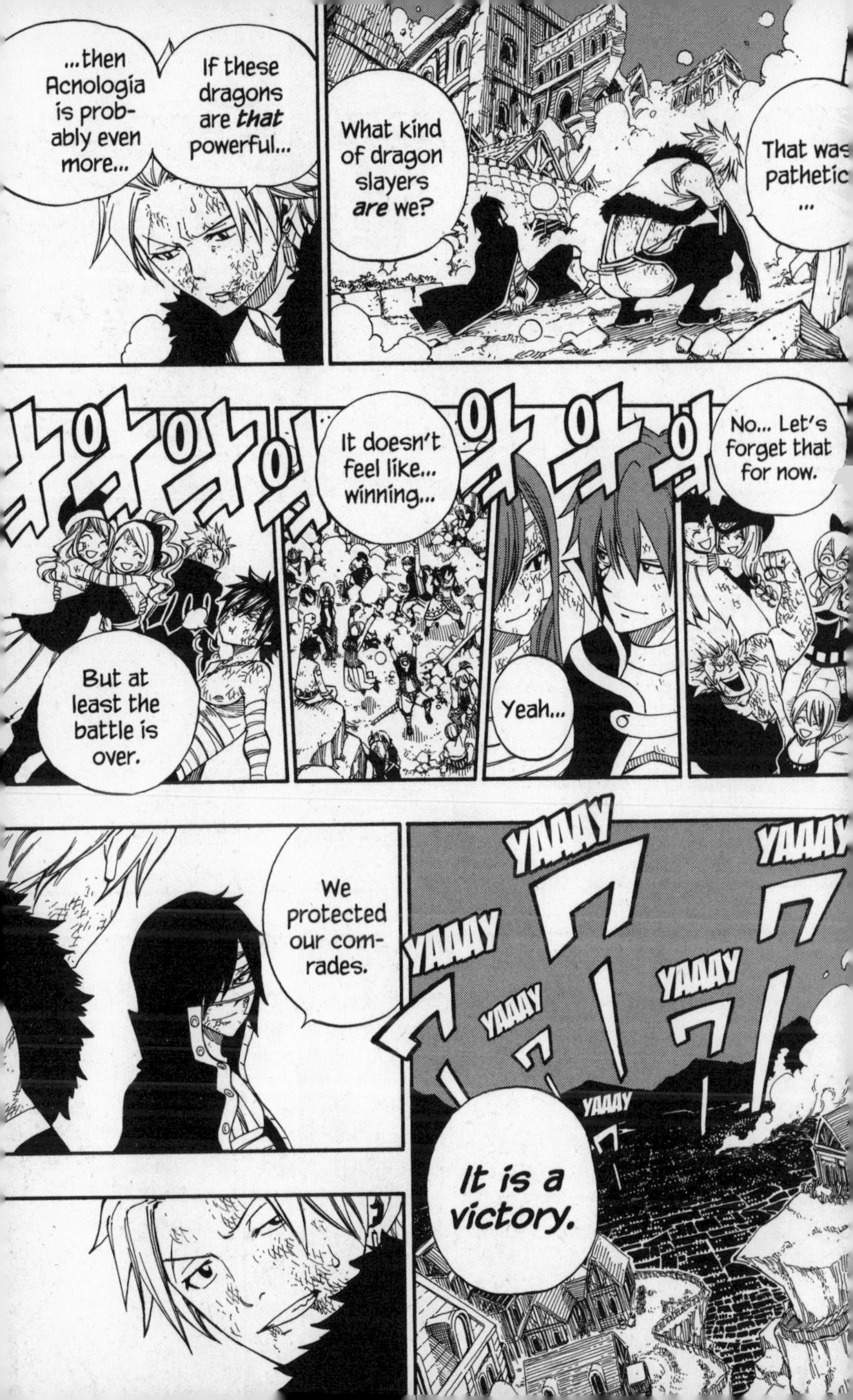
That was pathetic...
What kind of dragon slayers *are* we?
If these dragons are *that* powerful...
...then Acnologia is probably even more...
No... Let's forget that for now.
Yeah...
It doesn't feel like... winning...
But at least the battle is over.
YAAAY
YAAAY
YAAAY
YAAAY
YAAAY
YAAAY
It is a victory.
We protected our comrades.

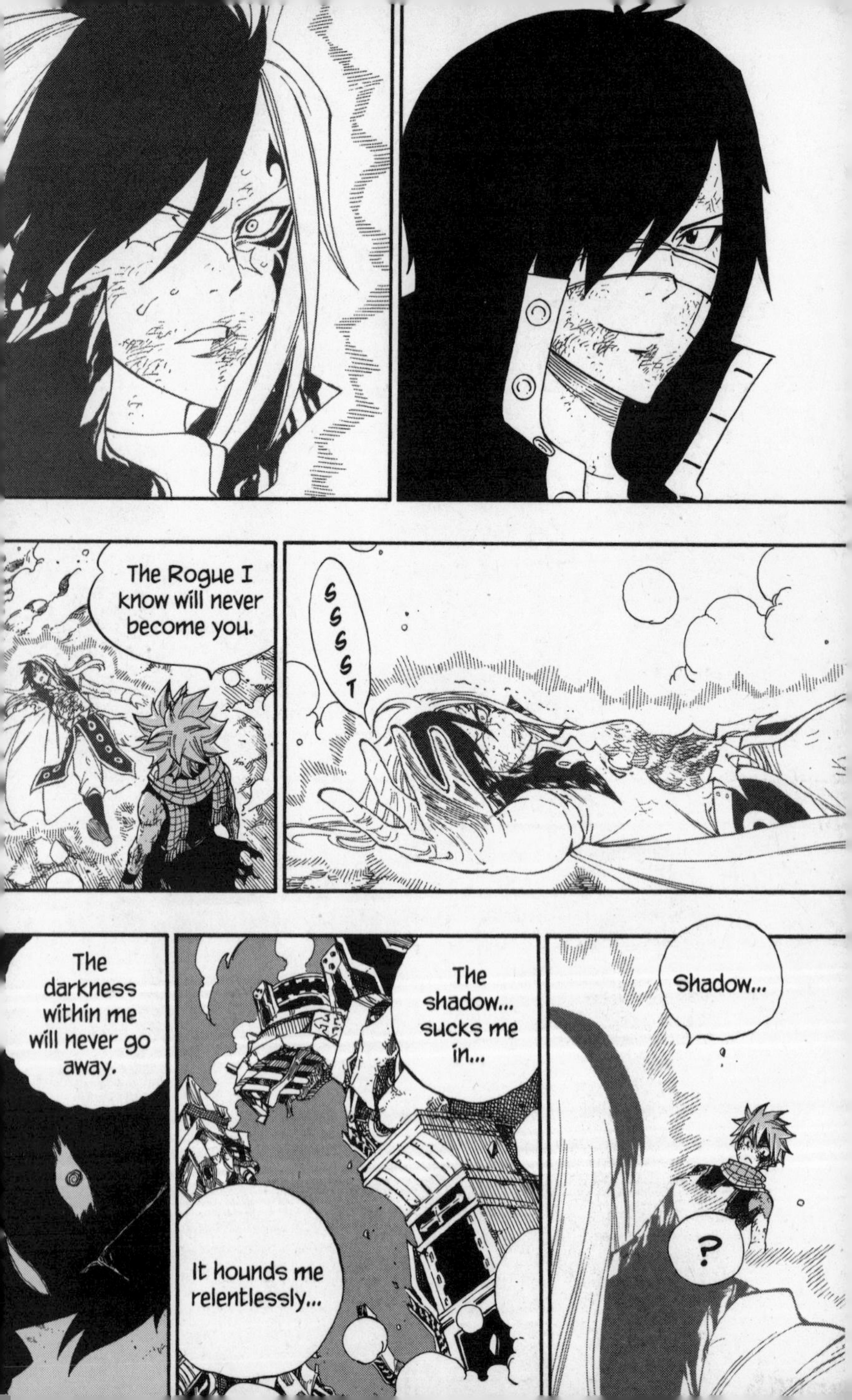
SSSST
The Rogue I know will never become you.
Shadow...
?
The shadow... sucks me in...
It hounds me relentlessly...
The darkness within me will never go away.

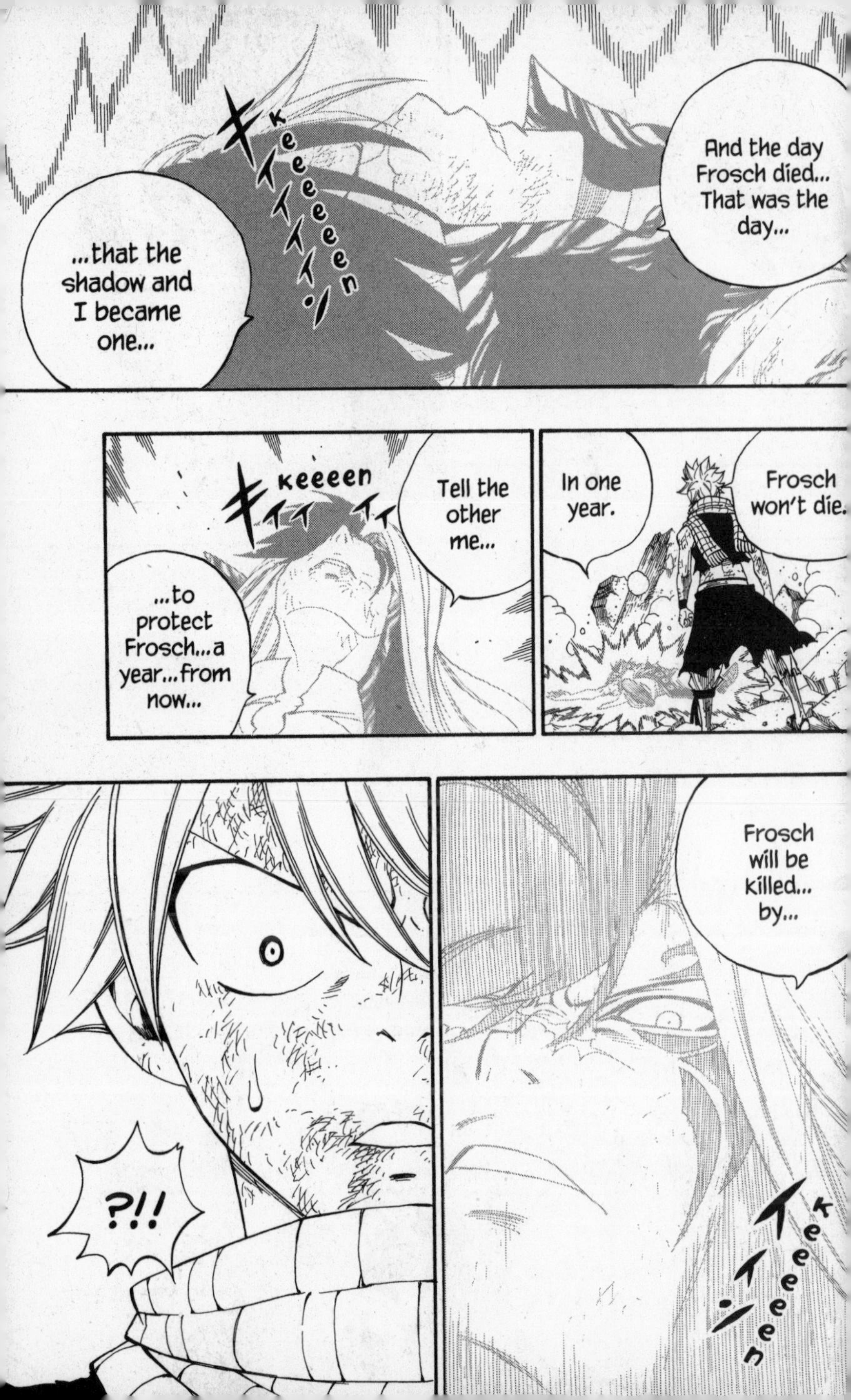
And the day Frosch died... That was the day...
Keeeeeeen
...that the shadow and I became one...
Frosch won't die.
In one year.
Tell the other me...
Keeeen
...to protect Frosch...a year...from now...
Frosch will be killed... by...
Keeeeeen
?!!

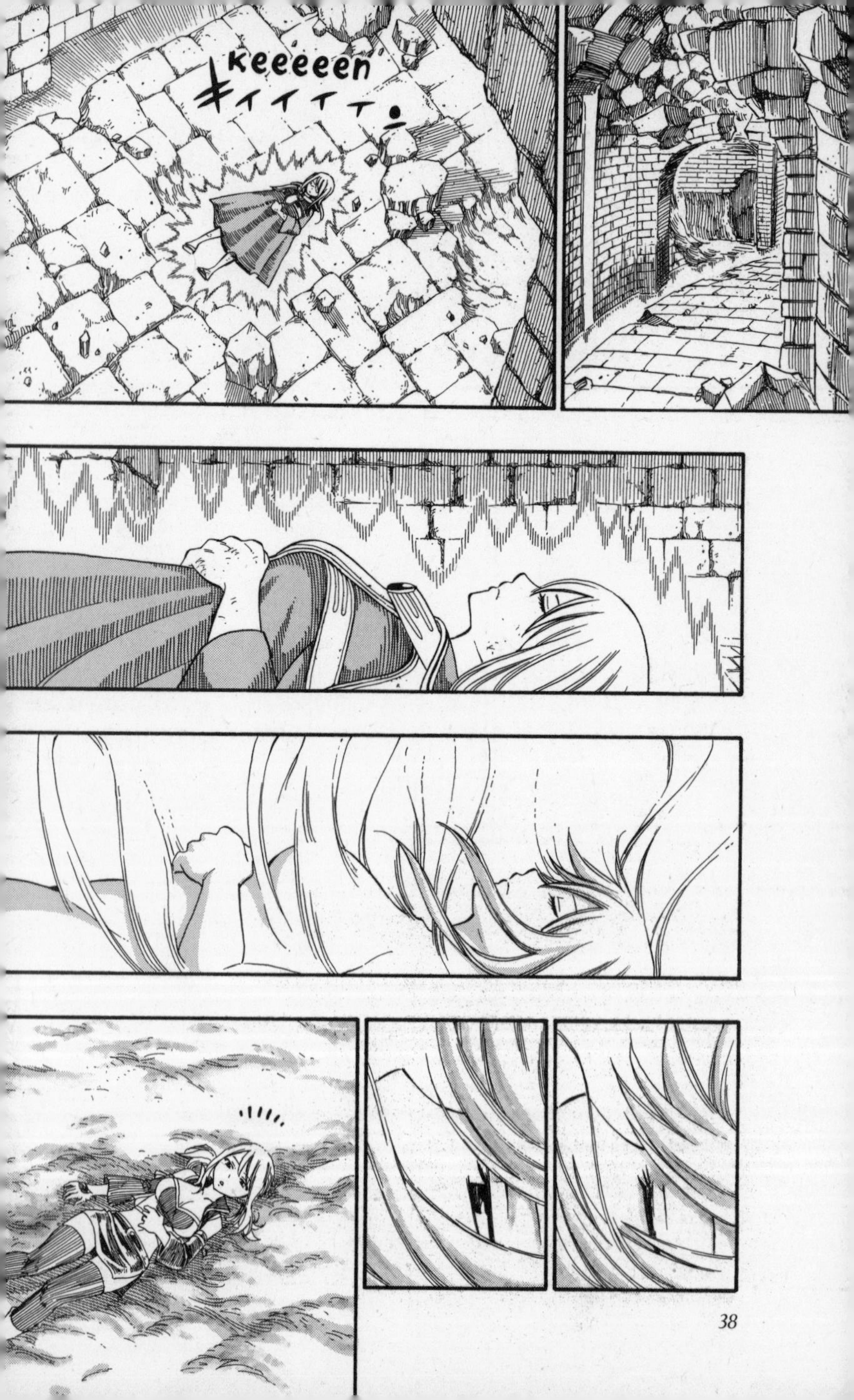
keeeeeen
キイイイイ…

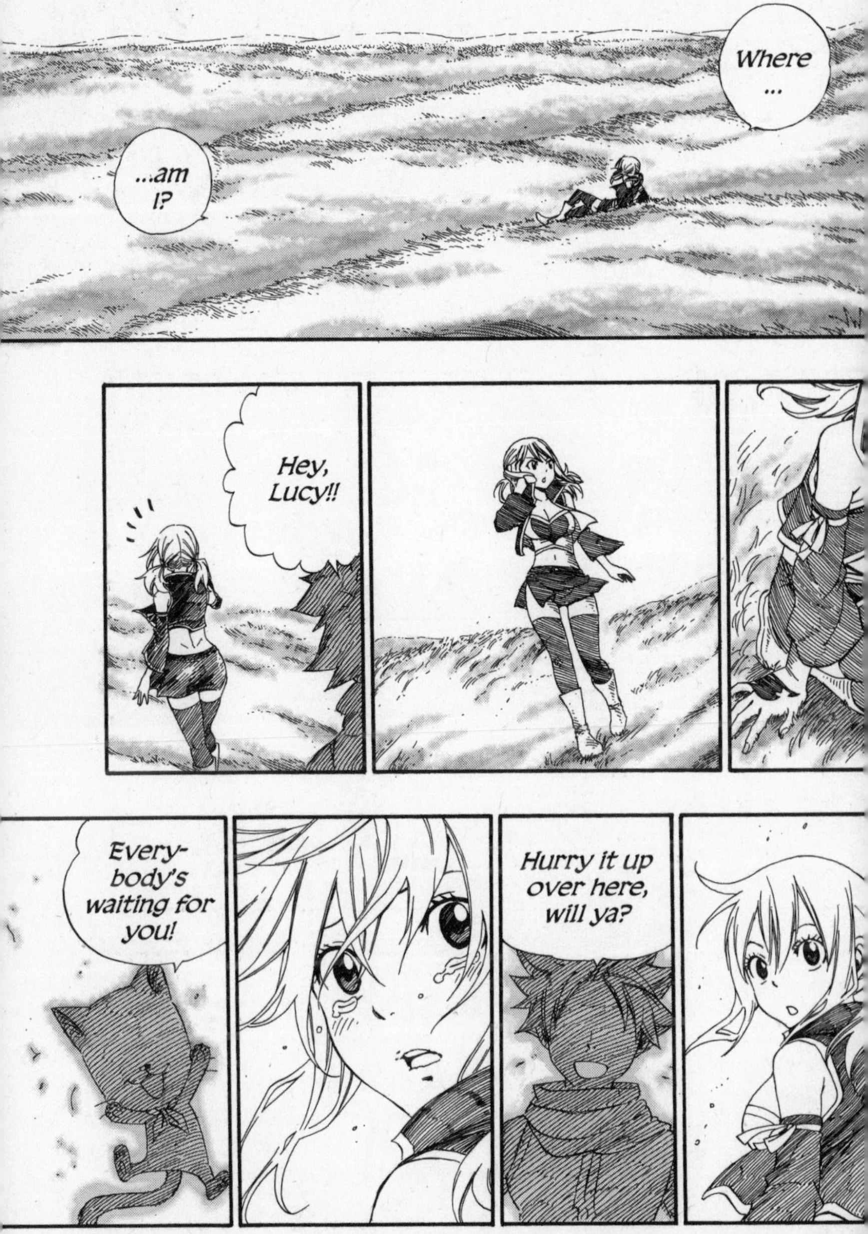
Where ...
...am I?
Hey, Lucy!!
Hurry it up over here, will ya?
Every-body's waiting for you!

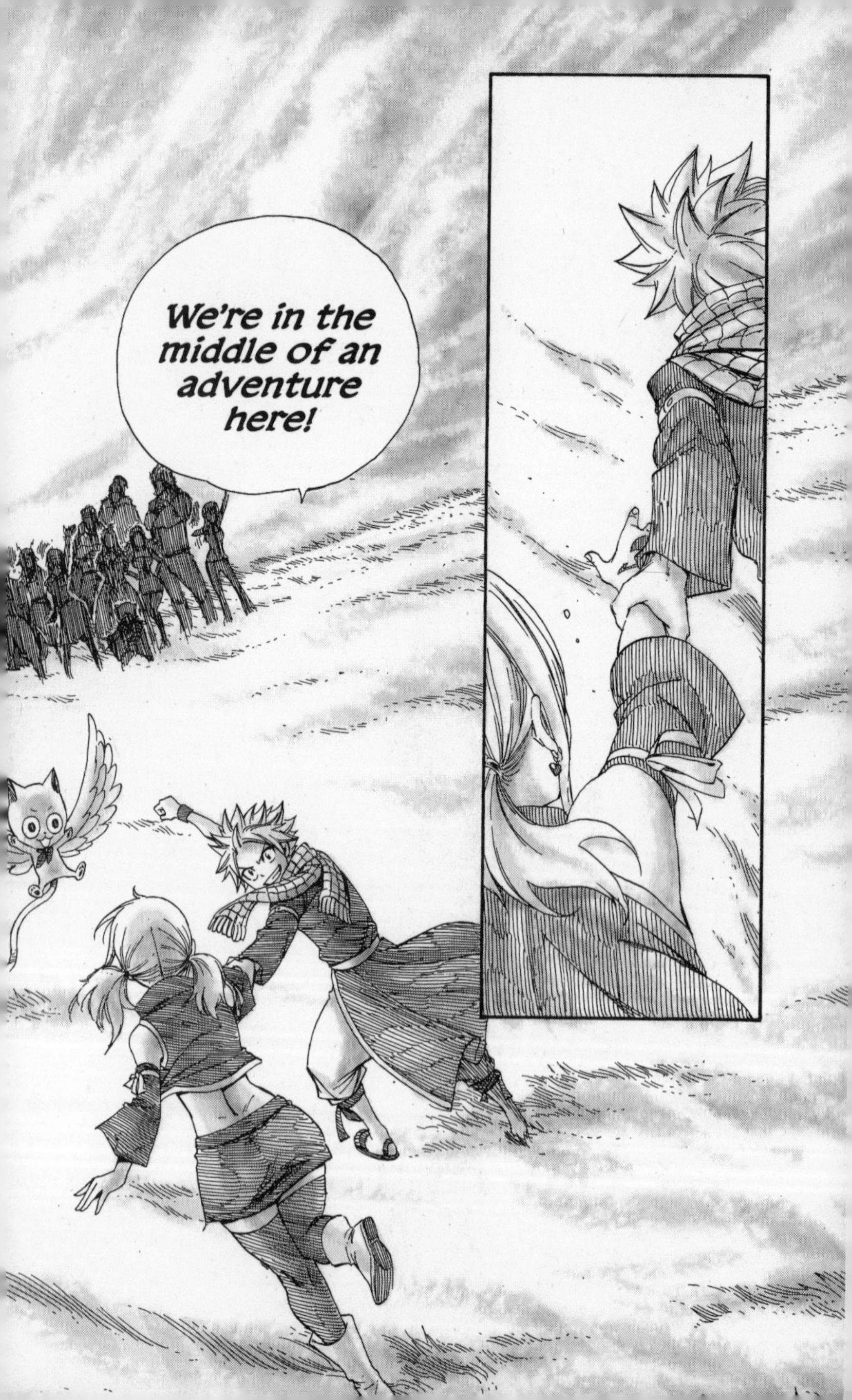
We're in the middle of an adventure here!

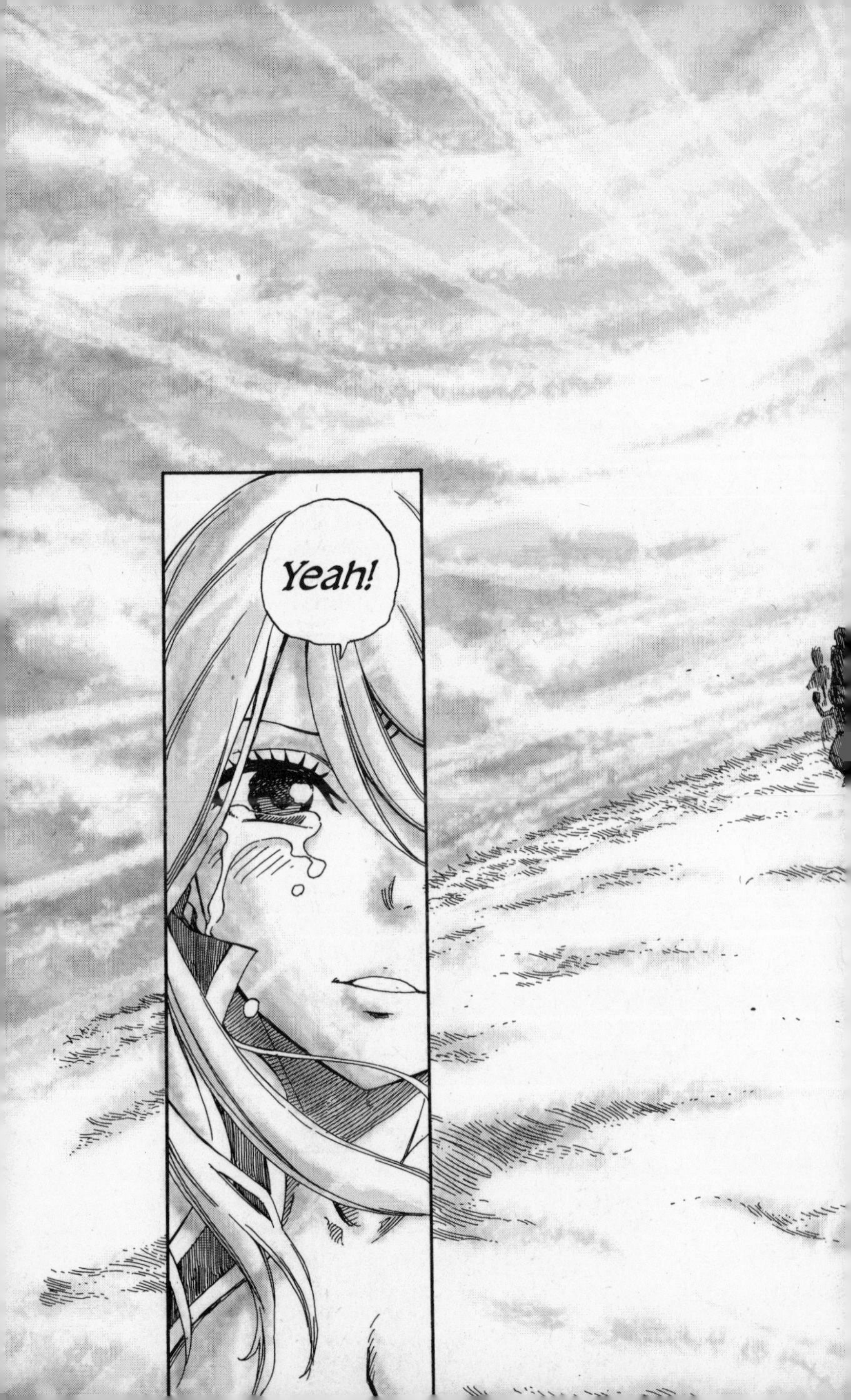
Yeah!

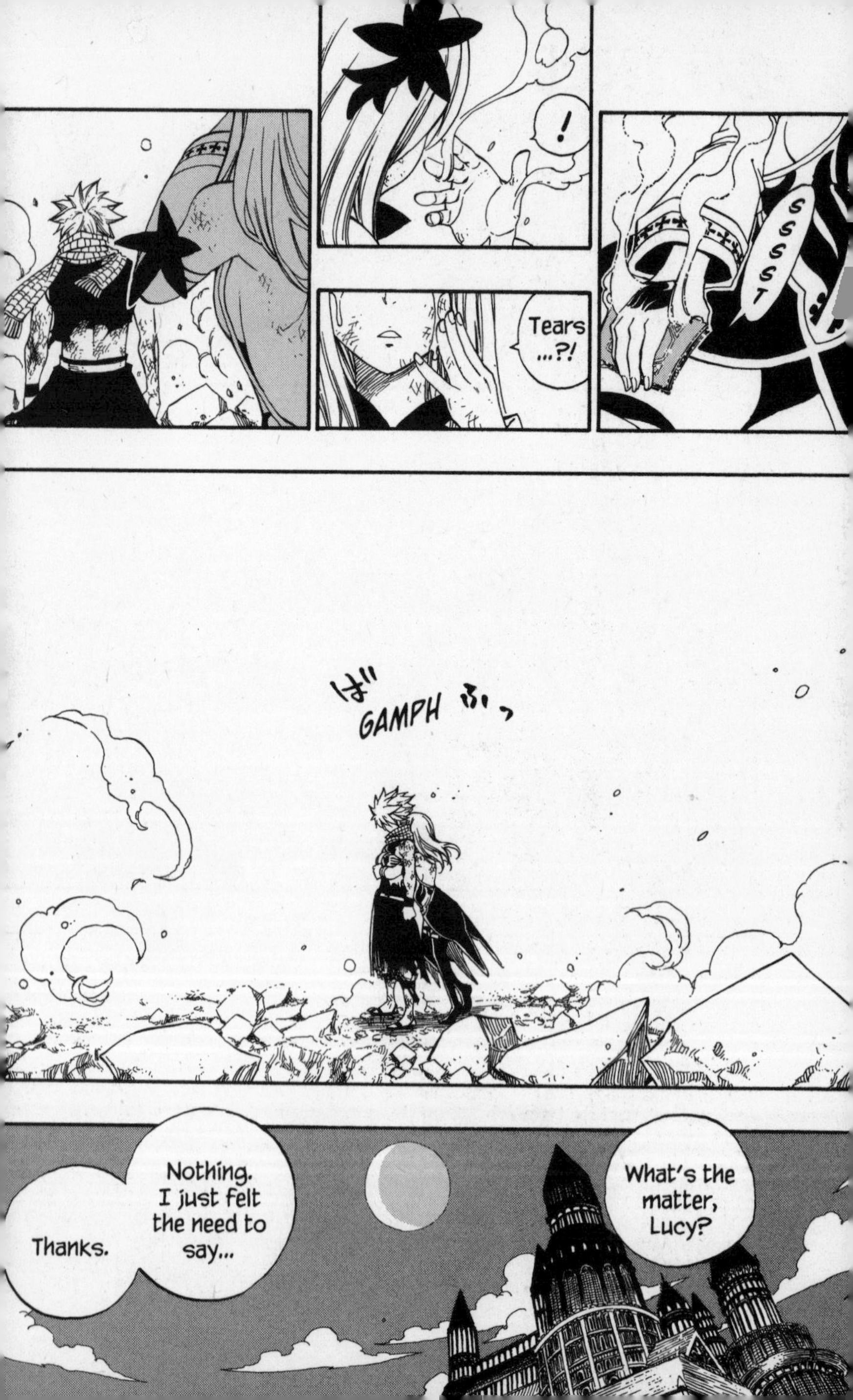
SSSST
!
Tears ...?!
ば
GAMPH
ふっ
What's the matter, Lucy?
Nothing. I just felt the need to say...
Thanks.

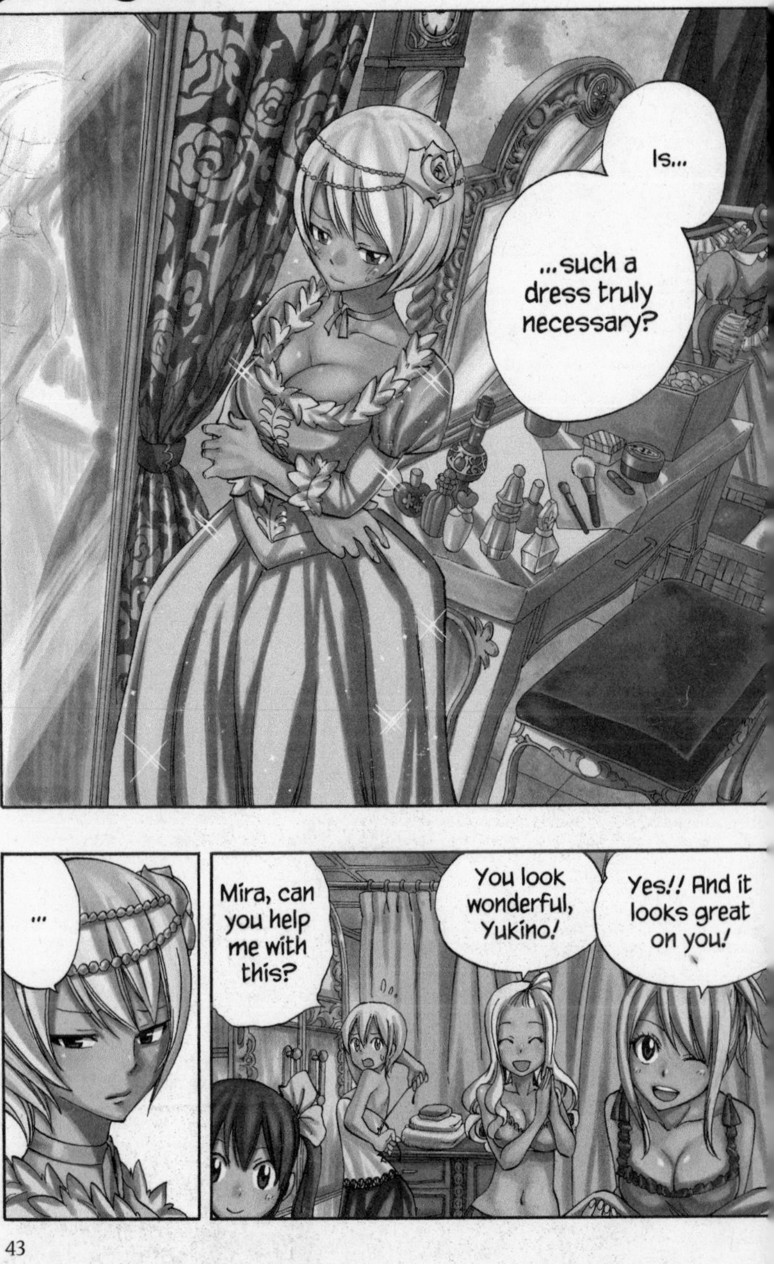
Is...
...such a dress truly necessary?
Yes!! And it looks great on you!
You look wonderful, Yukino!
Mira, can you help me with this?
...

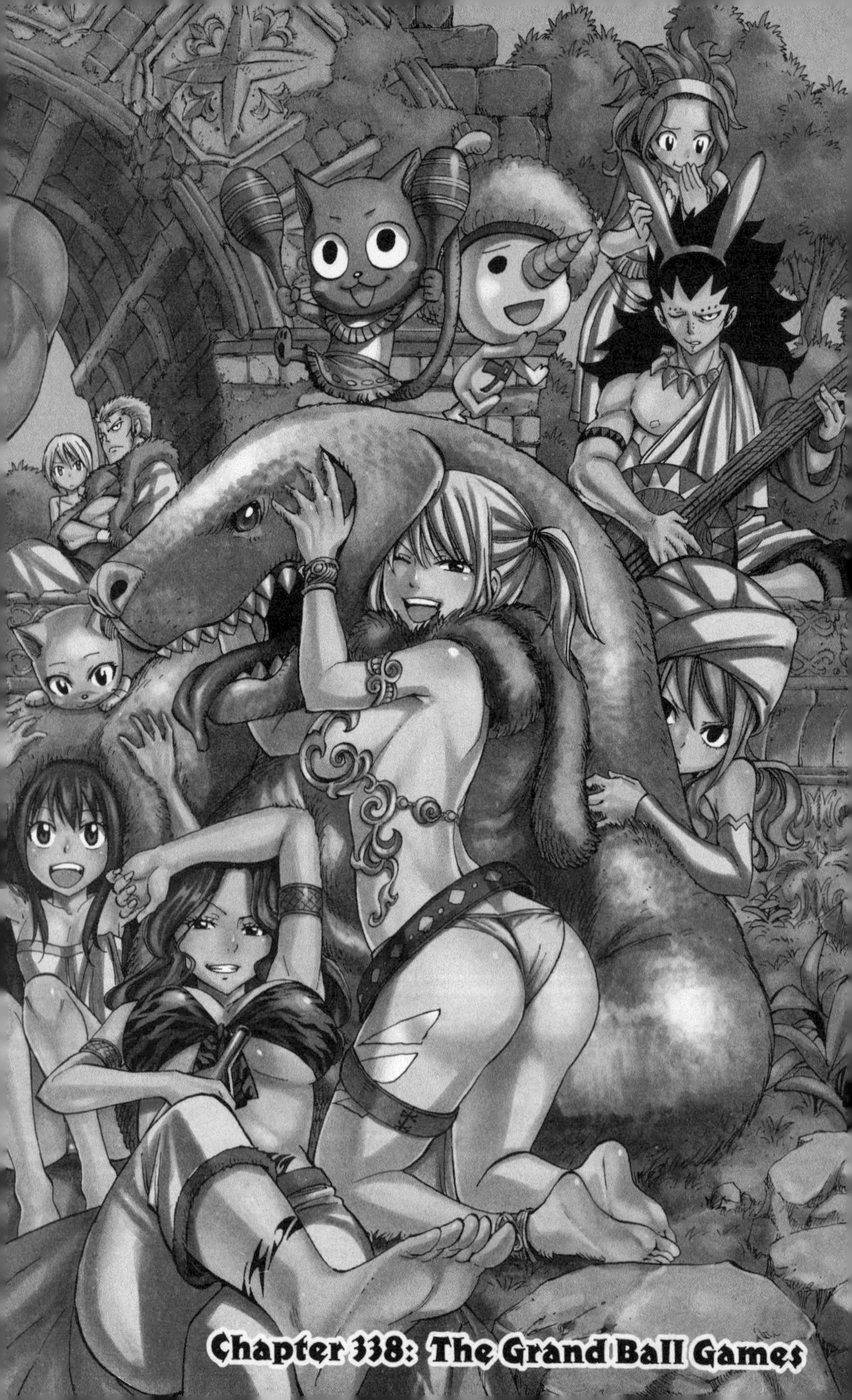

Chapter 338: The Grand Ball Games

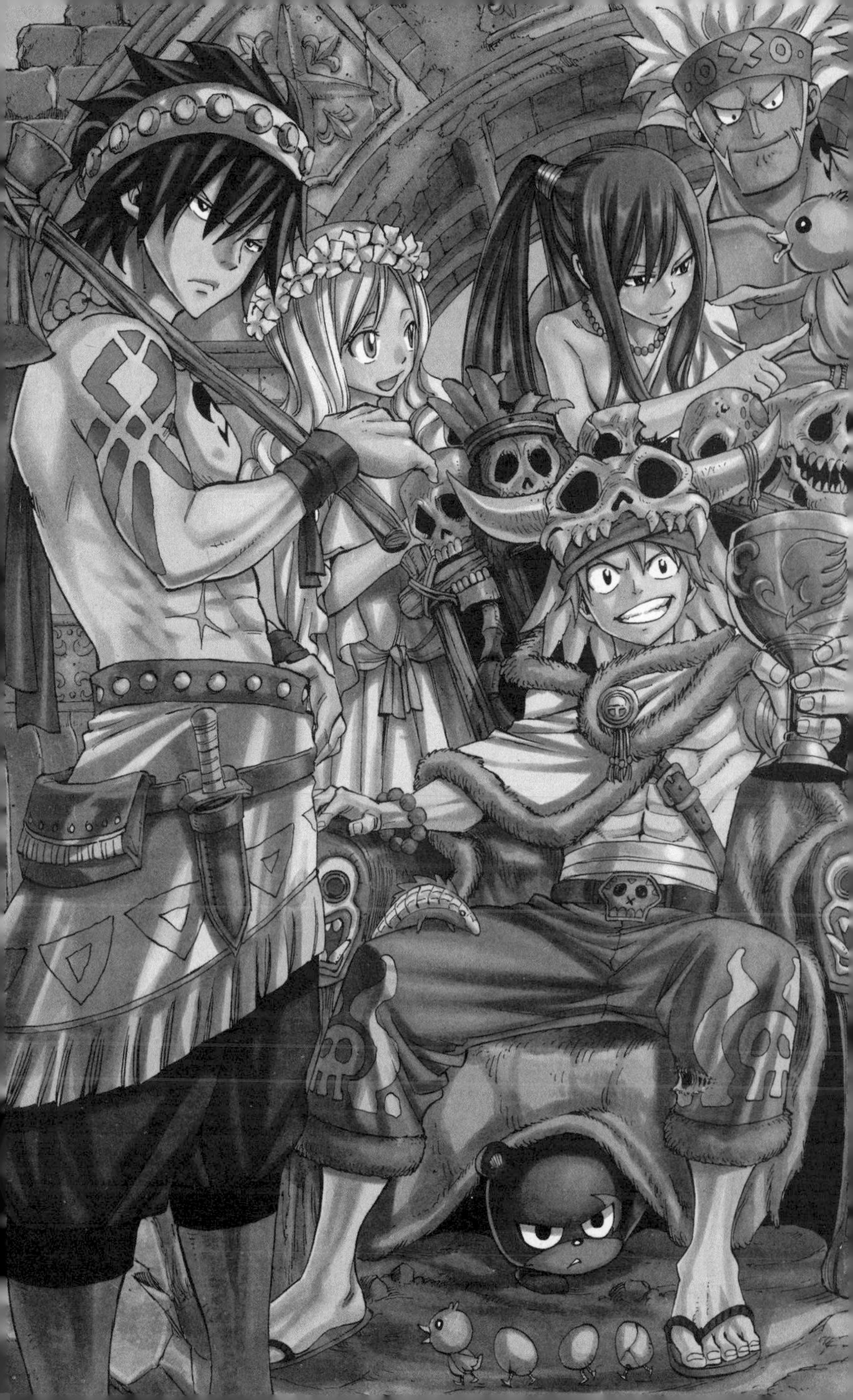

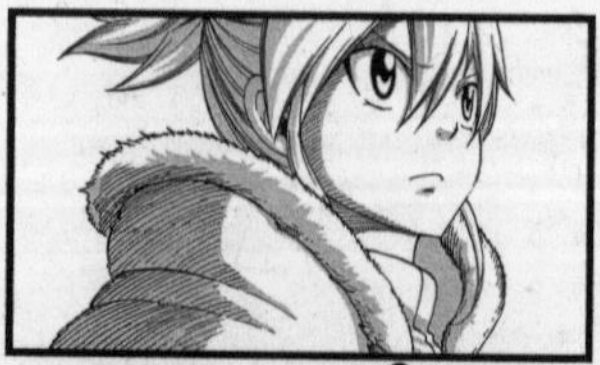

FAIRY TAIL

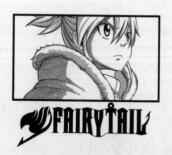

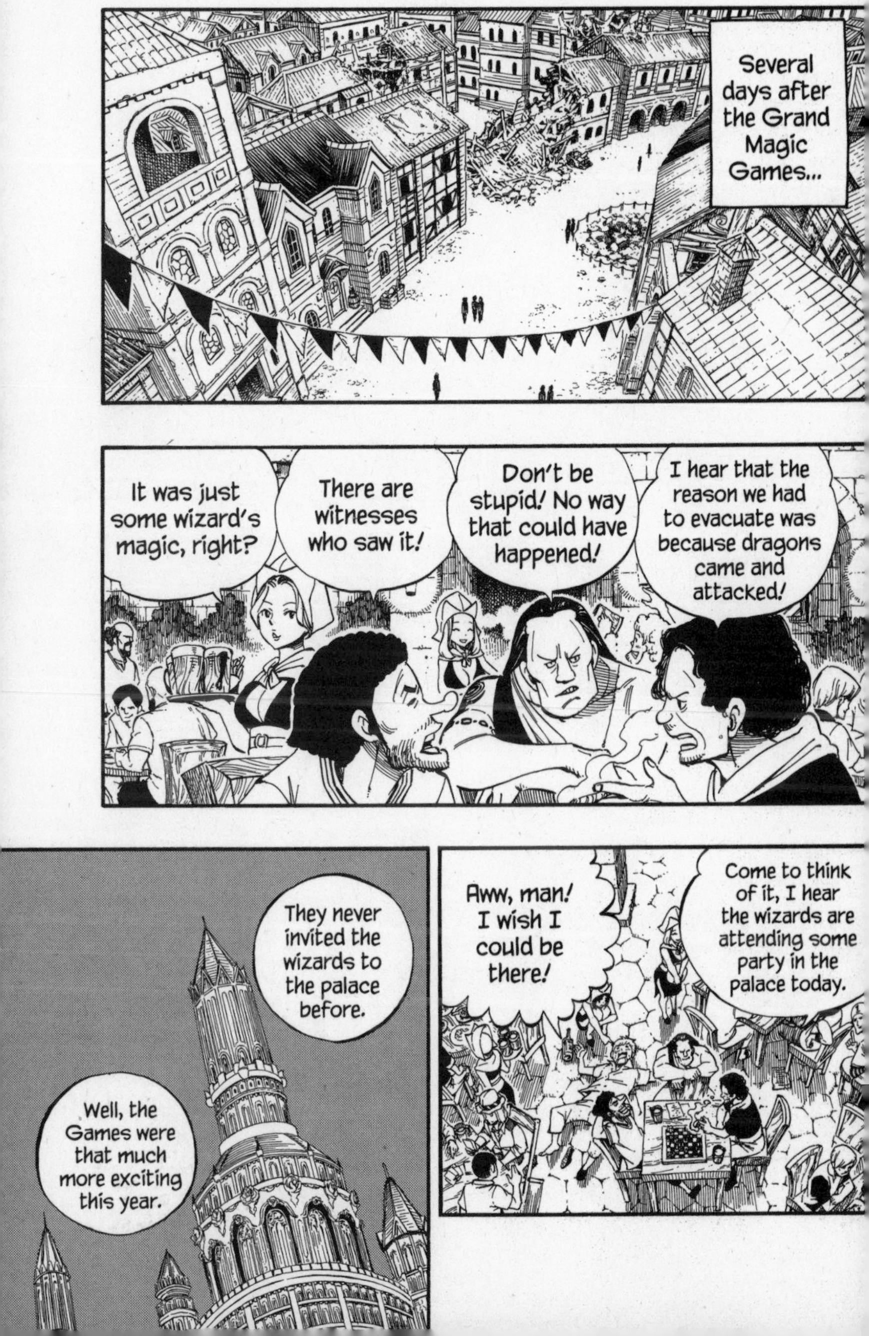
Several days after the Grand Magic Games...
I hear that the reason we had to evacuate was because dragons came and attacked!
Don't be stupid! No way that could have happened!
There are witnesses who saw it!
It was just some wizard's magic, right?
Come to think of it, I hear the wizards are attending some party in the palace today.
Aww, man! I wish I could be there!
They never invited the wizards to the palace before.
Well, the Games were that much more exciting this year.

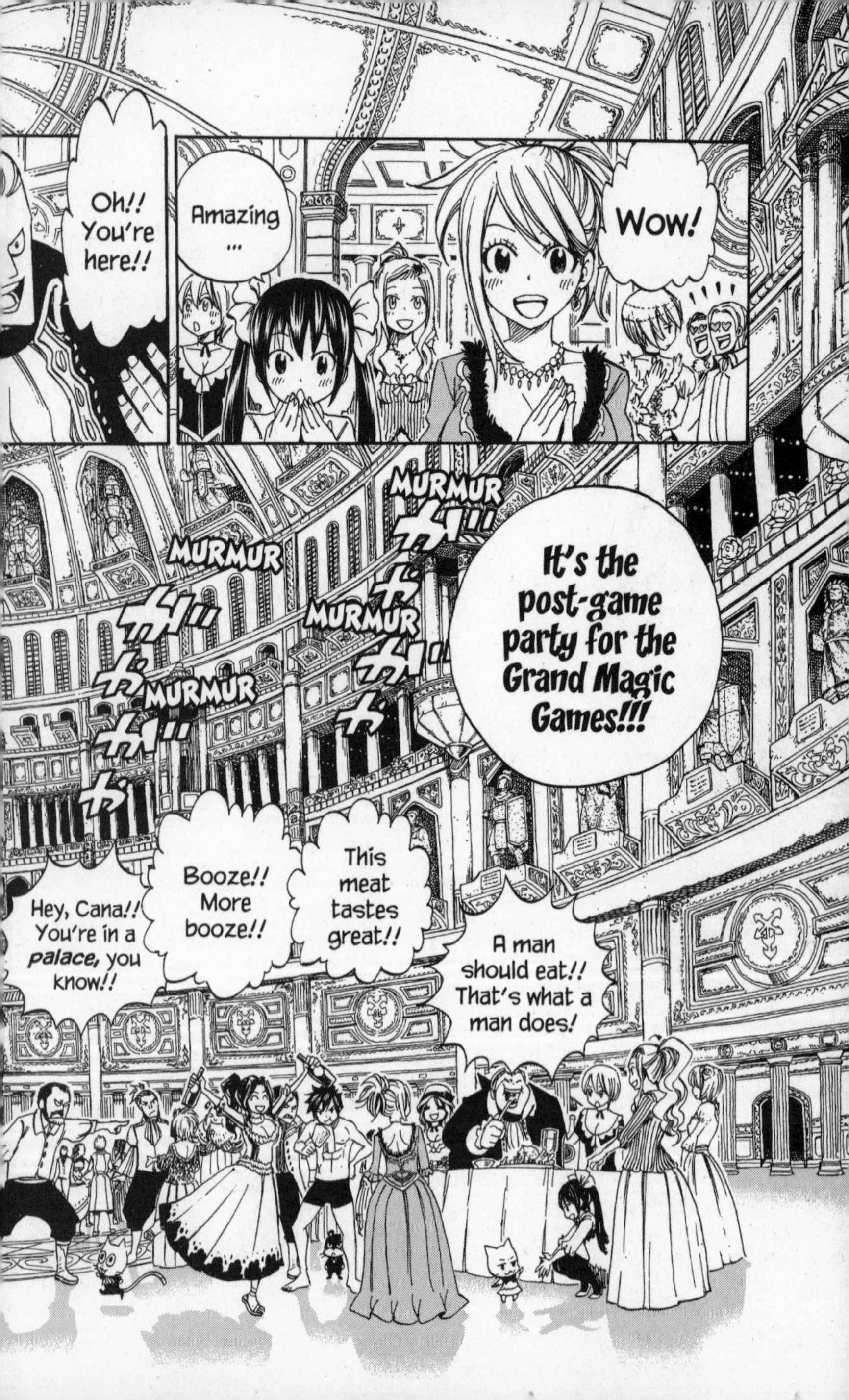
Wow!
Amazing ...
Oh!! You're here!!
MURMUR
MURMUR
It's the post-game party for the Grand Magic Games!!!
MURMUR
MURMUR
A man should eat!! That's what a man does!
This meat tastes great!!
Booze!! More booze!!
Hey, Cana!! You're in a *palace*, you know!!

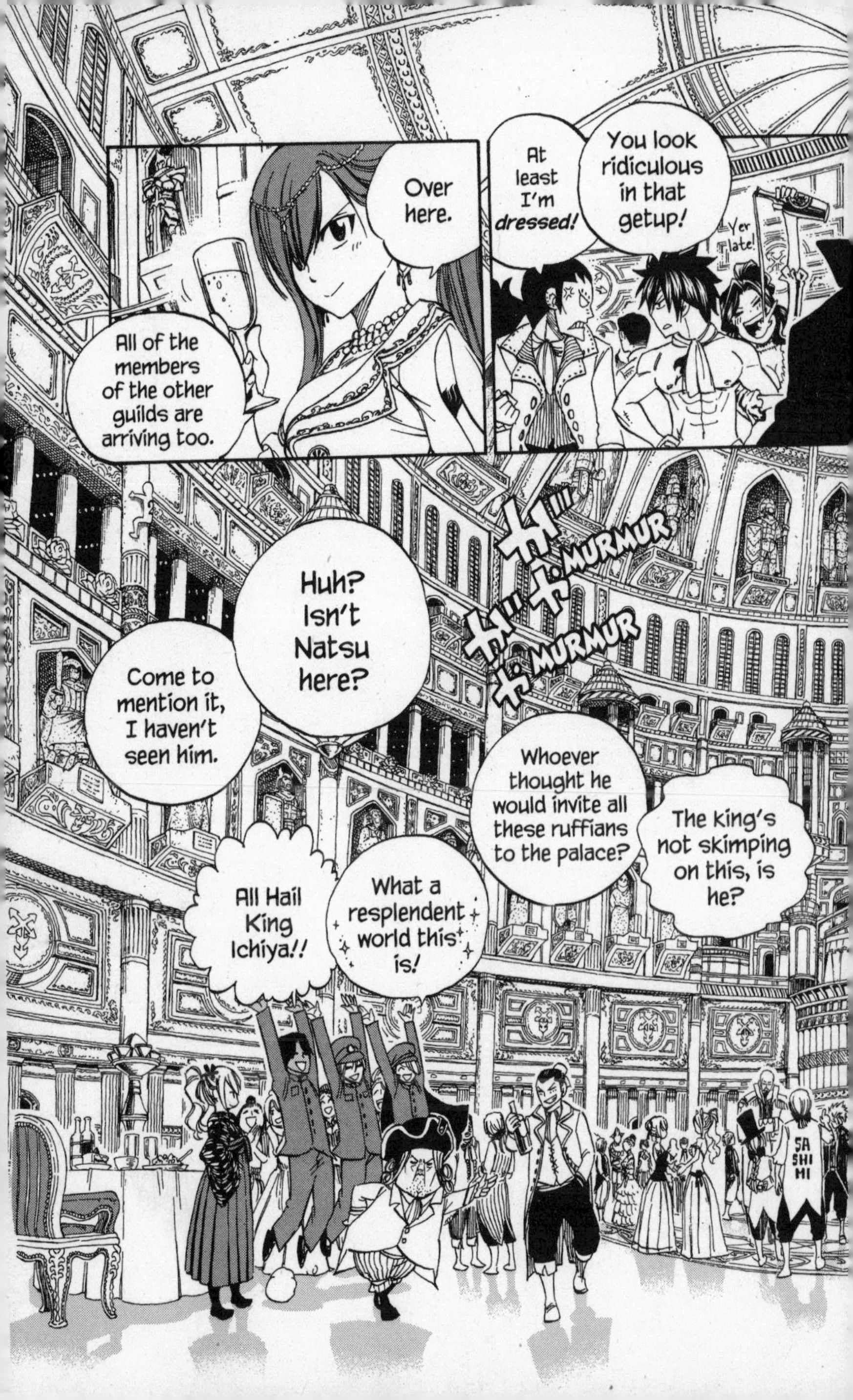
Yer late!
You look ridiculous in that getup!
At least I'm *dressed!*
Over here.
All of the members of the other guilds are arriving too.
MURMUR
MURMUR
Huh? Isn't Natsu here?
Come to mention it, I haven't seen him.
The king's not skimping on this, is he?
Whoever thought he would invite all these ruffians to the palace?
What a resplendent world this is!
All Hail King Ichiya!!
SASHIMI

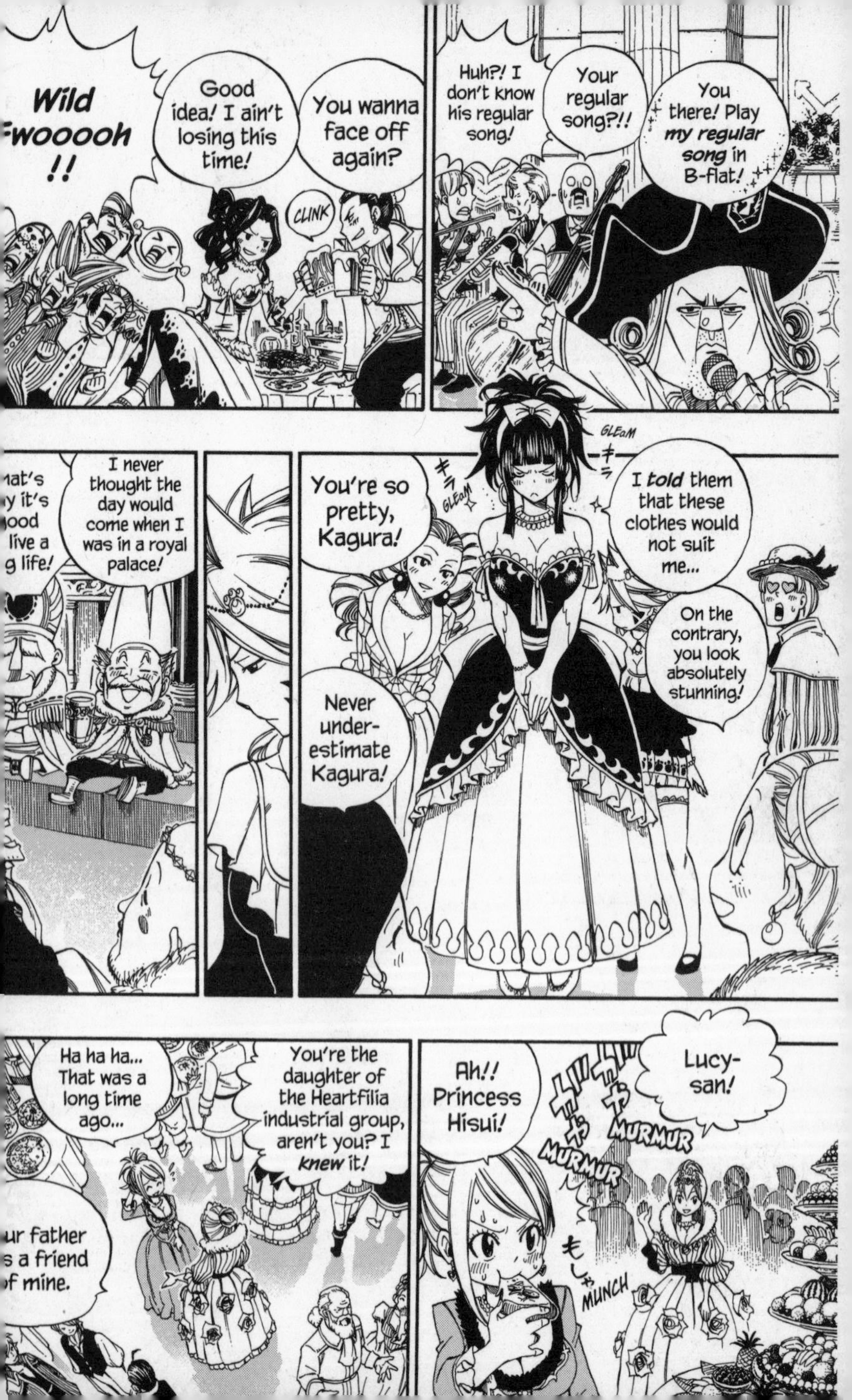
You there! Play my regular song in B-flat!
Your regular song?!!
Huh?! I don't know his regular song!
You wanna face off again?
CLINK
Good idea! I ain't losing this time!
Wild Fwooooh !!
GLEaM
I told them that these clothes would not suit me...
On the contrary, you look absolutely stunning!
GLEaM
You're so pretty, Kagura!
Never under-estimate Kagura!
I never thought the day would come when I was in a royal palace!
Lucy-san!
Ah!! Princess Hisui!
MURMUR
MURMUR
MUNCH
You're the daughter of the Heartfilia industrial group, aren't you? I knew it!
Ha ha ha... That was a long time ago...

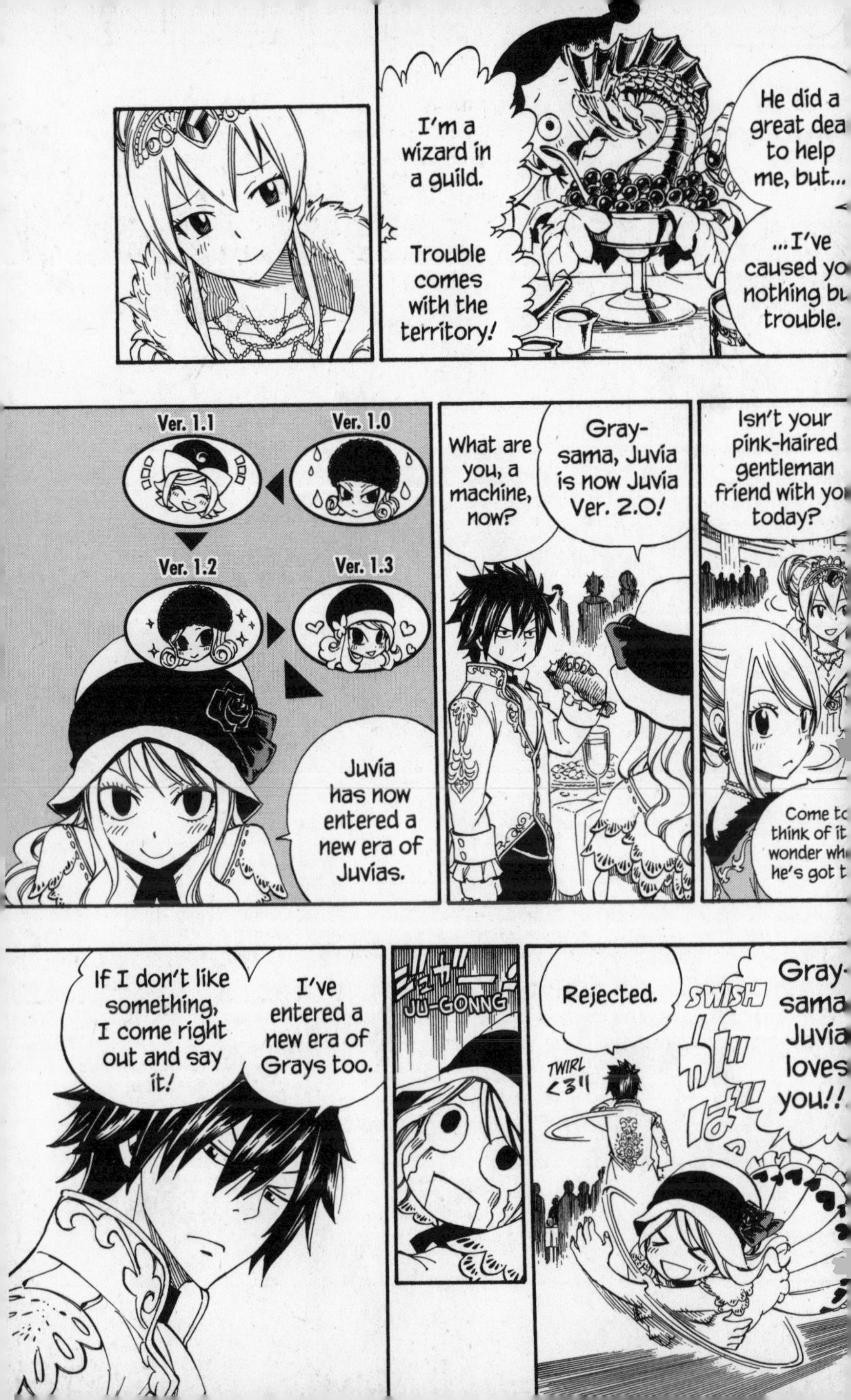
He did a great dea to help me, but...
...I've caused yo nothing bu trouble.
I'm a wizard in a guild.
Trouble comes with the territory!
Isn't your pink-haired gentleman friend with yo today?
Come tc think of it wonder wh he's got t
Gray-sama, Juvia is now Juvia Ver. 2.0!
What are you, a machine, now?
Ver. 1.0
Ver. 1.1
Ver. 1.2
Ver. 1.3
Juvia has now entered a new era of Juvias.
Gray-sama Juvia loves you!!
SWISH
Rejected.
TWIRL くるり
JU-GONNG
I've entered a new era of Grays too.
If I don't like something, I come right out and say it!

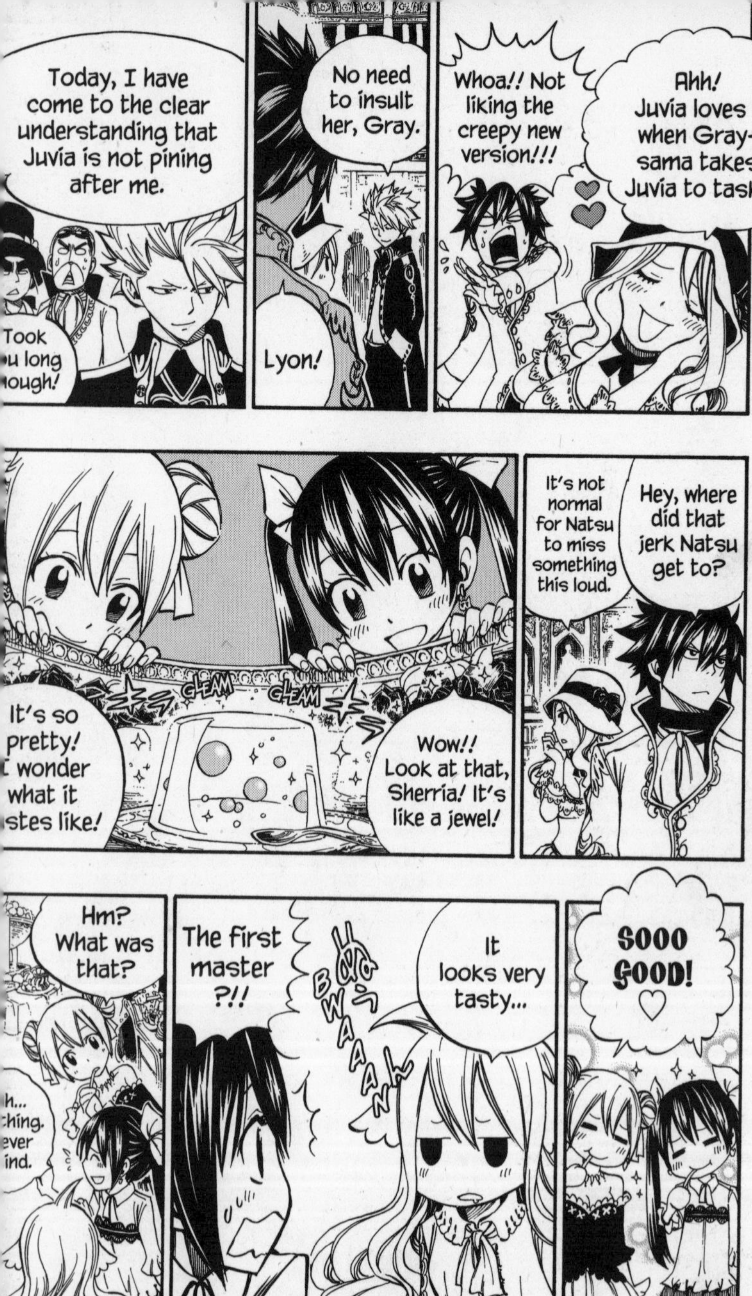
Ahh! Juvia loves it when Gray-sama takes Juvia to task!
Whoa!! Not liking the creepy new version!!!
No need to insult her, Gray.
Lyon!
Today, I have come to the clear understanding that Juvia is not pining after me.
Took
Hey, where did that jerk Natsu get to?
It's not normal for Natsu to miss something this loud.
Wow!! Look at that, Sherria! It's like a jewel!
GLEAM
GLEAM
It's so pretty!
wonder
what it
SOOO GOOD! ♥
It looks very tasty...
BWAAAN
The first master?!!
Hm? What was that?

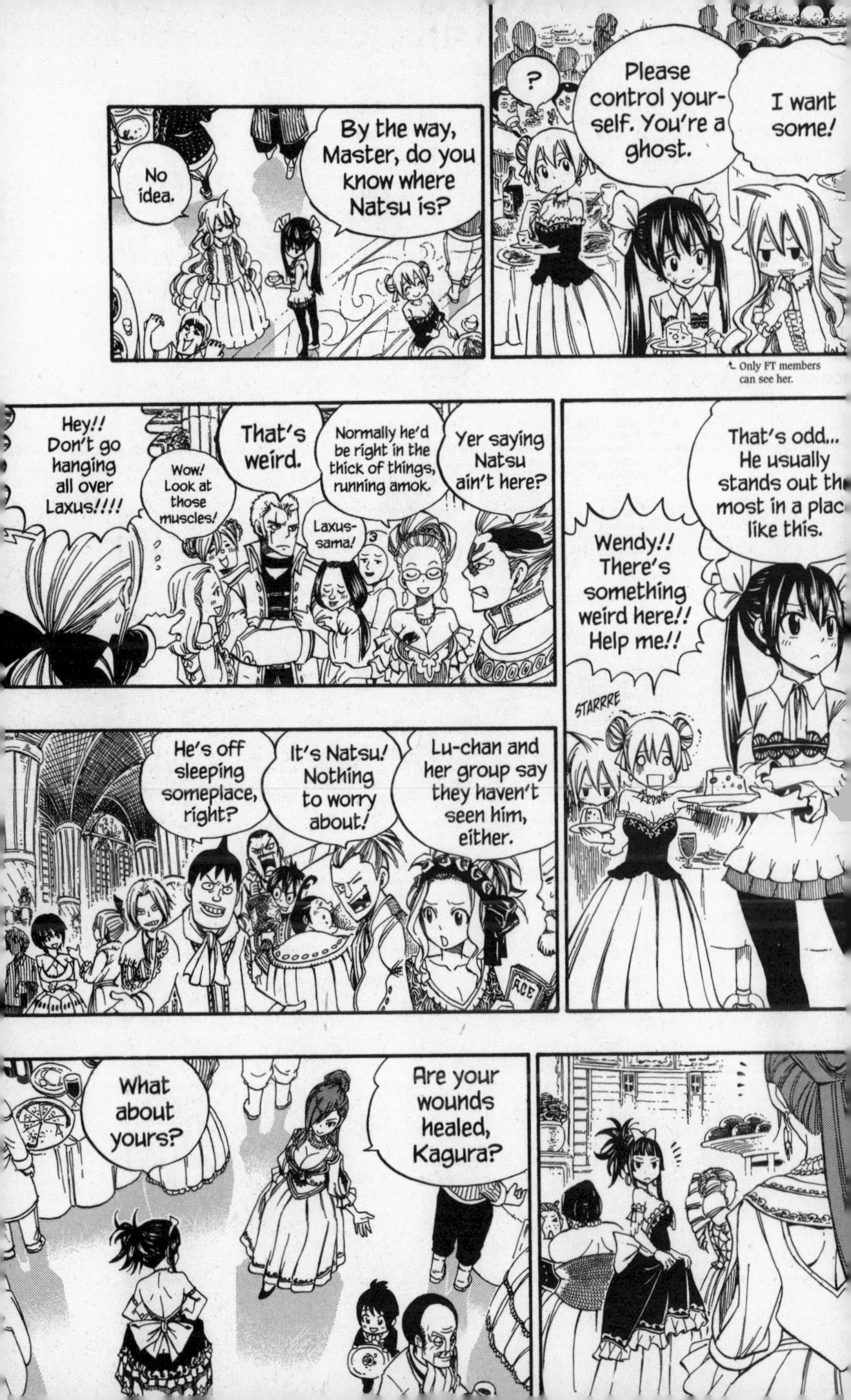
I want some!
Please control your-self. You're a ghost.
?
Only FT members can see her.
By the way, Master, do you know where Natsu is?
No idea.
That's odd... He usually stands out the most in a plac like this.
Wendy!! There's something weird here!! Help me!!
STARRRE
Yer saying Natsu ain't here?
Normally he'd be right in the thick of things, running amok.
That's weird.
Laxus-sama!
Wow! Look at those muscles!
Hey!! Don't go hanging all over Laxus!!!!
Lu-chan and her group say they haven't seen him, either.
It's Natsu! Nothing to worry about!
He's off sleeping someplace, right?
Are your wounds healed, Kagura?
What about yours?

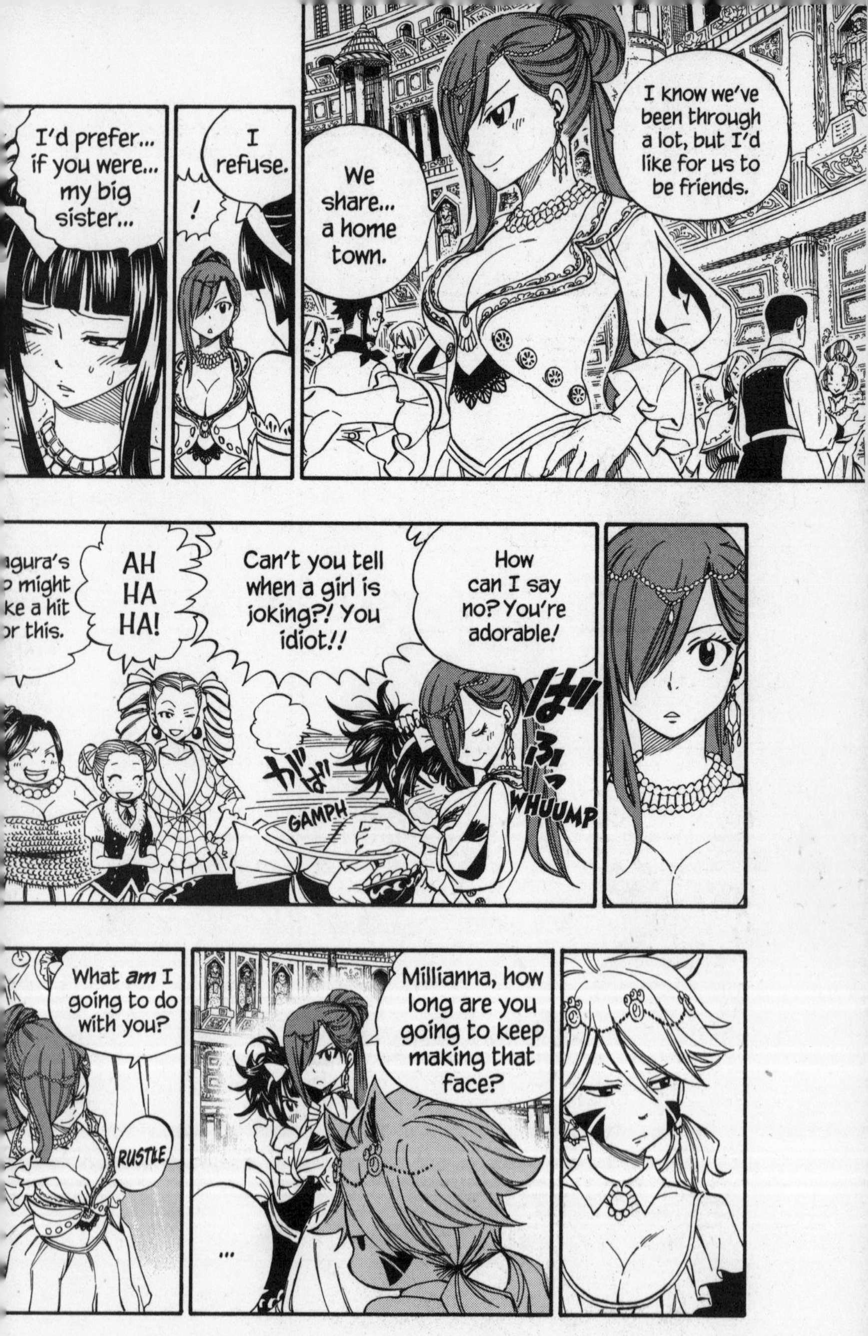
I know we've been through a lot, but I'd like for us to be friends.
We share... a home town.
I refuse.
!
I'd prefer... if you were... my big sister...
How can I say no? You're adorable!
はふっ
WHUUMP
Can't you tell when a girl is joking?! You idiot!!
がばっ
GAMPH
AH HA HA!
agura's
might
ke a hit
or this.
Millianna, how long are you going to keep making that face?
...
What *am* I going to do with you?
RUSTLE

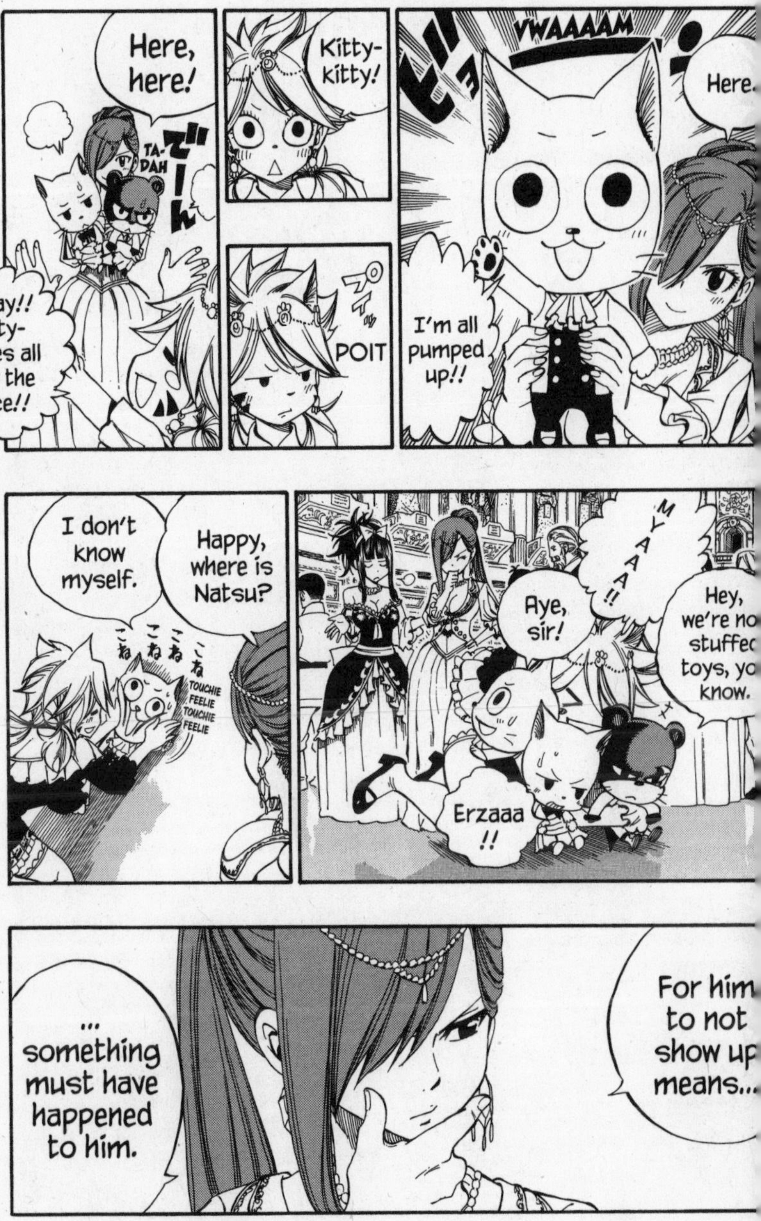
VWAAAAM
Here.
I'm all pumped up!!
Kitty-kitty!
POIT
Here, here!
TA-DAH
Yaaay!! Kitty-kitties all over the place!!
Hey, we're no stuffec toys, yo know.
MYAAAA!!
Aye, sir!
Erzaaa!!
Happy, where is Natsu?
I don't know myself.
TOUCHIE FEELIE TOUCHIE FEELIE
For him to not show up means...
... something must have happened to him.

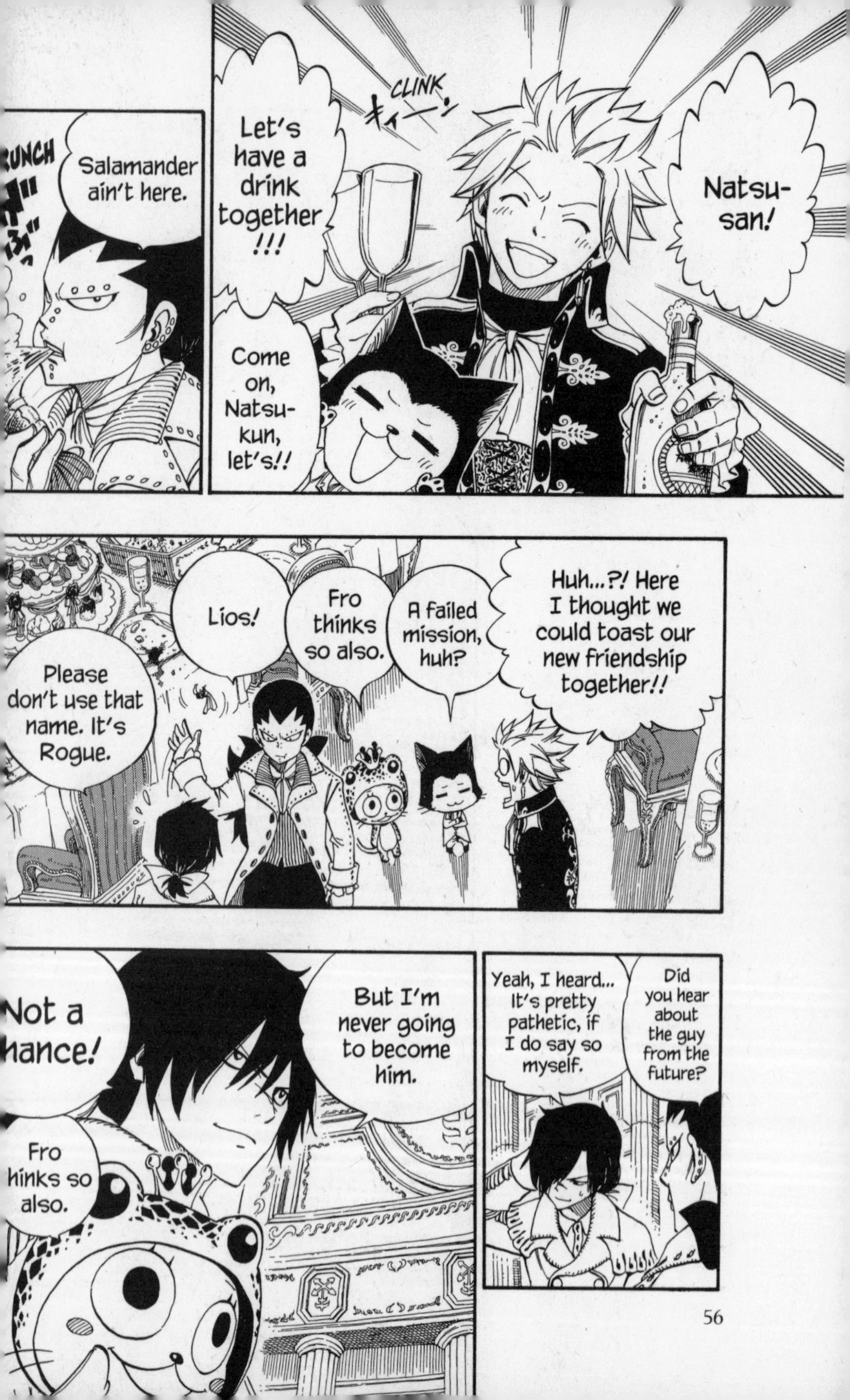
Natsu-san!
Let's have a drink together!!!
CLINK
Come on, Natsu-kun, let's!!
UNCH
Salamander ain't here.
Huh...?! Here I thought we could toast our new friendship together!!
A failed mission, huh?
Fro thinks so also.
Lios!
Please don't use that name. It's Rogue.
Did you hear about the guy from the future?
Yeah, I heard... It's pretty pathetic, if I do say so myself.
But I'm never going to become him.
Not a hance!
Fro hinks so also.

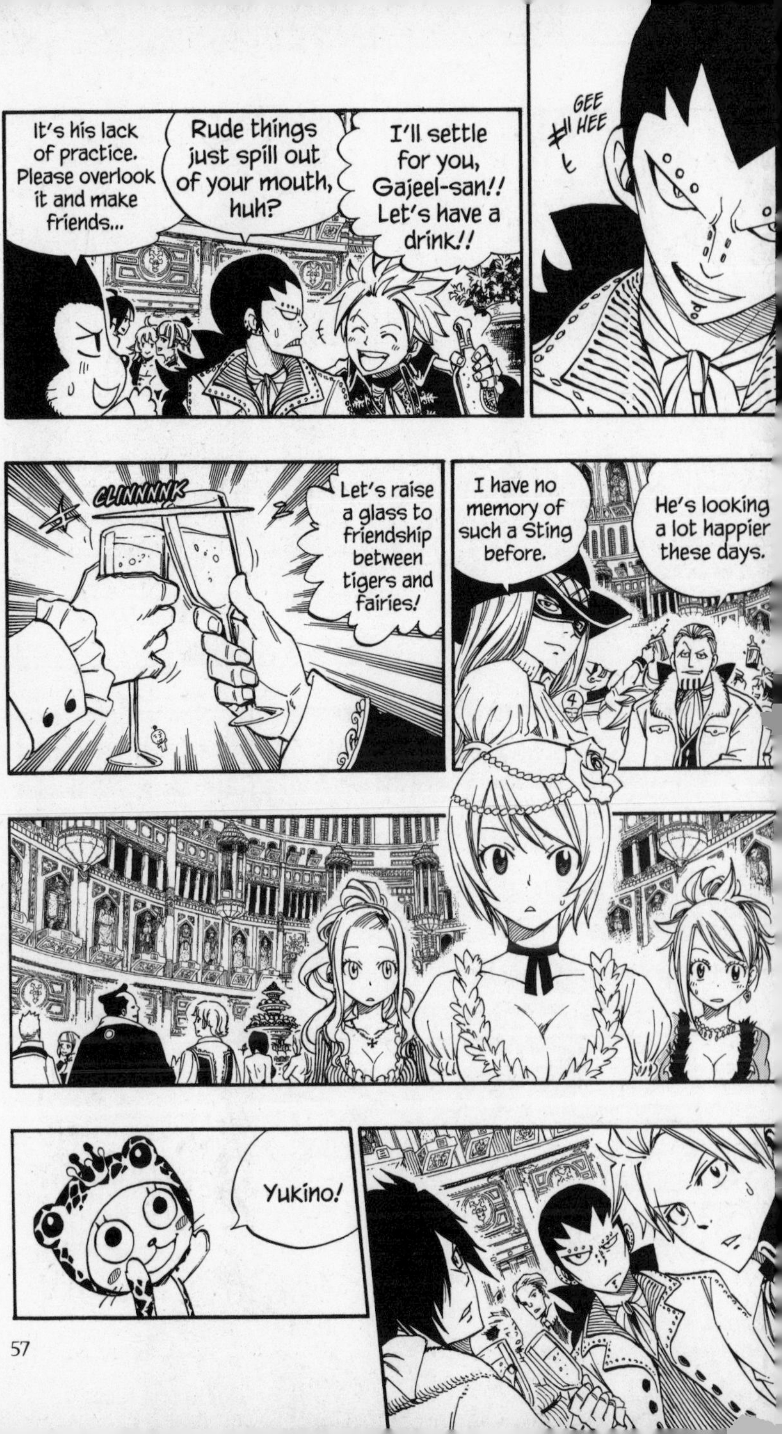
GEE HEE
I'll settle for you, Gajeel-san!! Let's have a drink!!
Rude things just spill out of your mouth, huh?
It's his lack of practice. Please overlook it and make friends...
He's looking a lot happier these days.
I have no memory of such a Sting before.
Let's raise a glass to friendship between tigers and fairies!
CLINNNNK
Yukino!

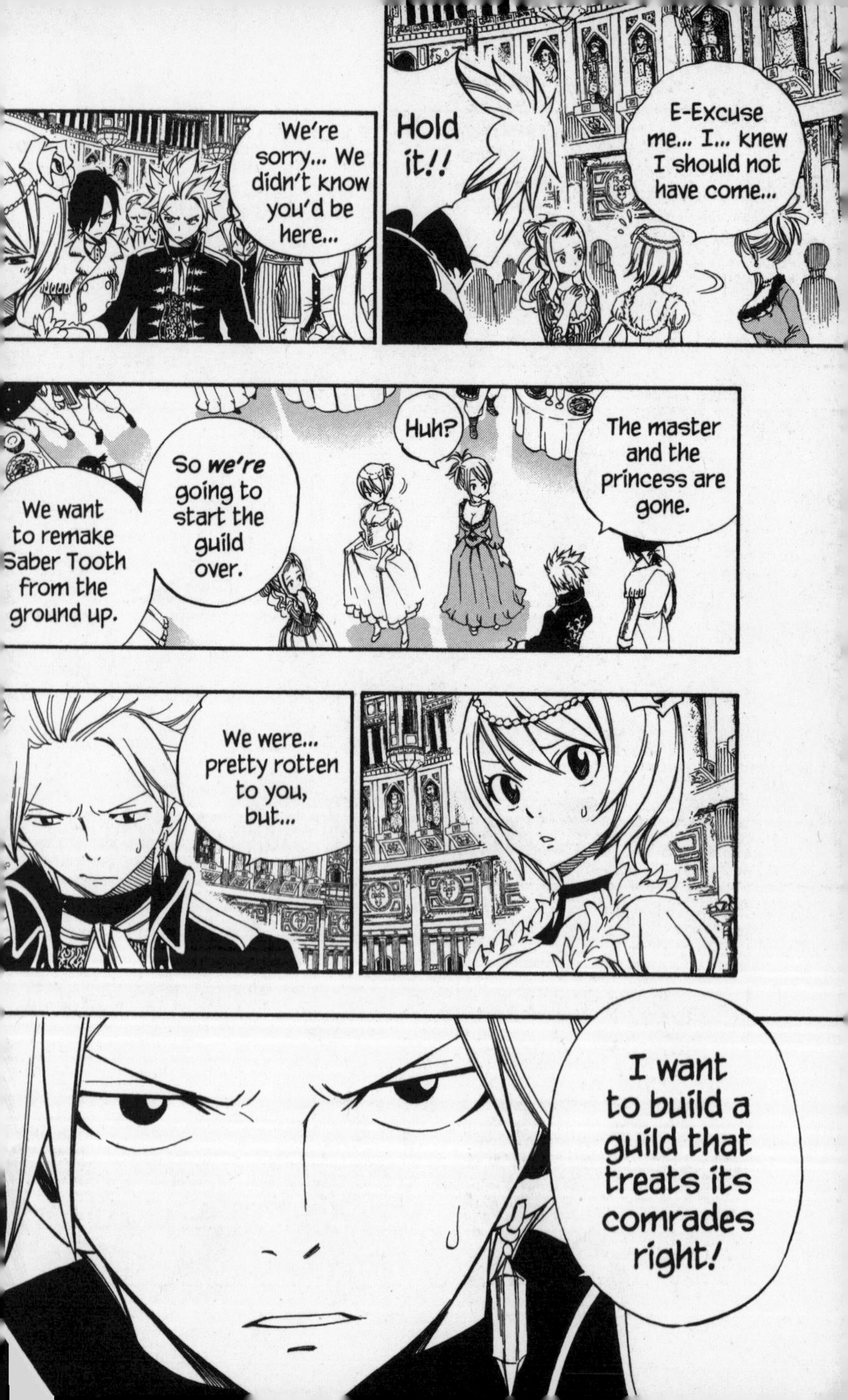
E-Excuse me... I... knew I should not have come...
Hold it!!
We're sorry... We didn't know you'd be here...
The master and the princess are gone.
Huh?
So *we're* going to start the guild over.
We want to remake Saber Tooth from the ground up.
We were... pretty rotten to you, but...
I want to build a guild that treats its comrades right!

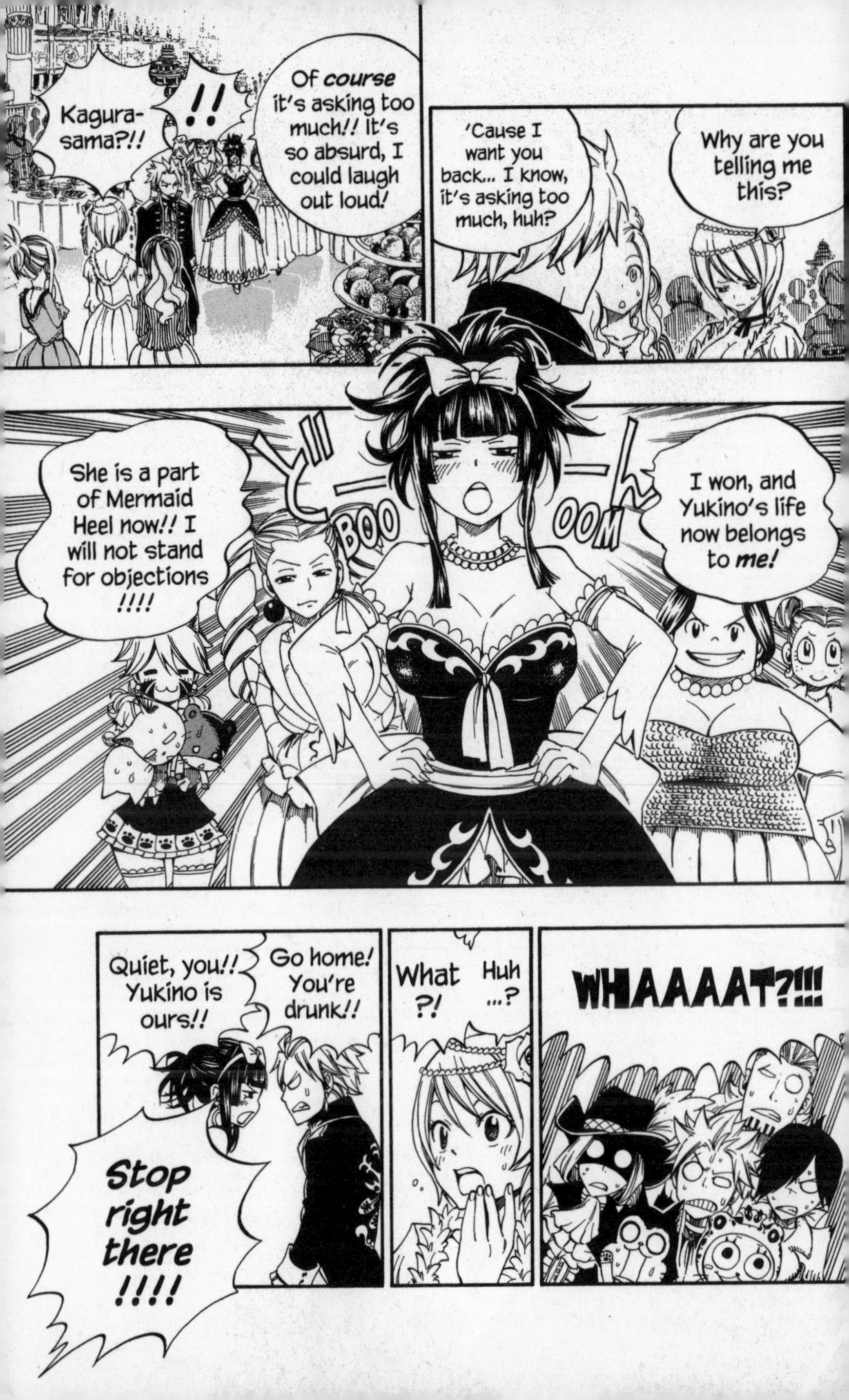

Why are you telling me this?
'Cause I want you back... I know, it's asking too much, huh?
Of *course* it's asking too much!! It's so absurd, I could laugh out loud!
!!
Kagura-sama?!!
I won, and Yukino's life now belongs to *me!*
BOO
OOM
She is a part of Mermaid Heel now!! I will not stand for objections!!!!
WHAAAAT?!!!
Huh ...?
What ?!
Go home! You're drunk!!
Quiet, you!! Yukino is ours!!
Stop right there!!!!

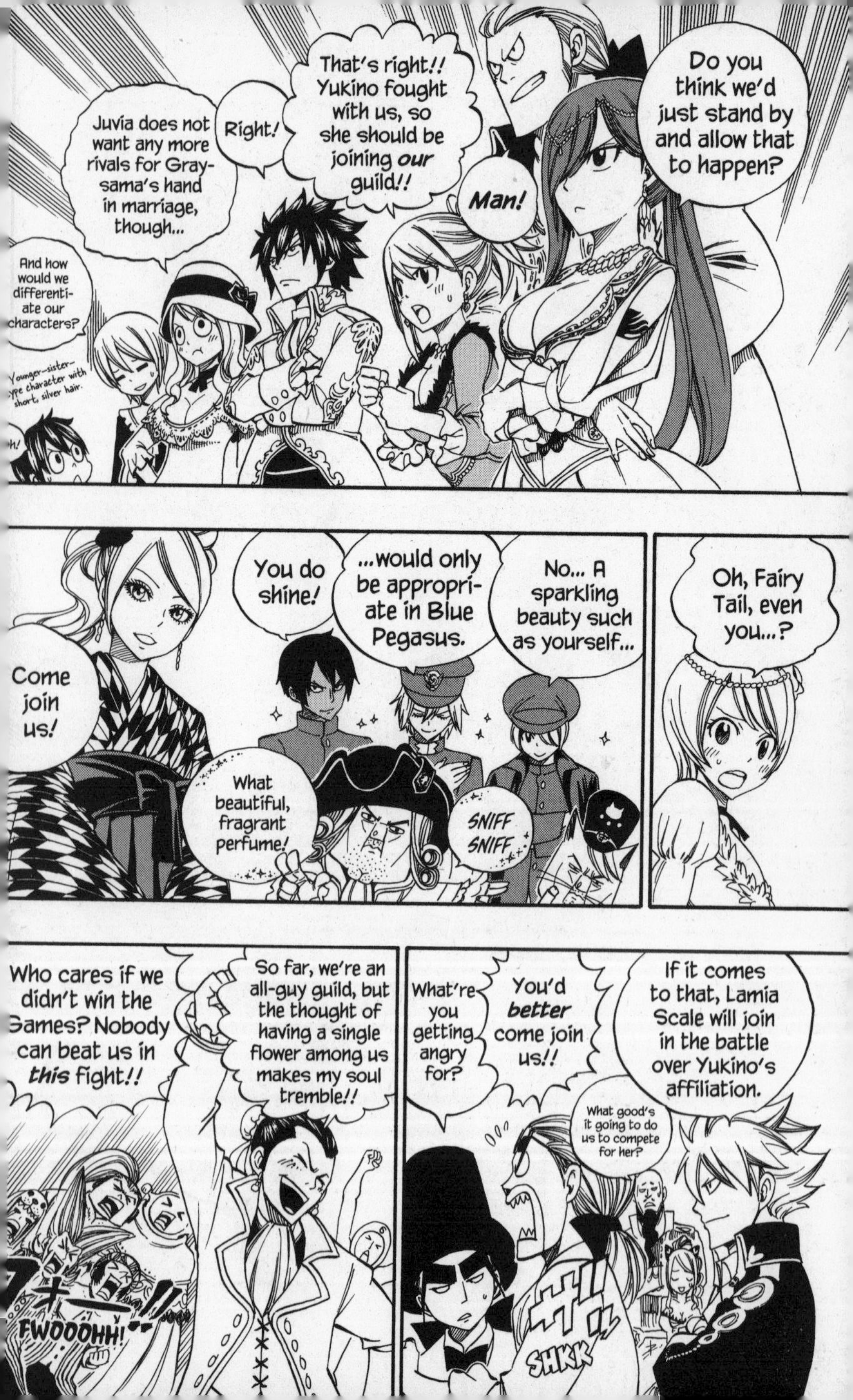
Do you think we'd just stand by and allow that to happen?
Man!
That's right!! Yukino fought with us, so she should be joining *our* guild!!
Right!
Juvia does not want any more rivals for Gray-sama's hand in marriage, though...
And how would we differenti-ate our characters?
Younger-sister-type character with short, silver hair.
Oh, Fairy Tail, even you...?
No... A sparkling beauty such as yourself...
...would only be appropri-ate in Blue Pegasus.
You do shine!
Come join us!
What beautiful, fragrant perfume!
SNIFF SNIFF
If it comes to that, Lamia Scale will join in the battle over Yukino's affiliation.
What good's it going to do us to compete for her?
You'd *better* come join us!!
What're you getting angry for?
SHKK
So far, we're an all-guy guild, but the thought of having a single flower among us makes my soul tremble!!
Who cares if we didn't win the Games? Nobody can beat us in *this* fight!!
FWOOOHH!

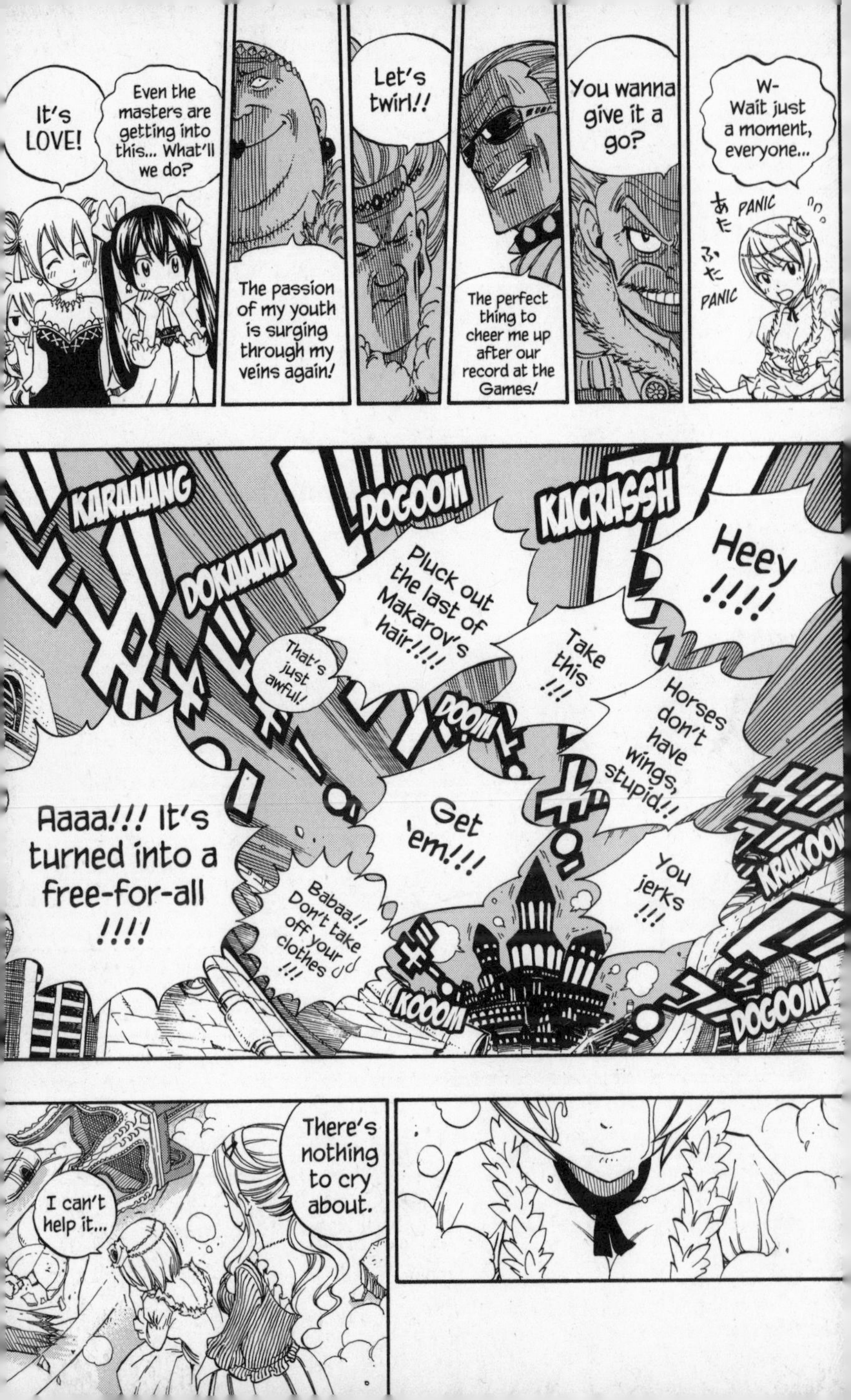

W- Wait just a moment, everyone...
あたふた
PANIC PANIC
You wanna give it a go?
The perfect thing to cheer me up after our record at the Games!
Let's twirl!!
The passion of my youth is surging through my veins again!
Even the masters are getting into this... What'll we do?
It's LOVE!
KACRASSH
Heey!!!!
DOGOOM
Pluck out the last of Makarov's hair!!!!
KARAAANG
DOKAAAM
Take this!!!
Horses don't have wings, stupid!!
That's just awful!
DOOM
KRAKOOM
Get 'em!!!
You jerks!!!
Aaaa!!! It's turned into a free-for-all!!!!
Babaa!! Don't take off your clothes♪!!!
DOGOOM
KOOOM
There's nothing to cry about.
I can't help it...

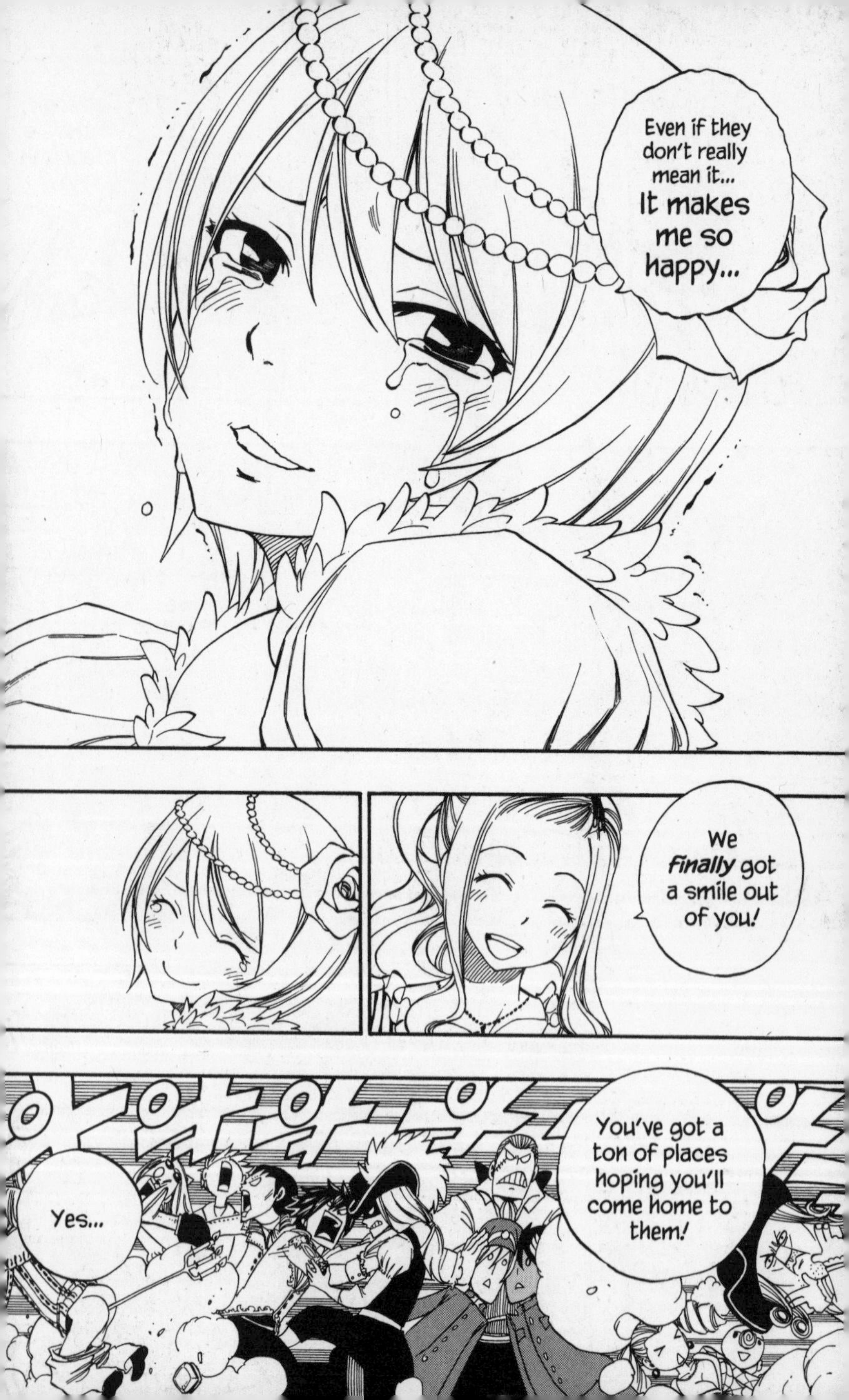
Even if they don't really mean it... It makes me so happy...
We *finally* got a smile out of you!
You've got a ton of places hoping you'll come home to them!
Yes...

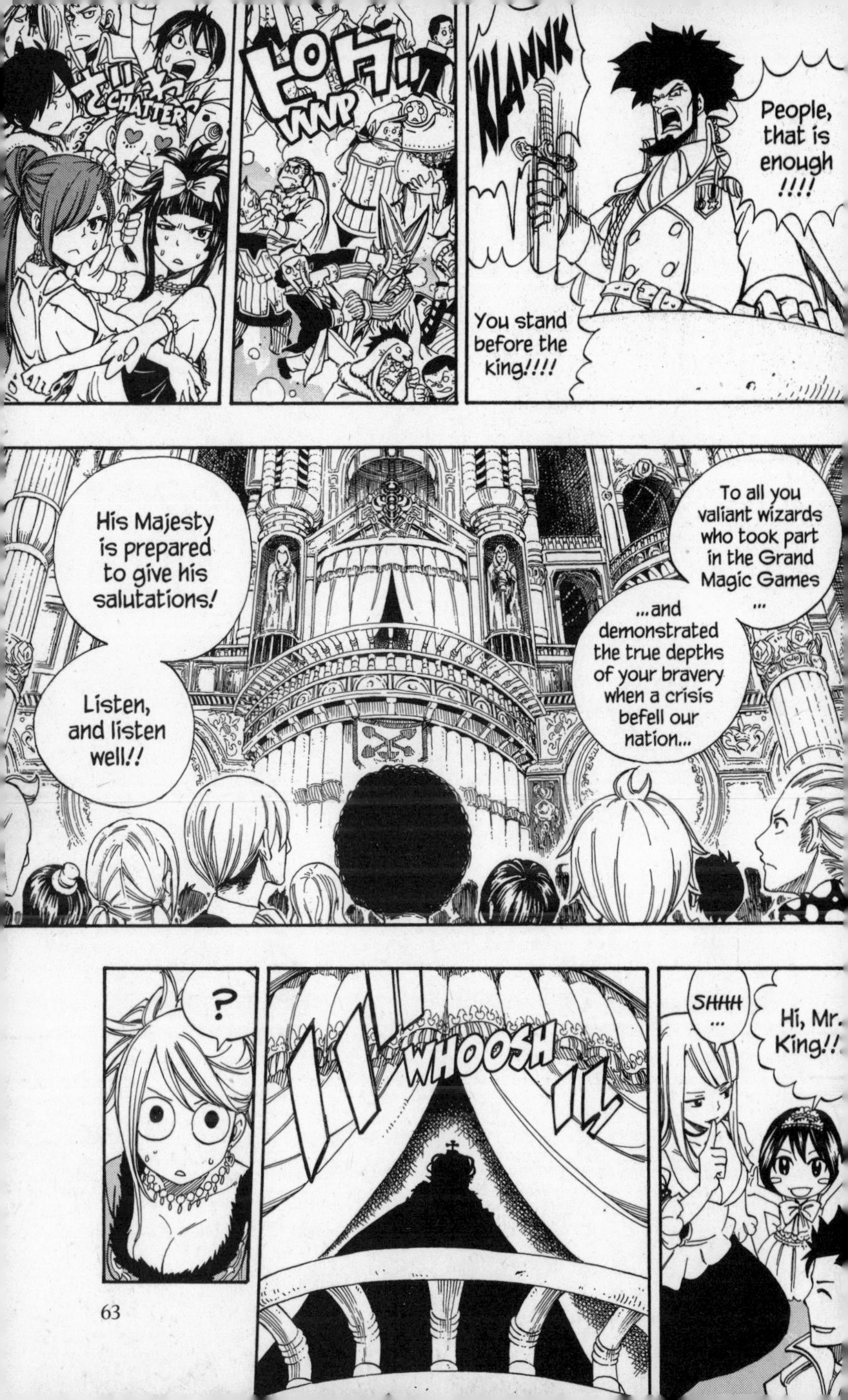
KLANNK
People, that is enough!!!!
You stand before the king!!!!
WWP
CHATTER
To all you valiant wizards who took part in the Grand Magic Games ...
...and demonstrated the true depths of your bravery when a crisis befell our nation...
His Majesty is prepared to give his salutations!
Listen, and listen well!!
Hi, Mr. King!!
SHHH ...
WHOOSH
?

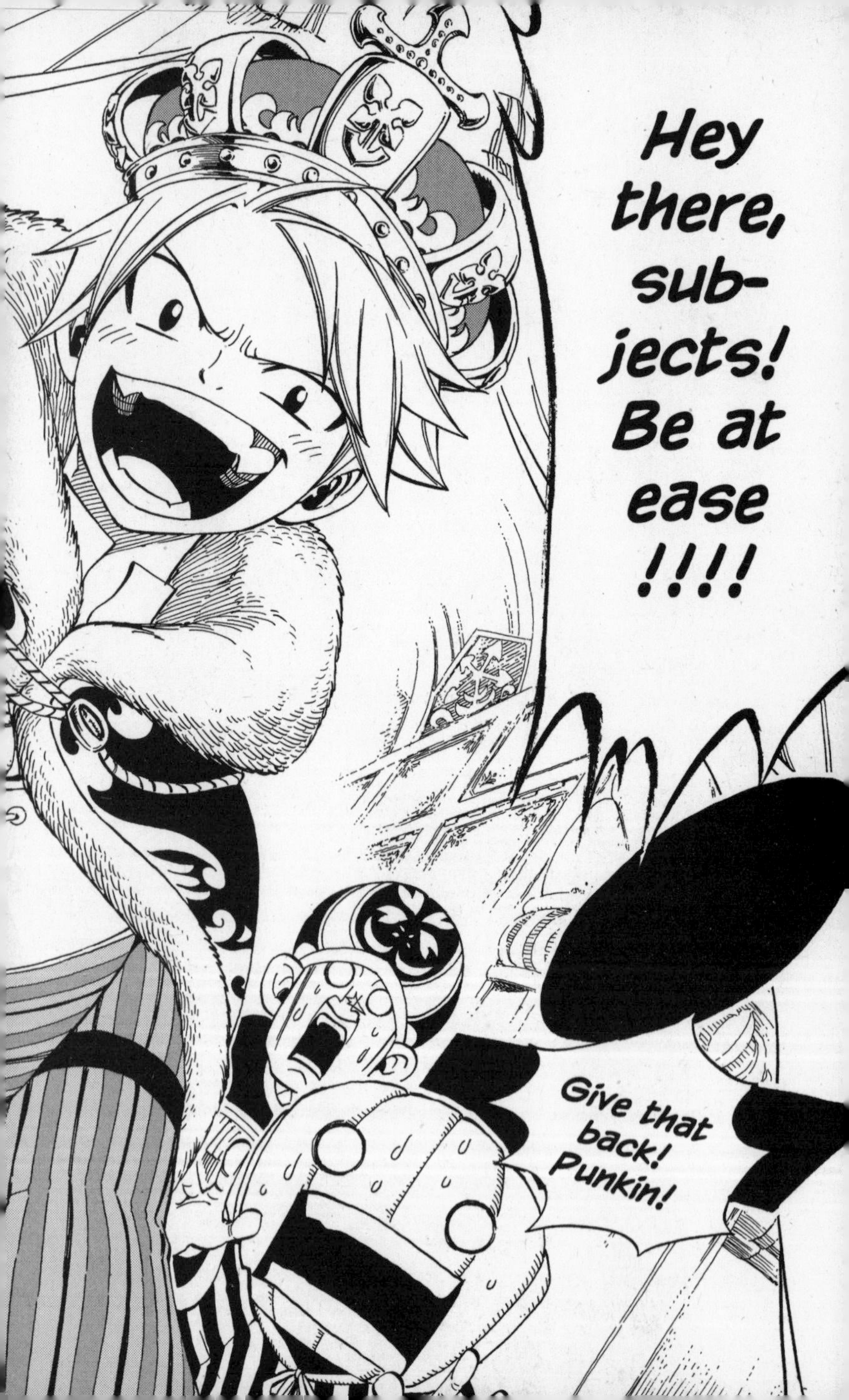
Hey there, sub-jects! Be at ease !!!!
Give that back! Punkin!

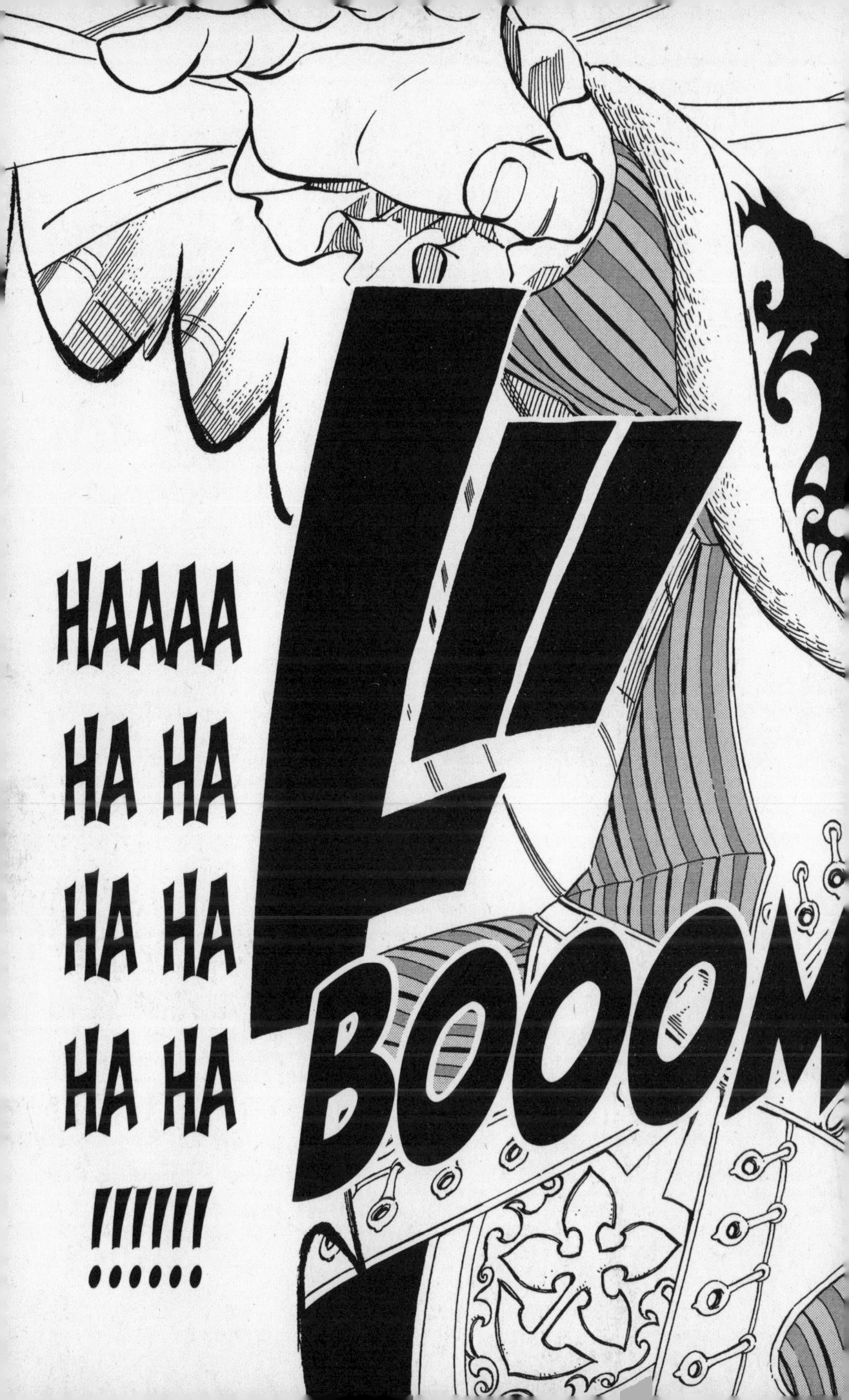
BOOOM
HAAAA HA HA HA HA HA HA !!!!!! ......

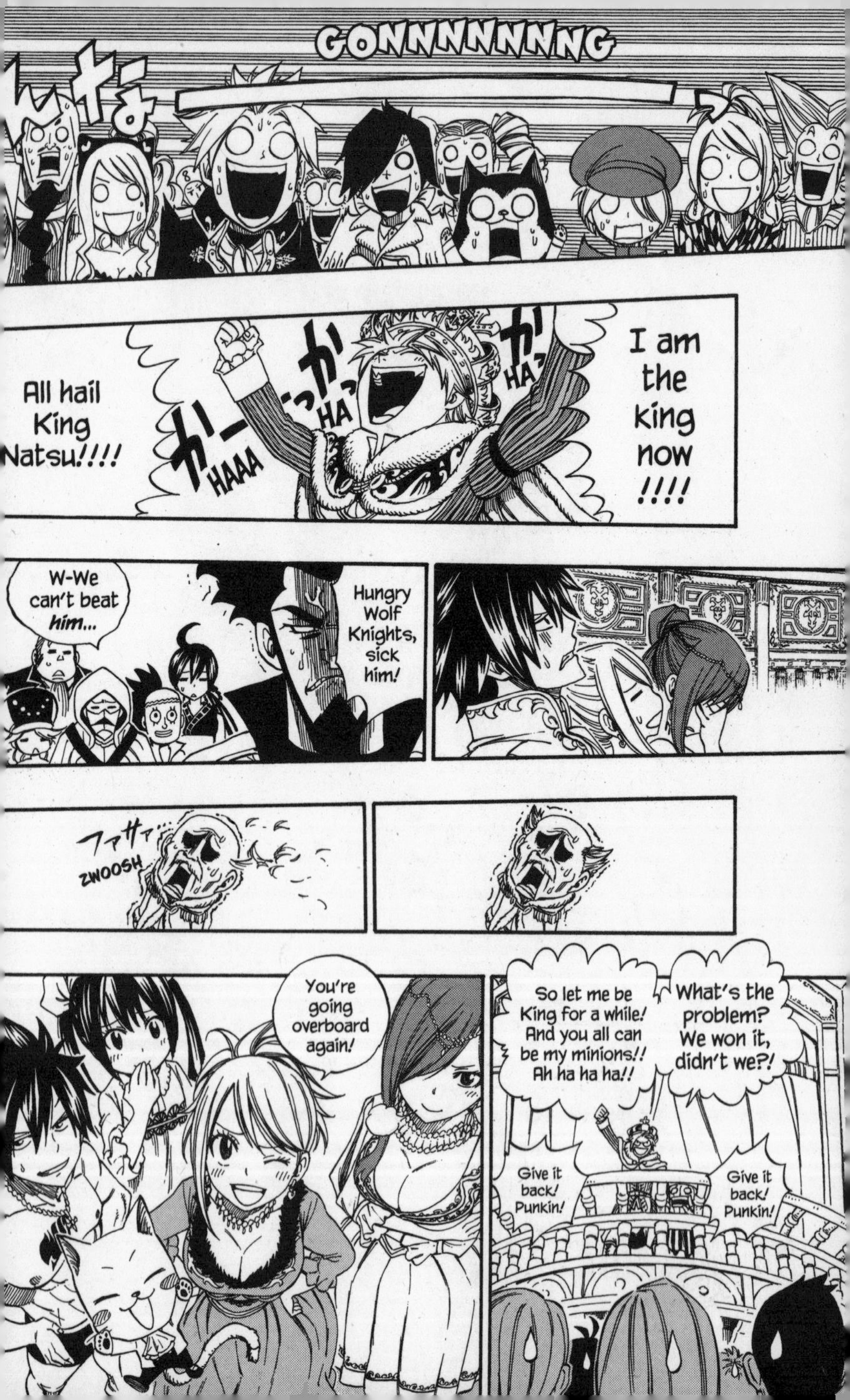
GONNNNNNNG
I am the king now!!!!
か
HA
かっ
HA
かー
HAAA
All hail King Natsu!!!!
Hungry Wolf Knights, sick him!
W-We can't beat *him*...
ファサァ
ZWOOSH
What's the problem? We won it, didn't we?!
So let me be King for a while! And you all can be my minions!! Ah ha ha ha!!
Give it back! Punkin!
Give it back! Punkin!
You're going overboard again!

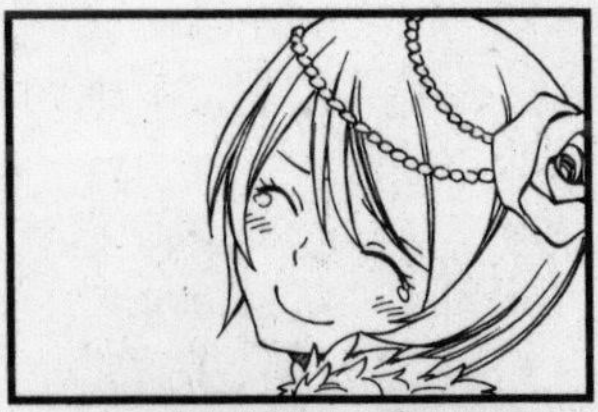

FAIRY TAIL

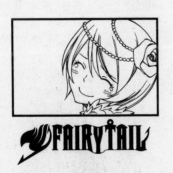

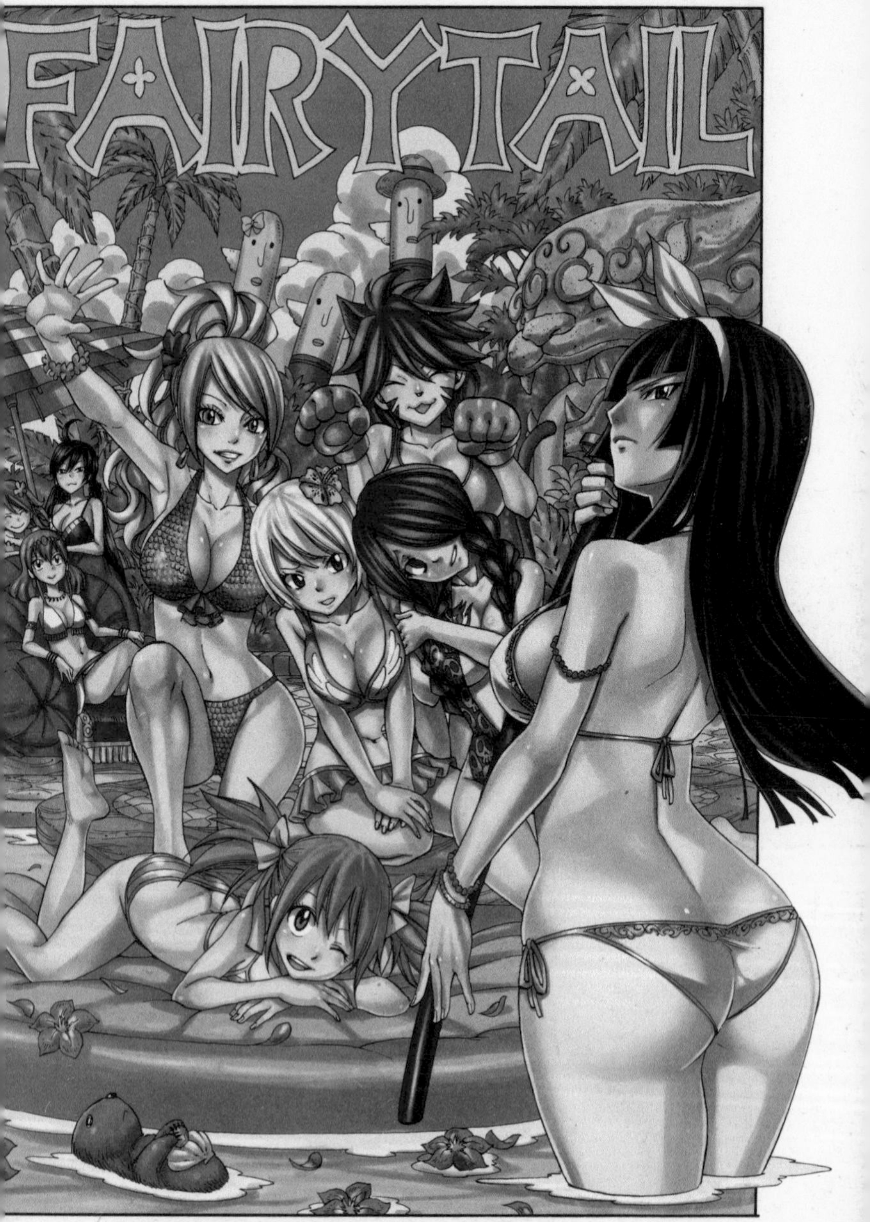
FAIRY TAIL

Chapter 339: Drops of Time

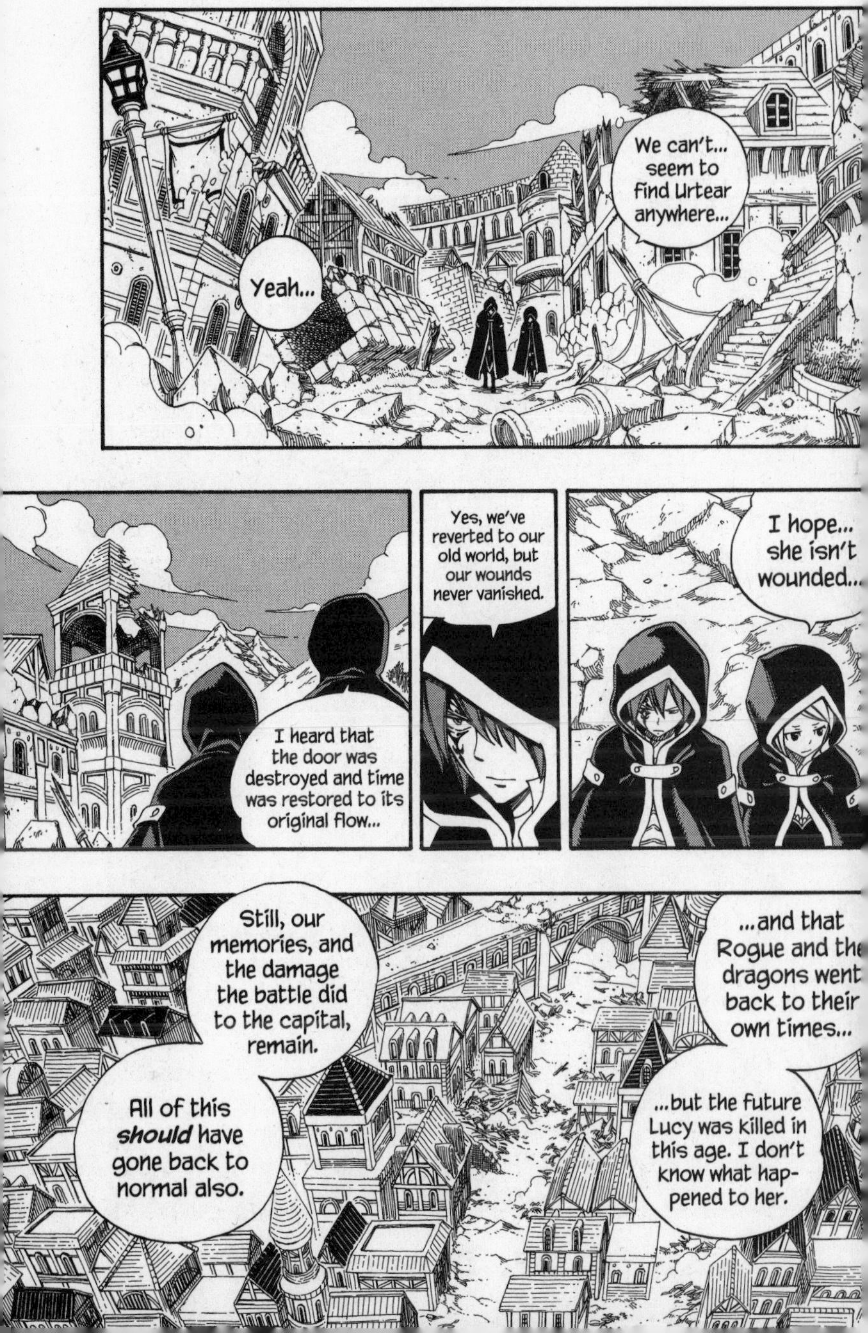
We can't... seem to find Urtear anywhere...
Yeah...
I hope... she isn't wounded...
Yes, we've reverted to our old world, but our wounds never vanished.
I heard that the door was destroyed and time was restored to its original flow...
...and that Rogue and the dragons went back to their own times...
...but the future Lucy was killed in this age. I don't know what hap-pened to her.
Still, our memories, and the damage the battle did to the capital, remain.
All of this *should* have gone back to normal also.

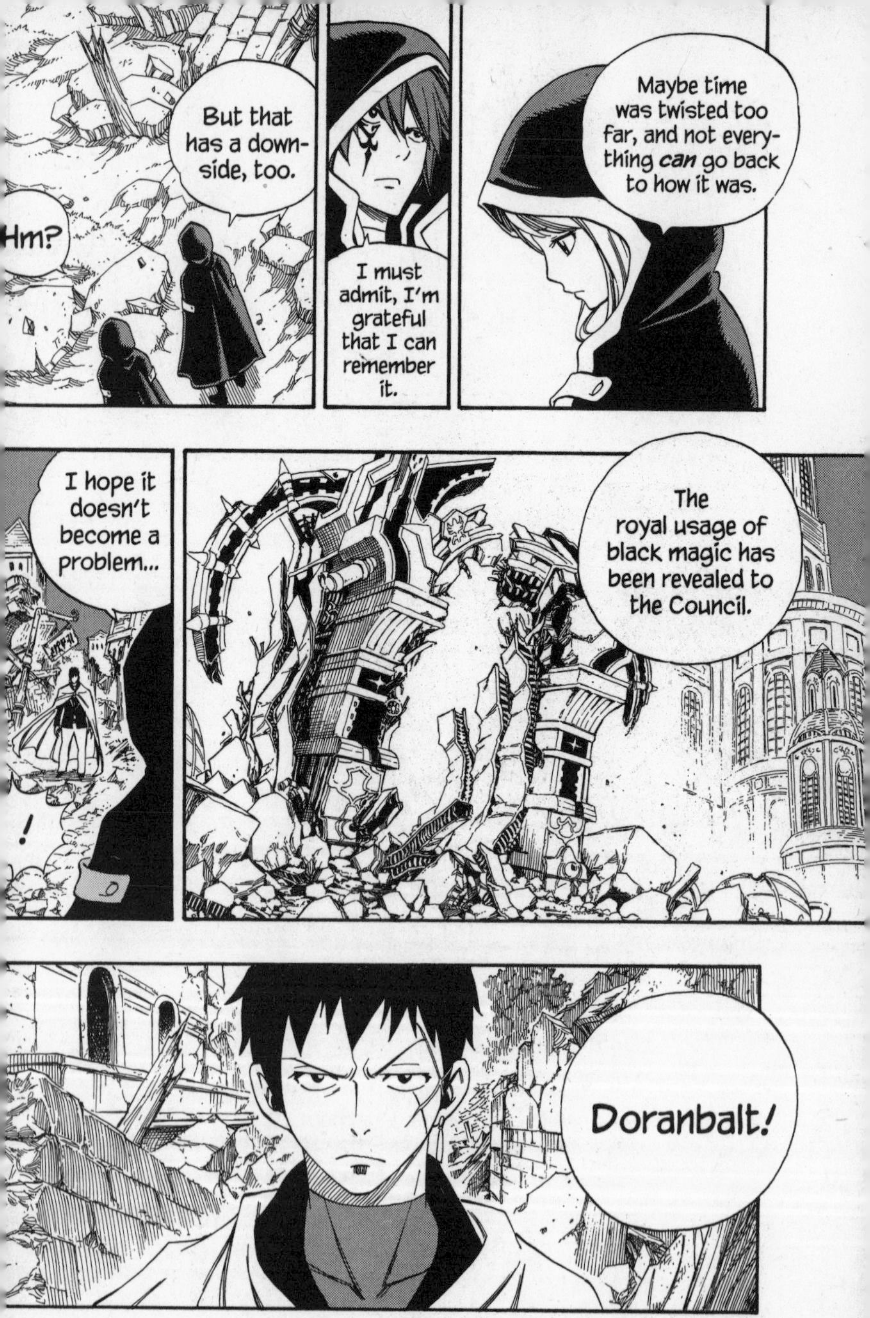
Maybe time was twisted too far, and not everything *can* go back to how it was.
I must admit, I'm grateful that I can remember it.
But that has a downside, too.
Hm?
The royal usage of black magic has been revealed to the Council.
I hope it doesn't become a problem...
!
Doranbalt!

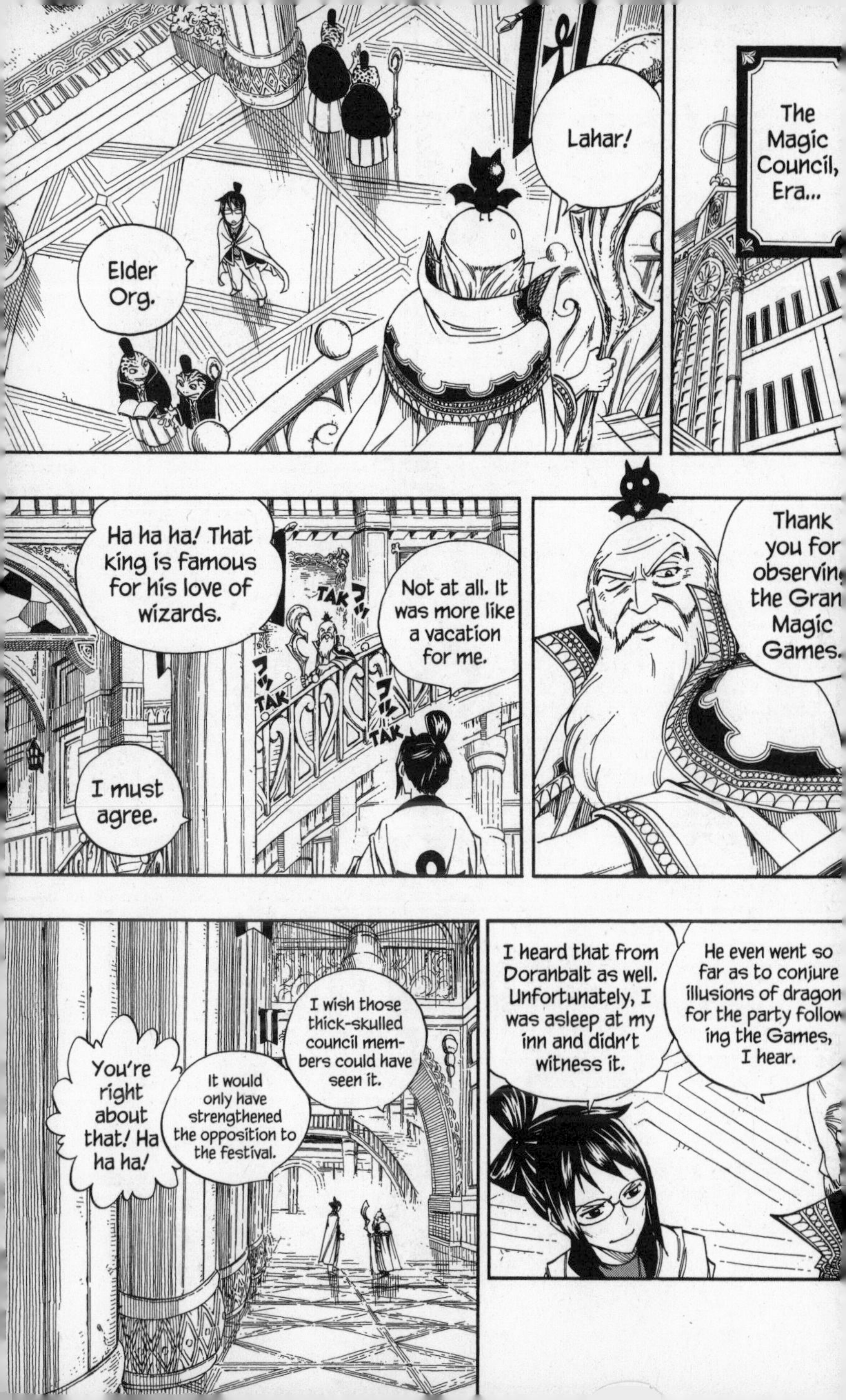
The Magic Council, Era...
Lahar!
Elder Org.
Thank you for observin the Gran Magic Games.
Not at all. It was more like a vacation for me.
TAK TAK TAK TAK
Ha ha ha! That king is famous for his love of wizards.
I must agree.
He even went so far as to conjure illusions of dragon for the party follow ing the Games, I hear.
I heard that from Doranbalt as well. Unfortunately, I was asleep at my inn and didn't witness it.
I wish those thick-skulled council mem- bers could have seen it.
It would only have strengthened the opposition to the festival.
You're right about that! Ha ha ha!

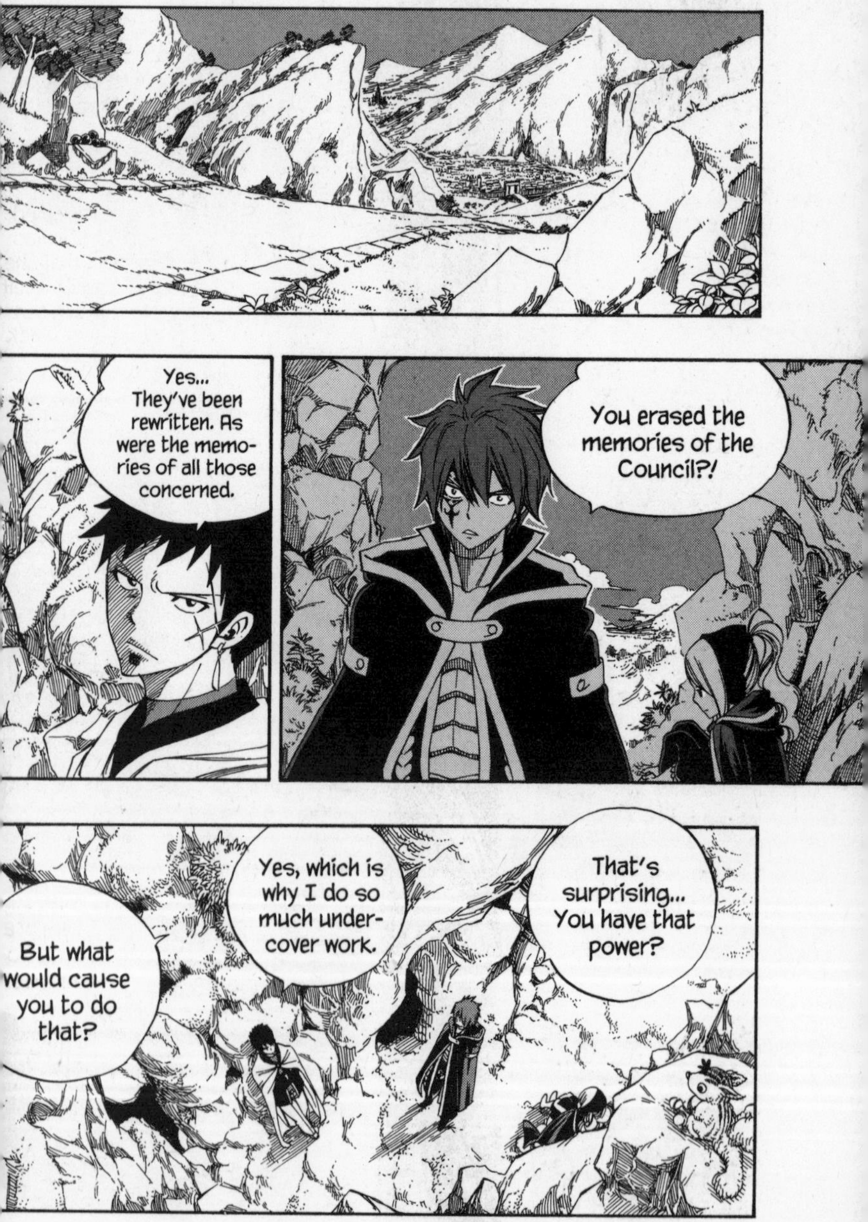
You erased the memories of the Council?!
Yes... They've been rewritten. As were the memories of all those concerned.
That's surprising... You have that power?
Yes, which is why I do so much undercover work.
But what would cause you to do that?

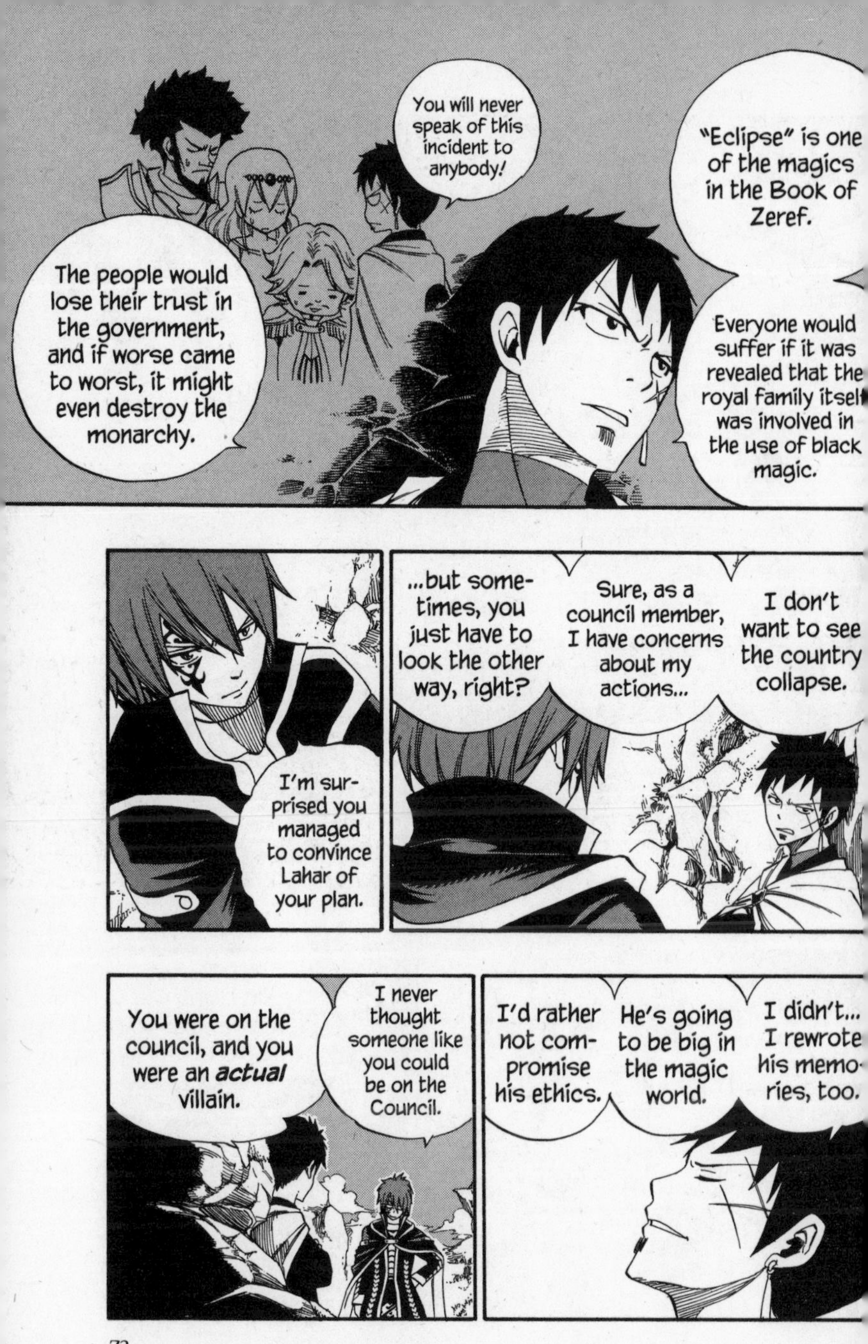
"Eclipse" is one of the magics in the Book of Zeref.
Everyone would suffer if it was revealed that the royal family itself was involved in the use of black magic.
You will never speak of this incident to anybody!
The people would lose their trust in the government, and if worse came to worst, it might even destroy the monarchy.
I don't want to see the country collapse.
Sure, as a council member, I have concerns about my actions...
...but some-times, you just have to look the other way, right?
I'm sur-prised you managed to convince Lahar of your plan.
I didn't... I rewrote his memo-ries, too.
He's going to be big in the magic world.
I'd rather not com-promise his ethics.
I never thought someone like you could be on the Council.
You were on the council, and you were an *actual* villain.

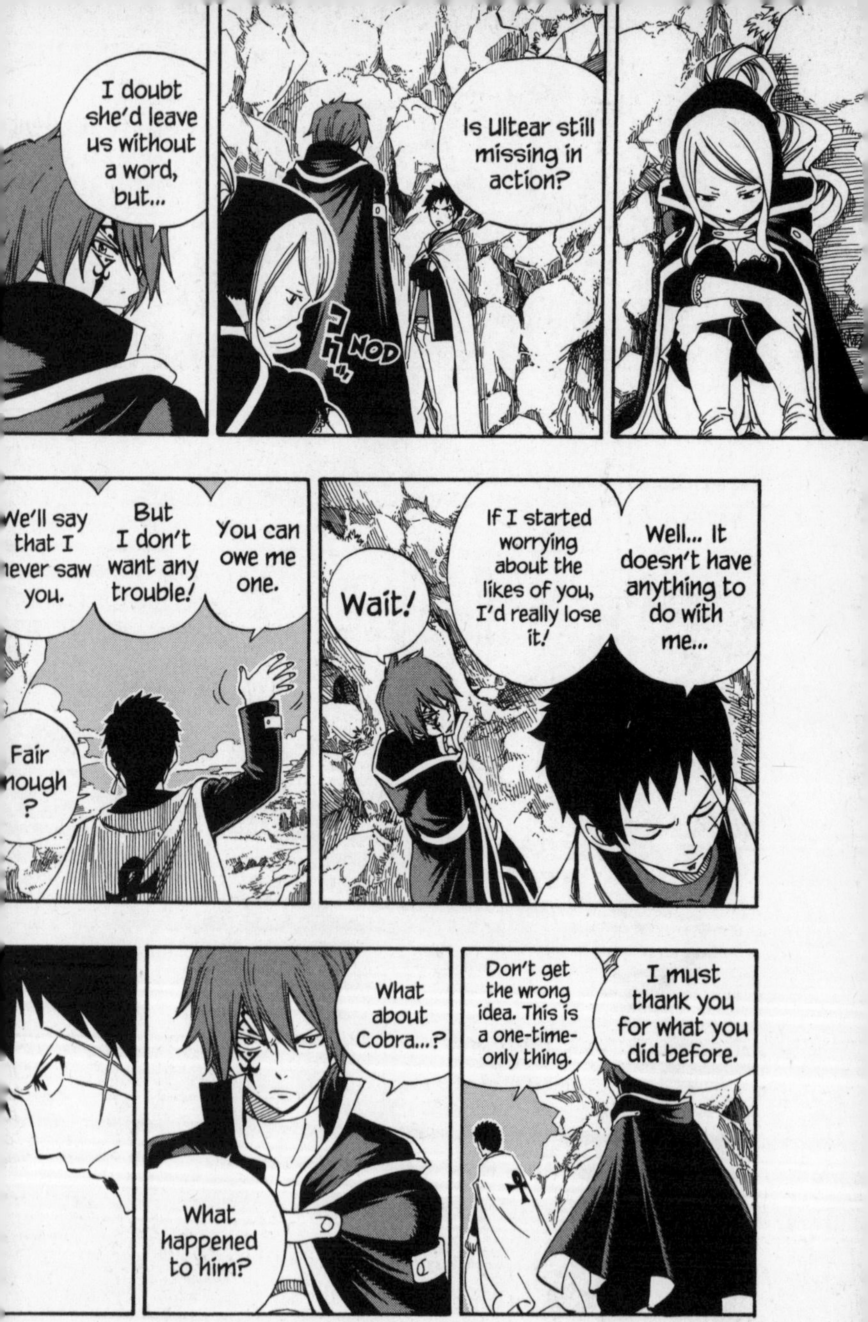
Is Ultear still missing in action?
NOD
I doubt she'd leave us without a word, but...
Well... It doesn't have anything to do with me...
If I started worrying about the likes of you, I'd really lose it!
Wait!
You can owe me one.
But I don't want any trouble!
We'll say that I never saw you.
Fair enough?
I must thank you for what you did before.
Don't get the wrong idea. This is a one-time-only thing.
What about Cobra...?
What happened to him?

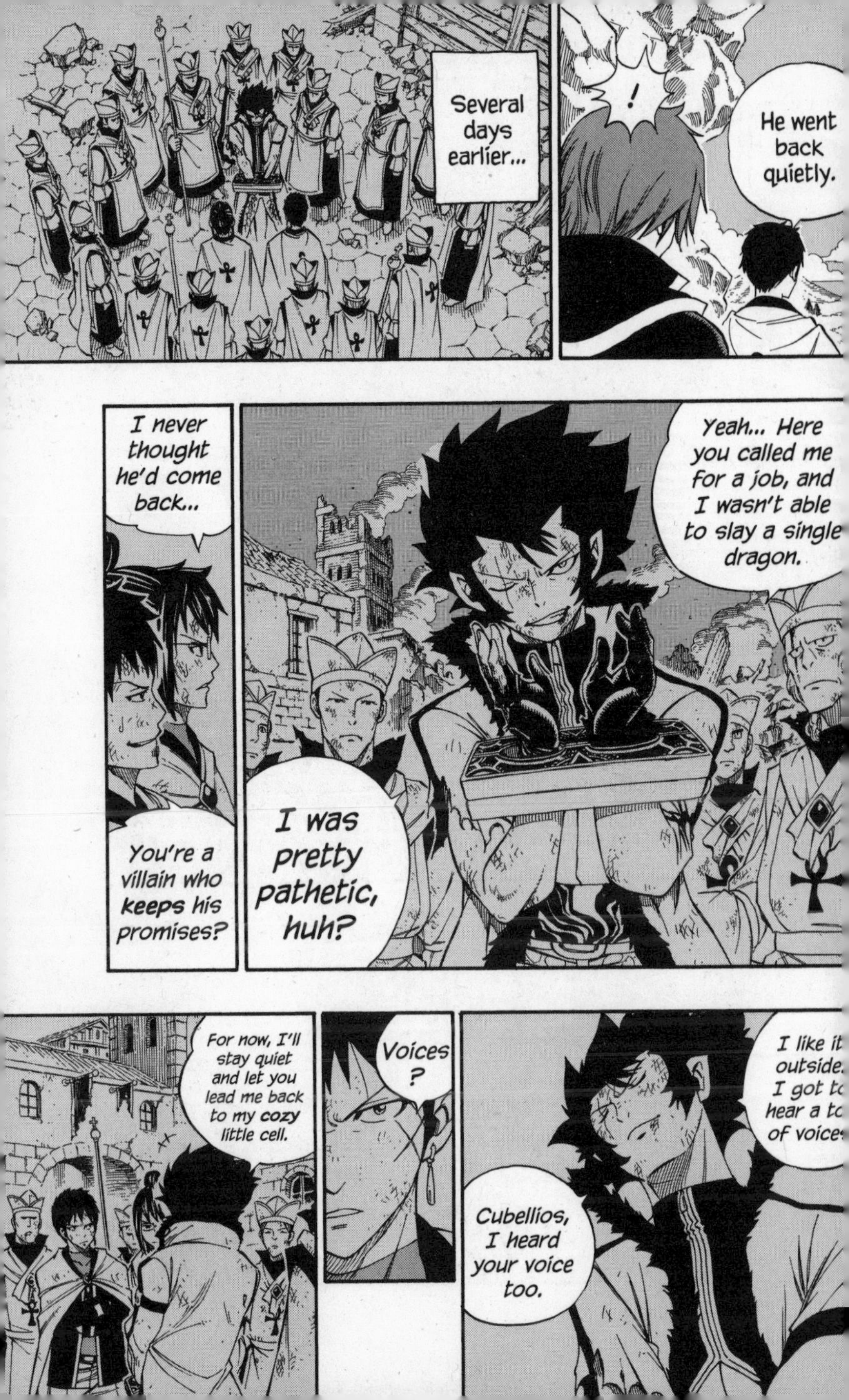
!
He went back quietly.
Several days earlier...
Yeah... Here you called me for a job, and I wasn't able to slay a single dragon.
I was pretty pathetic, huh?
I never thought he'd come back...
You're a villain who keeps his promises?
I like it outside. I got t hear a t of voices
Cubellios, I heard your voice too.
Voices?
For now, I'll stay quiet and let you lead me back to my cozy little cell.

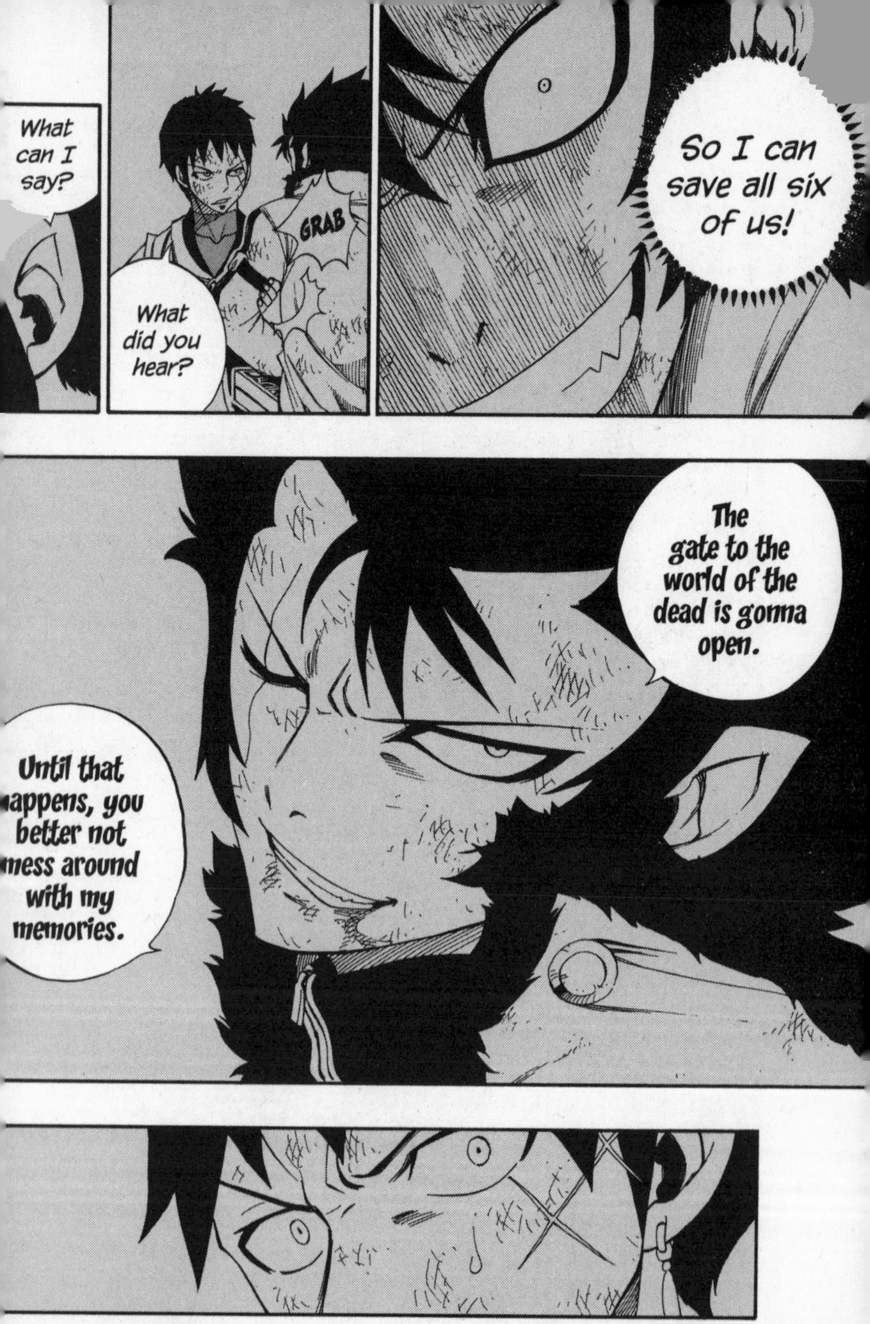
So I can save all six of us!
GRAB
What did you hear?
What can I say?
The gate to the world of the dead is gonna open.
Until that appens, you better not mess around with my memories.

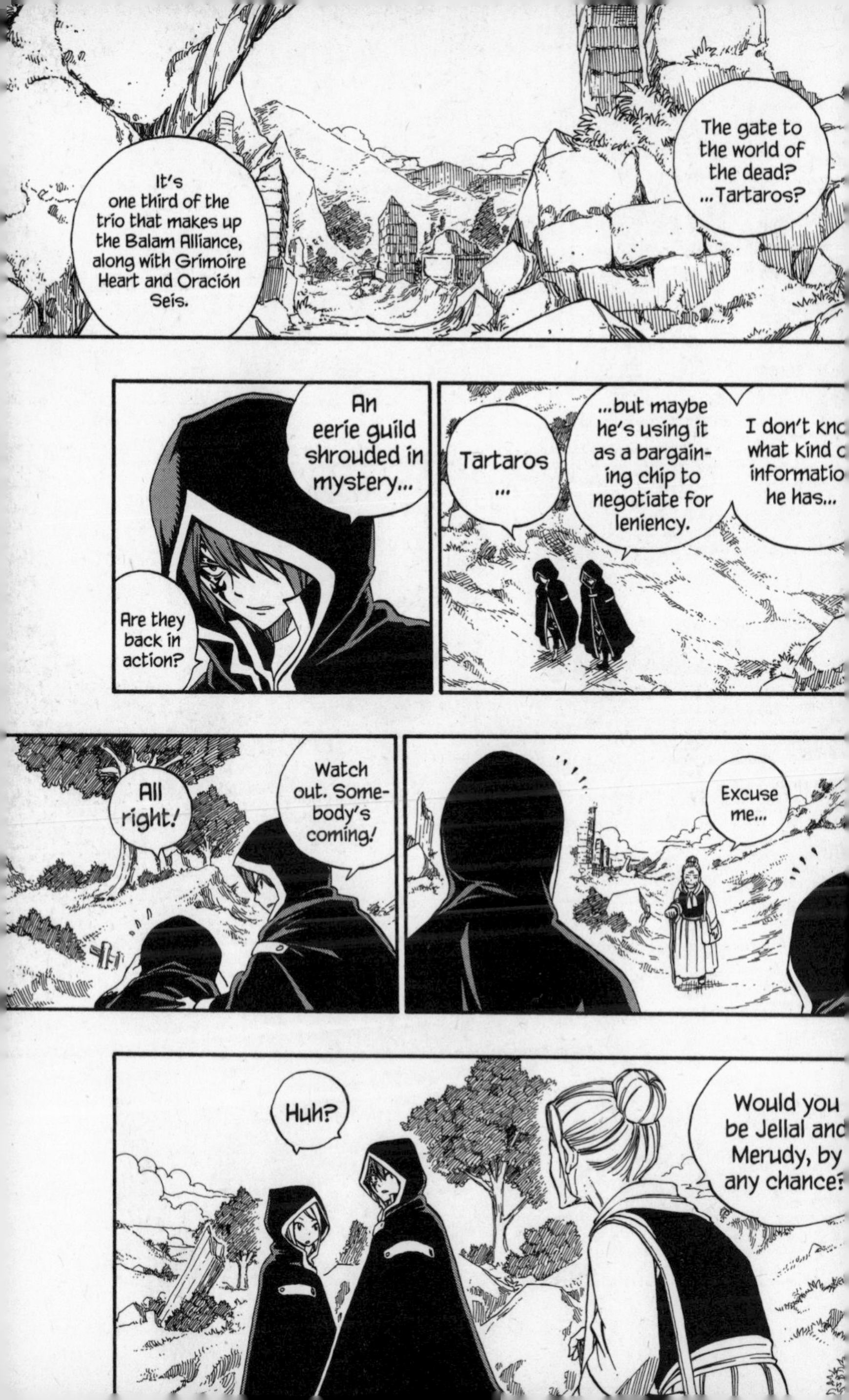
The gate to the world of the dead? ...Tartaros?
It's one third of the trio that makes up the Balam Alliance, along with Grimoire Heart and Oración Seis.
I don't kno what kind o informatio he has...
...but maybe he's using it as a bargain-ing chip to negotiate for leniency.
Tartaros ...
An eerie guild shrouded in mystery...
Are they back in action?
Excuse me...
Watch out. Some-body's coming!
All right!
Would you be Jellal and Merudy, by any chance?
Huh?

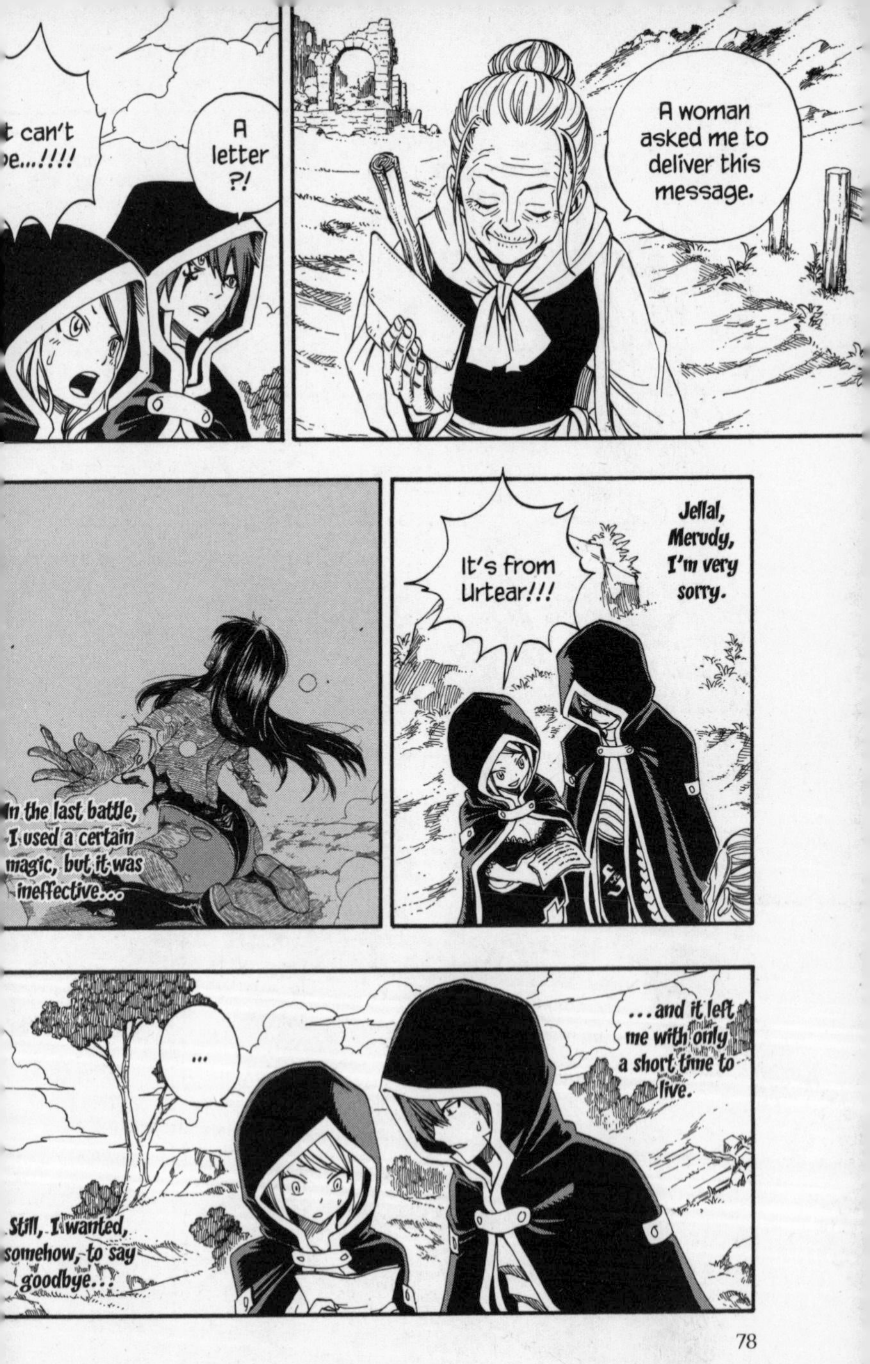
A woman asked me to deliver this message.
A letter ?!
t can't e...!!!!
Jellal, Merudy, I'm very sorry.
It's from Urtear!!!
In the last battle, I used a certain magic, but it was ineffective...
...and it left me with only a short time to live.
...
Still, I wanted, somehow, to say goodbye...

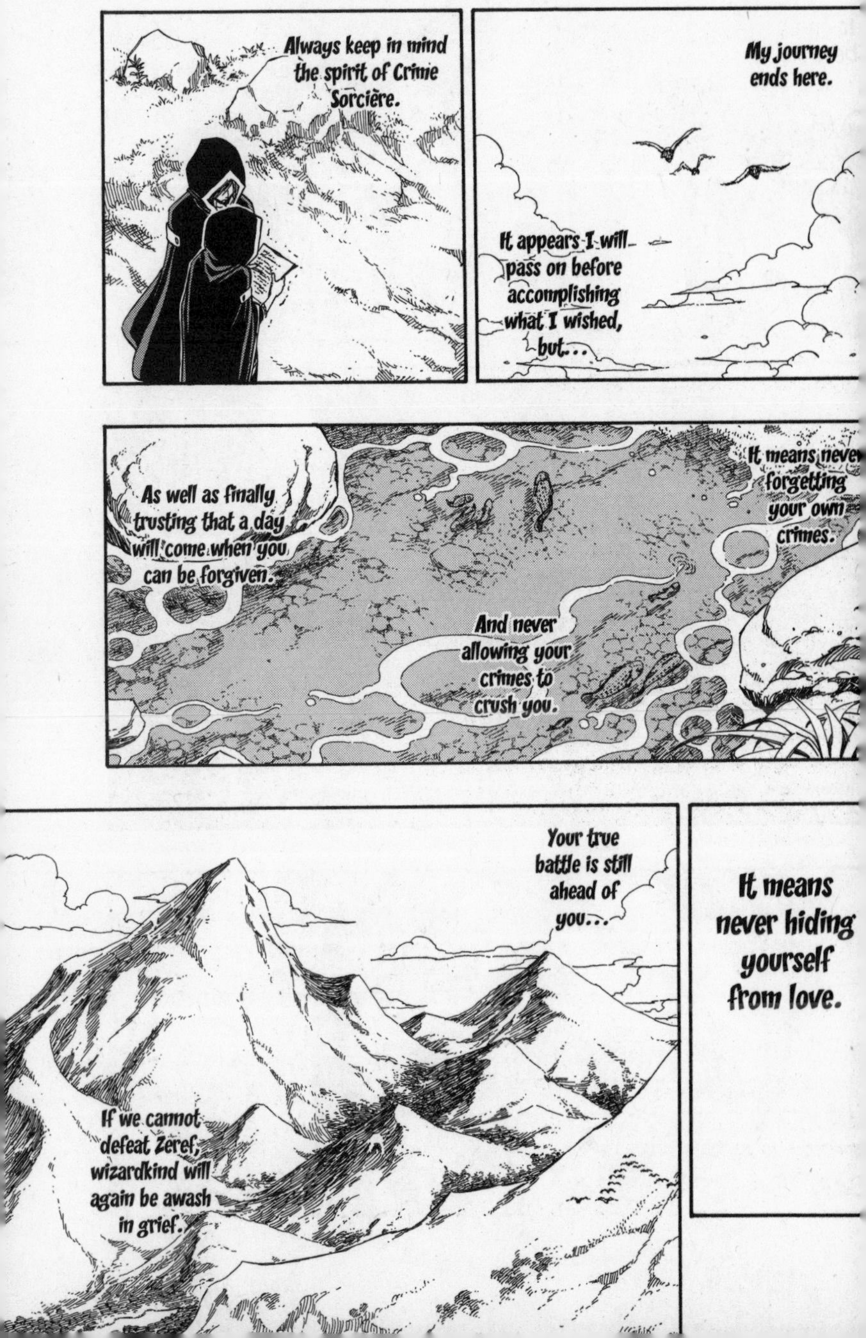
My journey ends here.
It appears I will pass on before accomplishing what I wished, but...
Always keep in mind the spirit of Crime Sorcière.
It means neve forgetting your own crimes.
And never allowing your crimes to crush you.
As well as finally trusting that a day will come when you can be forgiven.
It means never hiding yourself from love.
Your true battle is still ahead of you...
If we cannot defeat Zeref, wizardkind will again be awash in grief.

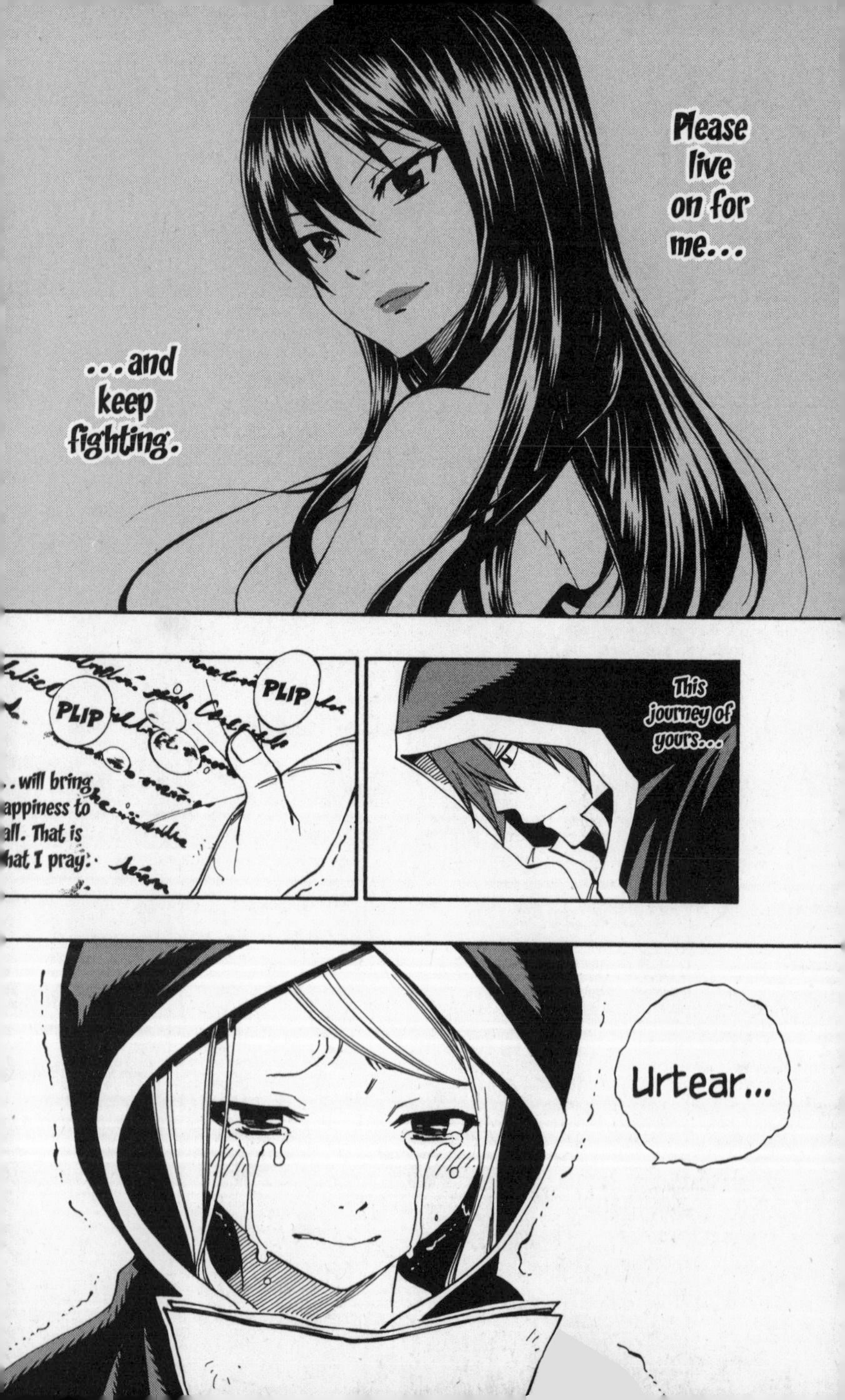
Please live on for me...
...and keep fighting.
This journey of yours...
PLIP
PLIP
...will bring appiness to all. That is hat I pray.
Urtear...

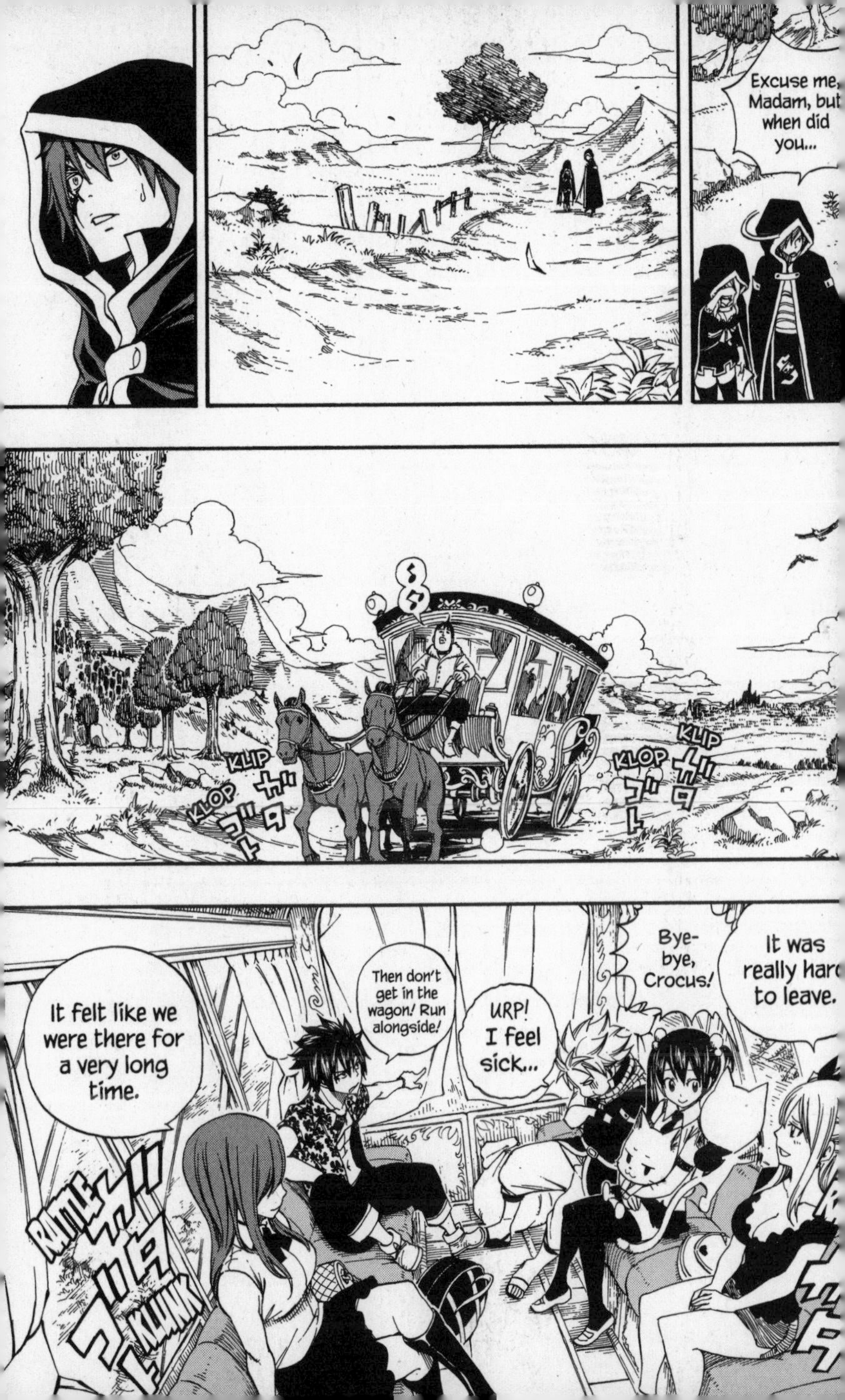
Excuse me, Madam, but when did you...
KLIP
KLOP
KLIP
KLOP
It was really har to leave.
Bye-bye, Crocus!
URP! I feel sick...
Then don't get in the wagon! Run alongside!
It felt like we were there for a very long time.
RUMBLE
KLUNK

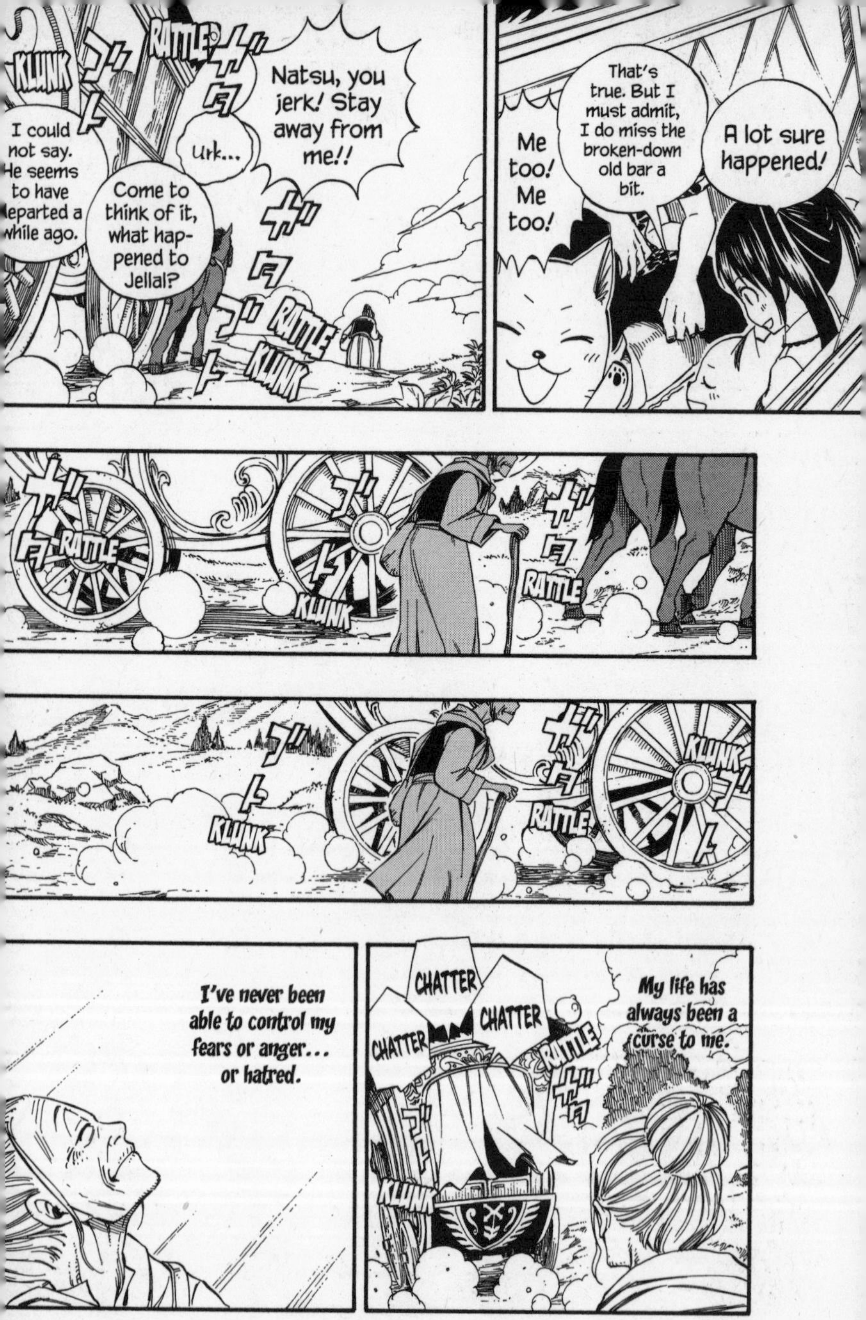
A lot sure happened!
That's true. But I must admit, I do miss the broken-down old bar a bit.
Me too! Me too!
RATTLE
KLUNK
Natsu, you jerk! Stay away from me!!
Urk...
Come to think of it, what happened to Jellal?
I could not say. He seems to have departed a while ago.
RATTLE
KLUNK
RATTLE
KLUNK
RATTLE
KLUNK
RATTLE
KLUNK
My life has always been a curse to me.
CHATTER
CHATTER
CHATTER
RATTLE
KLUNK
I've never been able to control my fears or anger... or hatred.

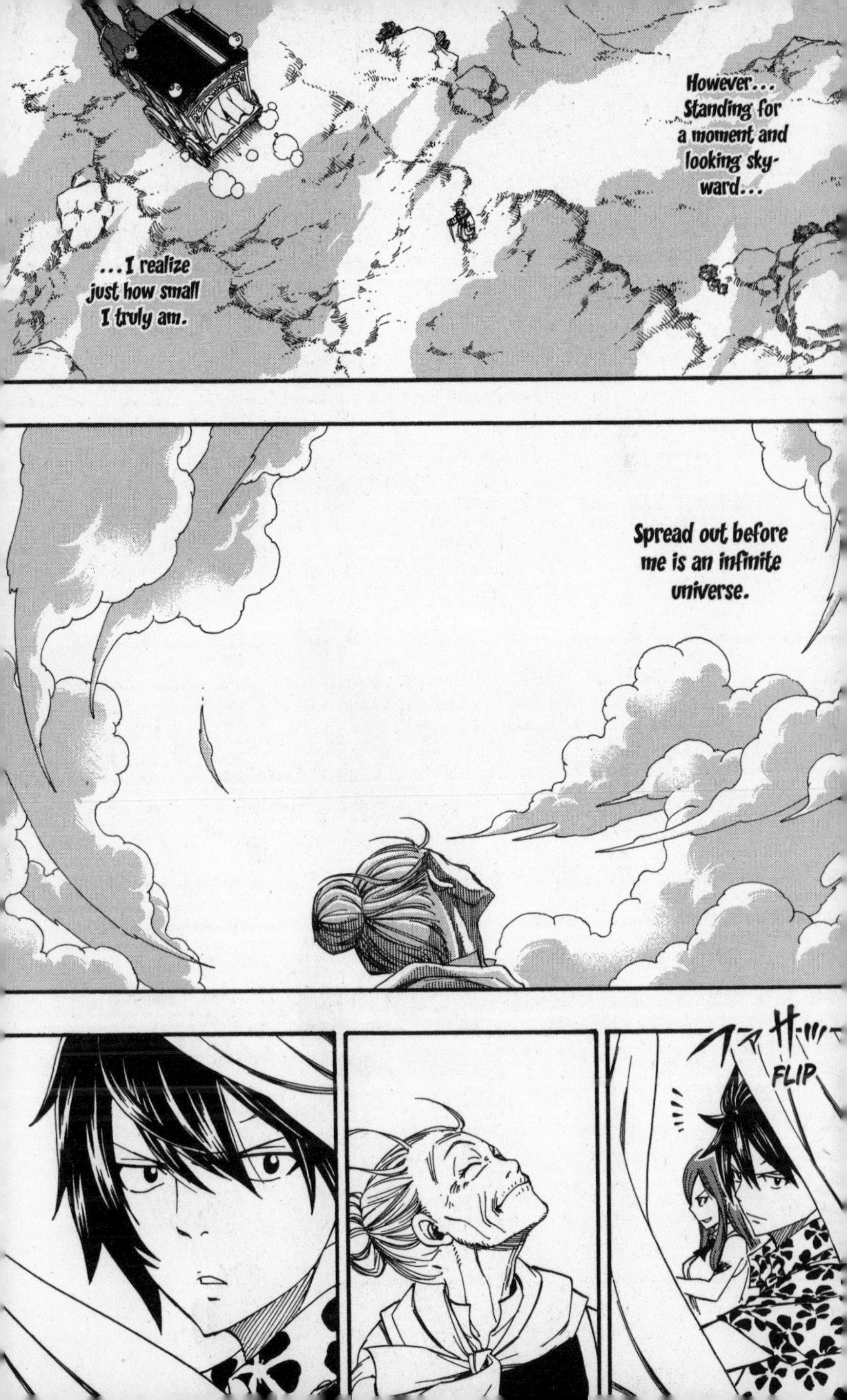
However... Standing for a moment and looking sky-ward...
...I realize just how small I truly am.
Spread out before me is an infinite universe.
FLIP

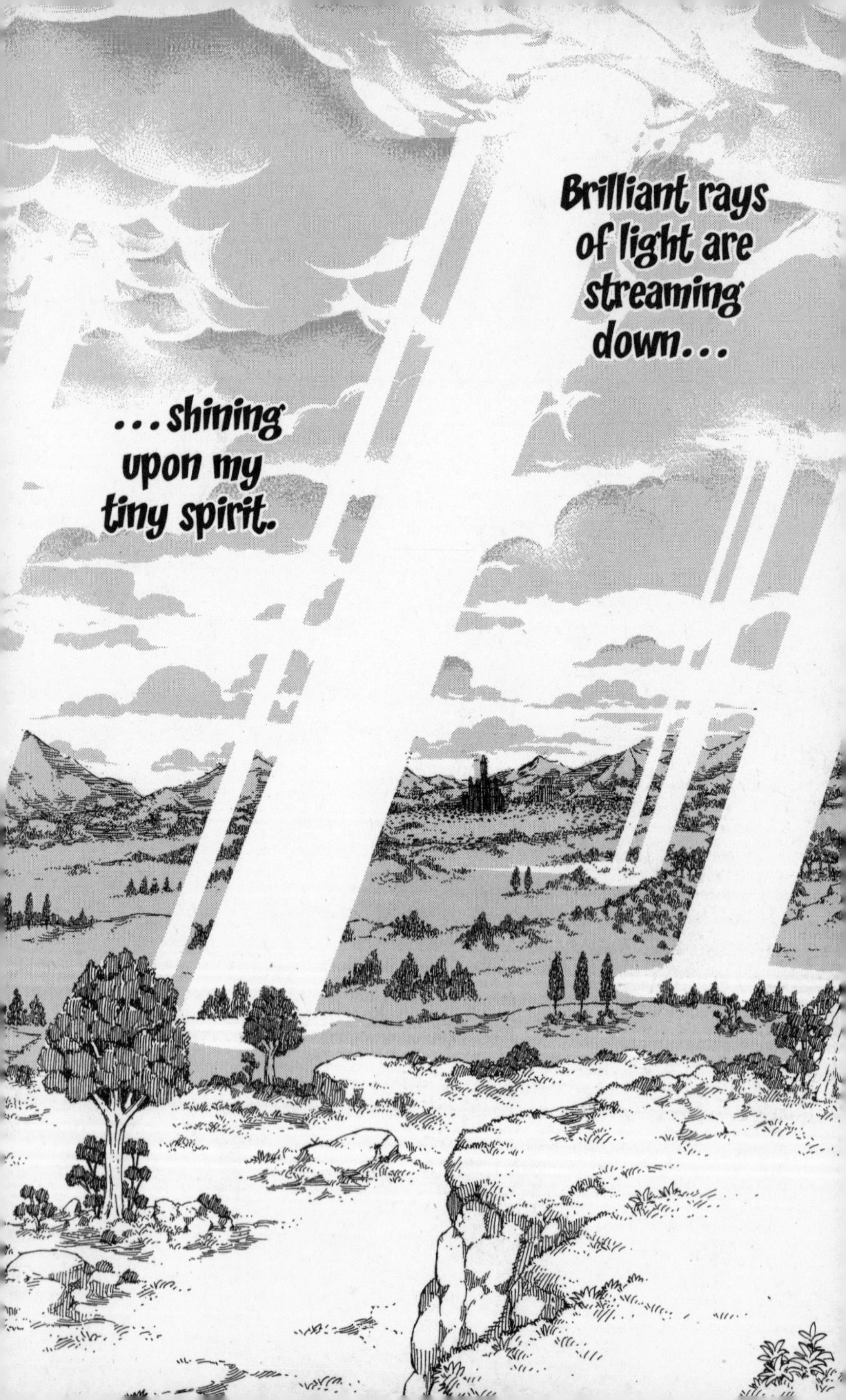
Brilliant rays of light are streaming down...
...shining upon my tiny spirit.

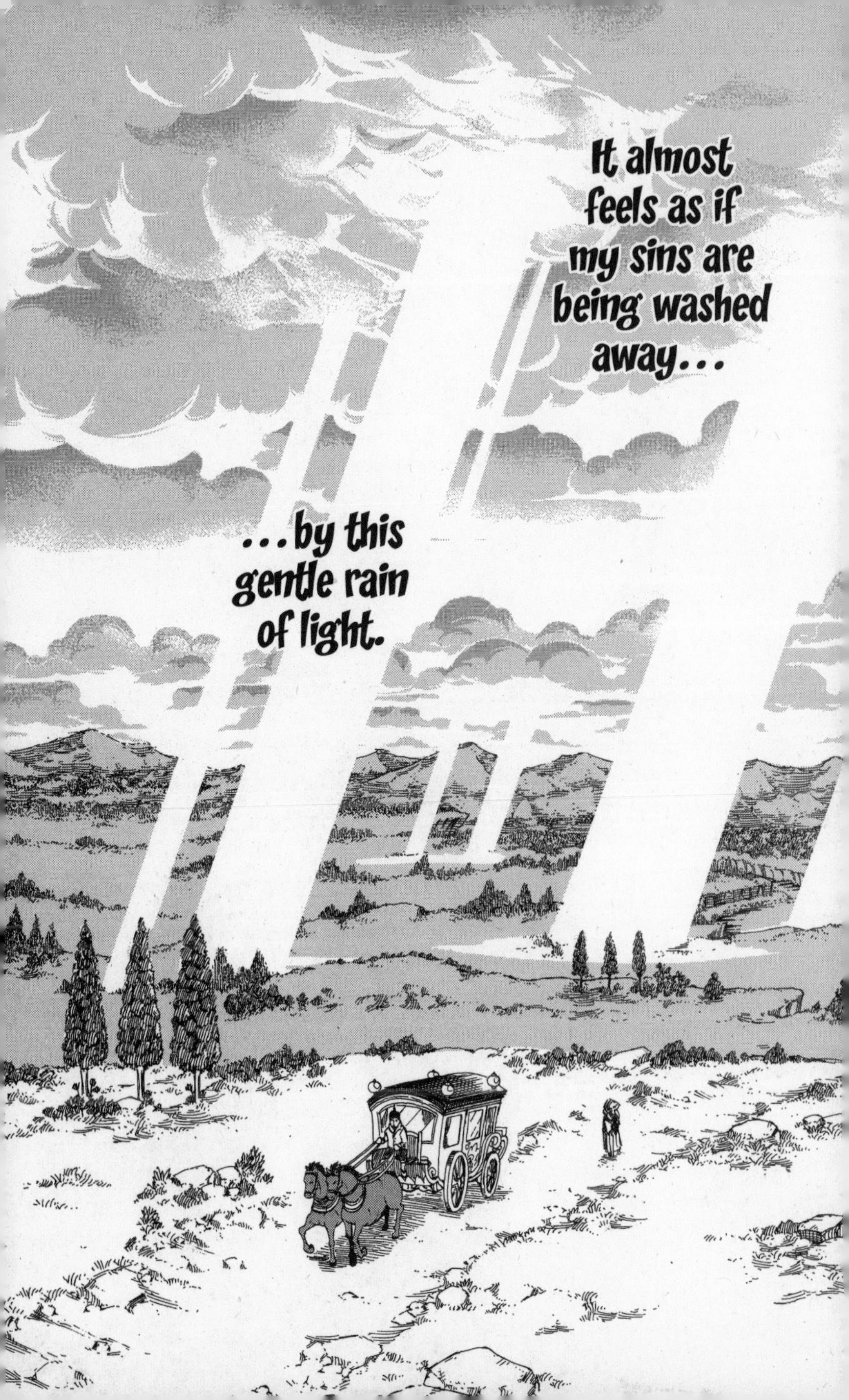
It almost feels as if my sins are being washed away...
...by this gentle rain of light.

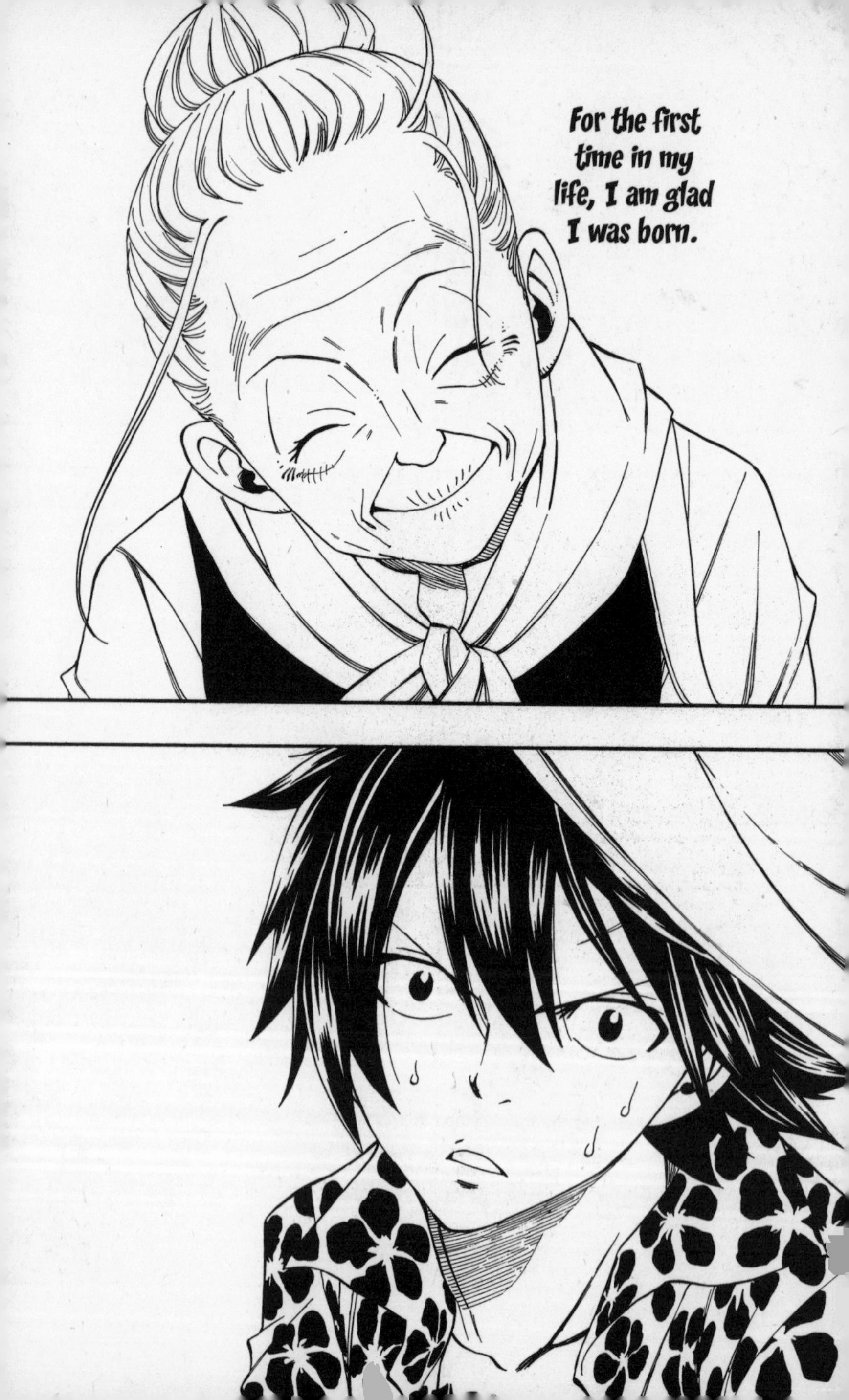
For the first time in my life, I am glad I was born.

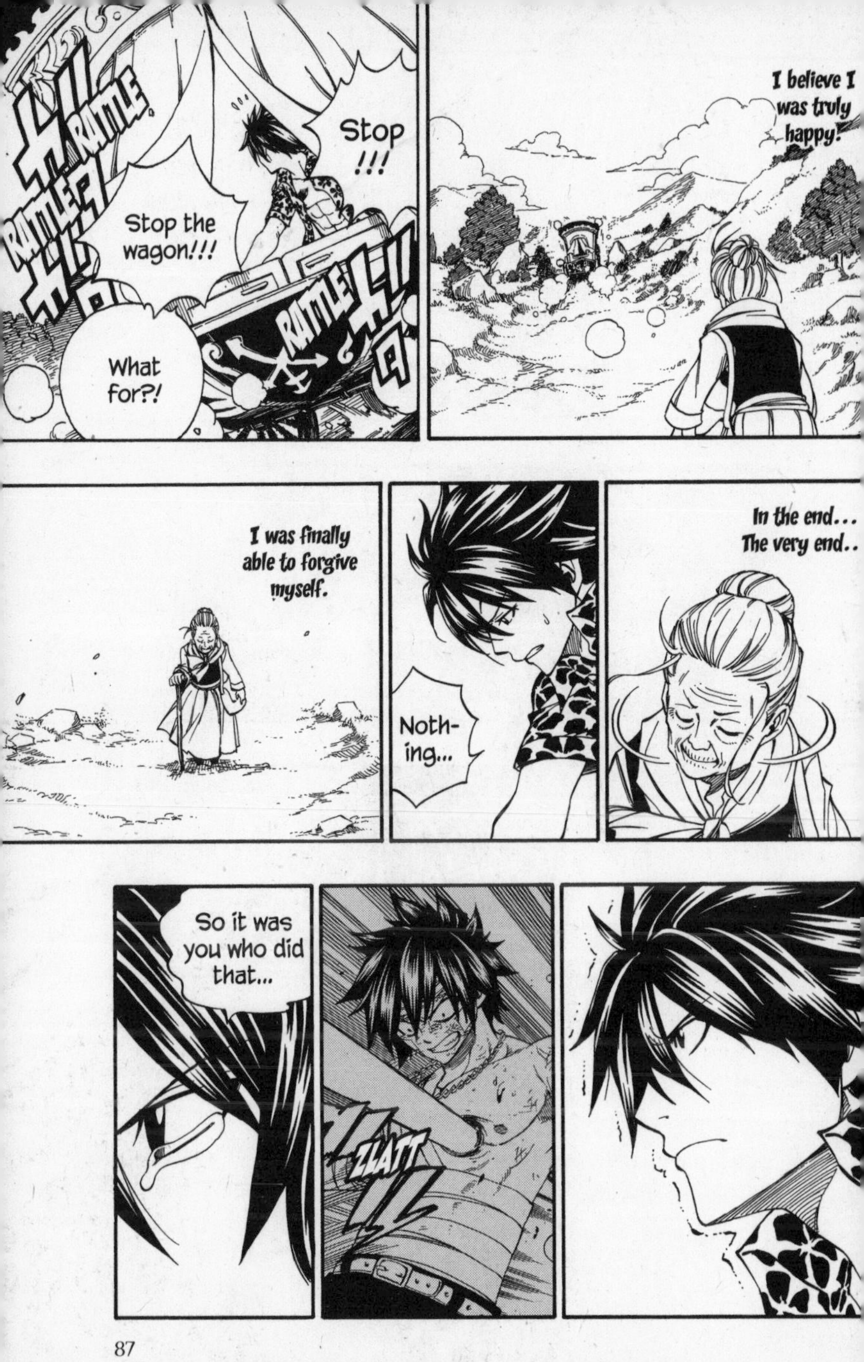
I believe I was truly happy!
Stop !!!
RATTLE
RATTLE
Stop the wagon!!!
RATTLE
What for?!
In the end... The very end..
Noth-ing...
I was finally able to forgive myself.
ZLATT
So it was you who did that...

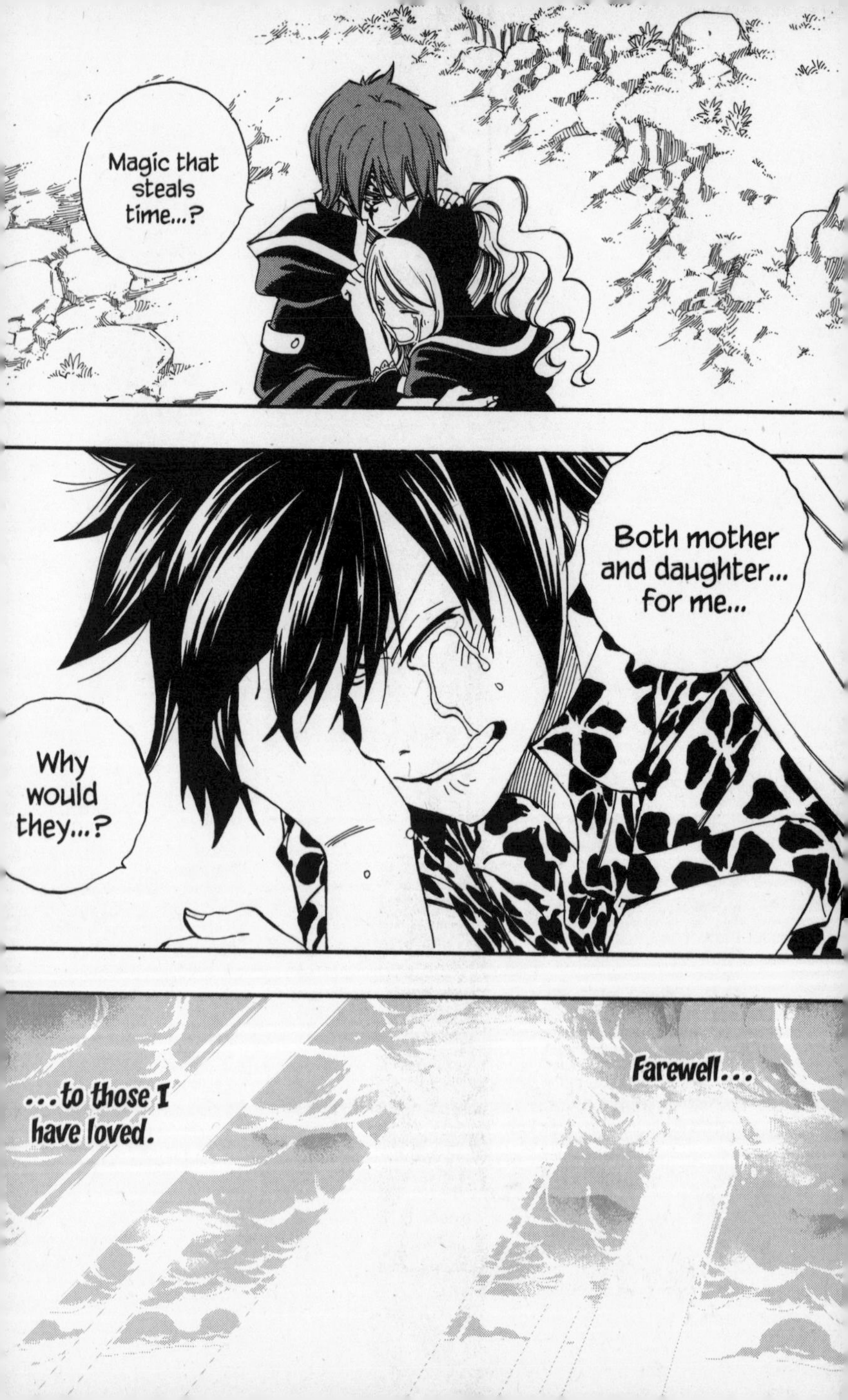
Magic that steals time...?
Both mother and daughter... for me...
Why would they...?
Farewell...
...to those I have loved.

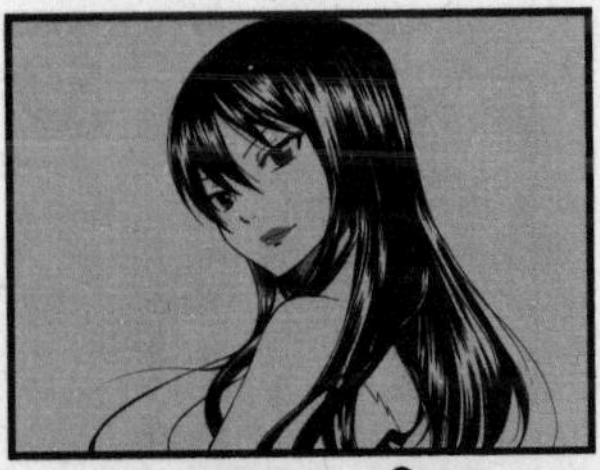

FAIRY TAIL

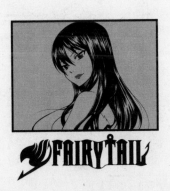

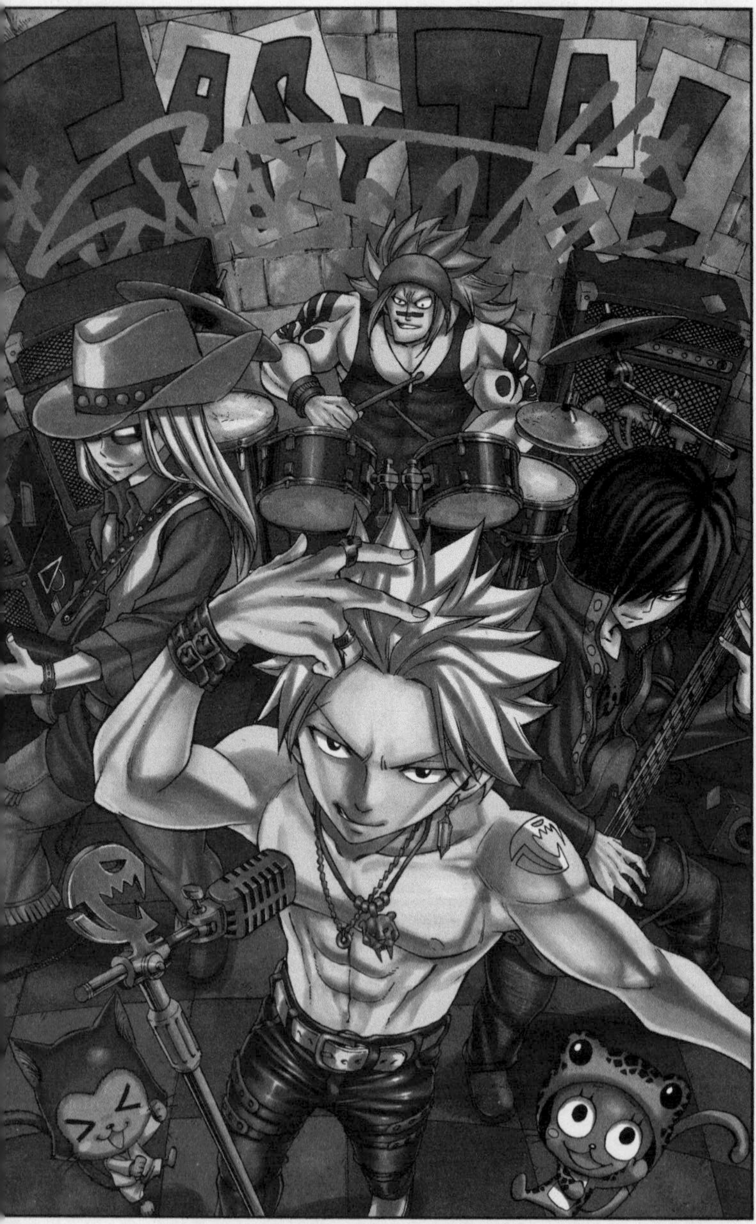

Chapter 340: Delivery

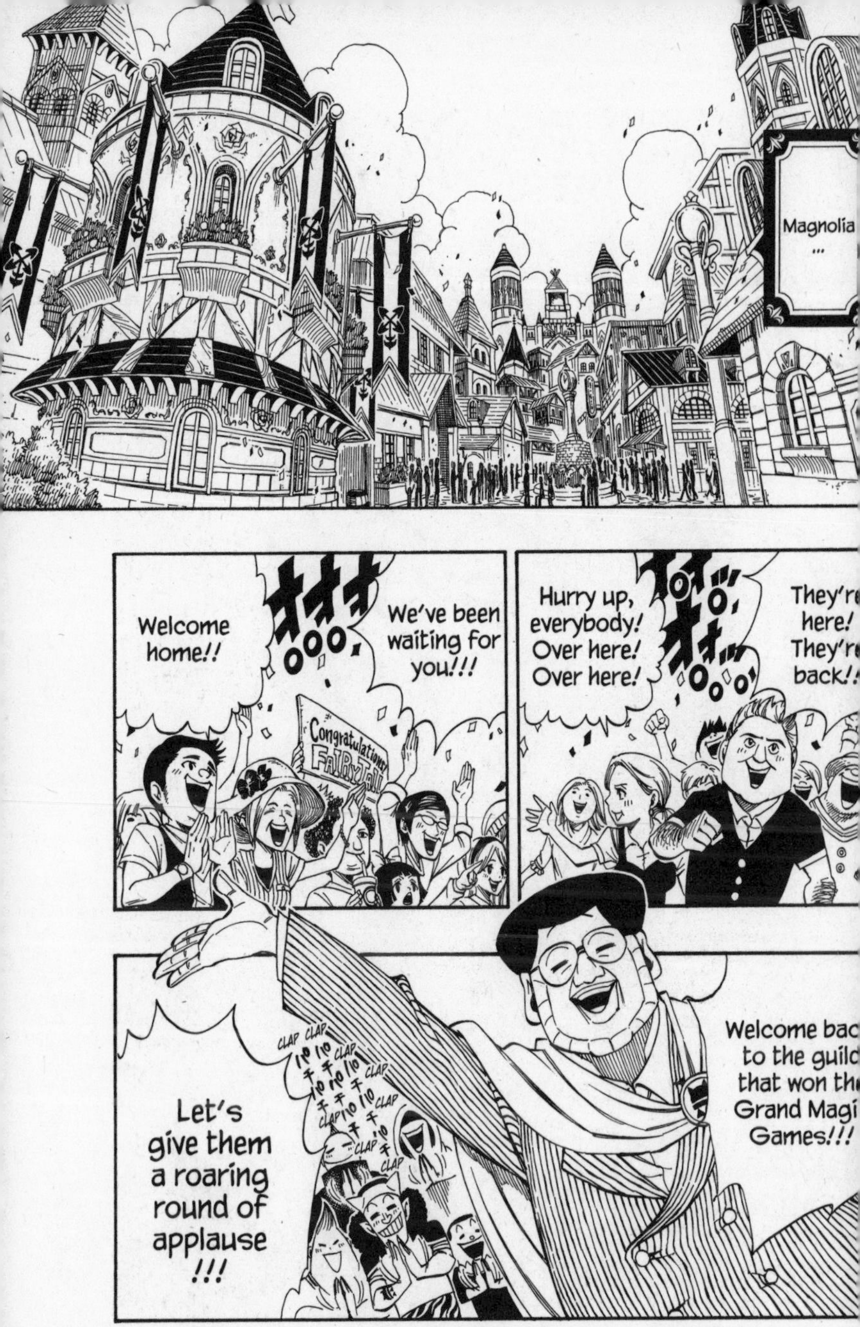
Magnolia
...
They'r here! They'r back!!
OOO
Hurry up, everybody! Over here! Over here!
We've been waiting for you!!!
OOO
Welcome home!!
Congratulations! FAIRY TAIL
Welcome bac to the guild that won th Grand Magi Games!!!
CLAP CLAP CLAP CLAP CLAP CLAP CLAP CLAP
Let's give them a roaring round of applause!!!

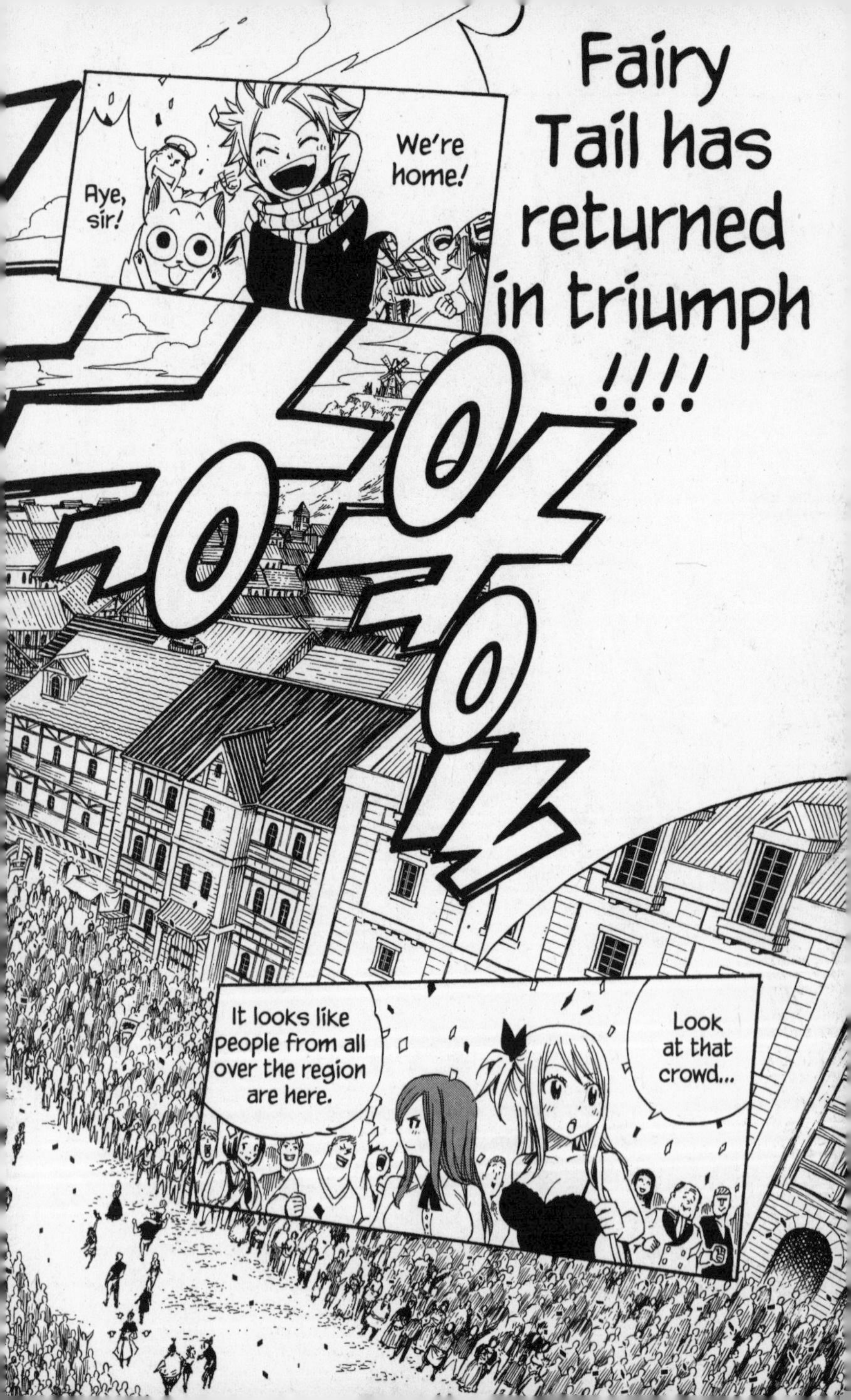
Fairy Tail has returned in triumph!!!!
We're home!
Aye, sir!
Look at that crowd...
It looks like people from all over the region are here.

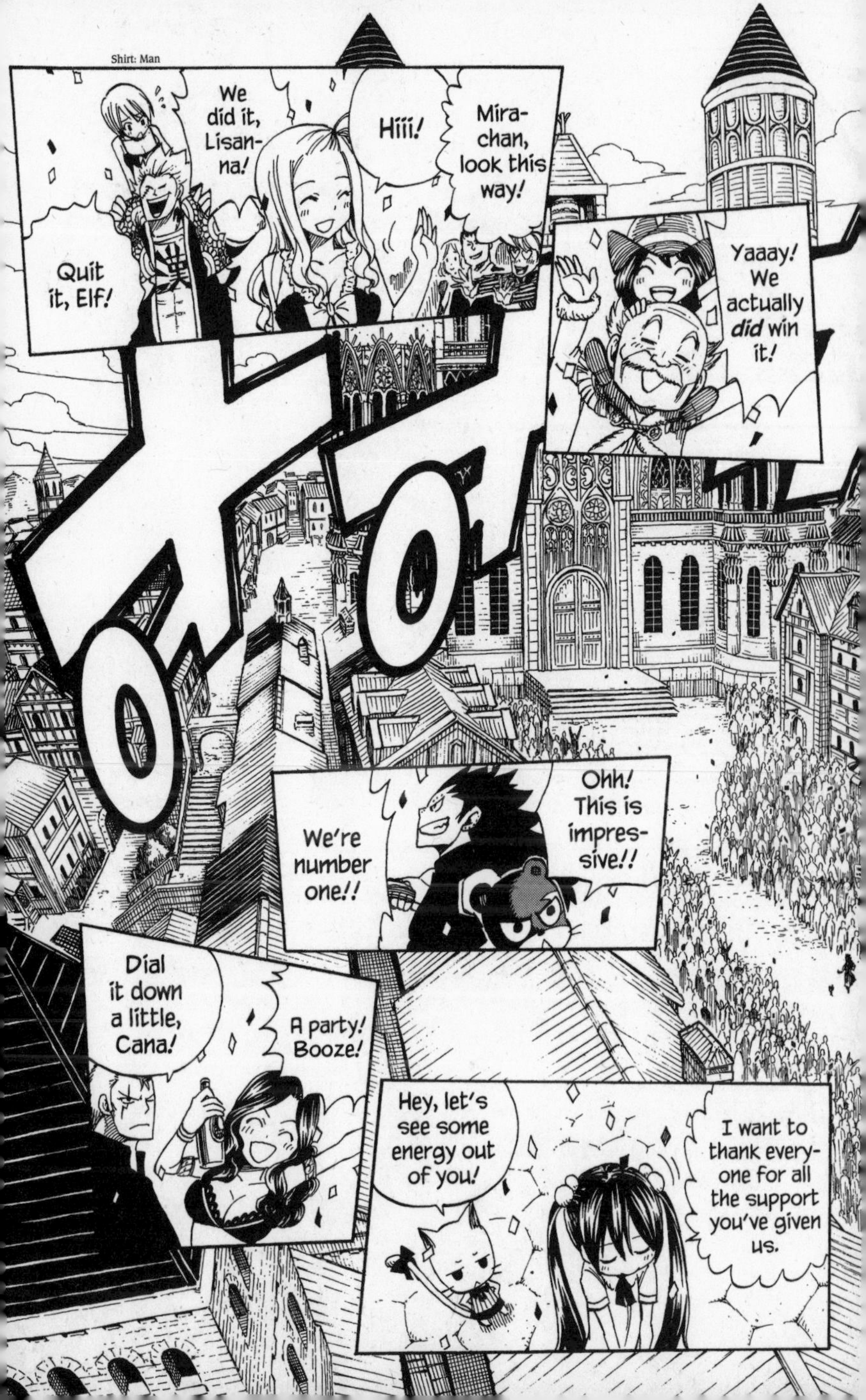
Shirt: Man
Mira-chan, look this way!
Hiii!
We did it, Lisanna!
Quit it, Elf!
Yaaay! We actually *did* win it!
Ohh! This is impressive!!
We're number one!!
A party! Booze!
Dial it down a little, Cana!
I want to thank everyone for all the support you've given us.
Hey, let's see some energy out of you!

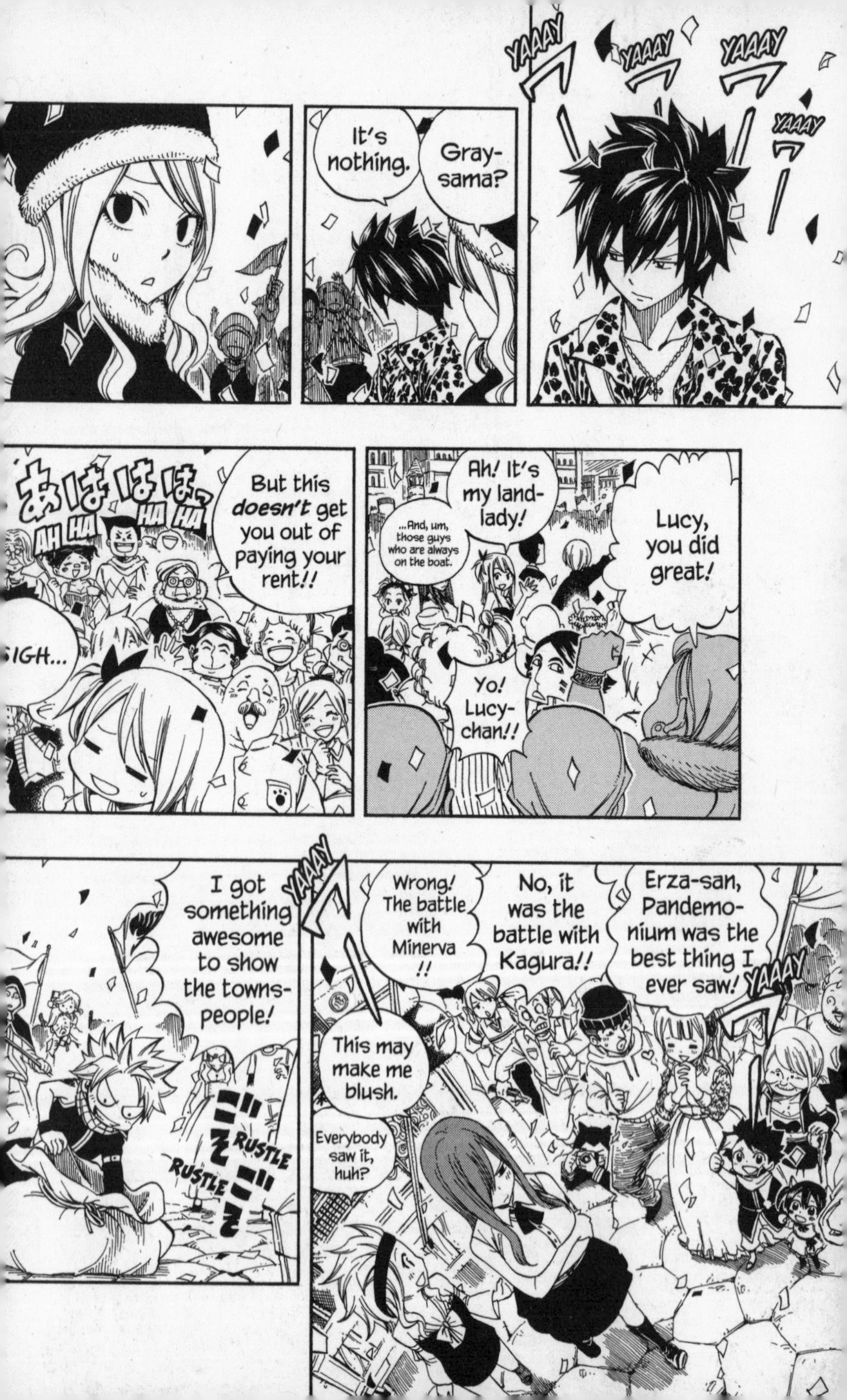
YAAAY
YAAAY
YAAAY
YAAAY
Gray-sama?
It's nothing.
Lucy, you did great!
Ah! It's my land-lady!
...And, um, those guys who are always on the boat.
Yo! Lucy-chan!!
あははは
AH HA HA HA
But this doesn't get you out of paying your rent!!
SIGH...
Erza-san, Pandemonium was the best thing I ever saw!
YAAAY
No, it was the battle with Kagura!!
Wrong! The battle with Minerva!!
YAAAY
This may make me blush.
Everybody saw it, huh?
I got something awesome to show the towns-people!
ごそ
RUSTLE
ごそ
RUSTLE

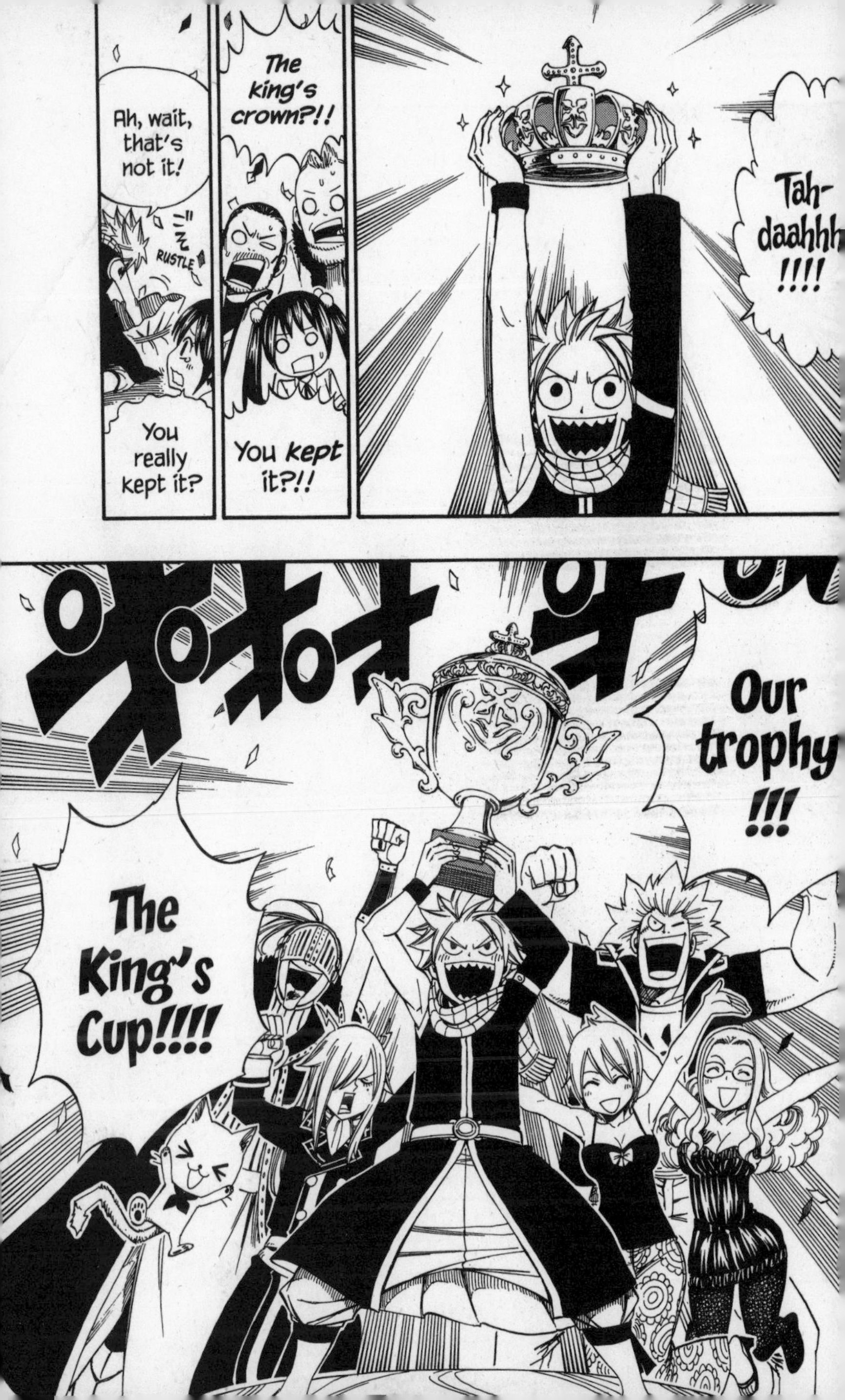
Tah-daahhh!!!!
The king's crown?!!
You kept it?!!
Ah, wait, that's not it!
RUSTLE
You really kept it?
Our trophy!!!
The King's Cup!!!!

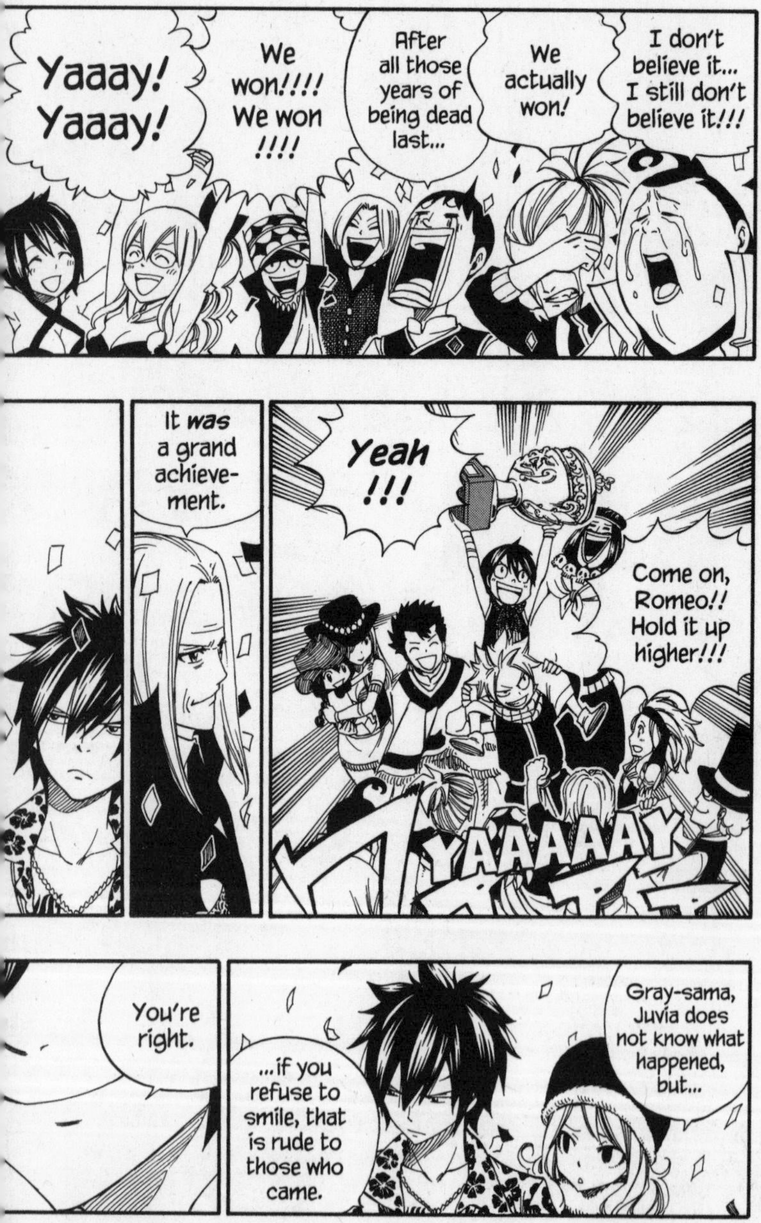
I don't believe it... I still don't believe it!!!
We actually won!
After all those years of being dead last...
We won!!!! We won !!!!
Yaaay! Yaaay!
Come on, Romeo!! Hold it up higher!!!
Yeah !!!
YAAAAAY
It *was* a grand achievement.
Gray-sama, Juvia does not know what happened, but...
...if you refuse to smile, that is rude to those who came.
You're right.

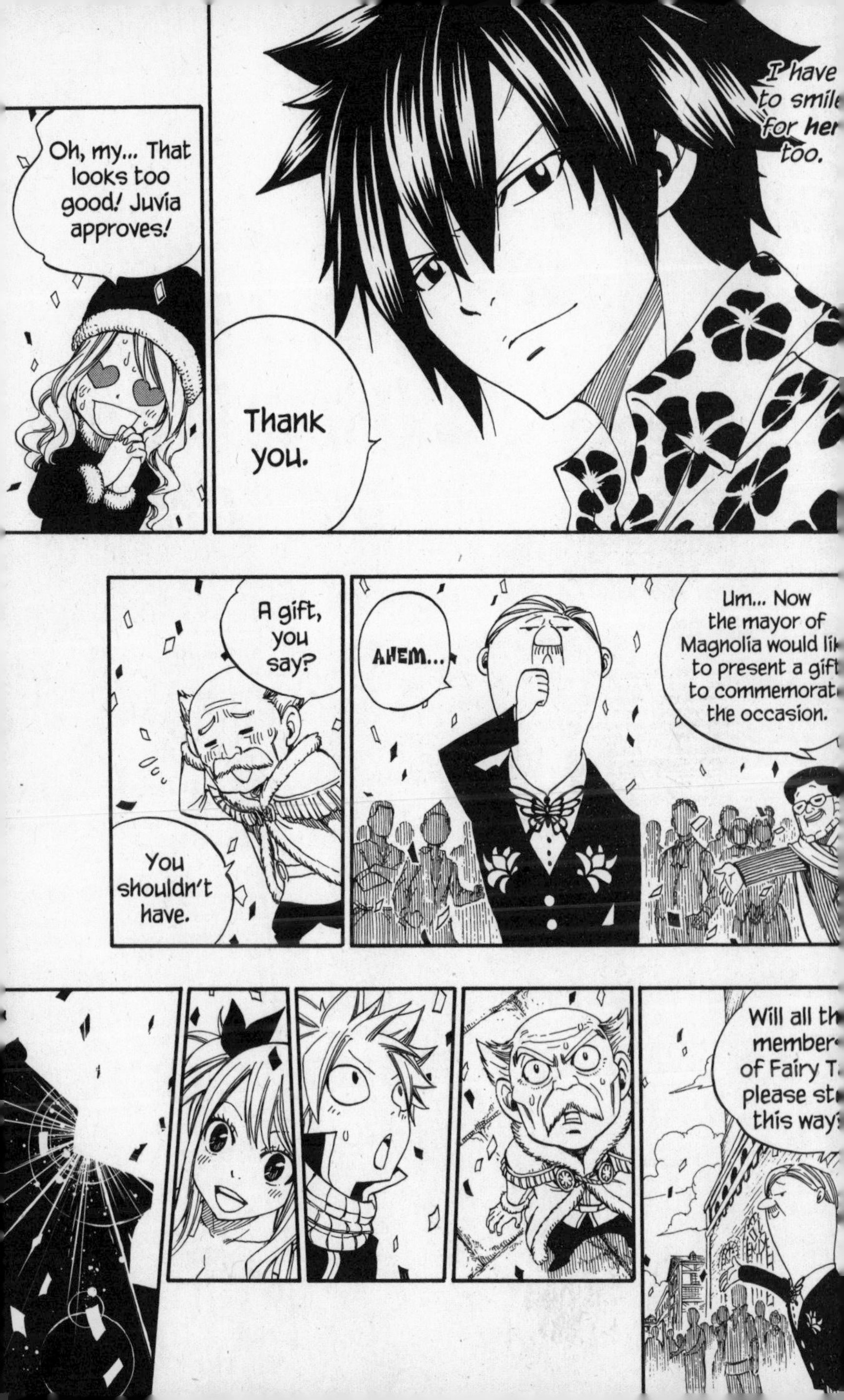
I have to smile for her too.
Thank you.
Oh, my... That looks too good! Juvia approves!
Um... Now the mayor of Magnolia would lik to present a gift to commemorat the occasion.
AHEM...
A gift, you say?
You shouldn't have.
Will all th member of Fairy T please st this way

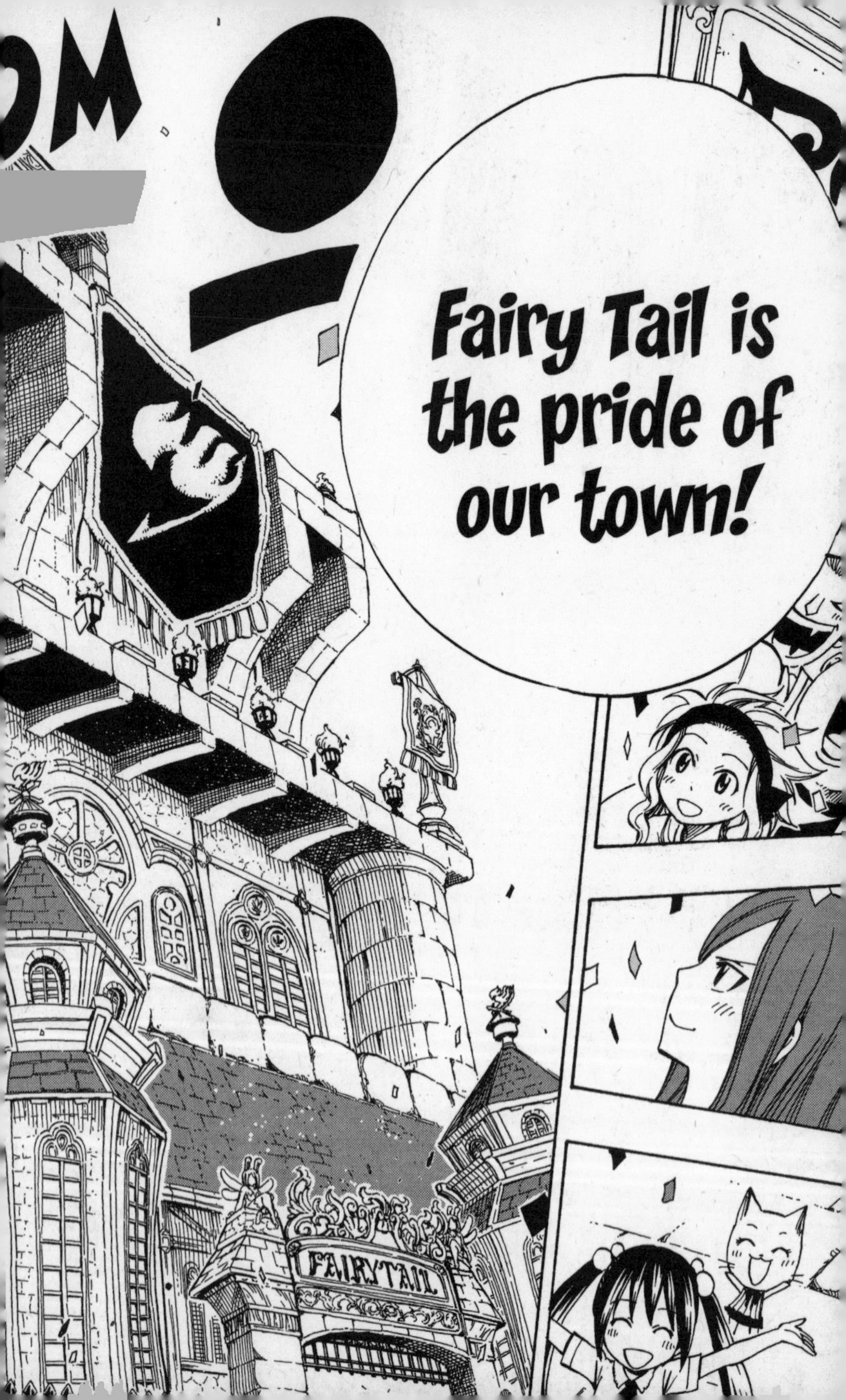
Fairy Tail is the pride of our town!
FAIRYTAIL

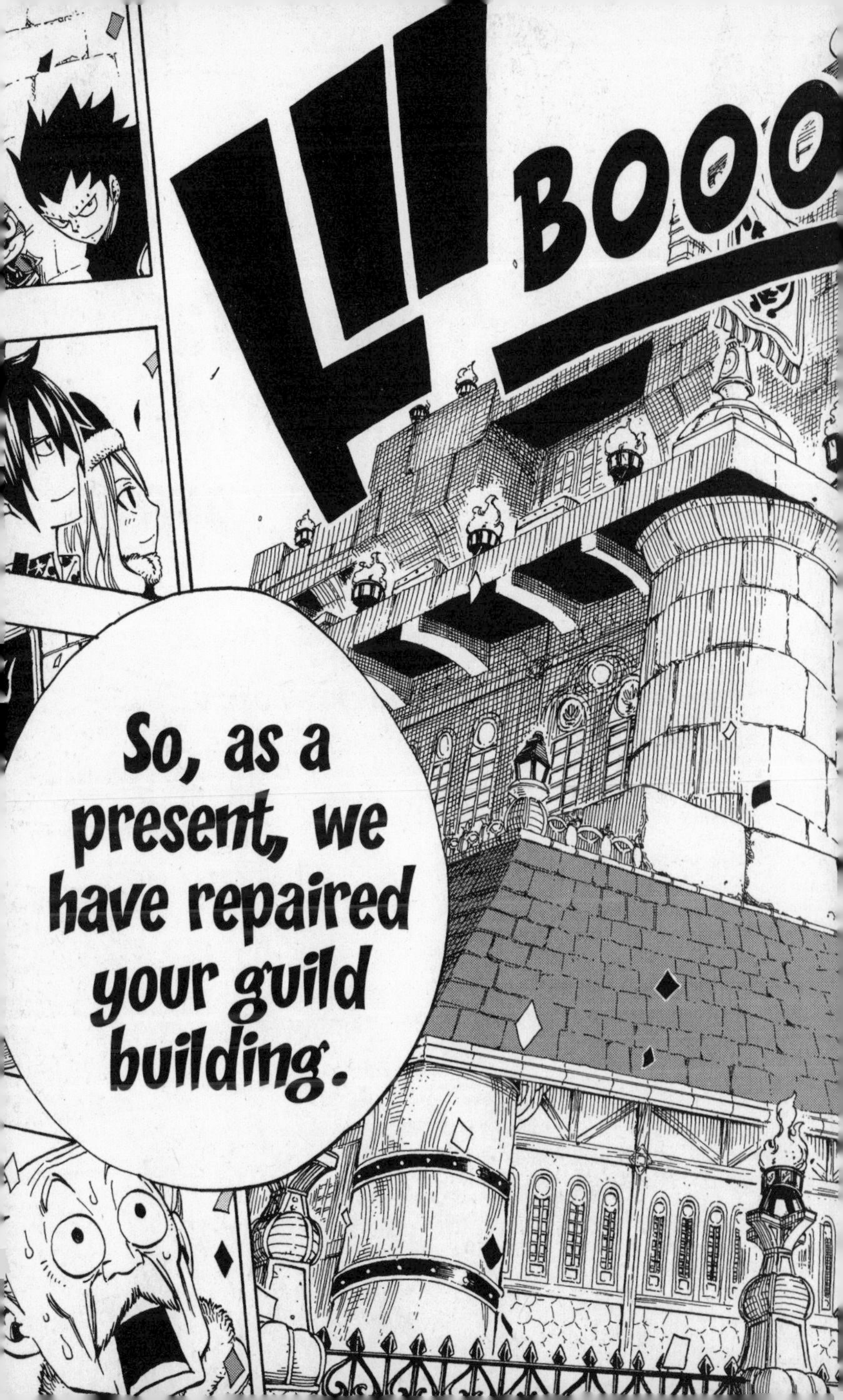
BOOOM!!
So, as a present, we have repaired your guild building.

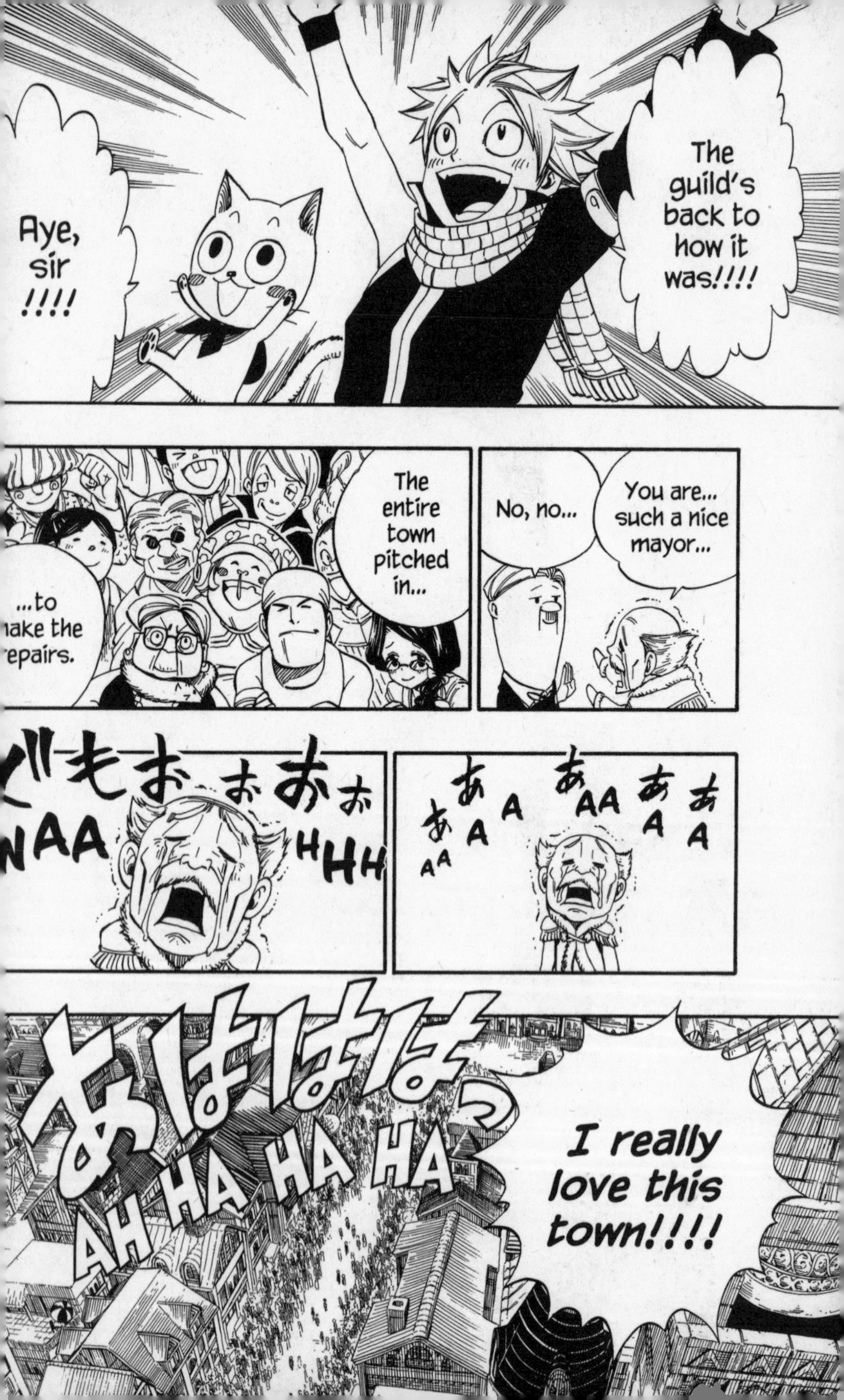

The guild's back to how it was!!!!
Aye, sir !!!!
You are... such a nice mayor...
No, no...
The entire town pitched in...
...to make the repairs.
あ あ あ あ あ あ
A A AA A A AA
ぐもおおおお
NAAHHH
I really love this town!!!!
あははははっ
AH HA HA HA HA

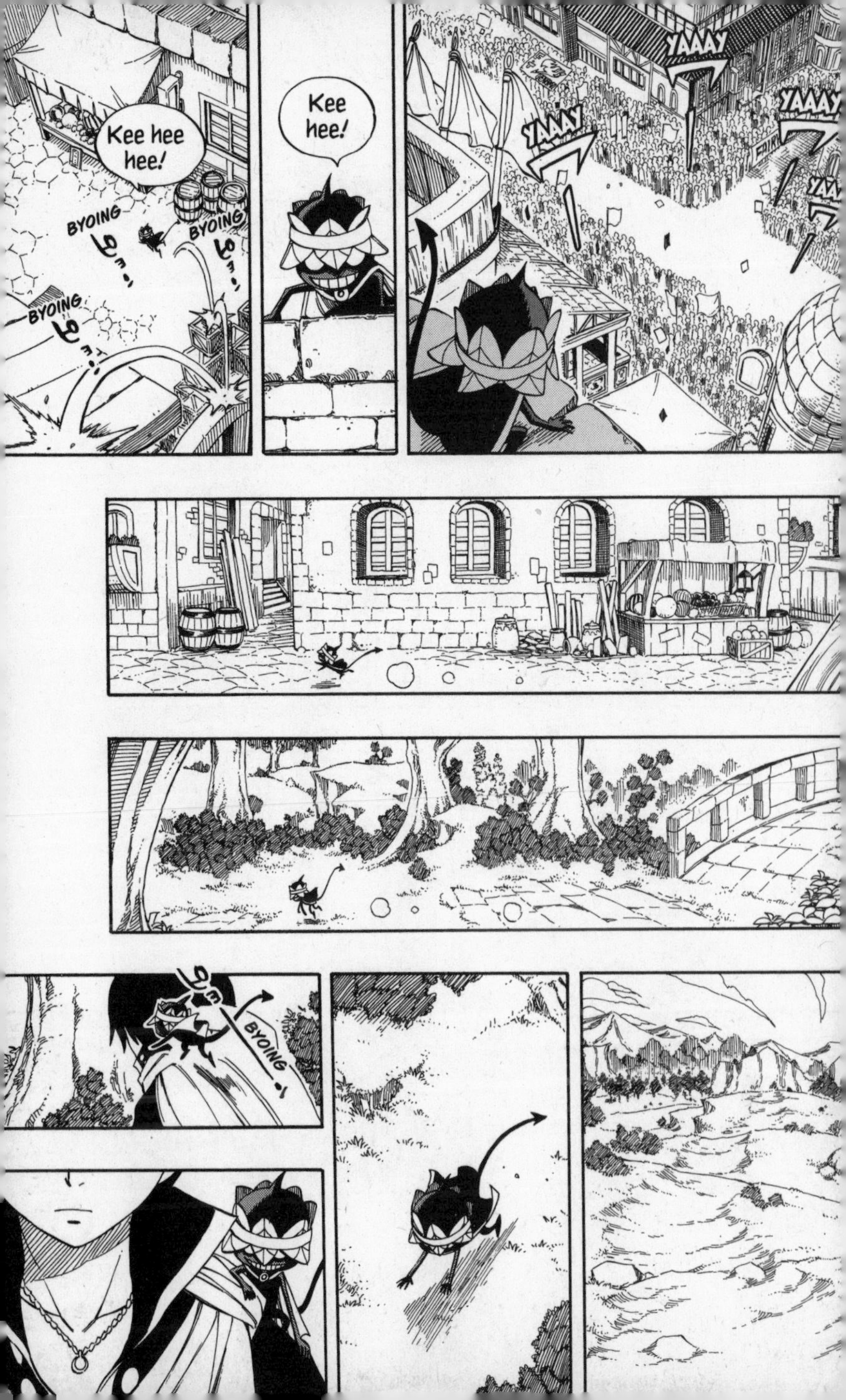
YAAAY
YAAAY
YAAAY
Kee hee!
Kee hee hee!
BYOING
BYOING
BYOING
BYOING

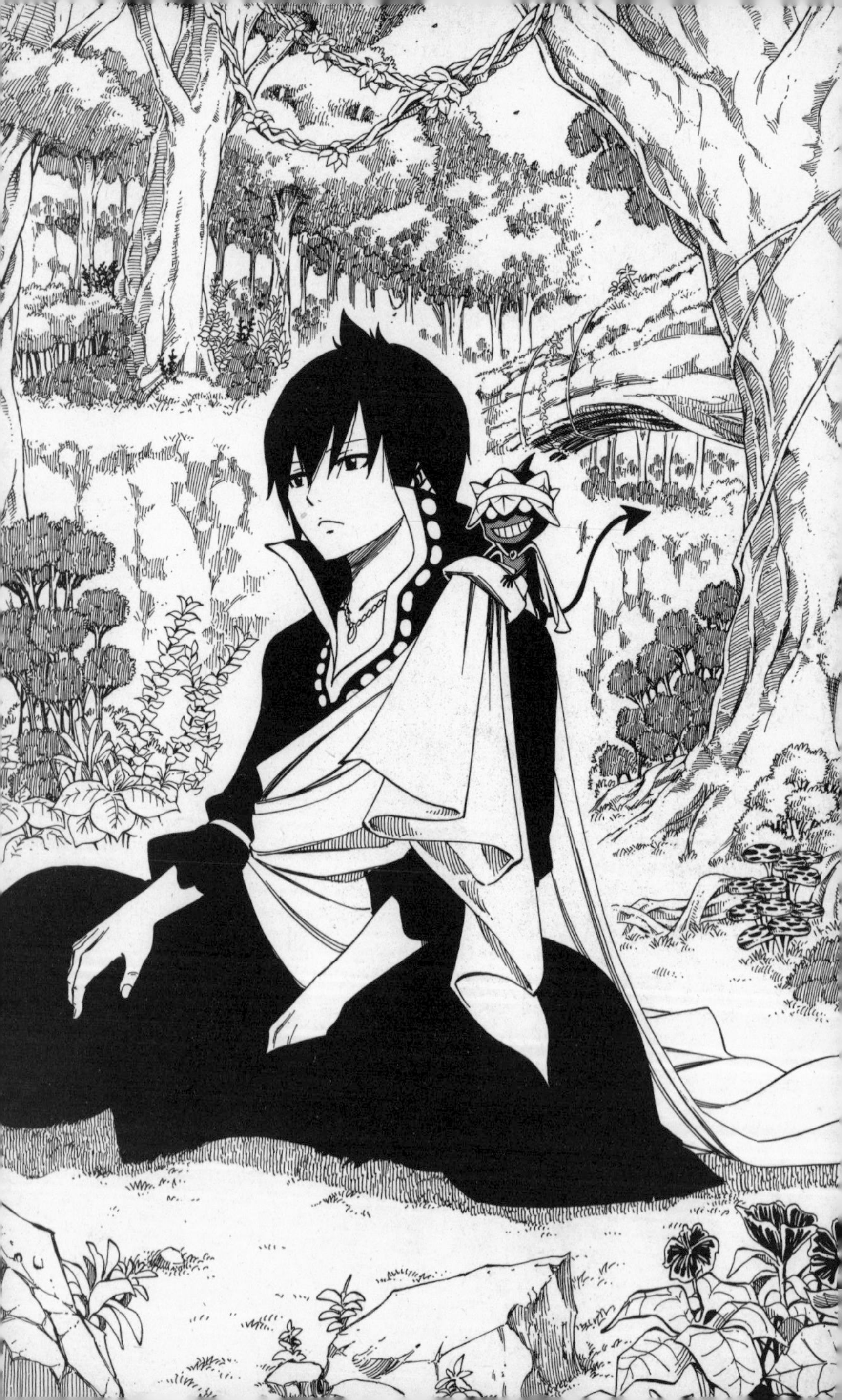

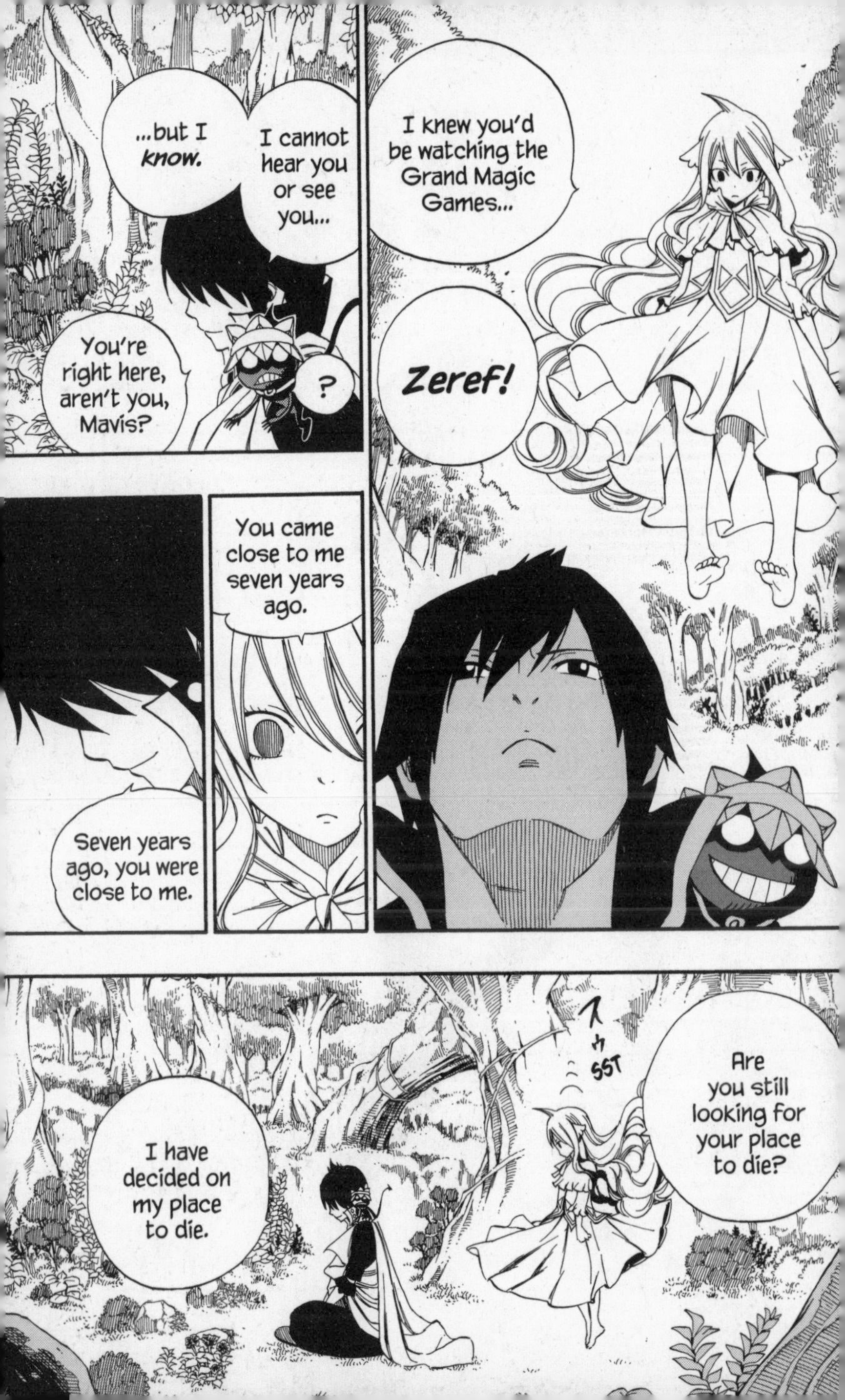
I knew you'd be watching the Grand Magic Games...
Zeref!
I cannot hear you or see you...
...but I *know.*
You're right here, aren't you, Mavis?
?
You came close to me seven years ago.
Seven years ago, you were close to me.
Are you still looking for your place to die?
スゥ SST
I have decided on my place to die.

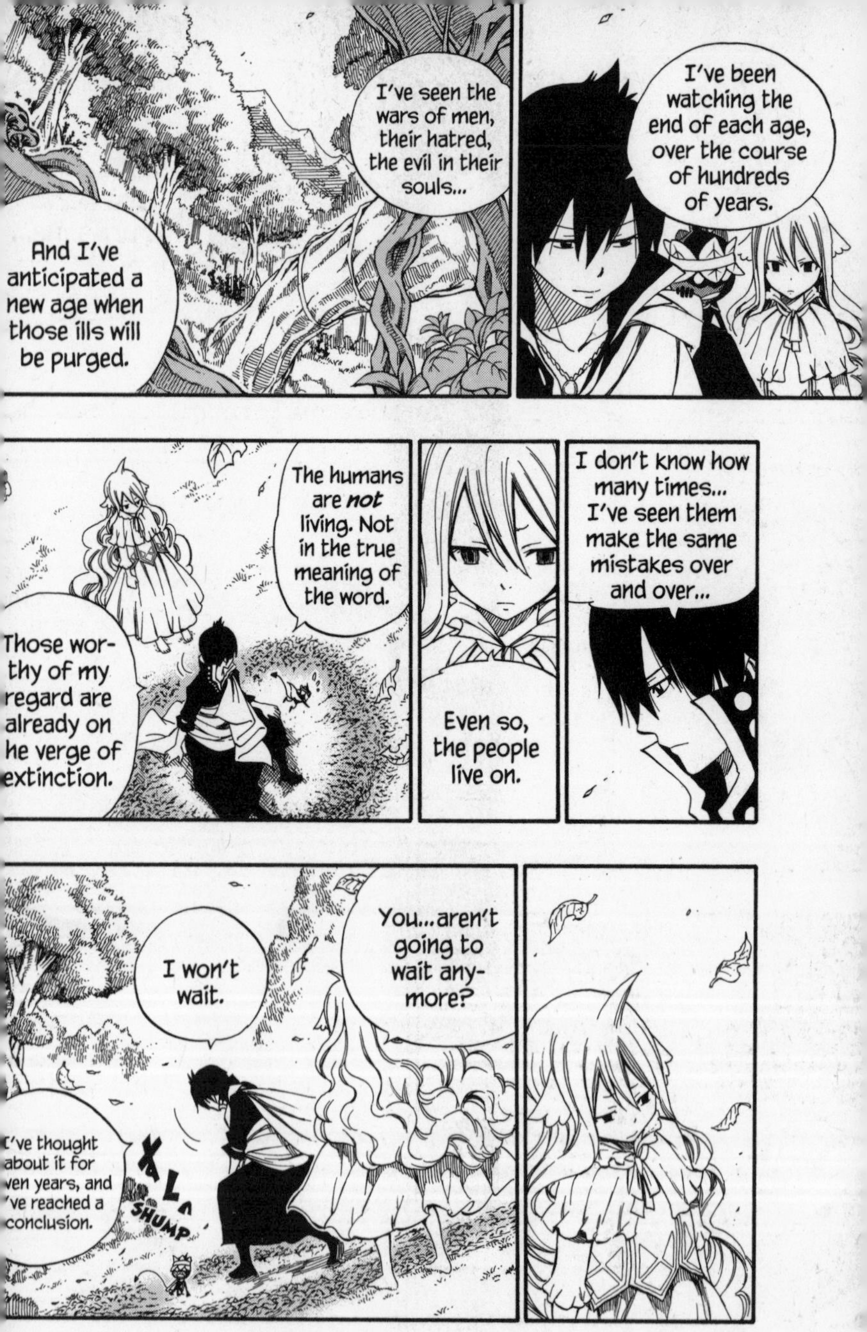

I've been watching the end of each age, over the course of hundreds of years.
I've seen the wars of men, their hatred, the evil in their souls...
And I've anticipated a new age when those ills will be purged.
I don't know how many times... I've seen them make the same mistakes over and over...
Even so, the people live on.
The humans are *not* living. Not in the true meaning of the word.
Those wor-thy of my regard are already on he verge of extinction.
You...aren't going to wait any-more?
I won't wait.
've thought about it for ven years, and 've reached a conclusion.
SHUMP

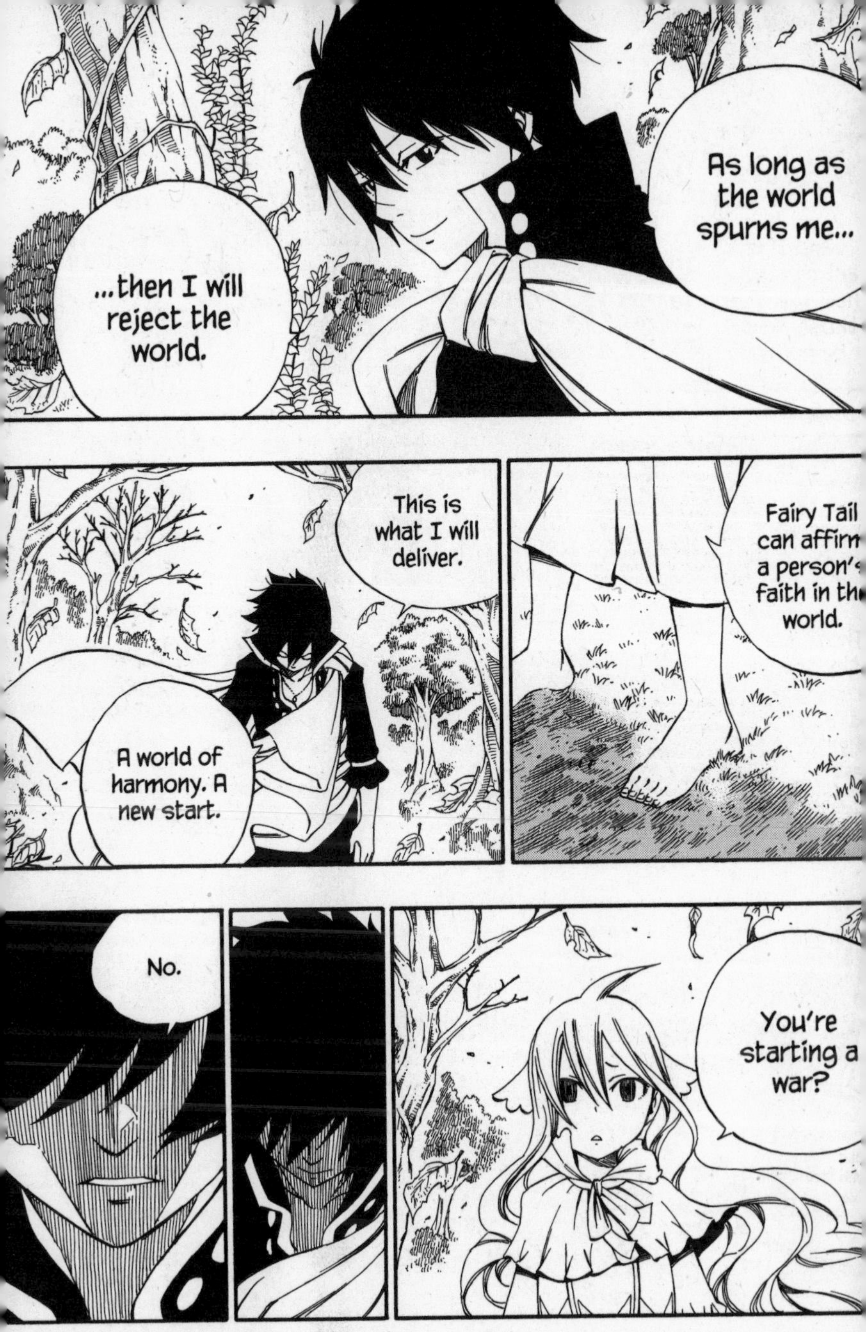
As long as the world spurns me...
...then I will reject the world.
Fairy Tail can affirm a person's faith in the world.
This is what I will deliver.
A world of harmony. A new start.
You're starting a war?
No.

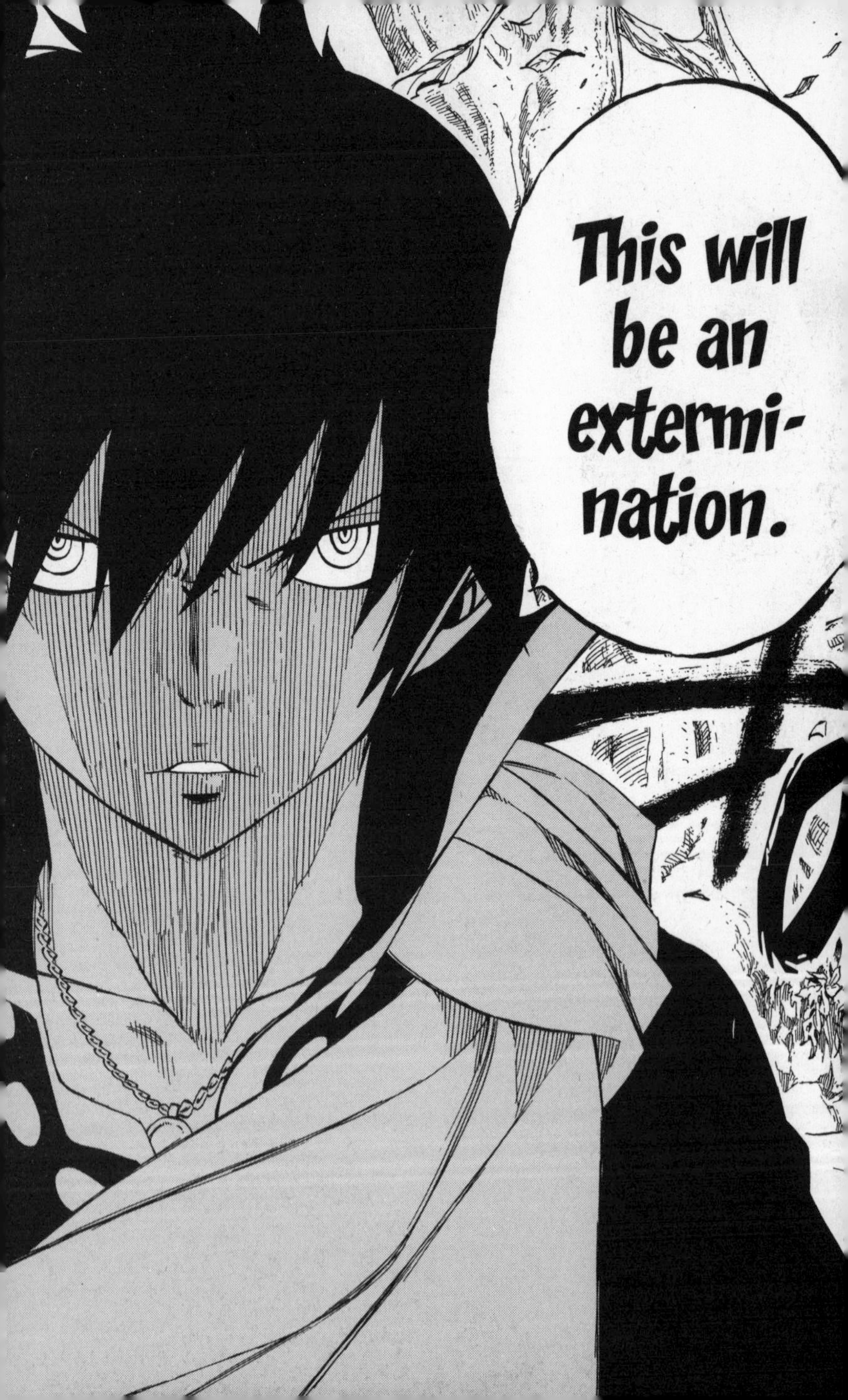
This will be an extermi-nation.

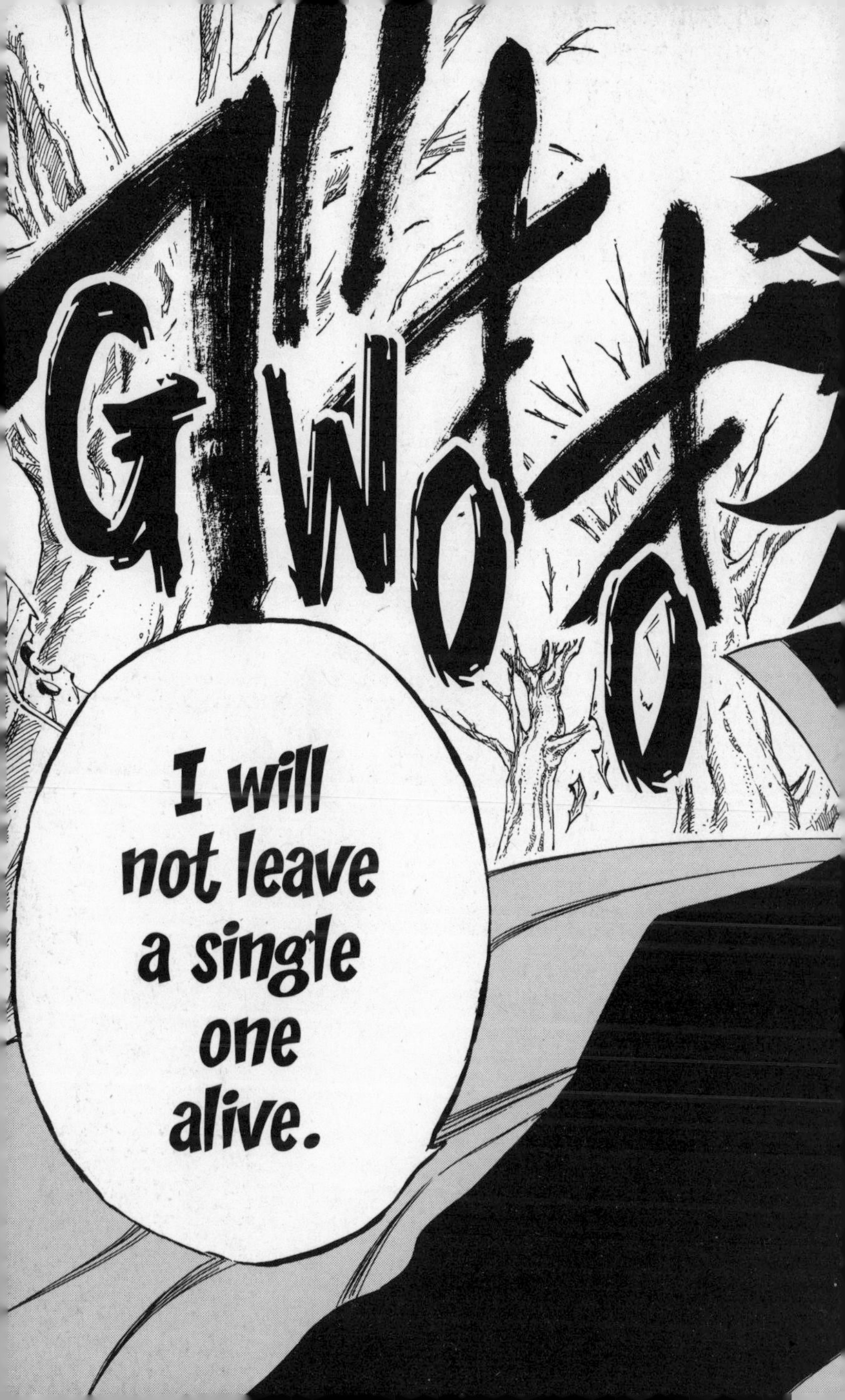
GWOOO
I will not leave a single one alive.

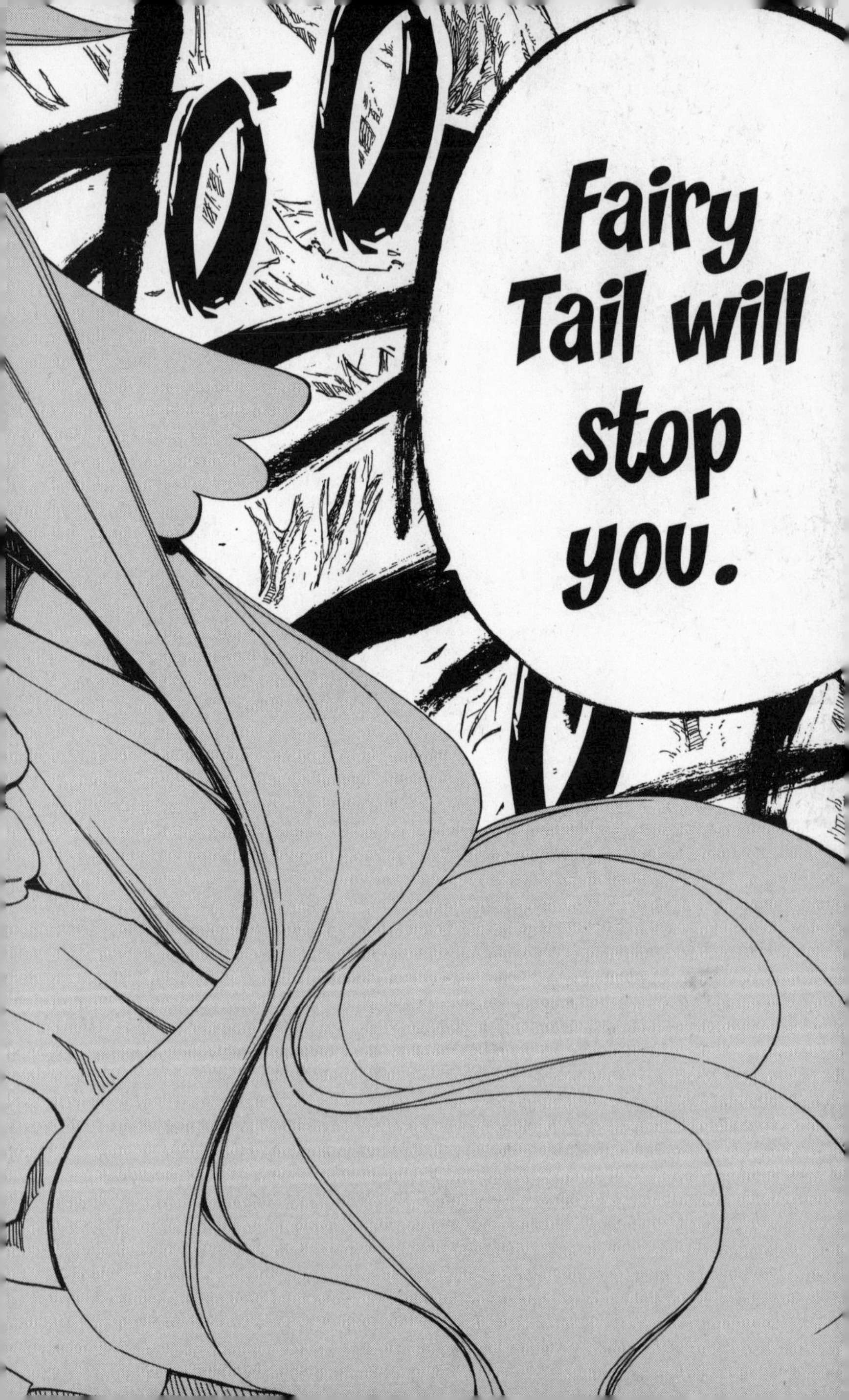
Fairy Tail will stop you.

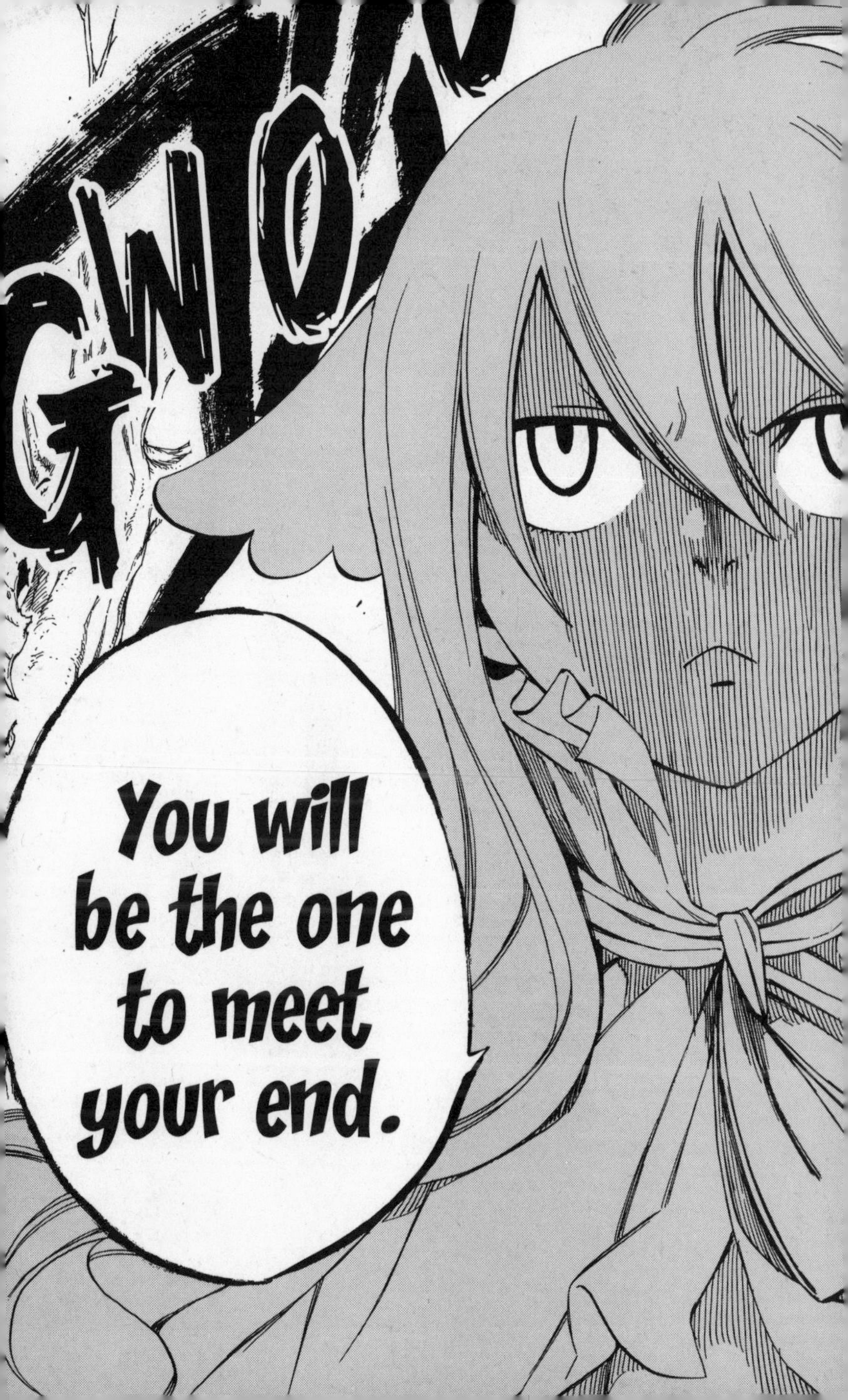
You will be the one to meet your end.

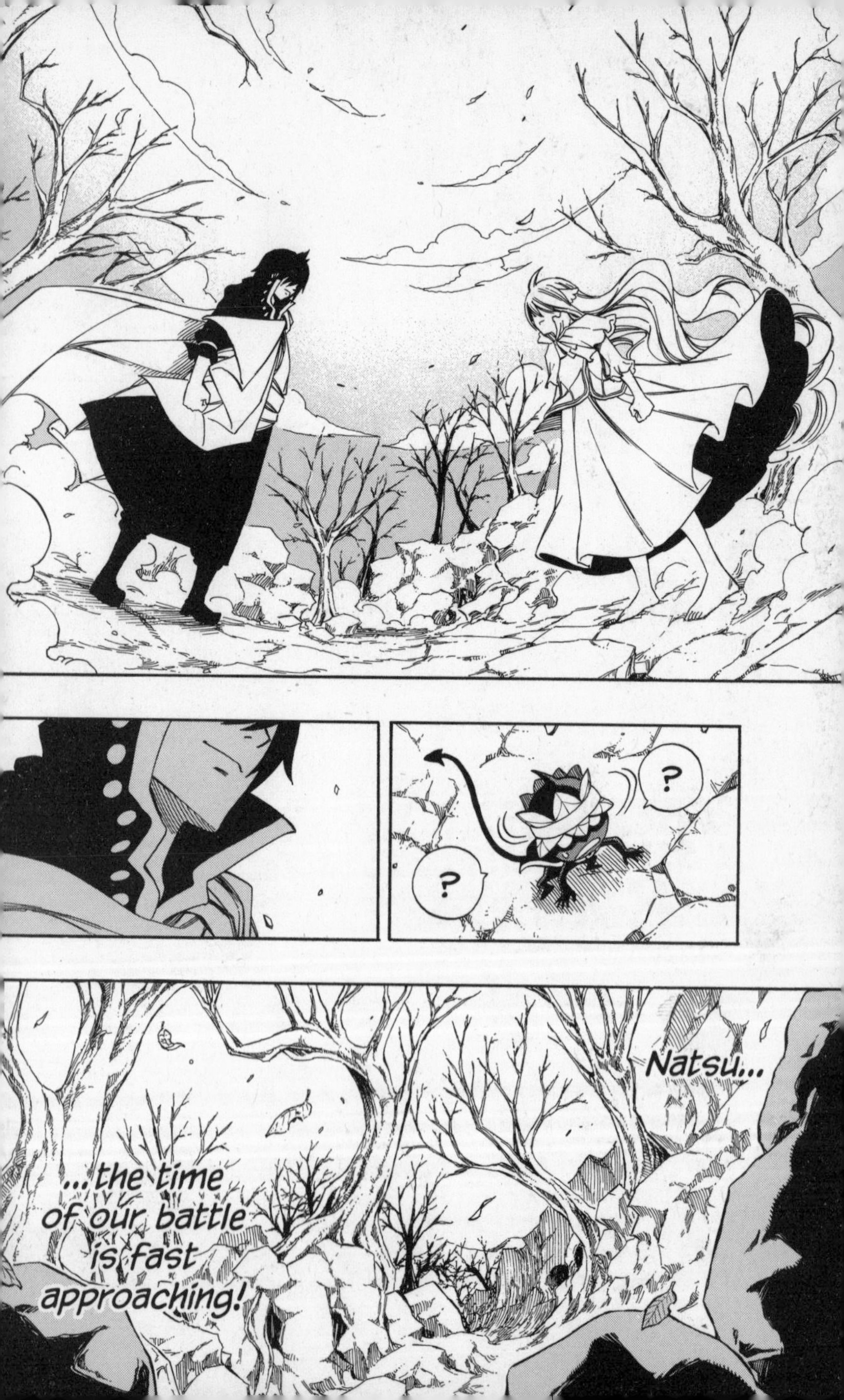
?
?
Natsu...
...the time of our battle is fast approaching!

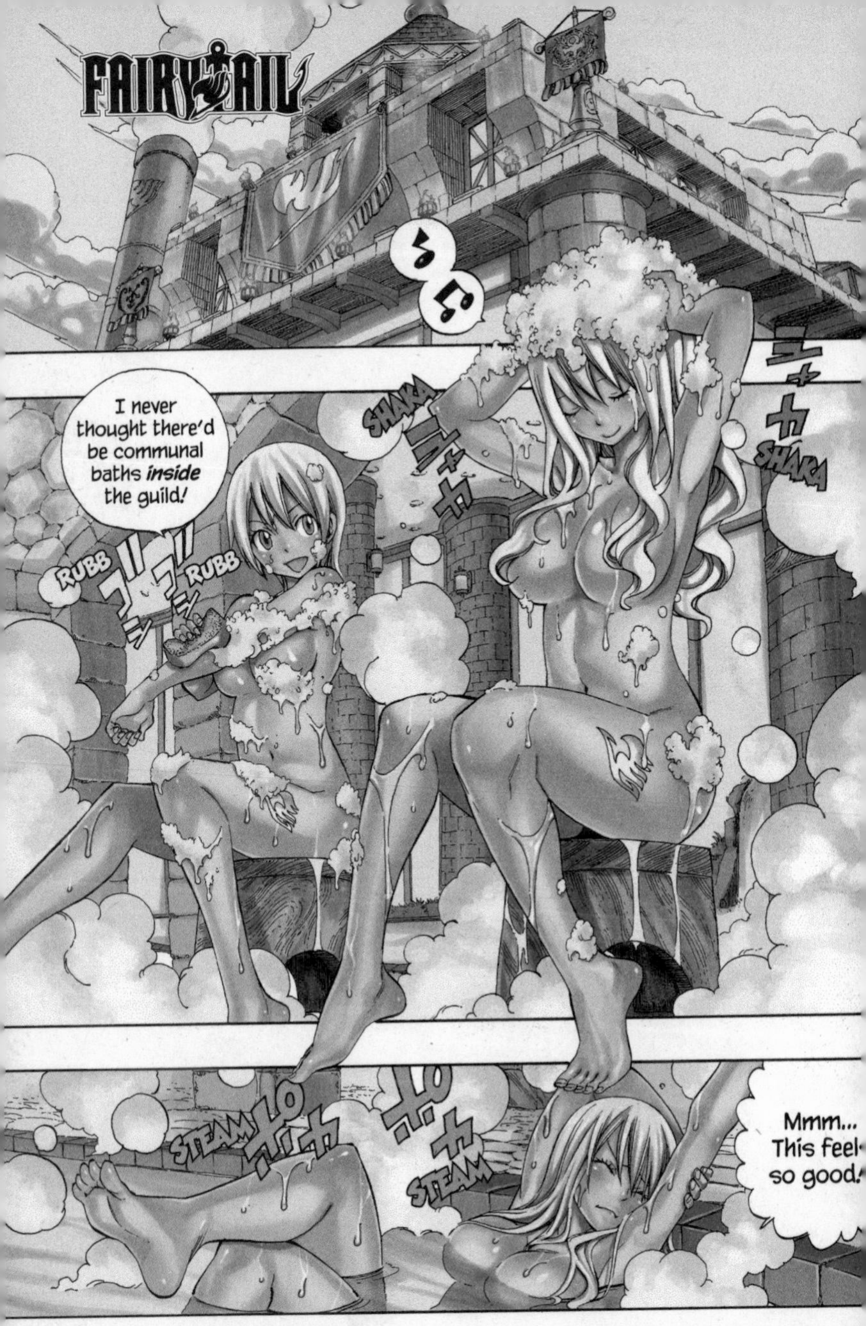
FAIRY TAIL
SHAKA
SHAKA
I never thought there'd be communal baths *inside* the guild!
RUBB RUBB
Mmm... This feel so good!
STEAM
STEAM

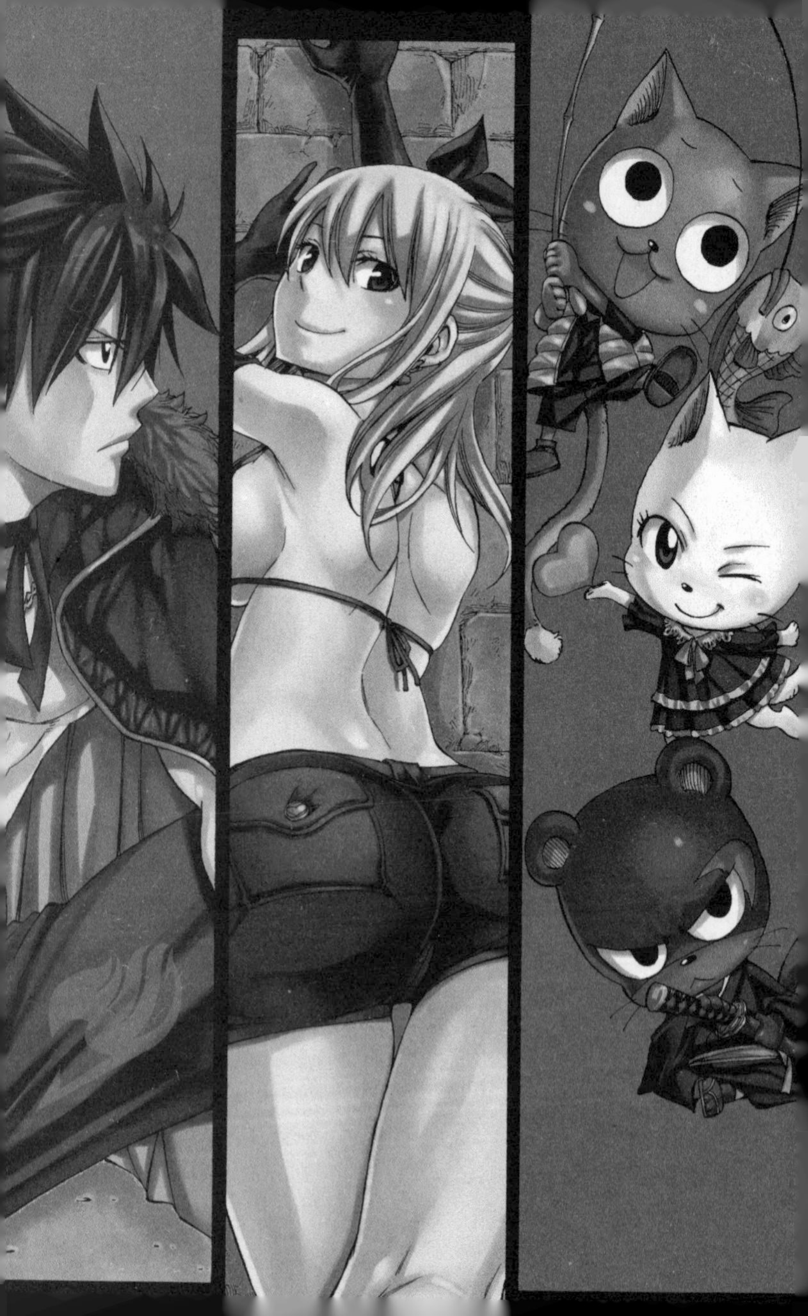

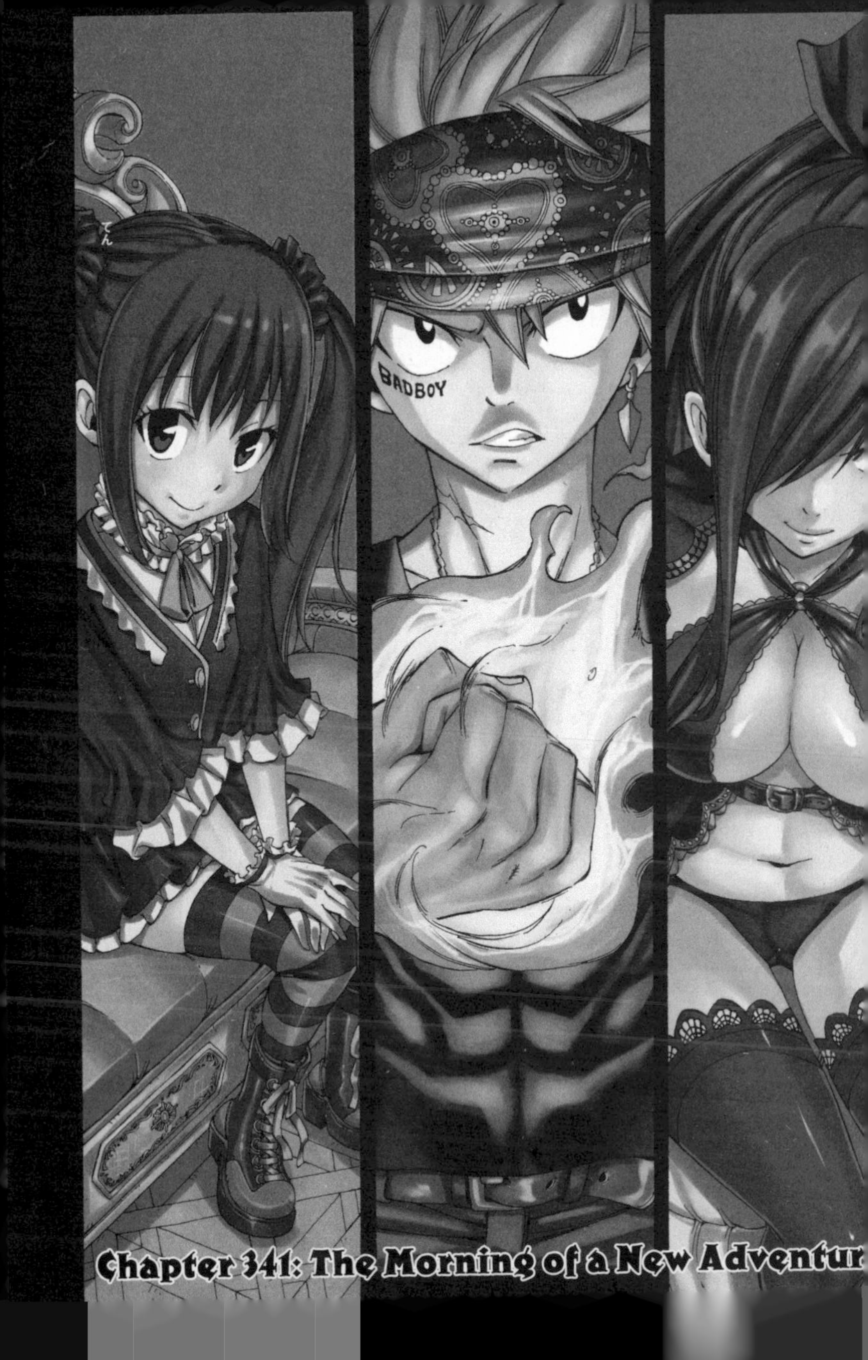
BADBOY
Chapter 341: The Morning of a New Adventur

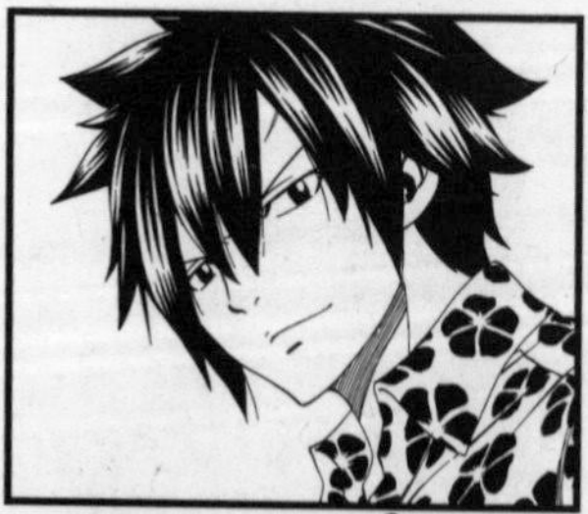

FAIRY TAIL

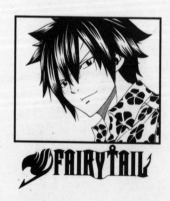

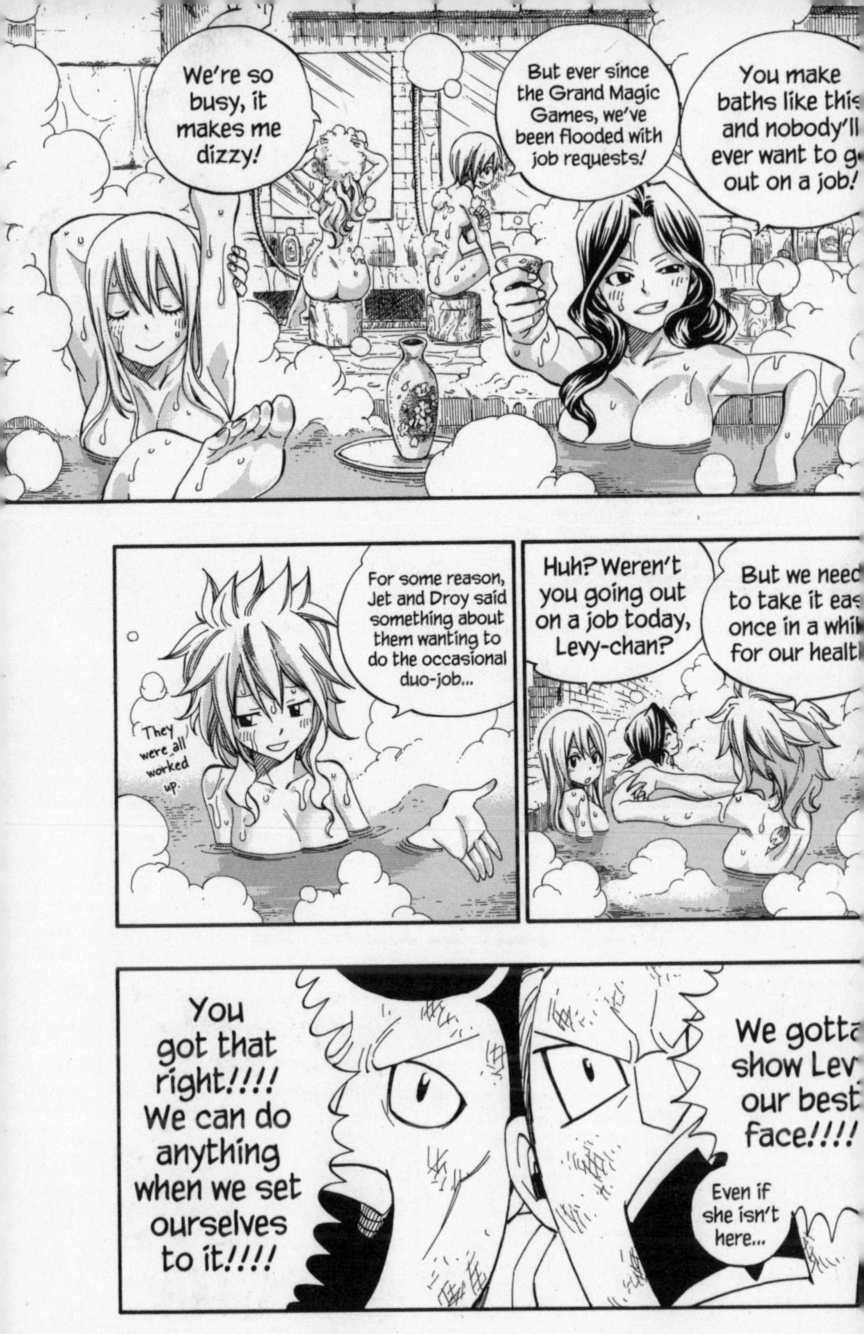
You make baths like this and nobody'll ever want to g out on a job!
But ever since the Grand Magic Games, we've been flooded with job requests!
We're so busy, it makes me dizzy!
But we need to take it eas once in a whi for our healt
Huh? Weren't you going out on a job today, Levy-chan?
For some reason, Jet and Droy said something about them wanting to do the occasional duo-job...
They were all worked up.
We gotta show Lev our best face!!!!
Even if she isn't here...
You got that right!!!! We can do anything when we set ourselves to it!!!!

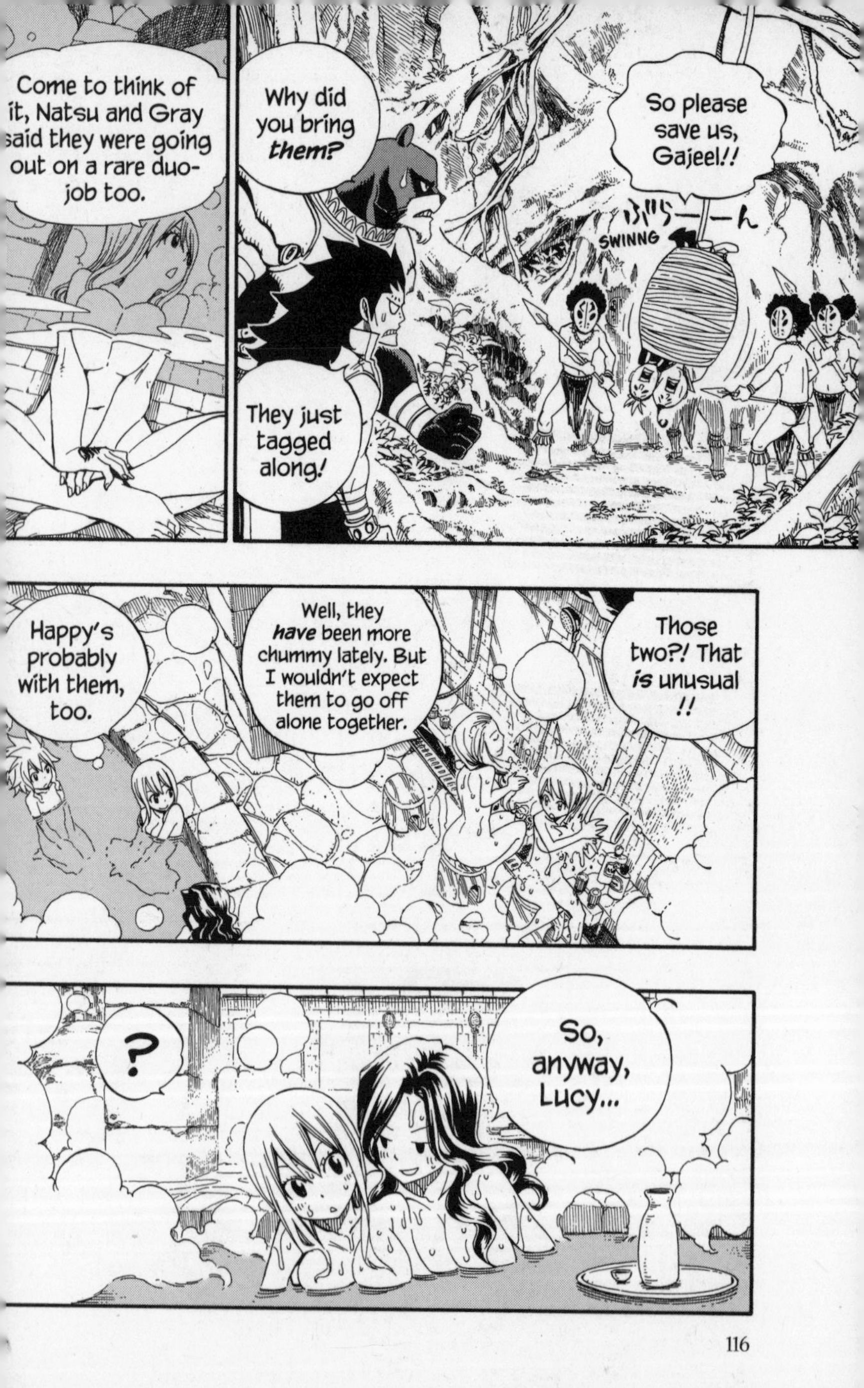

So please save us, Gajeel!!
ぶらーーーん
SWINNG
Why did you bring *them?*
They just tagged along!
Come to think of it, Natsu and Gray said they were going out on a rare duo-job too.
Those two?! That *is* unusual!!
Well, they *have* been more chummy lately. But I wouldn't expect them to go off alone together.
Happy's probably with them, too.
So, anyway, Lucy...
?

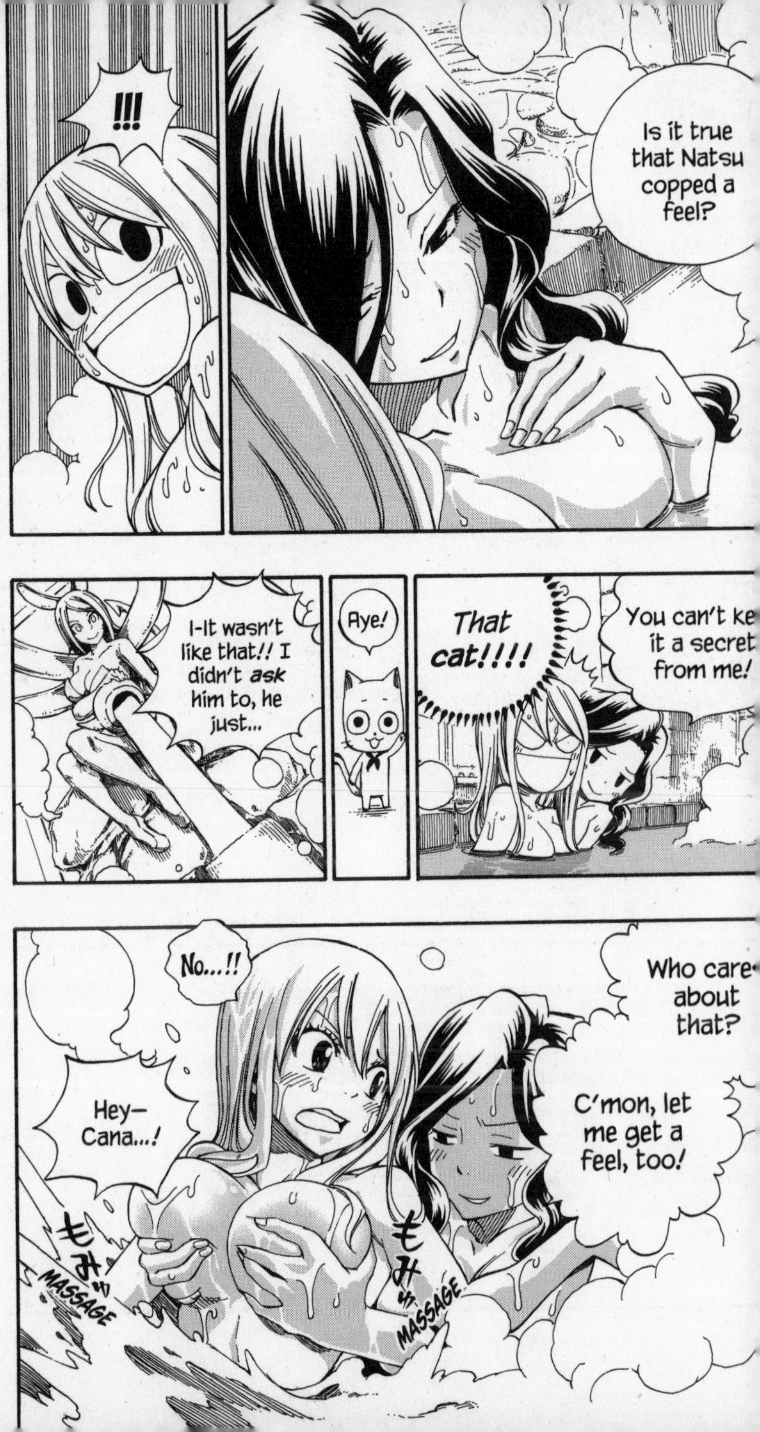

Is it true that Natsu copped a feel?
!!!
You can't ke it a secret from me!
That cat!!!!
Aye!
I-It wasn't like that!! I didn't ask him to, he just...
Who care about that?
C'mon, let me get a feel, too!
No...!!
Hey— Cana...!
もみ MASSAGE
もみ MASSAGE

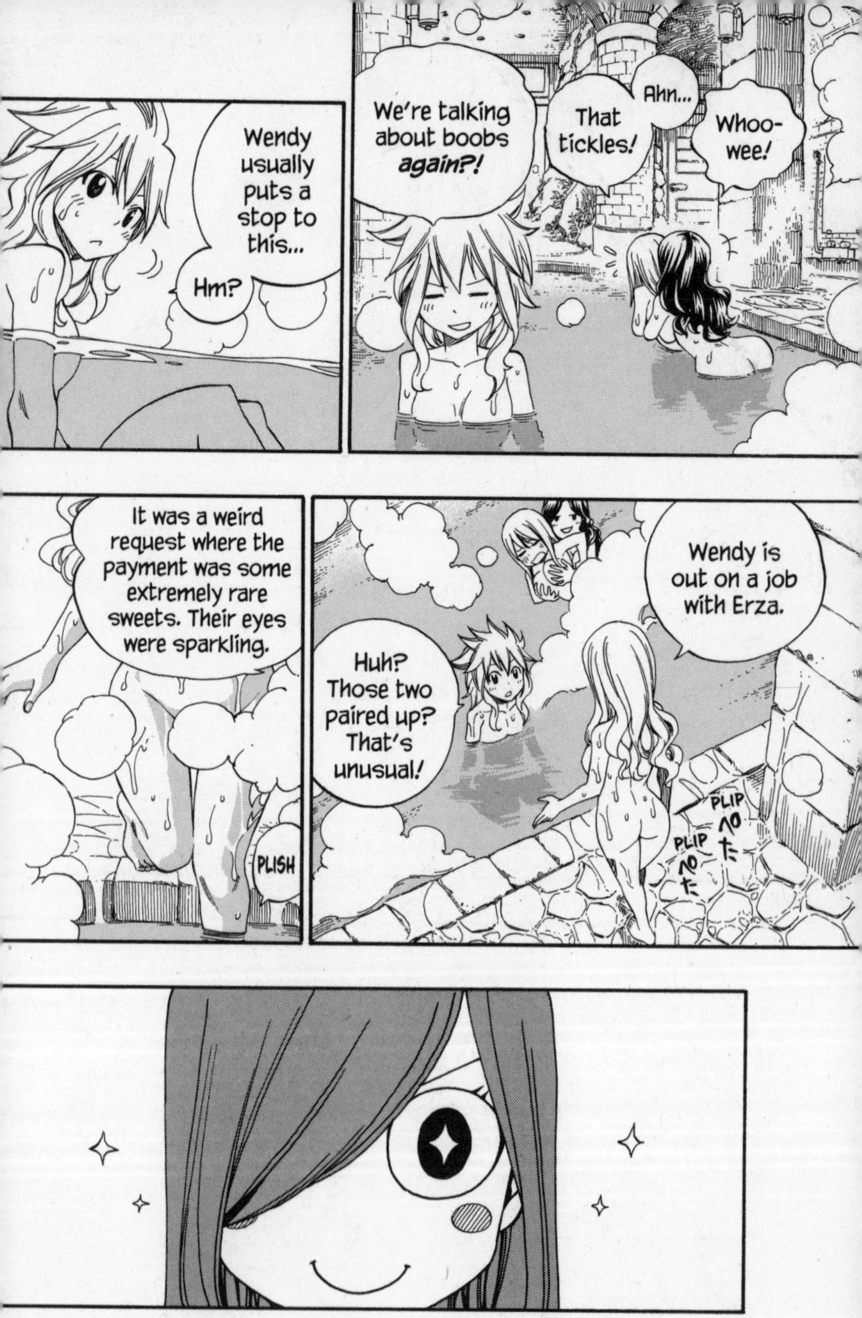
Whoo-wee!
Ahn...
That tickles!
We're talking about boobs *again?!*
Wendy usually puts a stop to this...
Hm?
Wendy is out on a job with Erza.
Huh? Those two paired up? That's unusual!
PLIP
PLIP
It was a weird request where the payment was some extremely rare sweets. Their eyes were sparkling.
PLISH

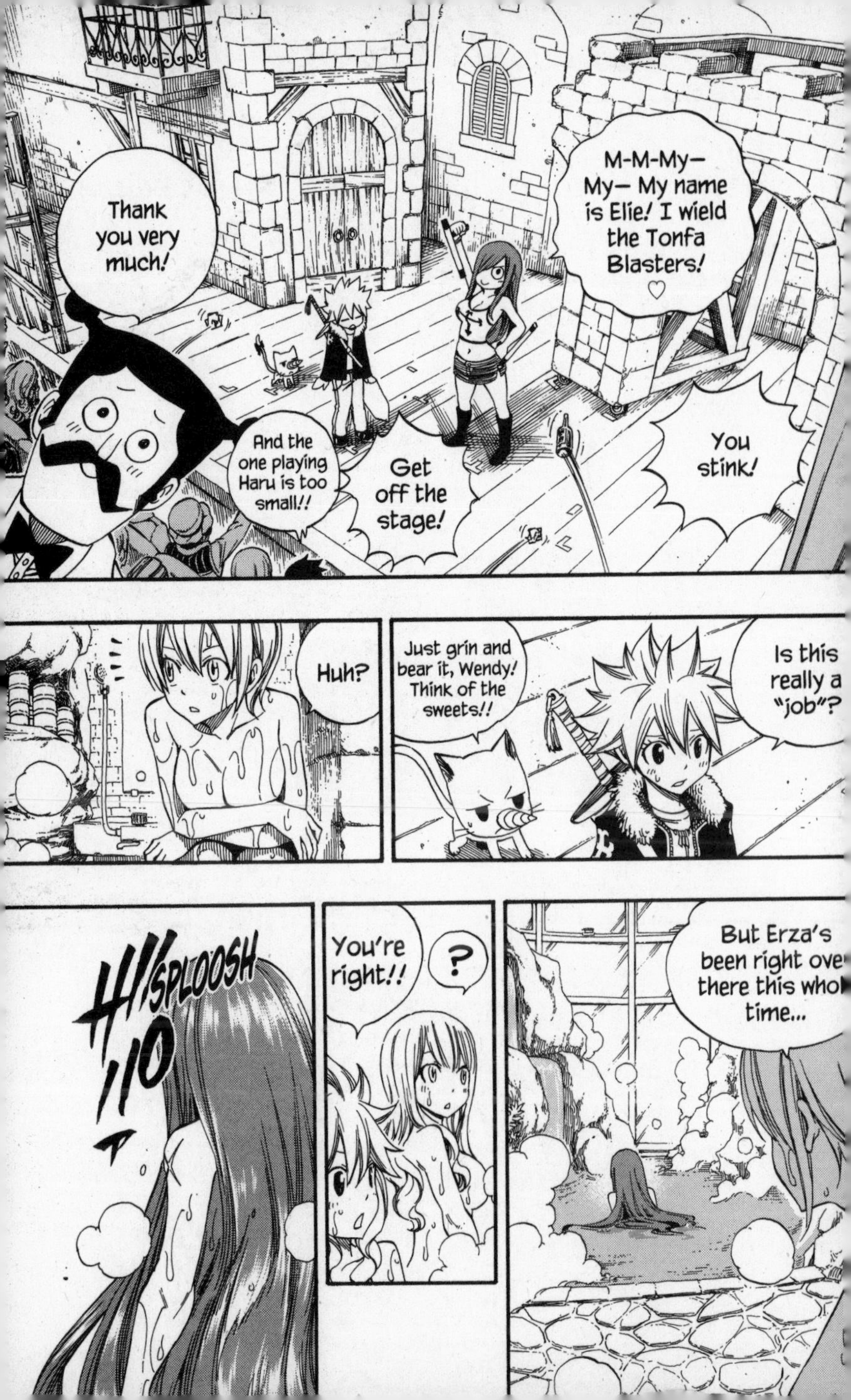
M-M-My— My— My name is Elie! I wield the Tonfa Blasters! ♡
Thank you very much!
You stink!
Get off the stage!
And the one playing Haru is too small!!
Is this really a "job"?
Just grin and bear it, Wendy! Think of the sweets!!
Huh?
But Erza's been right ove there this who time...
?
You're right!!
SPLOOSH

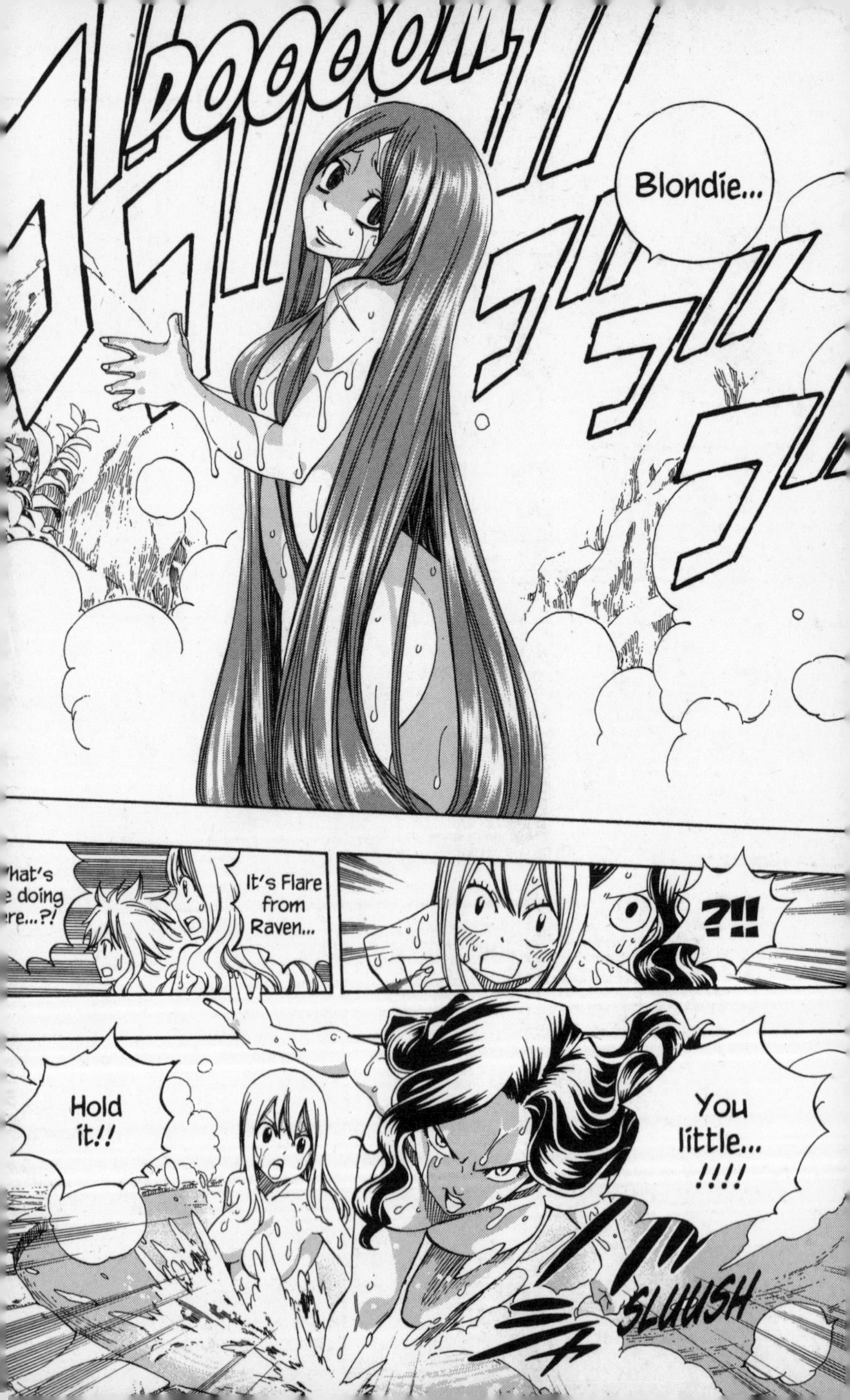
DOOOOM
Blondie...
?!!
It's Flare from Raven...
hat's e doing ere...?!
You little...!!!!
Hold it!!
SLUUSH

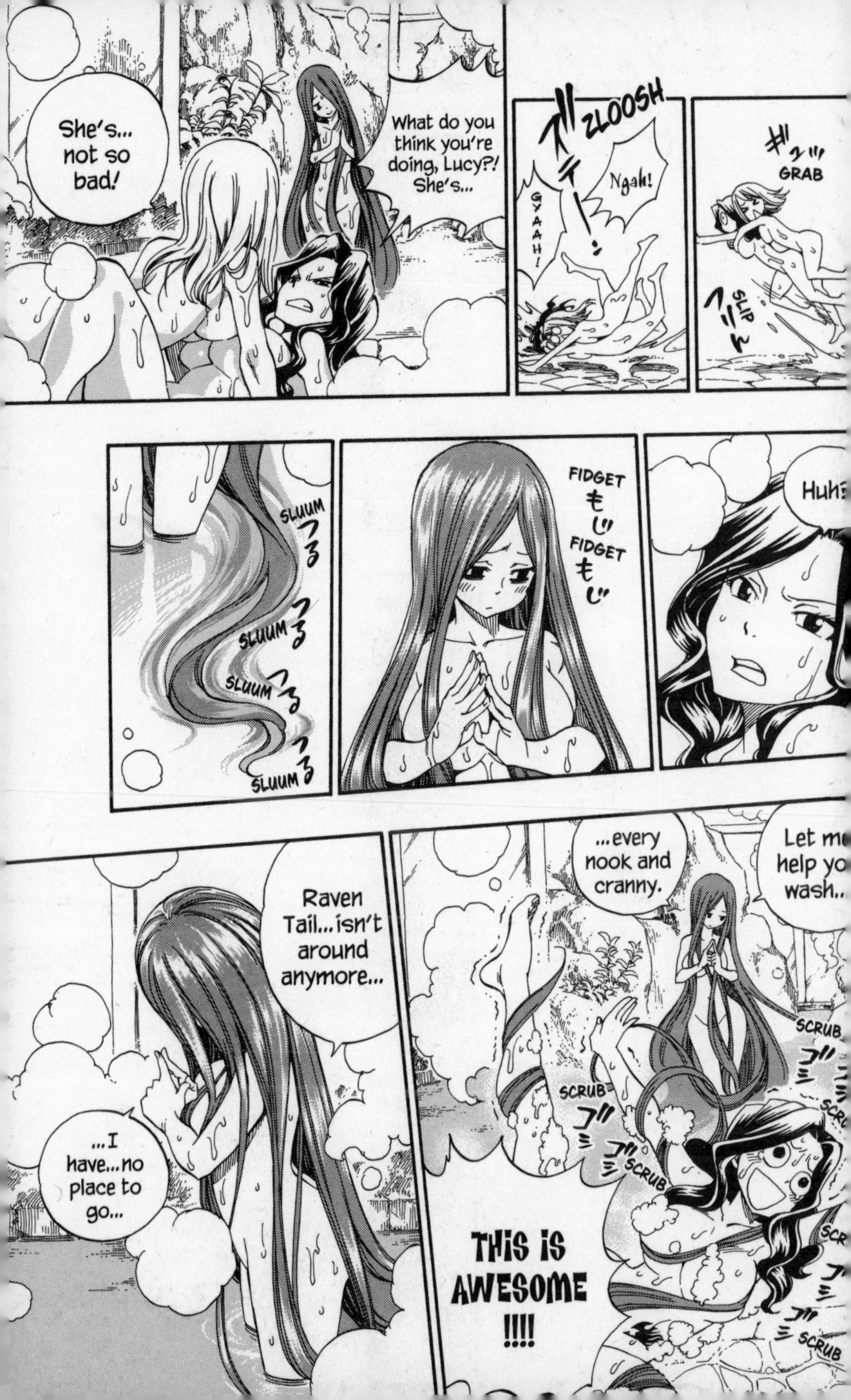
GRAB
SLIP
ZLOOSH
Ngah!
GYAAH!
What do you think you're doing, Lucy?! She's...
She's... not so bad!
Huh?
FIDGET
FIDGET
SLUUM
SLUUM
SLUUM
SLUUM
Let me help yo wash...
...every nook and cranny.
SCRUB
SCRUB
SCRUB
SCRUB
SCRUB
THIS IS AWESOME !!!!
Raven Tail...isn't around anymore...
...I have...no place to go...

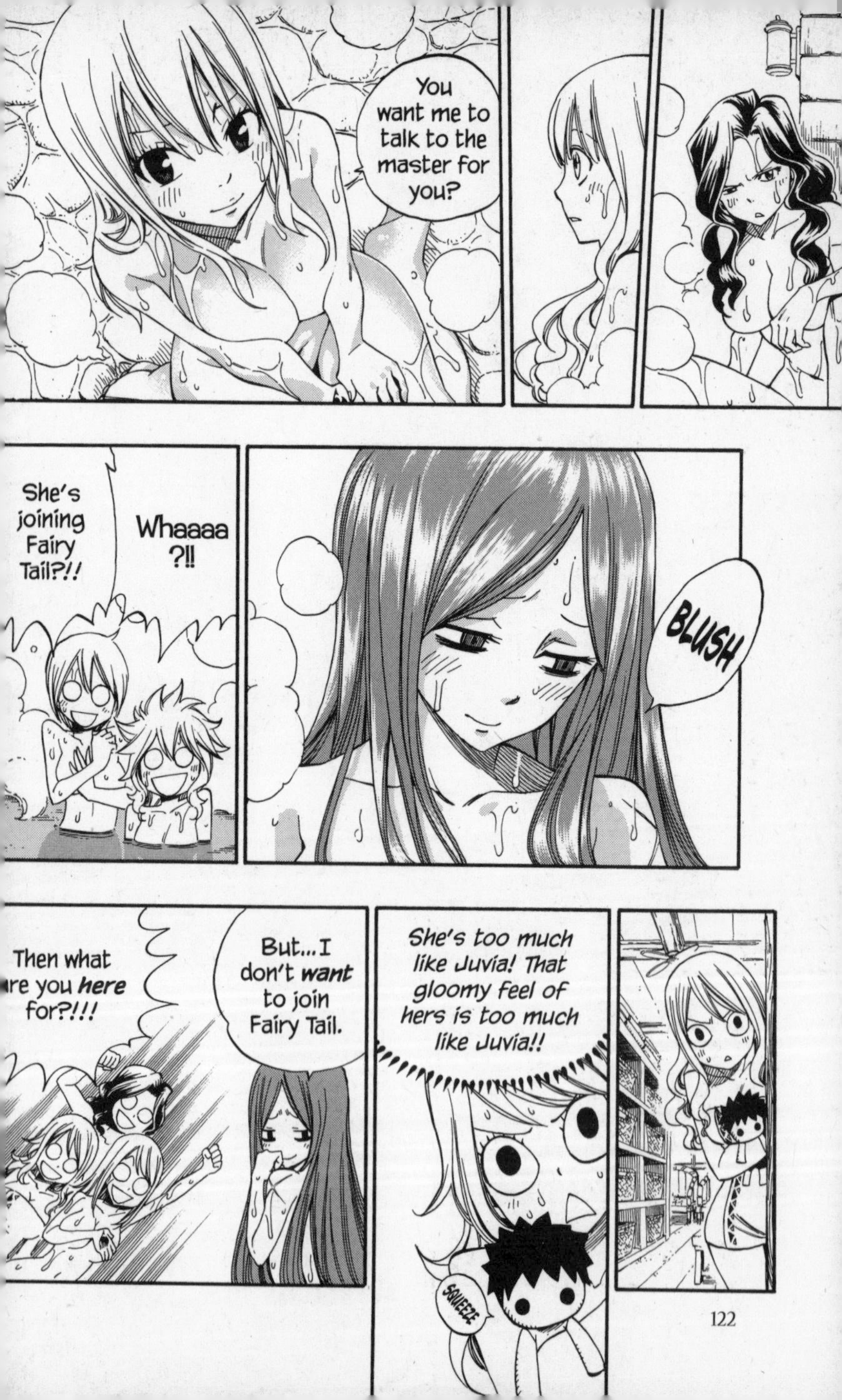
You want me to talk to the master for you?
BLUSH
Whaaaa ?!!
She's joining Fairy Tail?!!
She's too much like Juvia! That gloomy feel of hers is too much like Juvia!!
SQUEEZE
But...I don't *want* to join Fairy Tail.
Then what re you *here* for?!!!

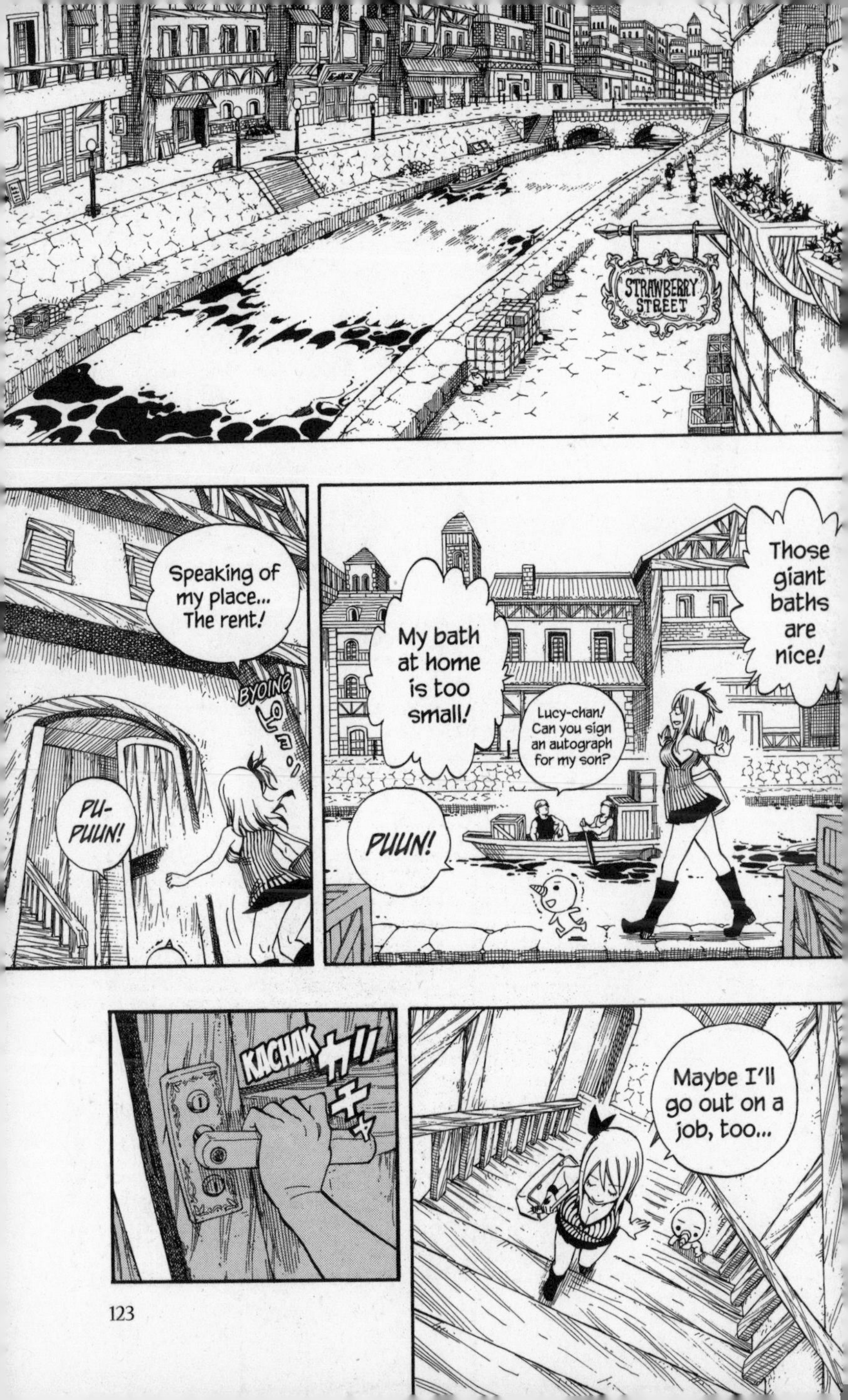
STRAWBERRY STREET
Those giant baths are nice!
My bath at home is too small!
Lucy-chan! Can you sign an autograph for my son?
PUUN!
Speaking of my place... The rent!
BYOING
PU-PUUN!
Maybe I'll go out on a job, too...
KACHAK

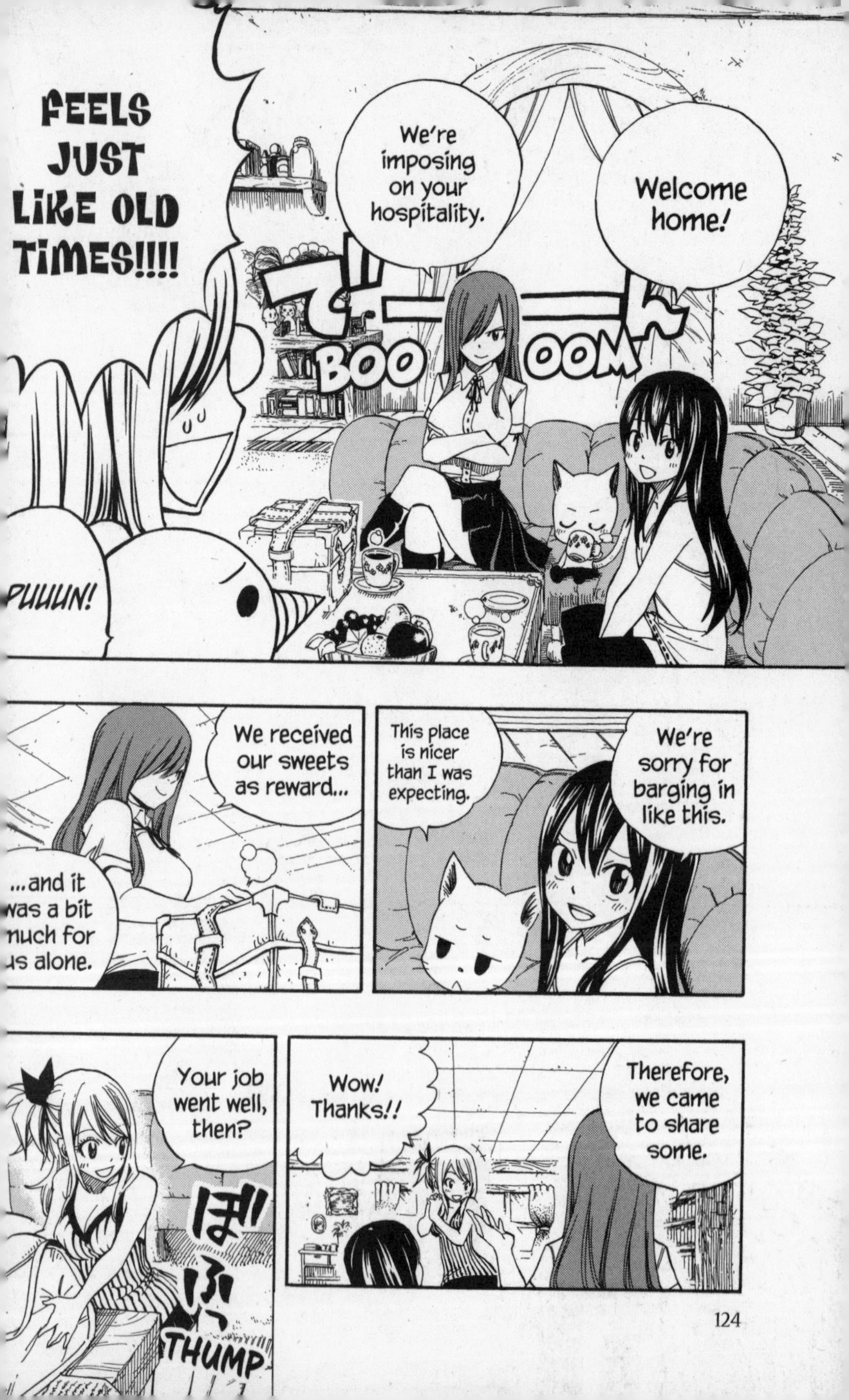

Welcome home!
We're imposing on your hospitality.
BOOOOM
FEELS JUST LIKE OLD TIMES!!!!
PUUUN!
We're sorry for barging in like this.
This place is nicer than I was expecting.
We received our sweets as reward...
...and it was a bit much for us alone.
Therefore, we came to share some.
Wow! Thanks!!
Your job went well, then?
THUMP

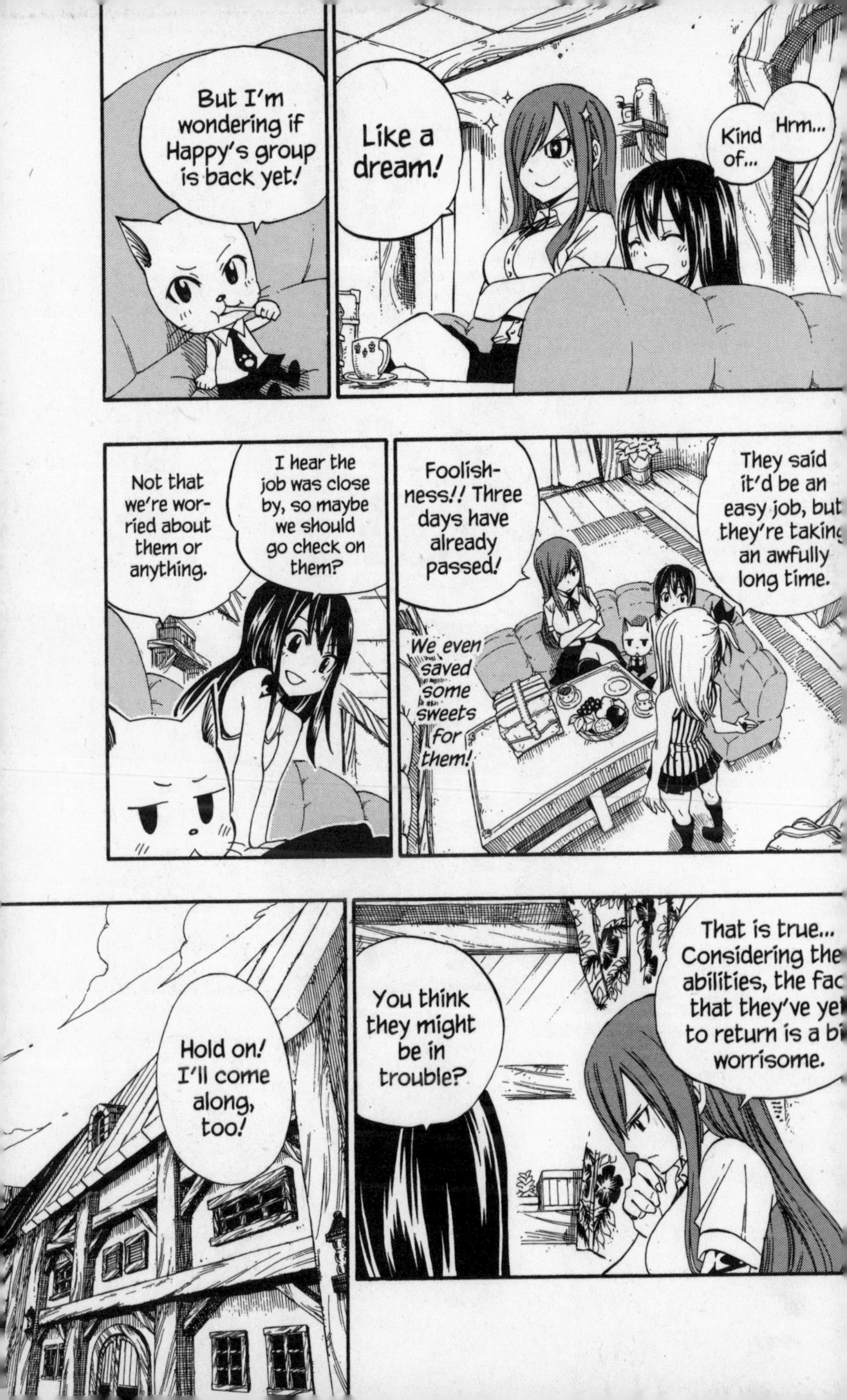
Hrm...
Kind of...
Like a dream!
But I'm wondering if Happy's group is back yet!
They said it'd be an easy job, but they're takin an awfully long time.
Foolish-ness!! Three days have already passed!
We even saved some sweets for them!
I hear the job was close by, so maybe we should go check on them?
Not that we're wor-ried about them or anything.
That is true... Considering the abilities, the fac that they've ye to return is a bi worrisome.
You think they might be in trouble?
Hold on! I'll come along, too!

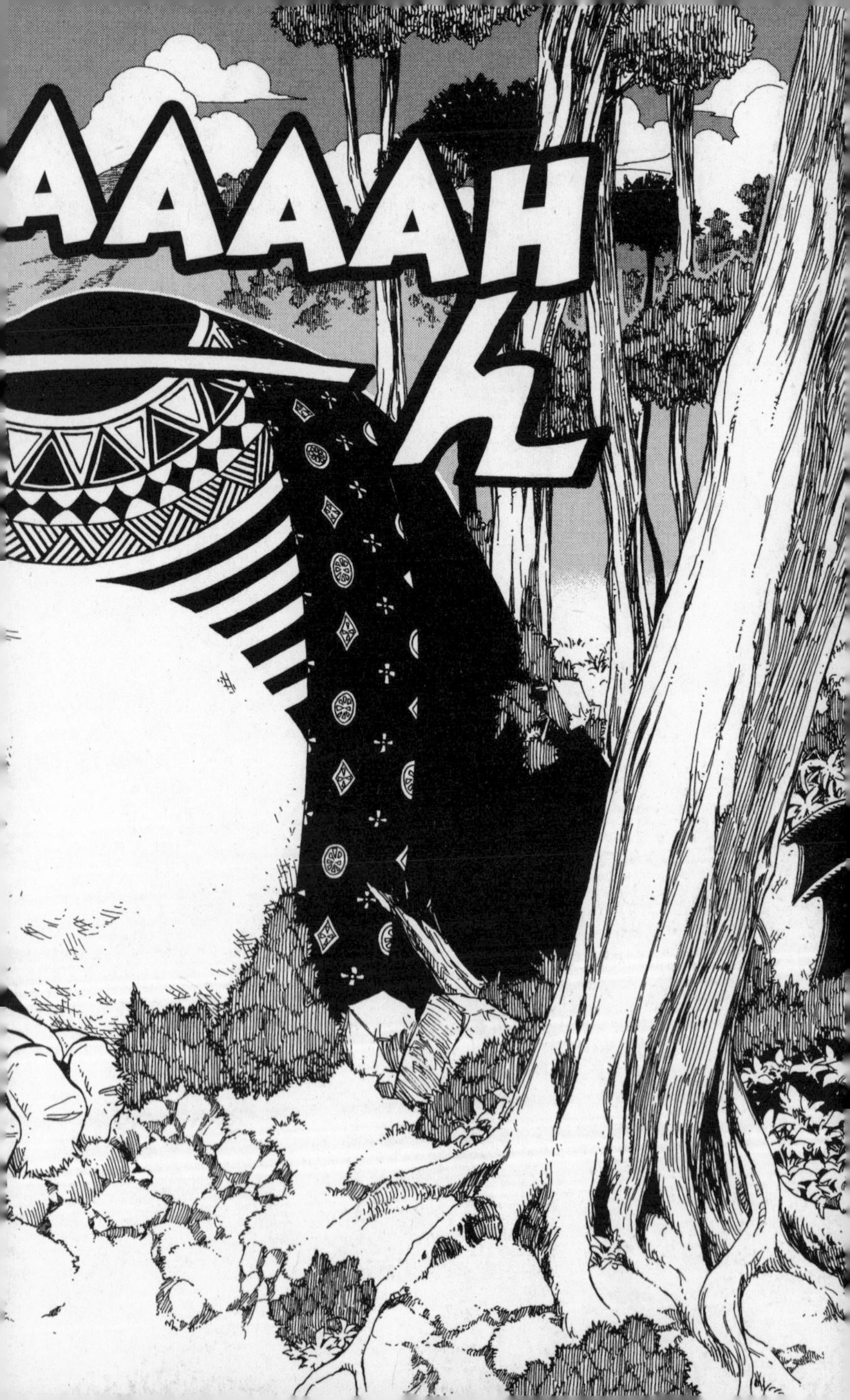
AAAAH

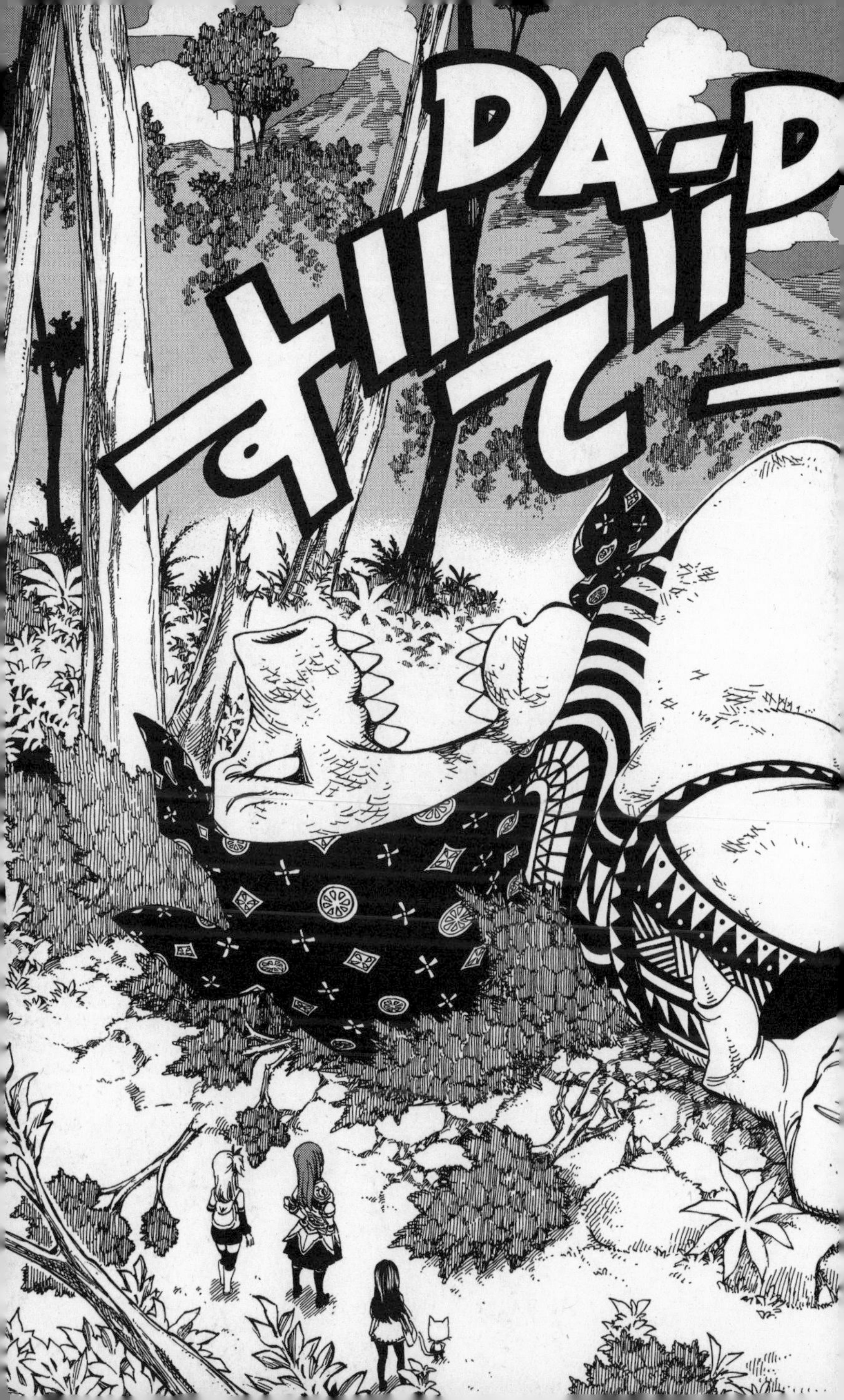
DA-D

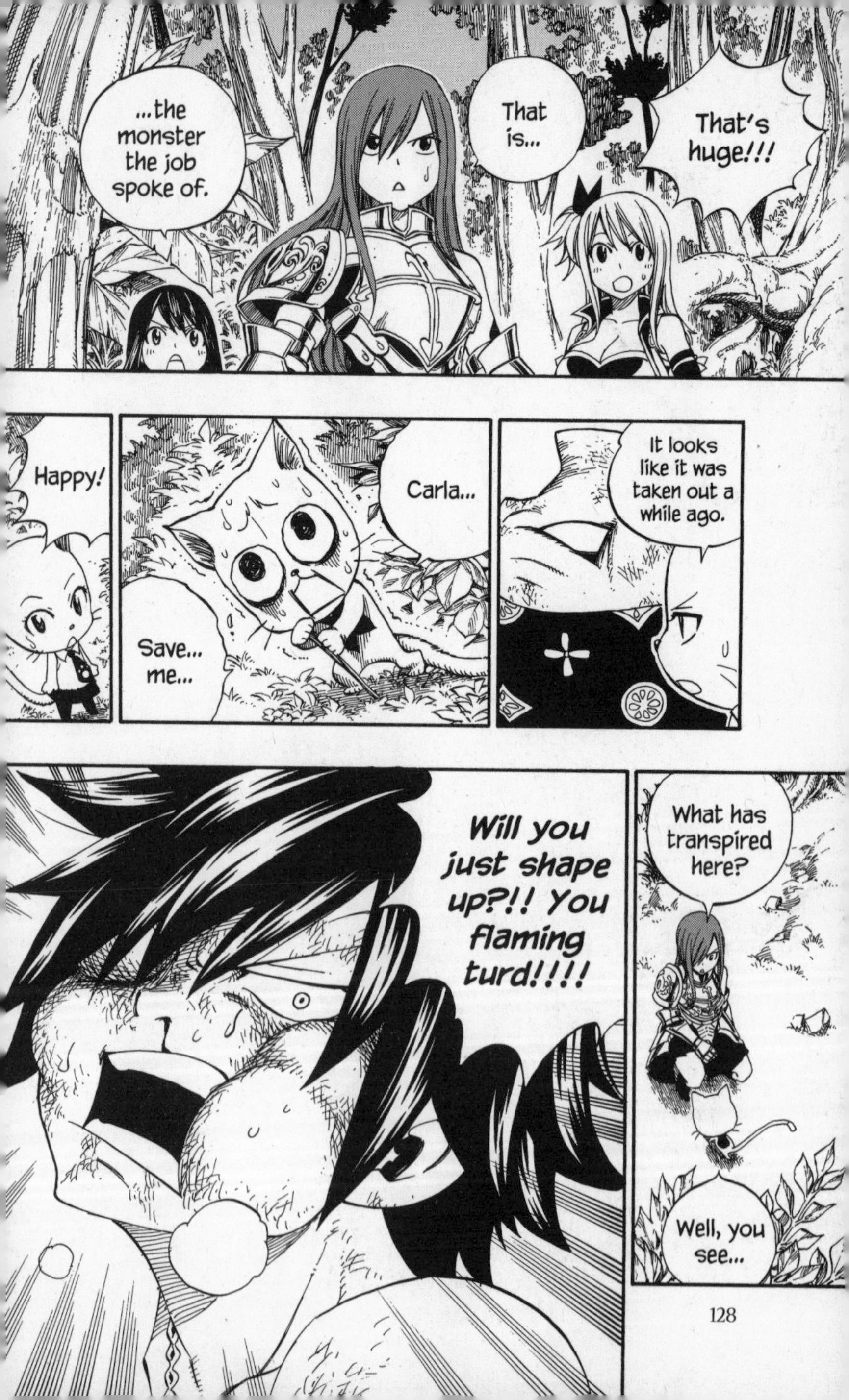
That's huge!!!
That is...
...the monster the job spoke of.
It looks like it was taken out a while ago.
Carla...
Save... me...
Happy!
What has transpired here?
Well, you see...
Will you just shape up?!! You flaming turd!!!!

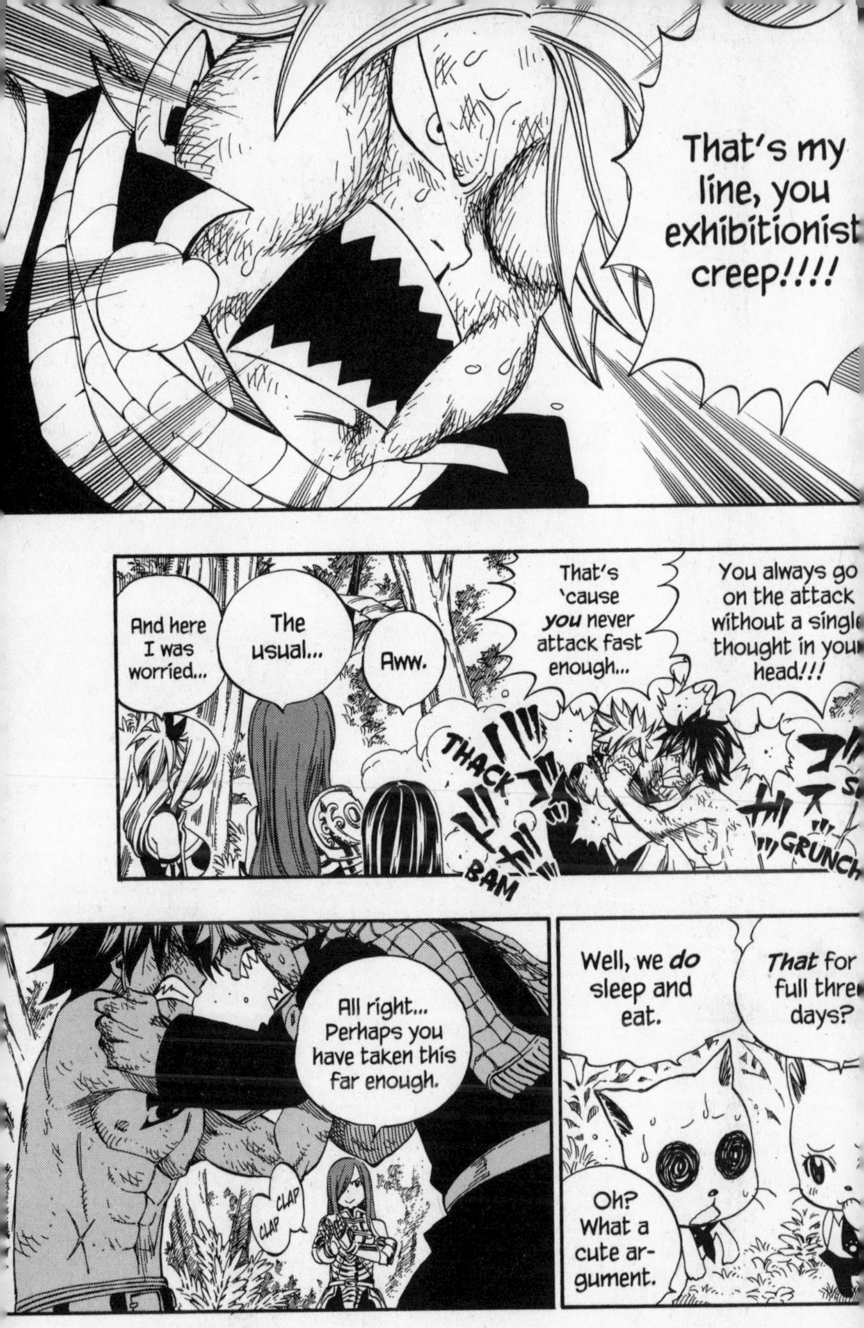
That's my line, you exhibitionist creep!!!!
You always go on the attack without a singl thought in you head!!!
That's 'cause *you* never attack fast enough...
GRUNCH
THACK
BAM
Aww.
The usual...
And here I was worried...
That for full thre days?
Well, we *do* sleep and eat.
Oh? What a cute argument.
All right... Perhaps you have taken this far enough.
CLAP CLAP

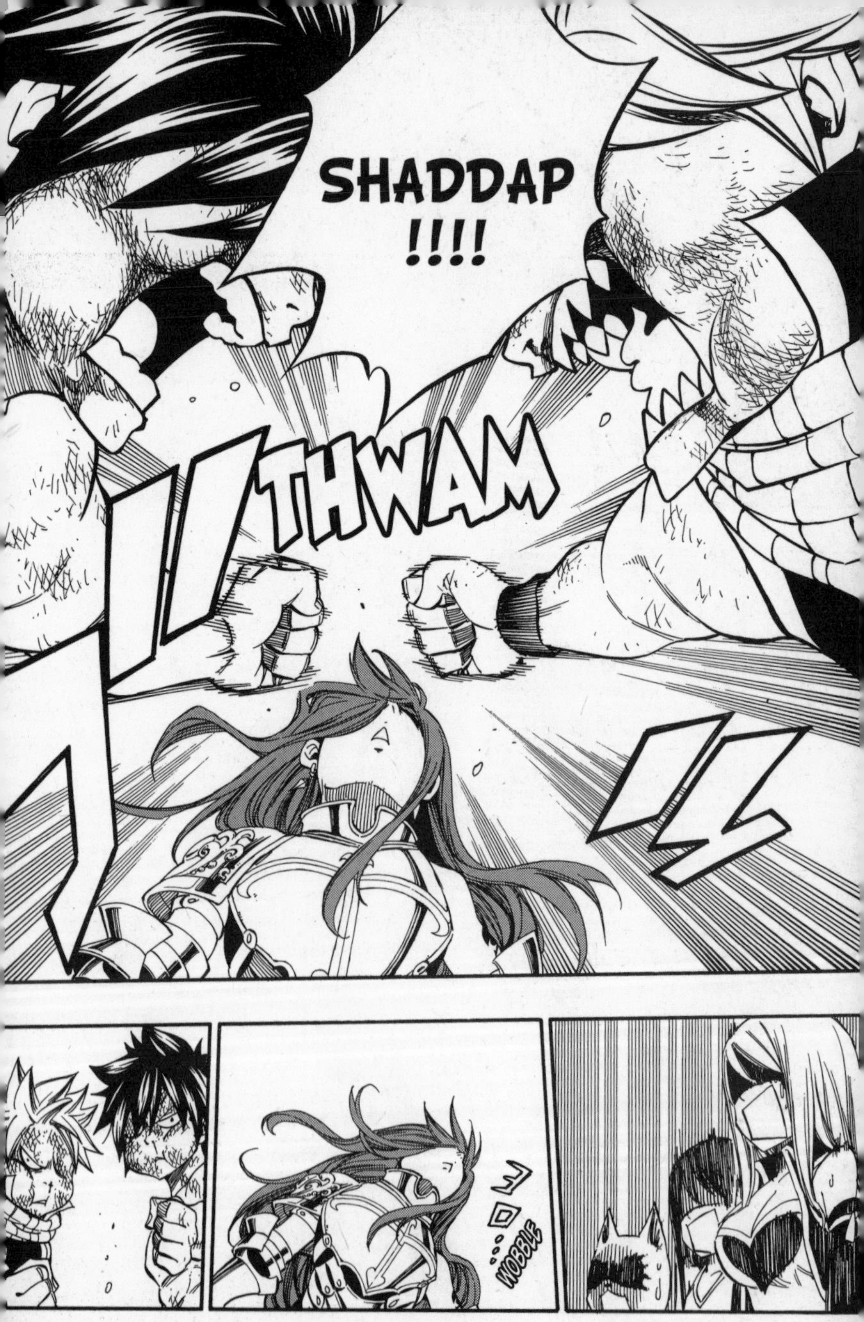
SHADDAP !!!!
THWAM
WOBBLE

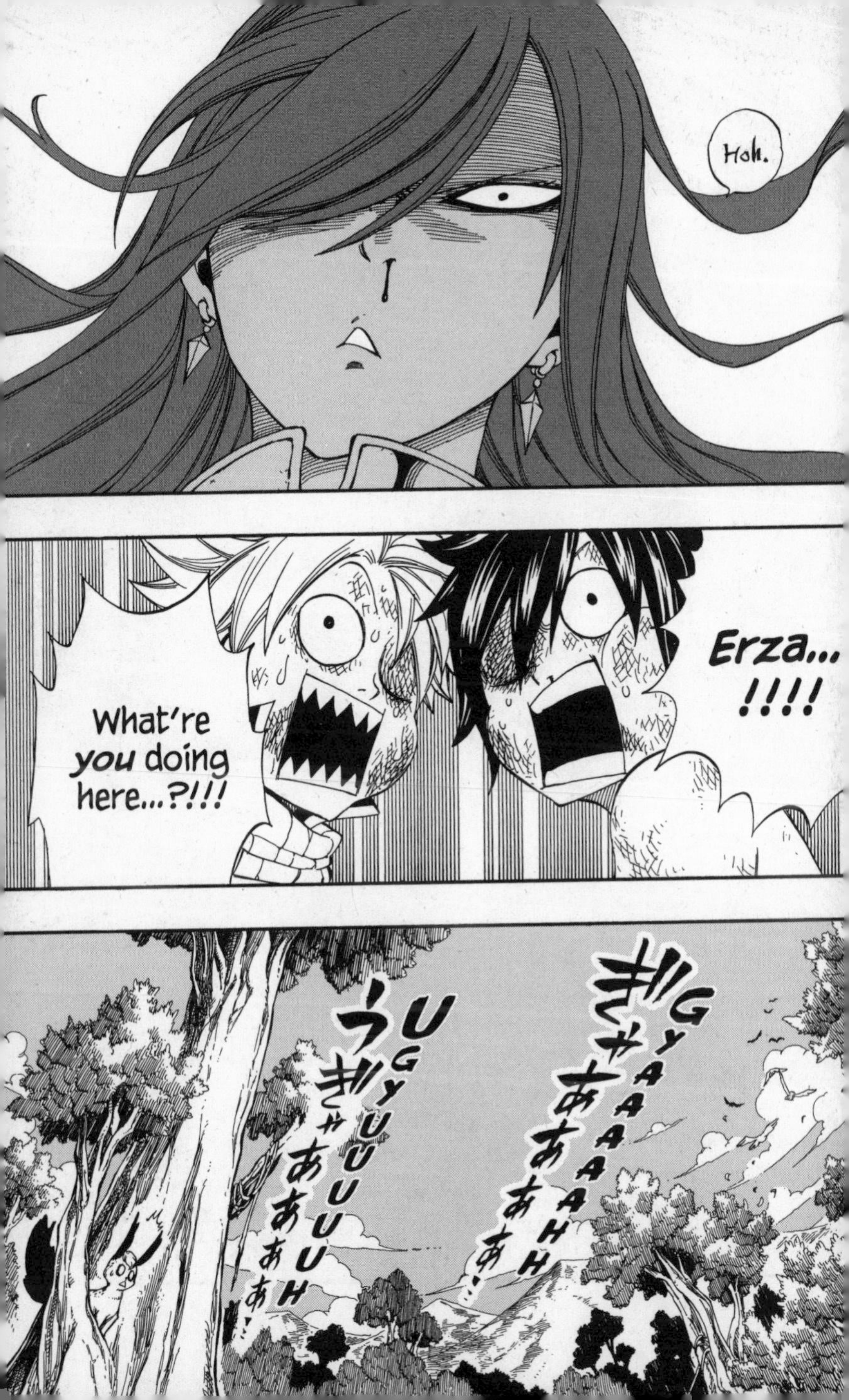

Hoh.
Erza... !!!!
What're *you* doing here...?!!!
GYAAAAAAHHH
UGYUUUUUH

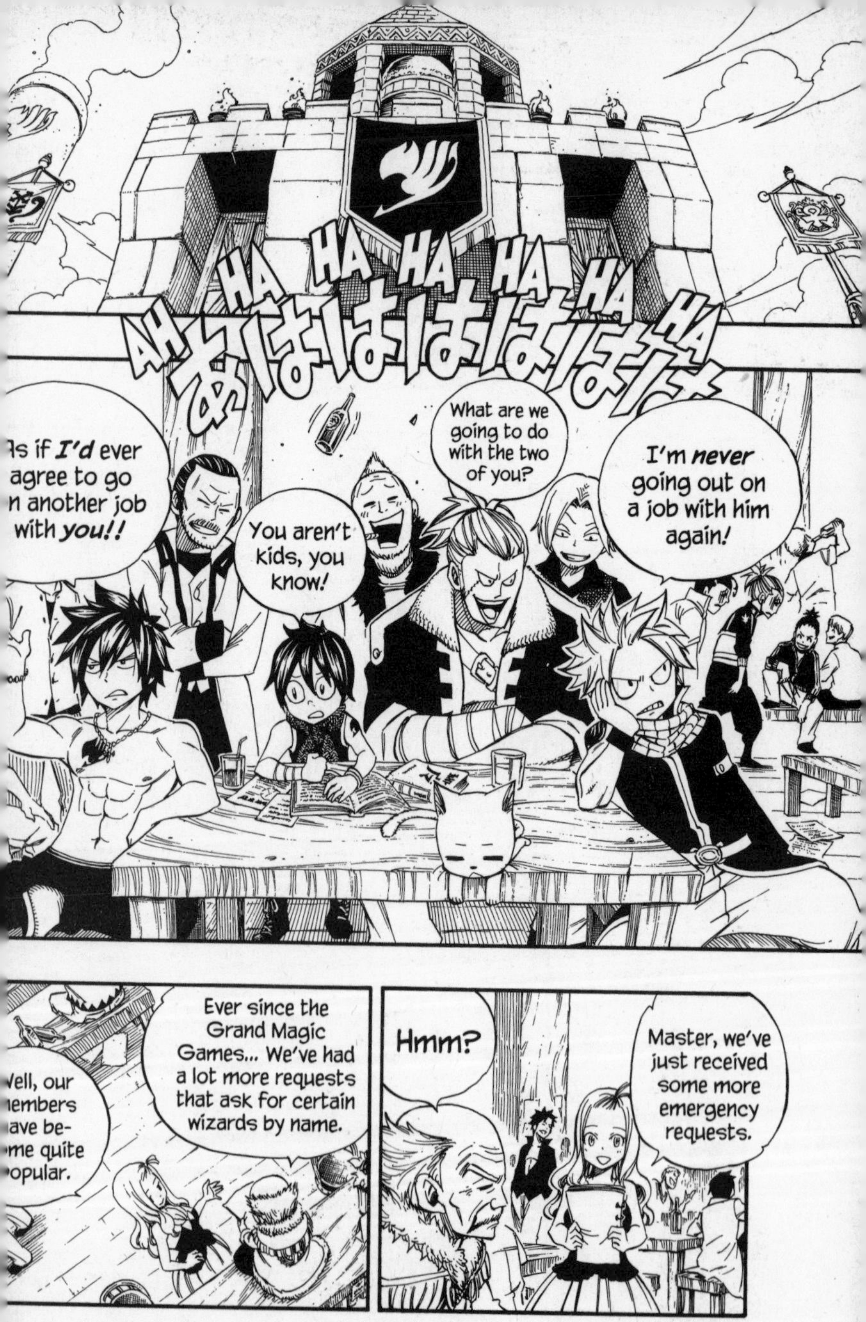
AH HA HA HA HA HA HA
I'm never going out on a job with him again!
What are we going to do with the two of you?
You aren't kids, you know!
ls if I'd ever agree to go n another job with you!!
Master, we've just received some more emergency requests.
Hmm?
Ever since the Grand Magic Games... We've had a lot more requests that ask for certain wizards by name.
Vell, our nembers ave be- me quite opular.

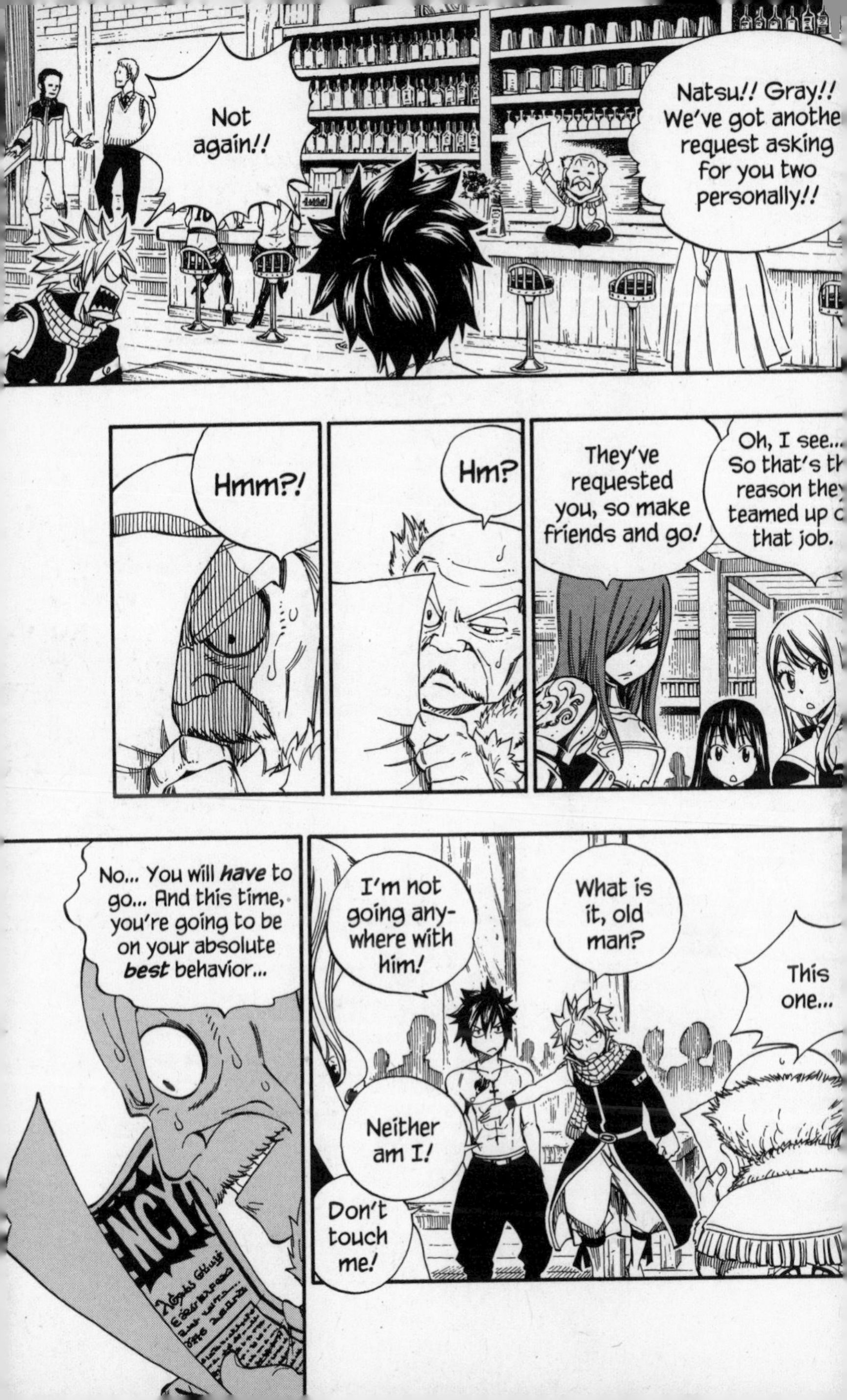
Natsu!! Gray!! We've got anothe request asking for you two personally!!
Not again!!
Oh, I see... So that's th reason the teamed up o that job.
They've requested you, so make friends and go!
Hm?
Hmm?!
This one...
What is it, old man?
I'm not going any-where with him!
Neither am I!
Don't touch me!
No... You will *have* to go... And this time, you're going to be on your absolute ***best*** behavior...

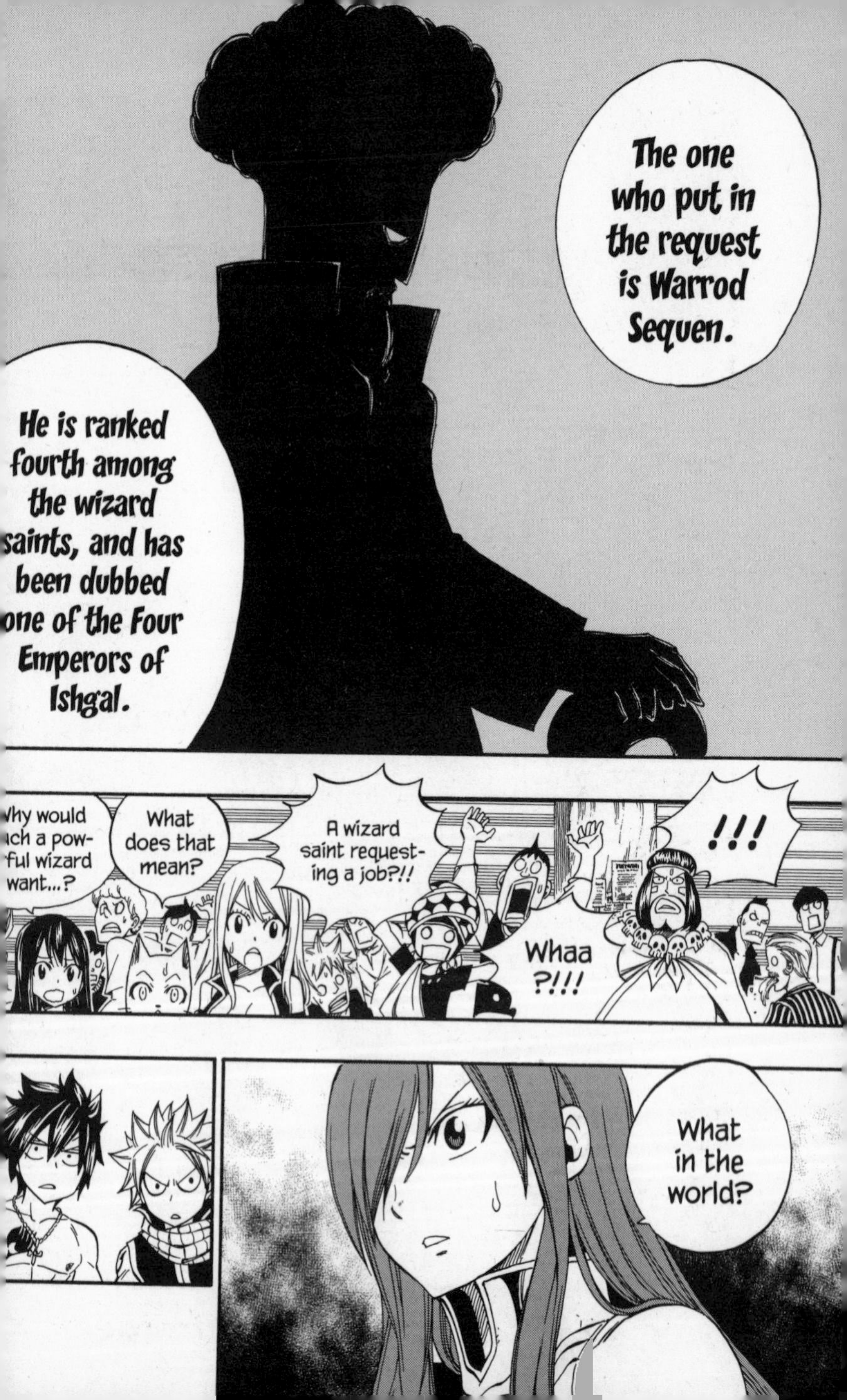
The one who put in the request is Warrod Sequen.
He is ranked fourth among the wizard saints, and has been dubbed one of the Four Emperors of Ishgal.
!!!
Whaa ?!!!
A wizard saint request-ing a job?!!
What does that mean?
hy would ch a pow- ful wizard want...?
What in the world?

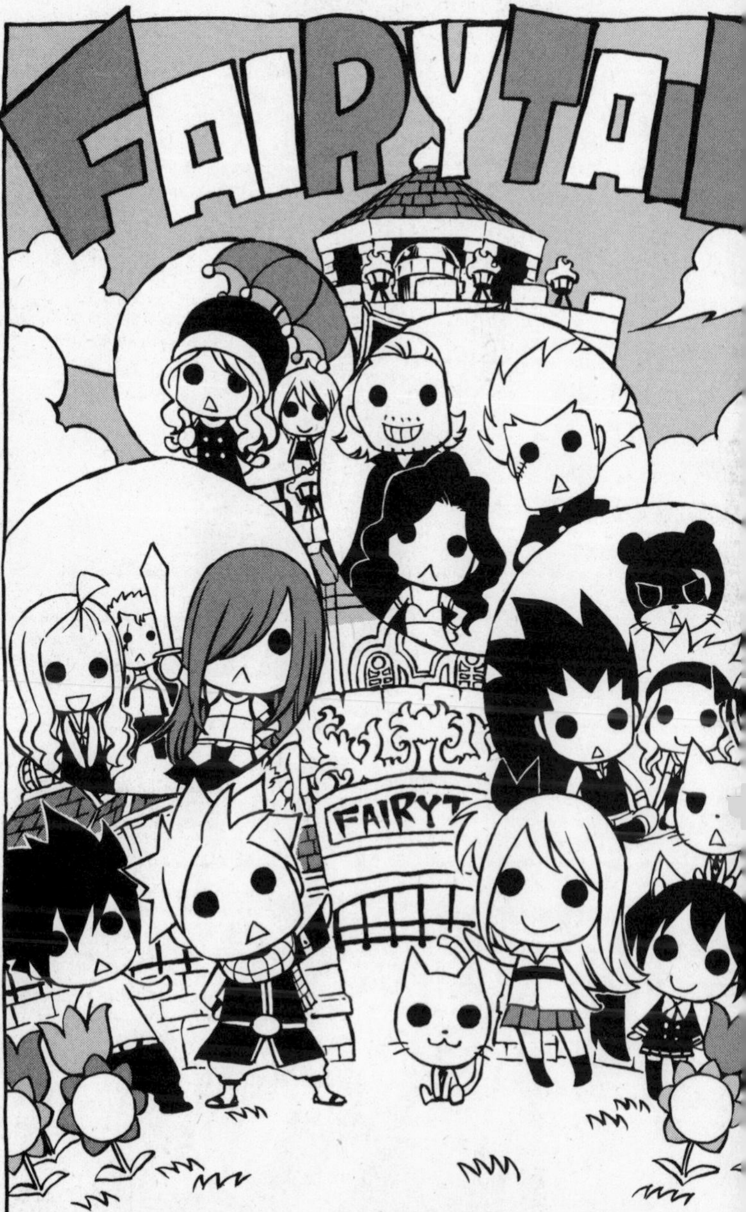
FAIRY TAIL
FAIRYT

Chapter 342: Warrod Sequen

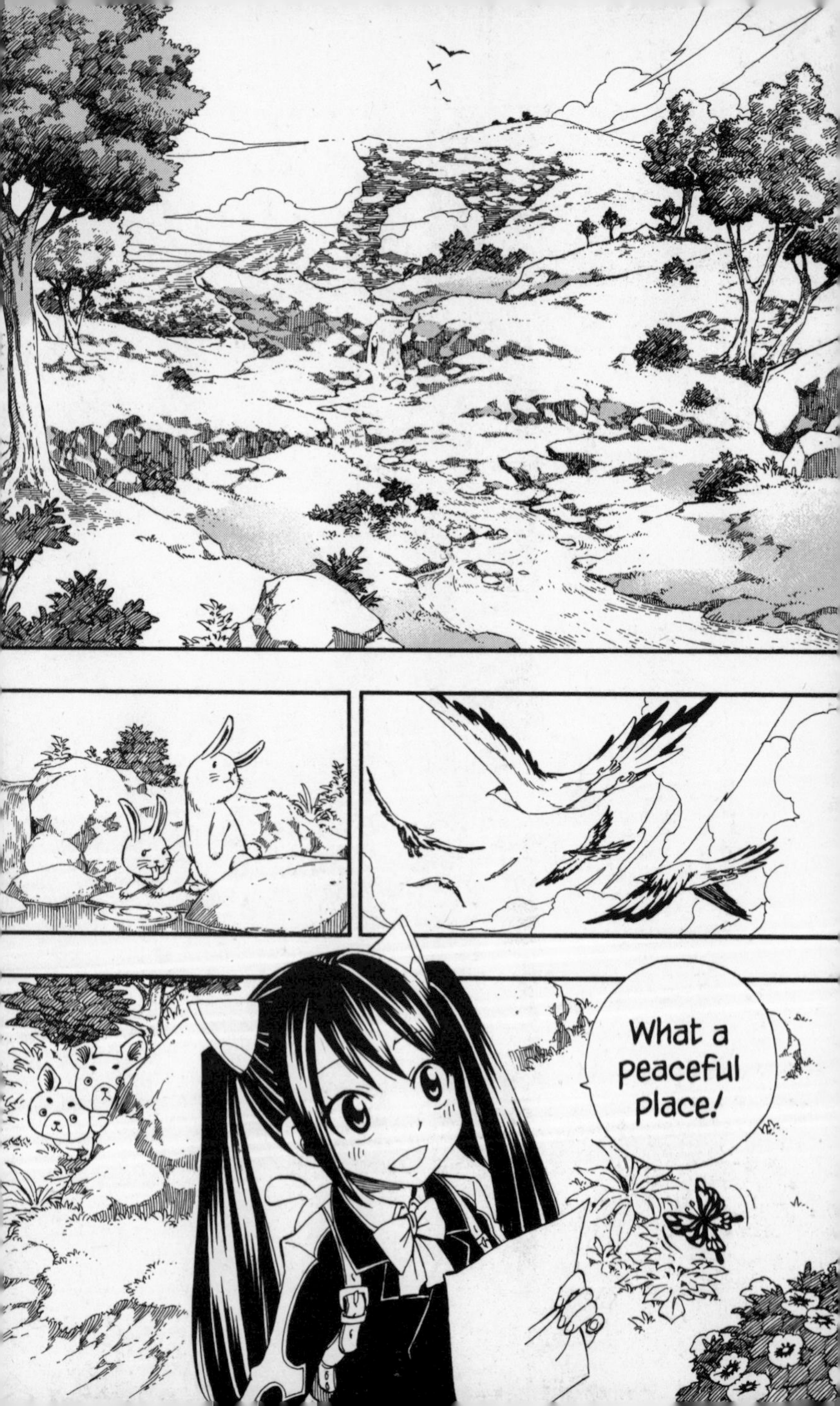
What a peaceful place!

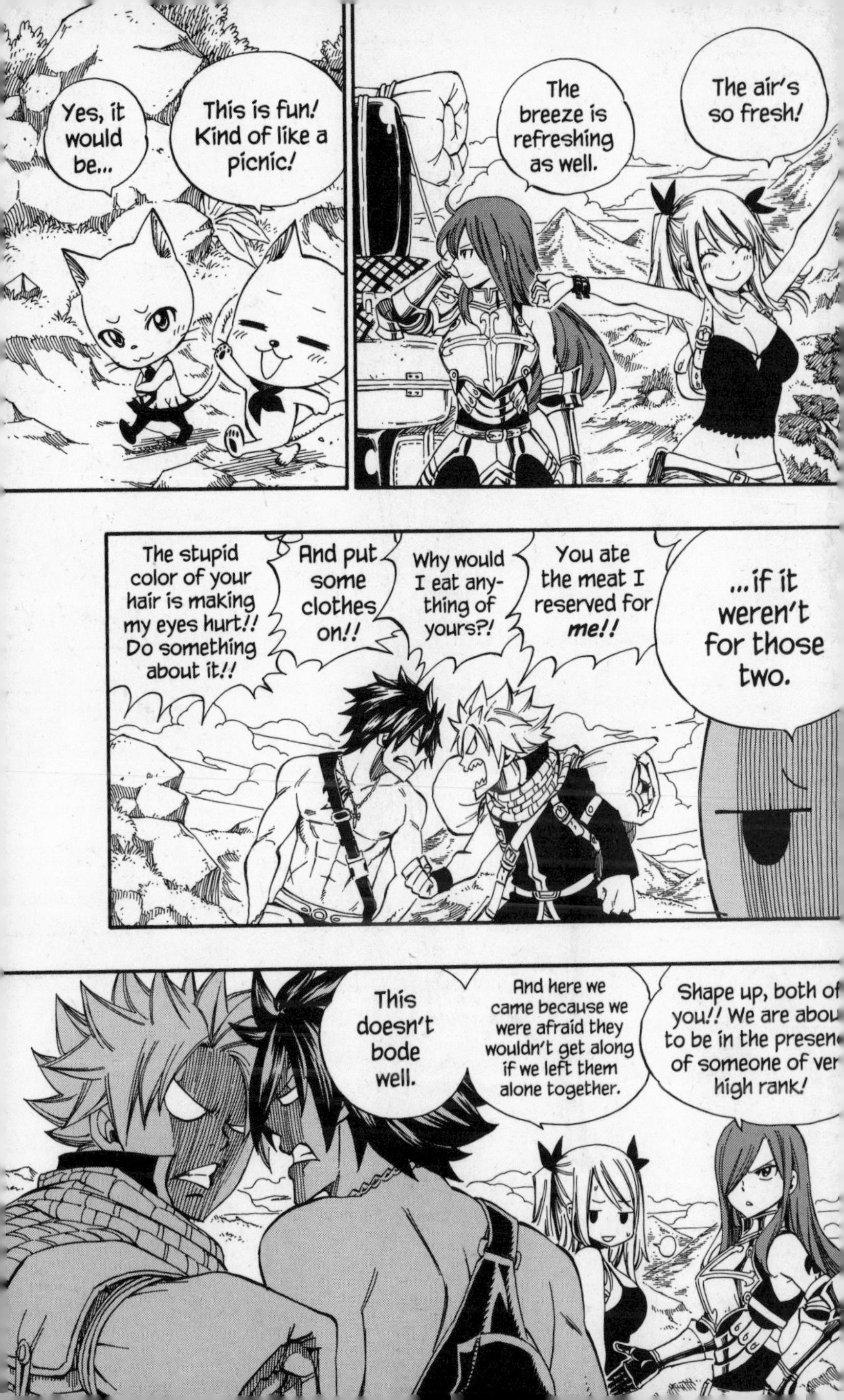
The air's so fresh!
The breeze is refreshing as well.
This is fun! Kind of like a picnic!
Yes, it would be...
...if it weren't for those two.
You ate the meat I reserved for *me!!*
Why would I eat any-thing of yours?!
And put some clothes on!!
The stupid color of your hair is making my eyes hurt!! Do something about it!!
Shape up, both of you!! We are abou to be in the presen of someone of ver high rank!
And here we came because we were afraid they wouldn't get along if we left them alone together.
This doesn't bode well.

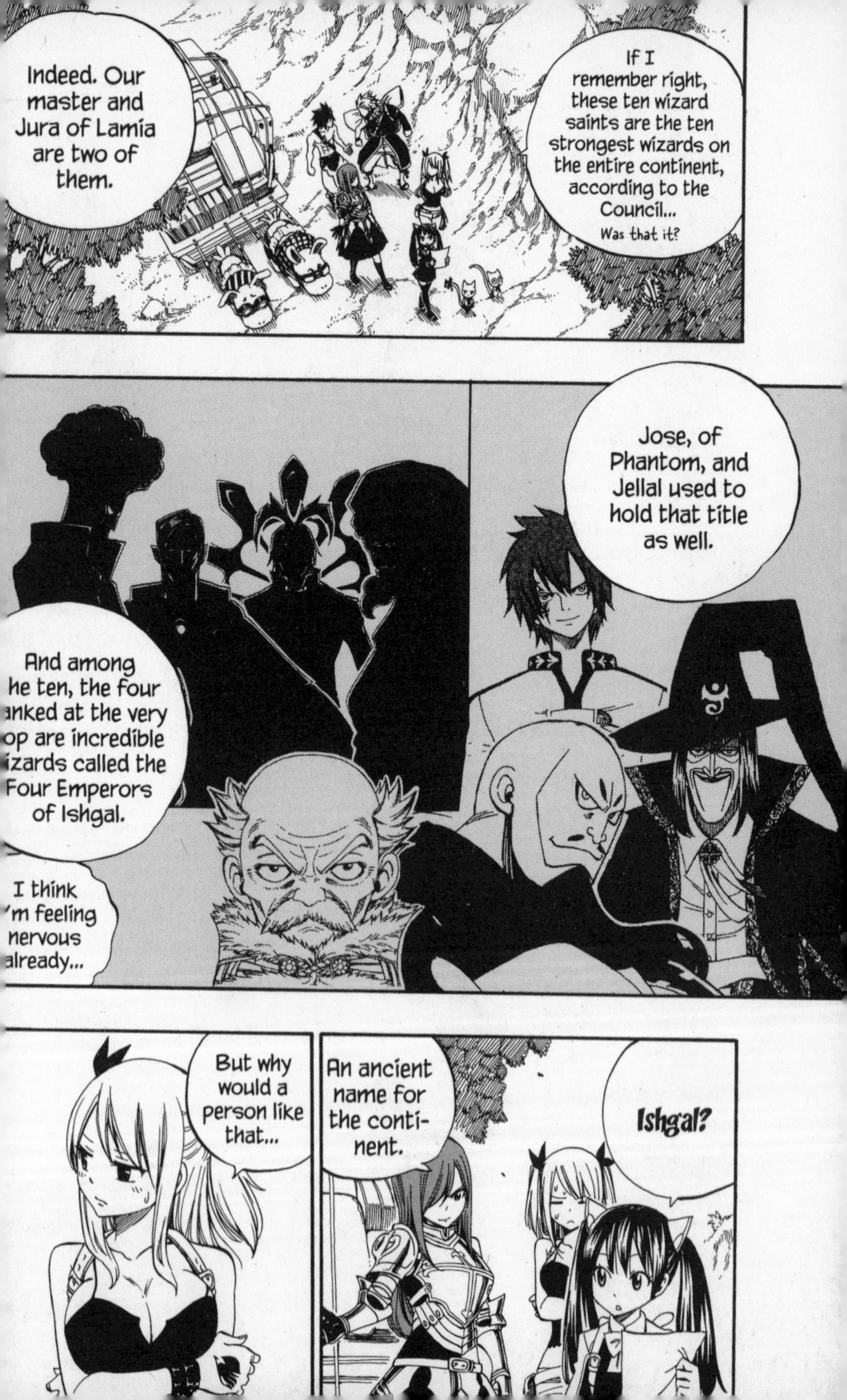
If I remember right, these ten wizard saints are the ten strongest wizards on the entire continent, according to the Council...
Was that it?
Indeed. Our master and Jura of Lamia are two of them.
Jose, of Phantom, and Jellal used to hold that title as well.
And among he ten, the four anked at the very op are incredible izards called the Four Emperors of Ishgal.
I think 'm feeling nervous already...
Ishgal?
An ancient name for the conti- nent.
But why would a person like that...

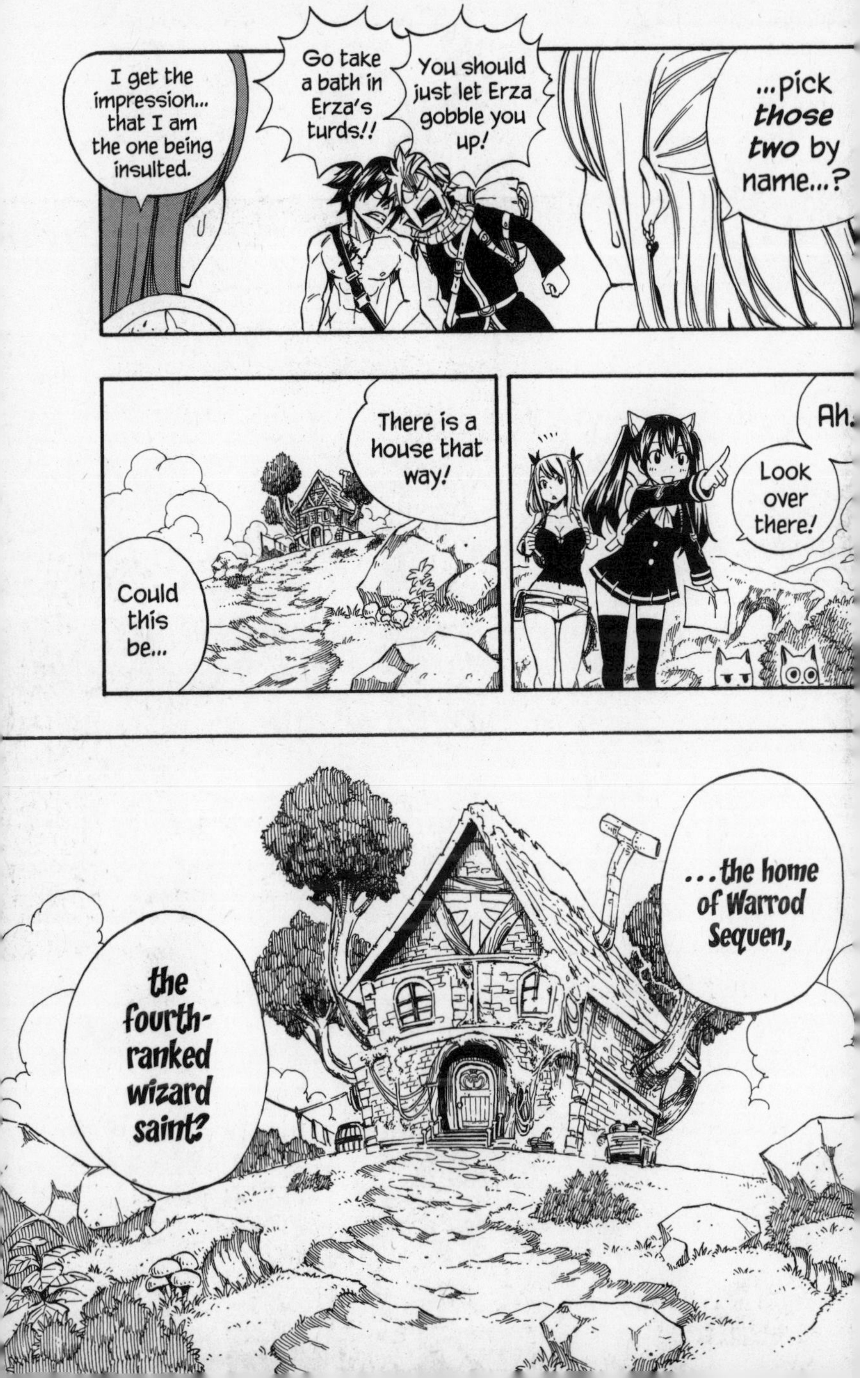
...pick those two by name...?
You should just let Erza gobble you up!
Go take a bath in Erza's turds!!
I get the impression... that I am the one being insulted.
Ah.
Look over there!
There is a house that way!
Could this be...
...the home of Warrod Sequen,
the fourth-ranked wizard saint?

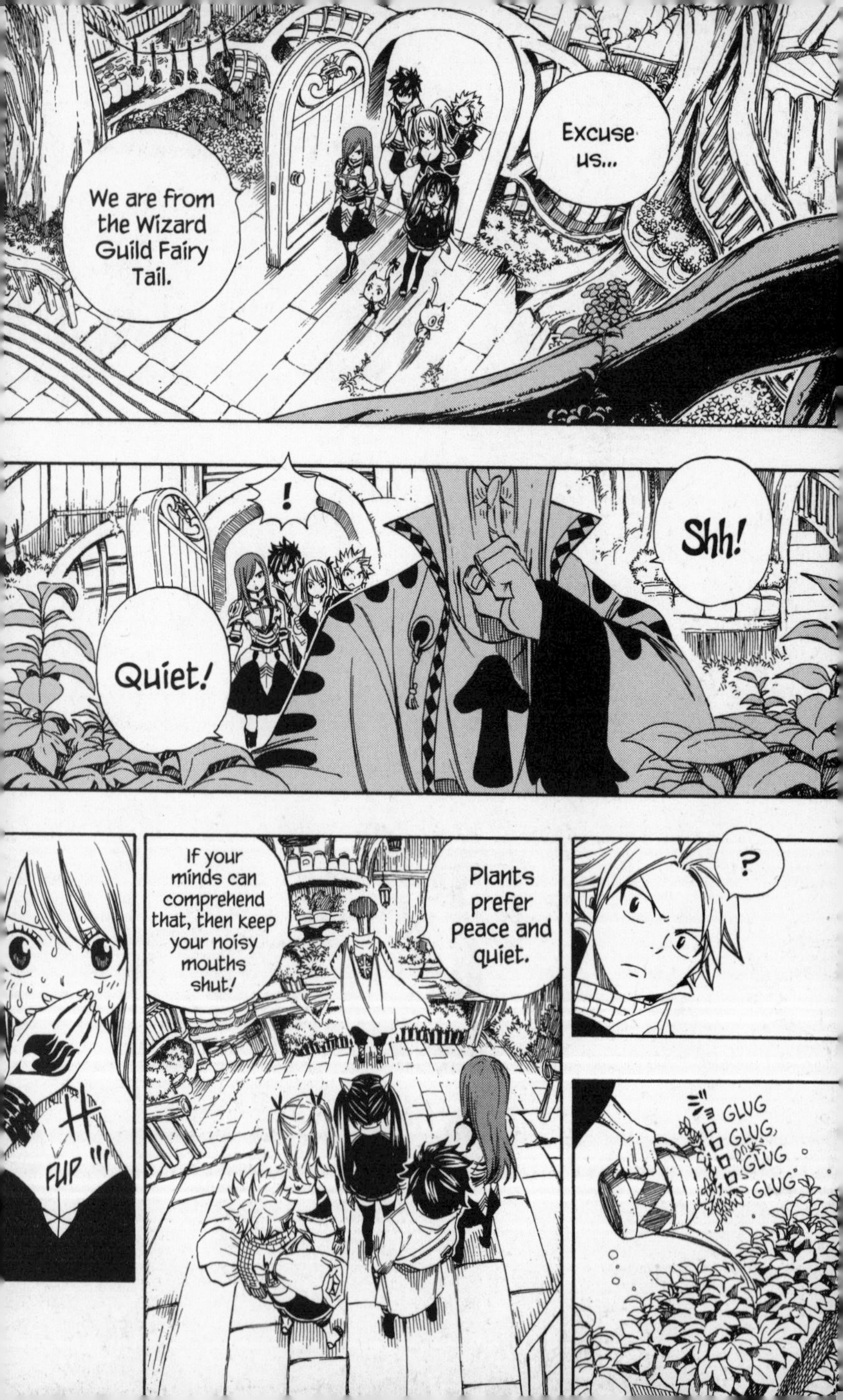

Excuse us...
We are from the Wizard Guild Fairy Tail.
Shh!
!
Quiet!
?
GLUG GLUG GLUG GLUG
Plants prefer peace and quiet.
If your minds can comprehend that, then keep your noisy mouths shut!
FUP

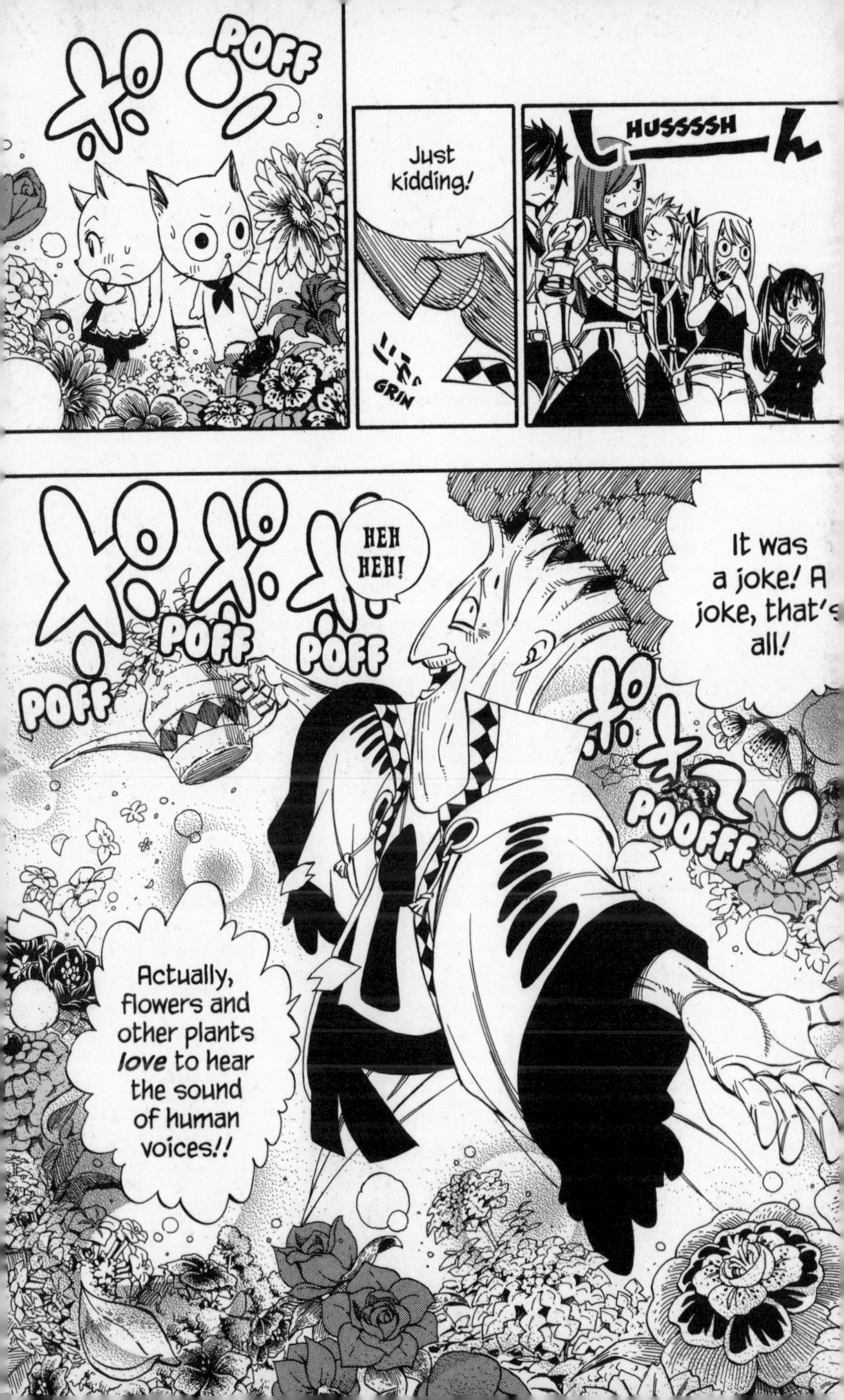

HUSSSSH
Just kidding!
GRIN
POFF
It was a joke! A joke, that's all!
POOFFF
HEH HEH!
POFF
POFF
POFF
Actually, flowers and other plants *love* to hear the sound of human voices!!

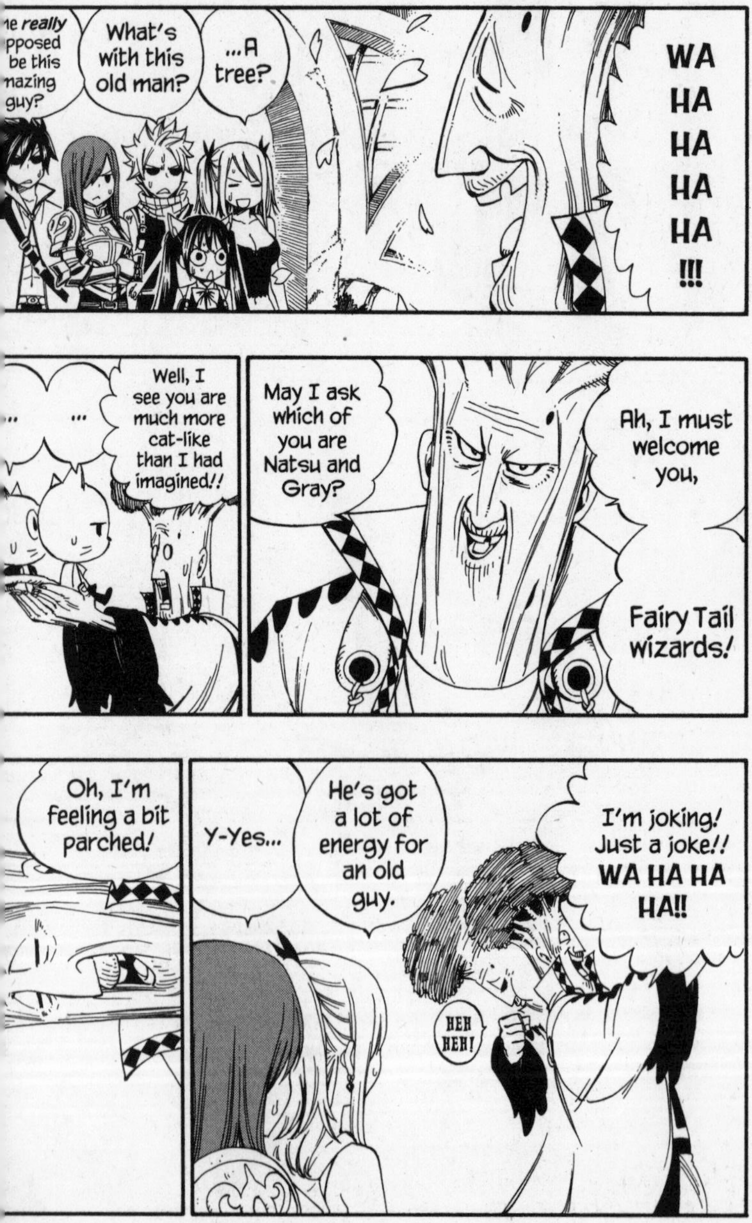
WA HA HA HA HA!!!
...A tree?
What's with this old man?
e really pposed be this mazing guy?
Ah, I must welcome you,
Fairy Tail wizards!
May I ask which of you are Natsu and Gray?
Well, I see you are much more cat-like than I had imagined!!
...
...
I'm joking! Just a joke!! WA HA HA HA!!
HEH HEH!
He's got a lot of energy for an old guy.
Y-Yes...
Oh, I'm feeling a bit parched!

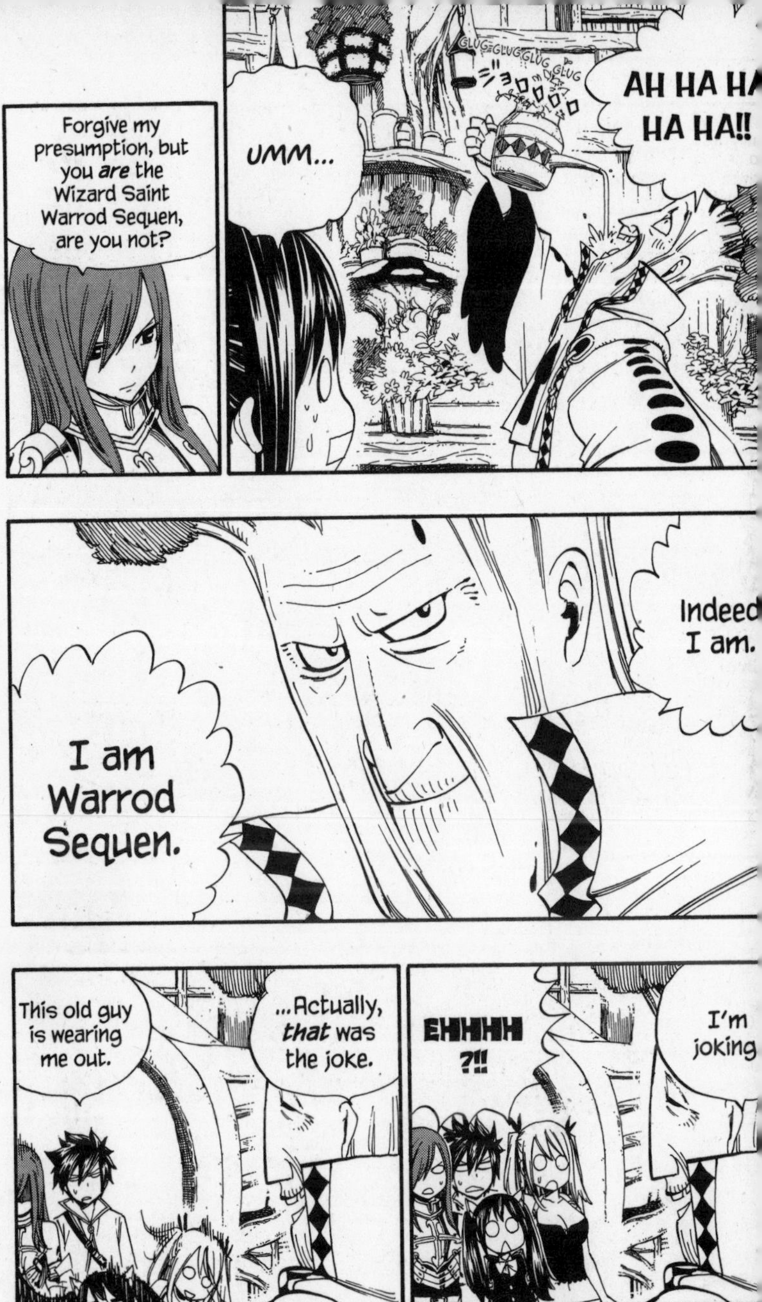
GLUG GLUG GLUG GLUG
AH HA HA HA HA!!
UMM...
Forgive my presumption, but you *are* the Wizard Saint Warrod Sequen, are you not?
Indeed I am.
I am Warrod Sequen.
I'm joking
EHHHH ?!!
...Actually, *that* was the joke.
This old guy is wearing me out.

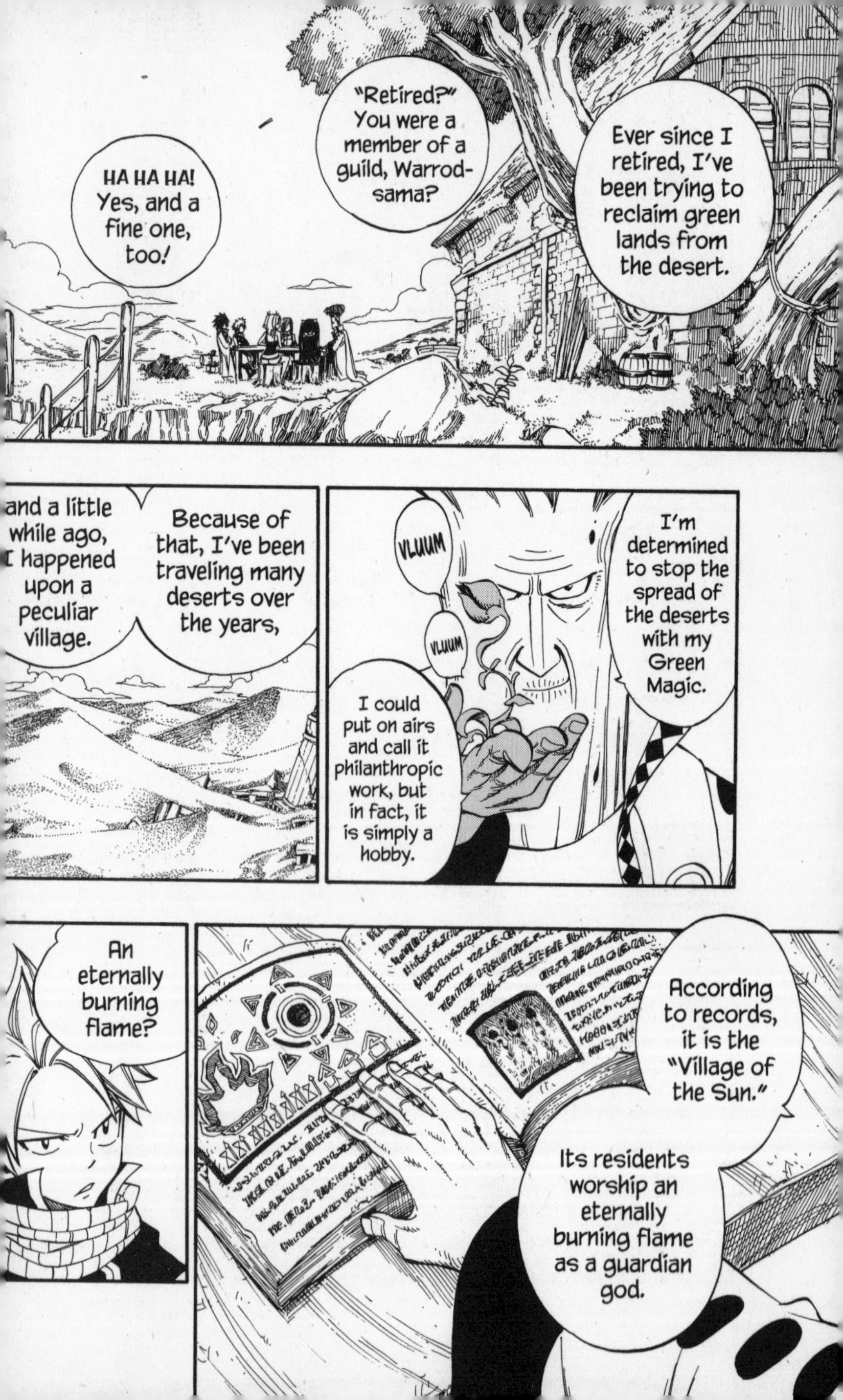
Ever since I retired, I've been trying to reclaim green lands from the desert.
"Retired?" You were a member of a guild, Warrod-sama?
HA HA HA! Yes, and a fine one, too!
I'm determined to stop the spread of the deserts with my Green Magic.
VLUUM
VLUUM
I could put on airs and call it philanthropic work, but in fact, it is simply a hobby.
Because of that, I've been traveling many deserts over the years,
and a little while ago, I happened upon a peculiar village.
According to records, it is the "Village of the Sun."
Its residents worship an eternally burning flame as a guardian god.
An eternally burning flame?

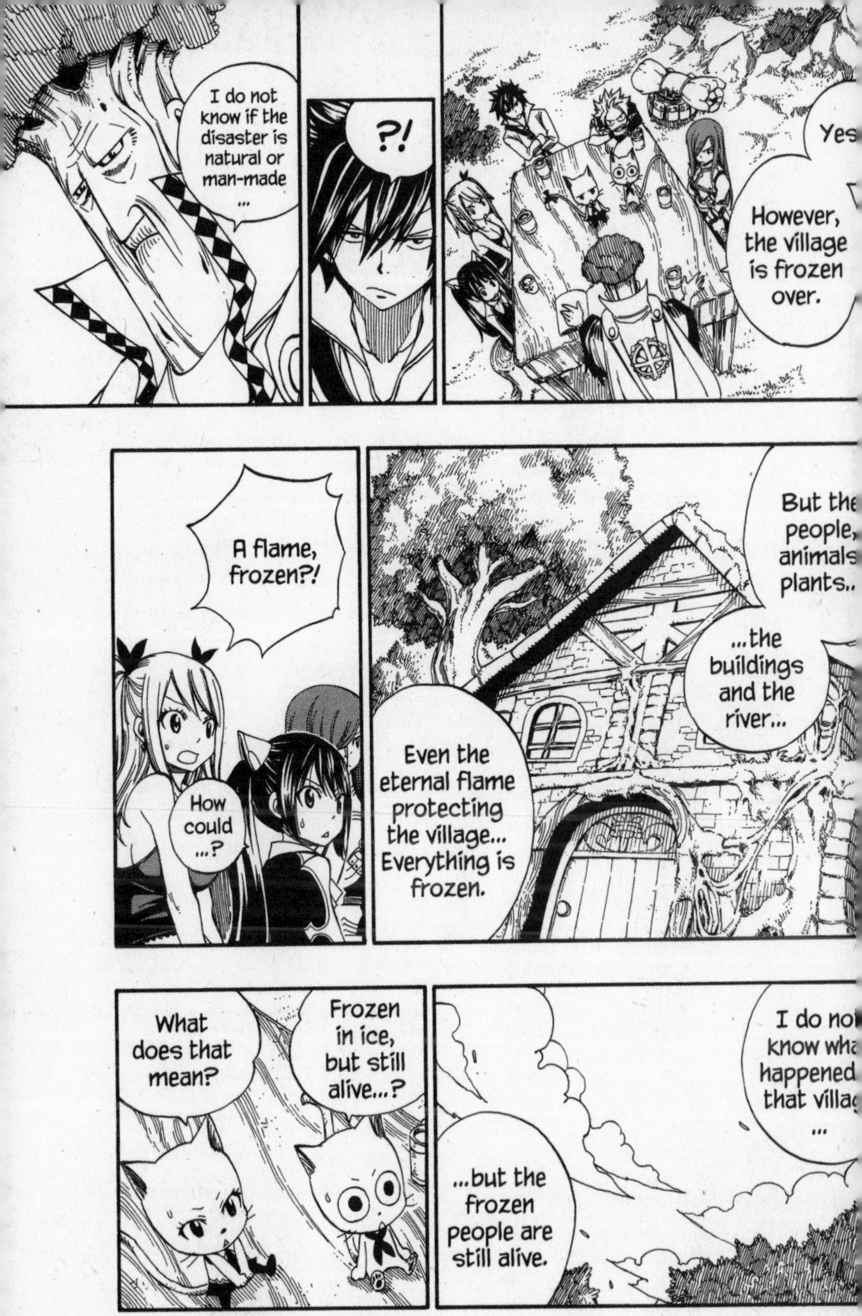
Yes
However, the village is frozen over.
?!
I do not know if the disaster is natural or man-made ...
But the people, animals plants..
...the buildings and the river...
Even the eternal flame protecting the village... Everything is frozen.
A flame, frozen?!
How could ...?
I do no know wha happened that villag ...
...but the frozen people are still alive.
Frozen in ice, but still alive...?
What does that mean?

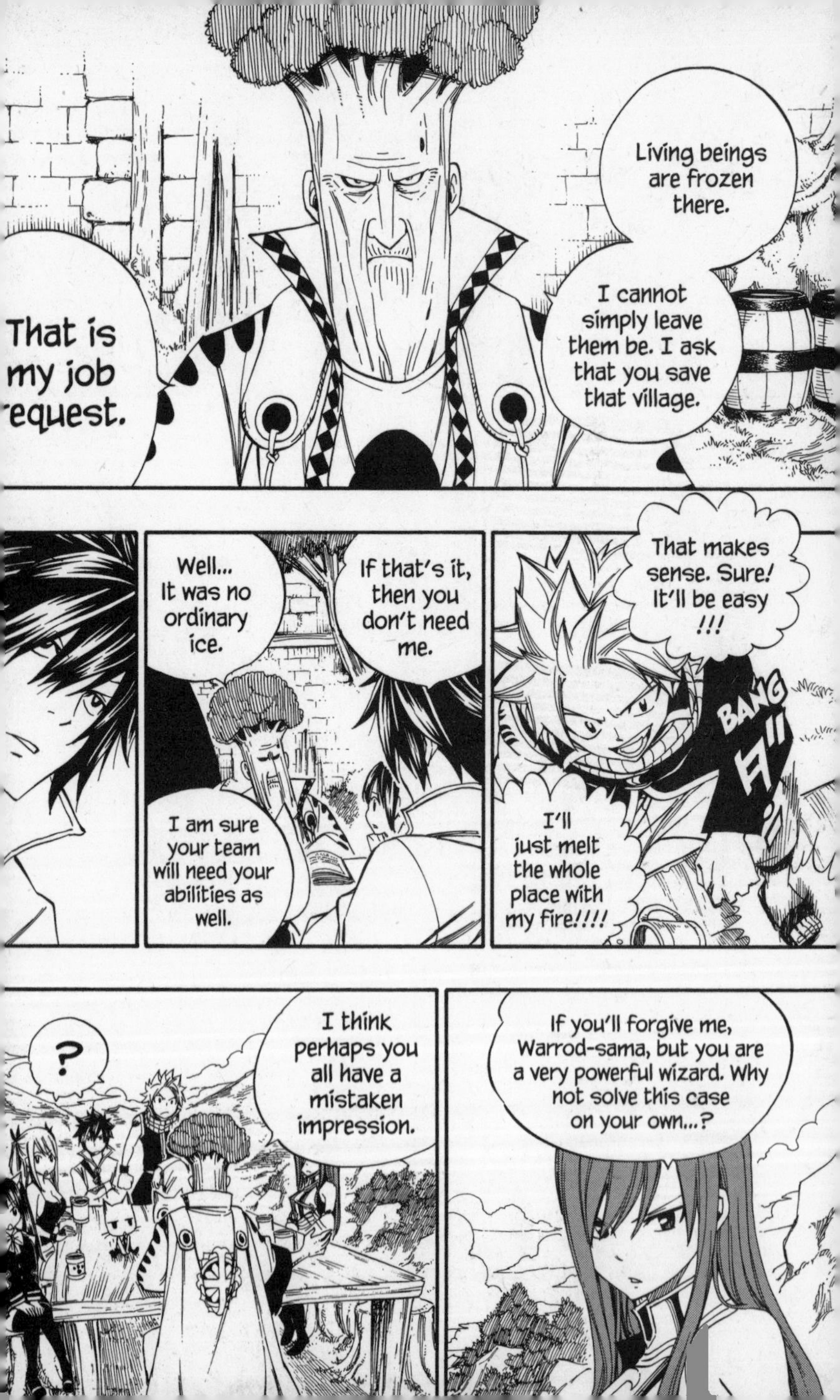
Living beings are frozen there.
I cannot simply leave them be. I ask that you save that village.
That is my job request.
That makes sense. Sure! It'll be easy!!!
BANG
I'll just melt the whole place with my fire!!!!
If that's it, then you don't need me.
Well... It was no ordinary ice.
I am sure your team will need your abilities as well.
If you'll forgive me, Warrod-sama, but you are a very powerful wizard. Why not solve this case on your own...?
I think perhaps you all have a mistaken impression.
?

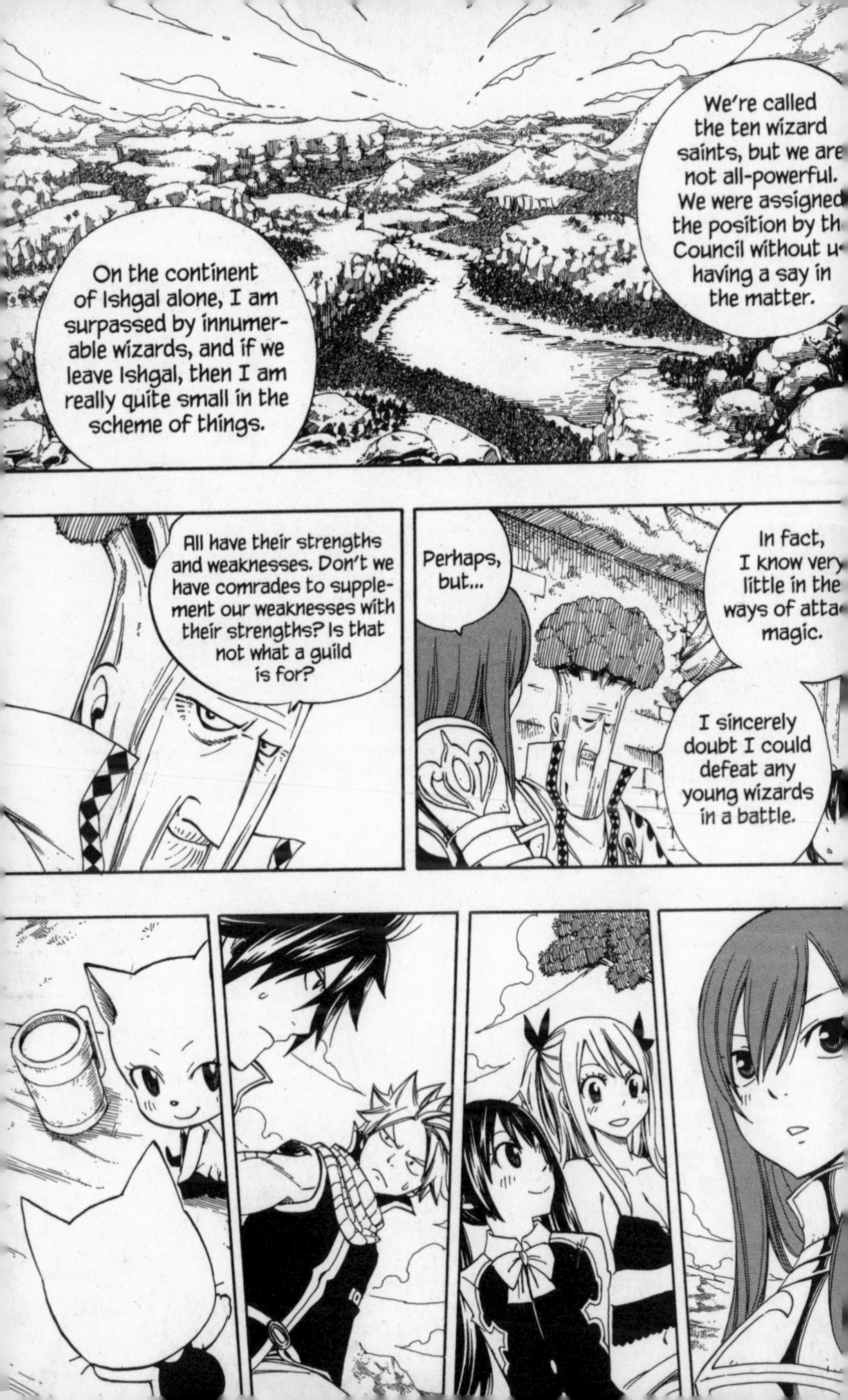
On the continent of Ishgal alone, I am surpassed by innumerable wizards, and if we leave Ishgal, then I am really quite small in the scheme of things.
We're called the ten wizard saints, but we are not all-powerful. We were assigned the position by th Council without u having a say in the matter.
All have their strengths and weaknesses. Don't we have comrades to supplement our weaknesses with their strengths? Is that not what a guild is for?
Perhaps, but...
In fact, I know very little in the ways of atta magic.
I sincerely doubt I could defeat any young wizards in a battle.

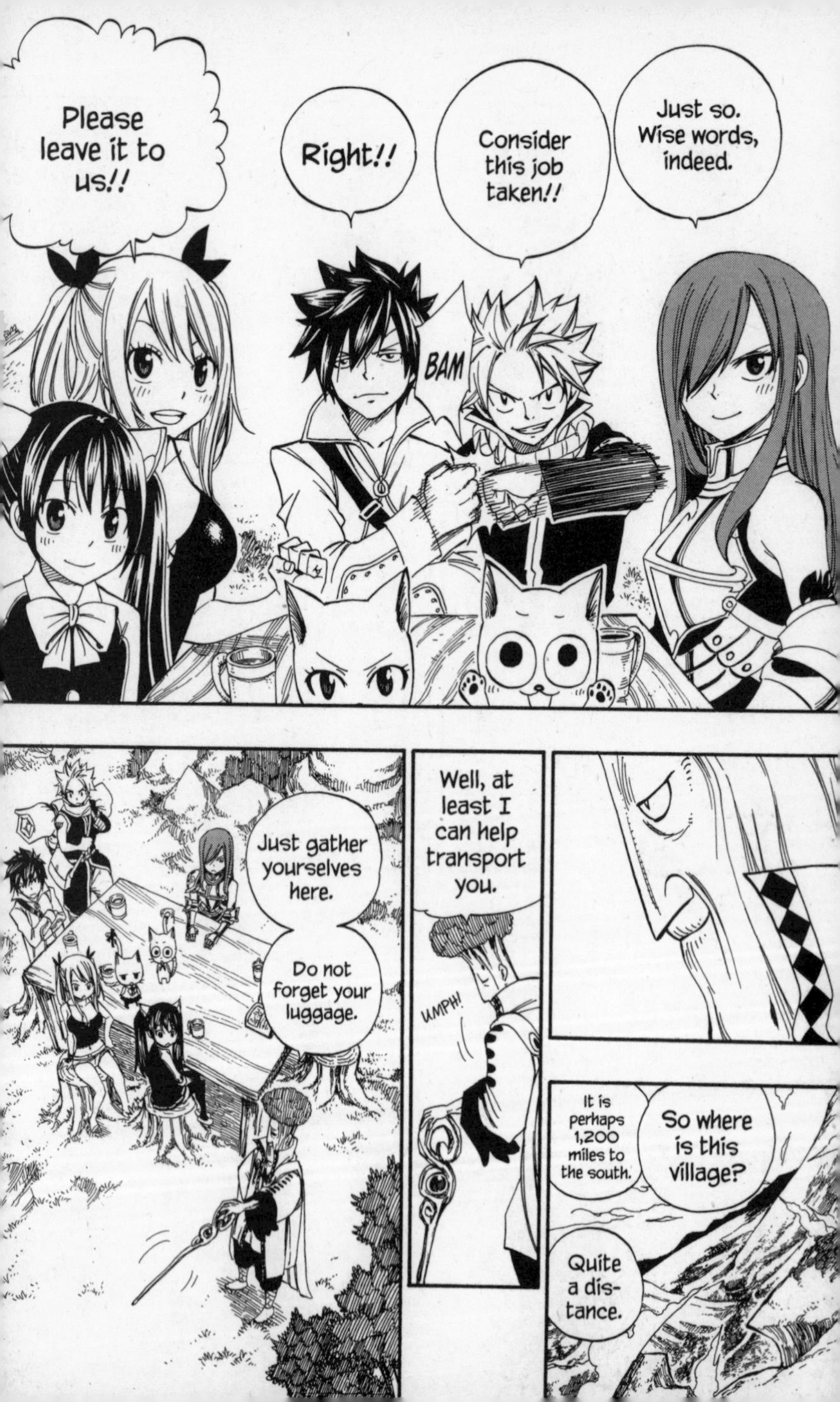
Just so. Wise words, indeed.
Consider this job taken!!
BAM
Right!!
Please leave it to us!!
So where is this village?
It is perhaps 1,200 miles to the south.
Quite a distance.
Well, at least I can help transport you.
UMPH!
Just gather yourselves here.
Do not forget your luggage.

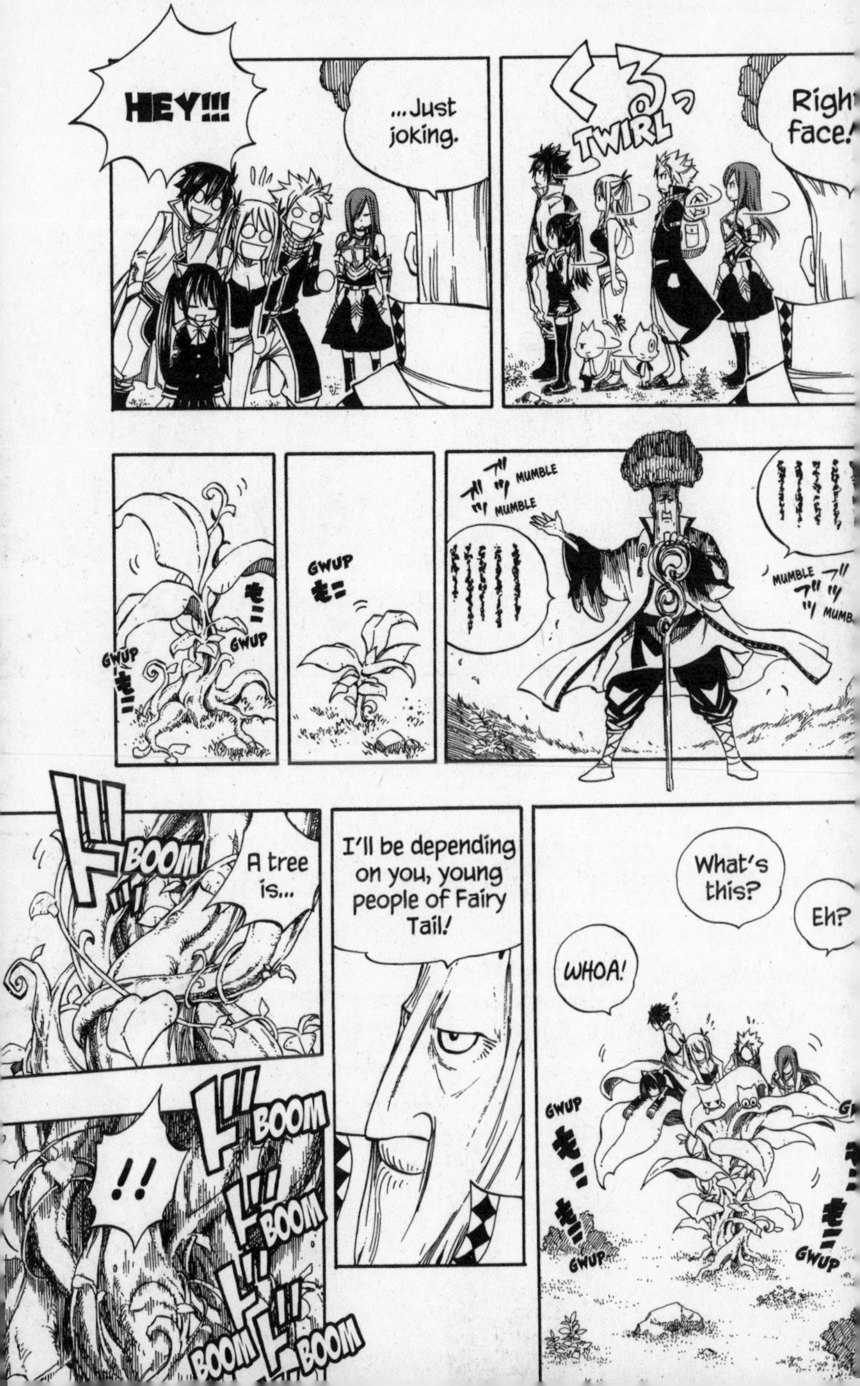

Right face!
TWIRL
...Just joking.
HEY!!!
MUMBLE
MUMBLE
MUMBLE
GWUP
GWUP
GWUP
Eh?
What's this?
WHOA!
GWUP
GWUP
I'll be depending on you, young people of Fairy Tail!
A tree is...
BOOM
!!
BOOM
BOOM
BOOM
BOOM

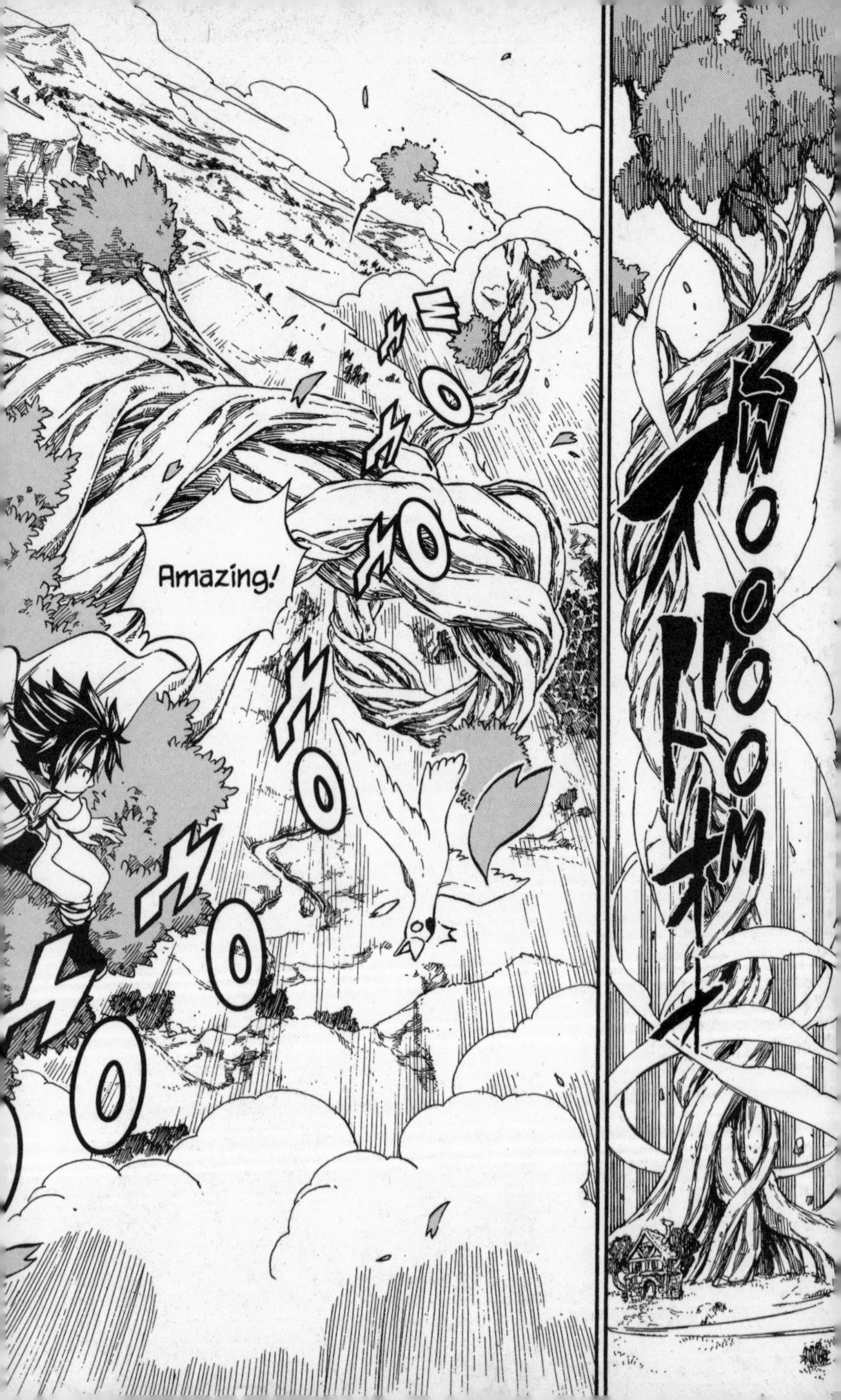
ZWOOOOM
Amazing!

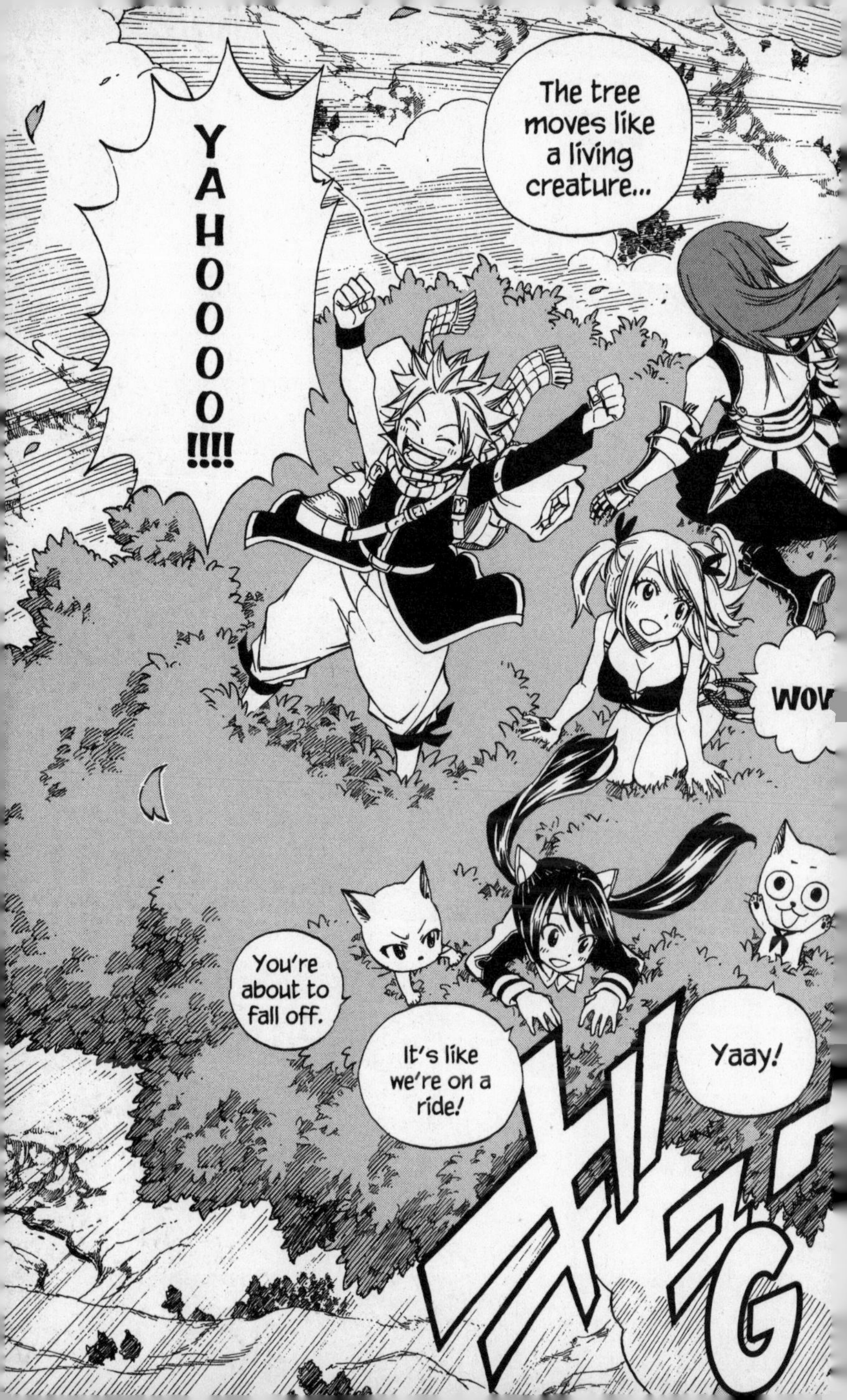
The tree moves like a living creature...
YAHOOOOO!!!!
Yaay!
It's like we're on a ride!
You're about to fall off.

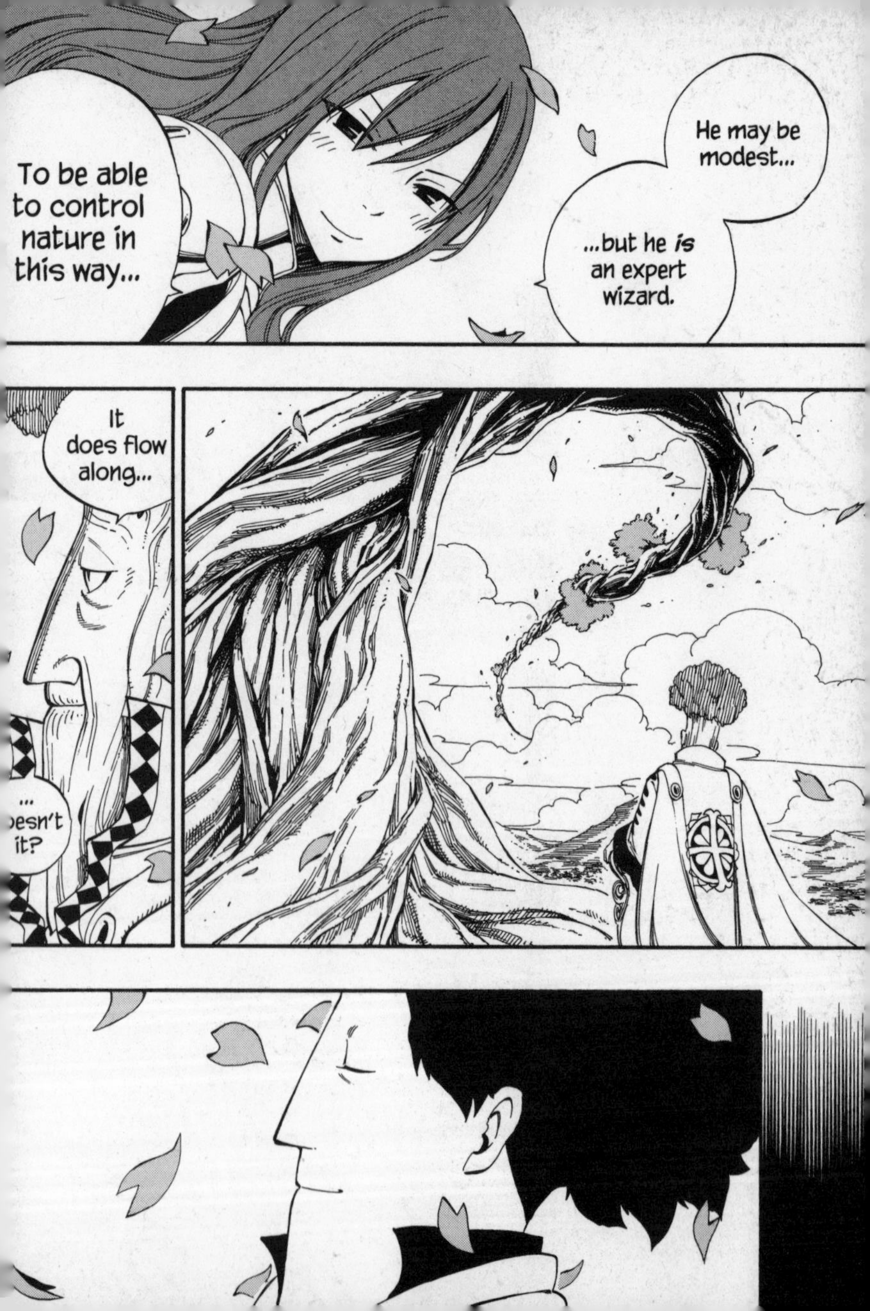
He may be modest...
...but he *is* an expert wizard.
To be able to control nature in this way...
It does flow along...
... oesn't it?

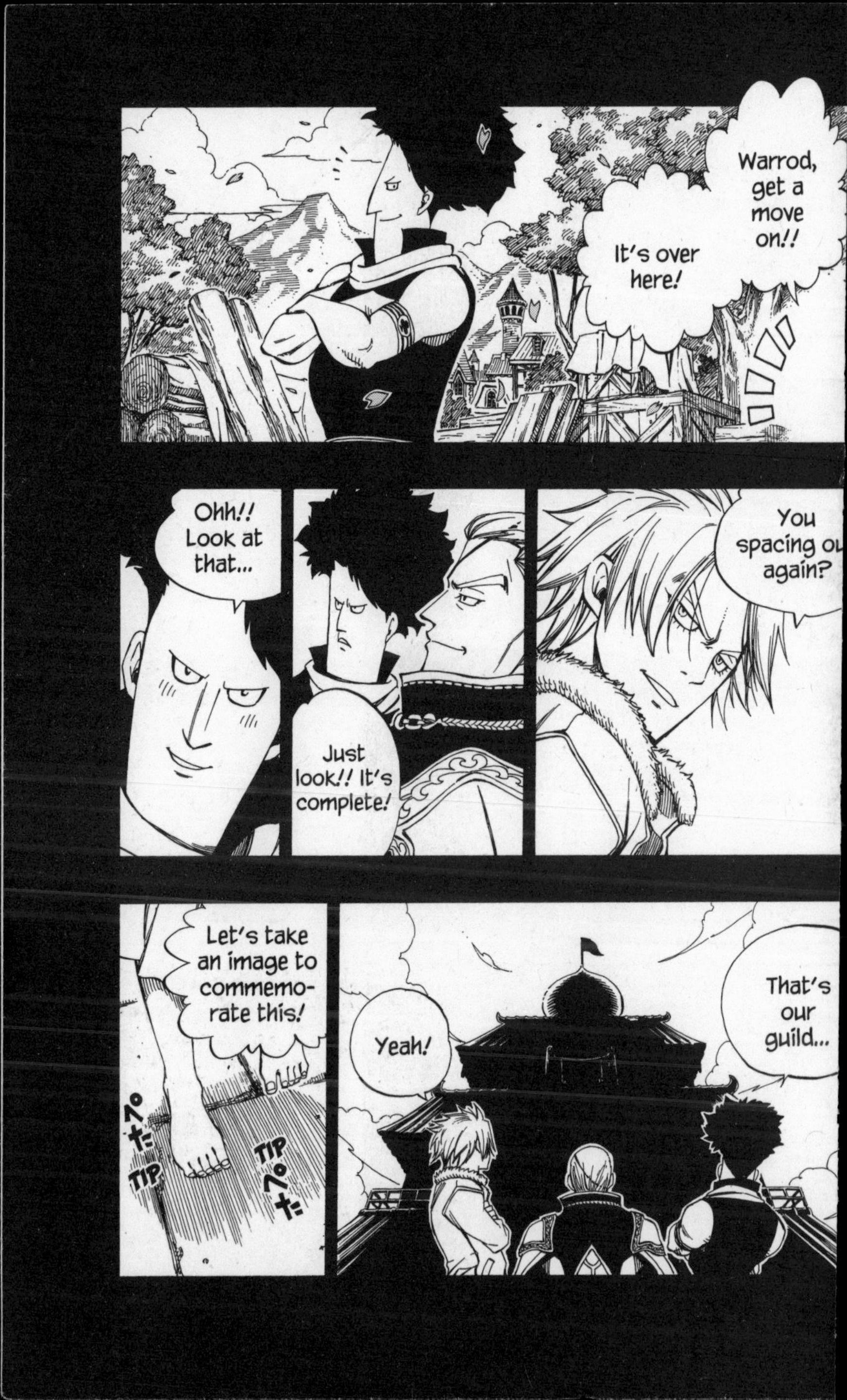
Warrod, get a move on!!
It's over here!
You spacing ou again?
Just look!! It's complete!
Ohh!! Look at that...
That's our guild...
Yeah!
Let's take an image to commemorate this!
TIP
TIP

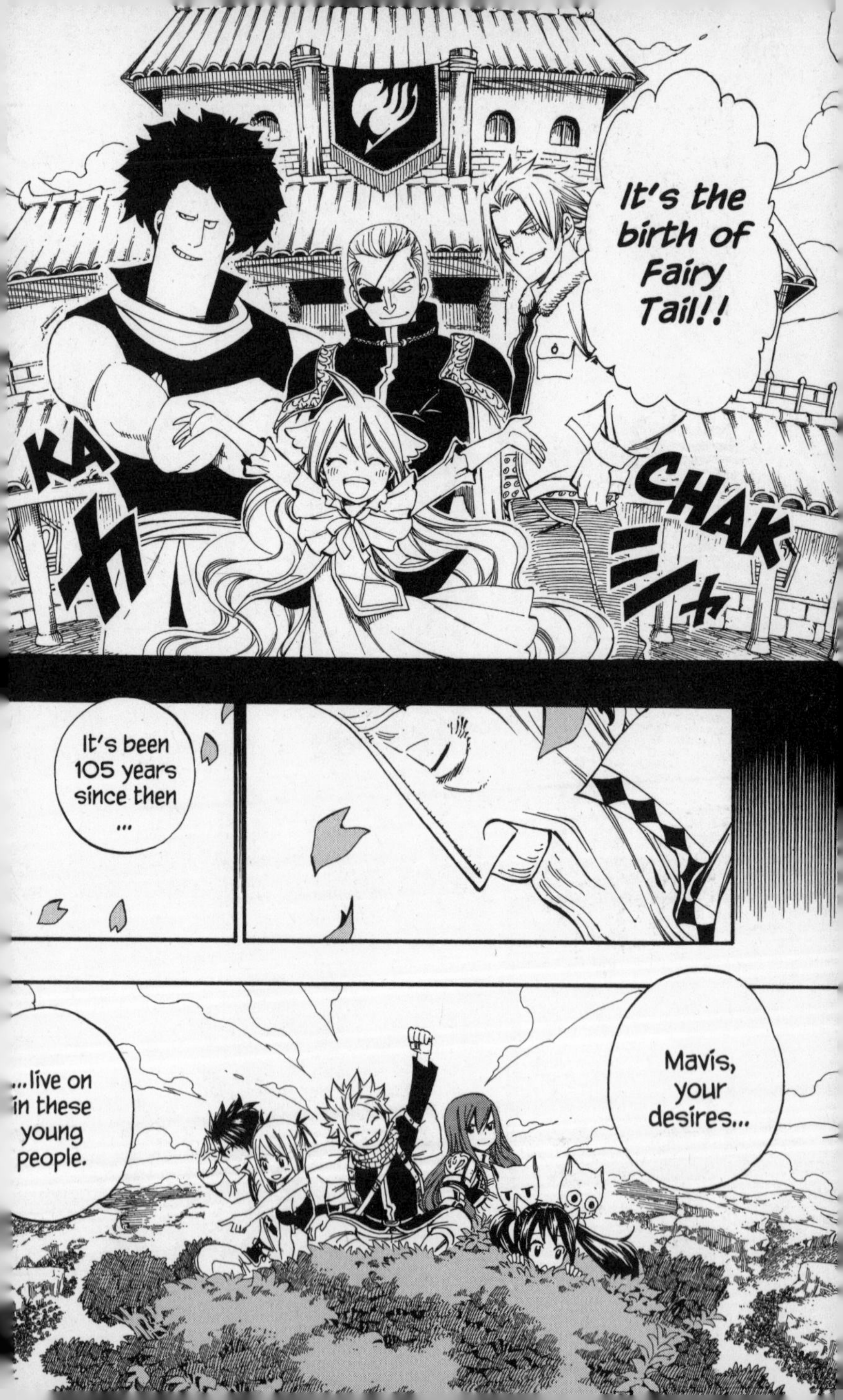
It's the birth of Fairy Tail!!
KA
CHAK
It's been 105 years since then ...
Mavis, your desires...
...live on in these young people.

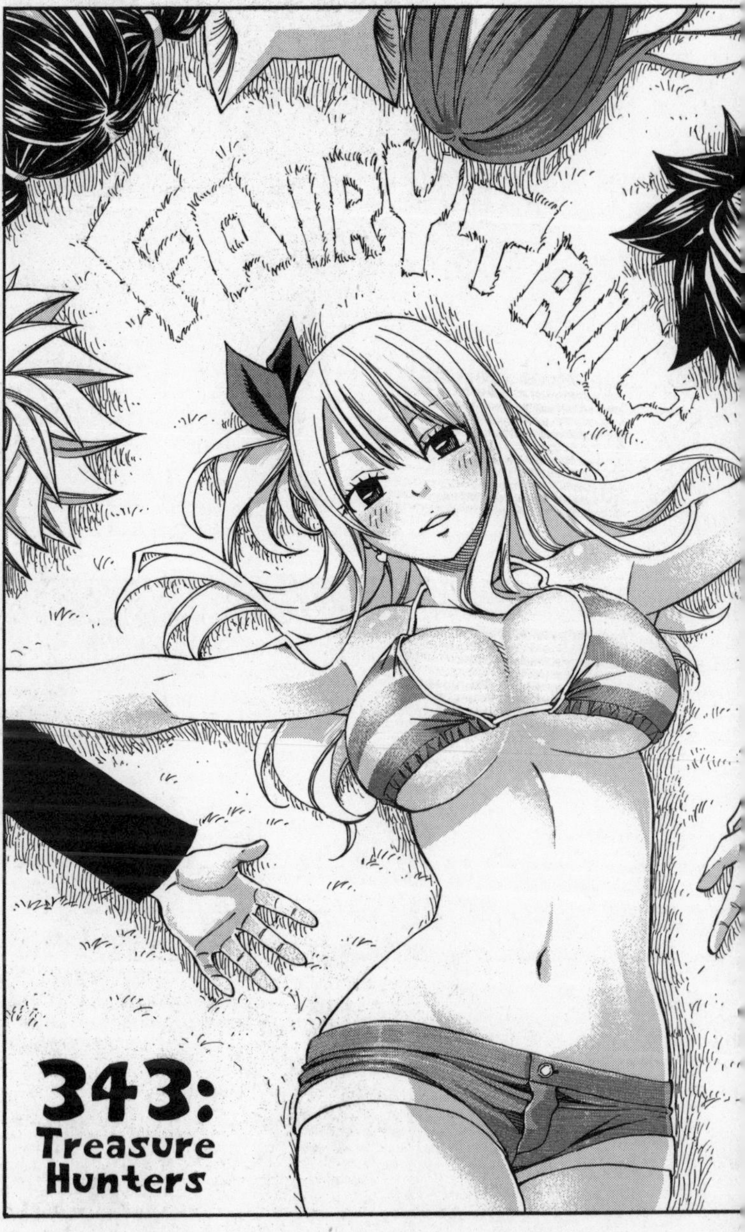
FAIRY TAIL
343: Treasure Hunters

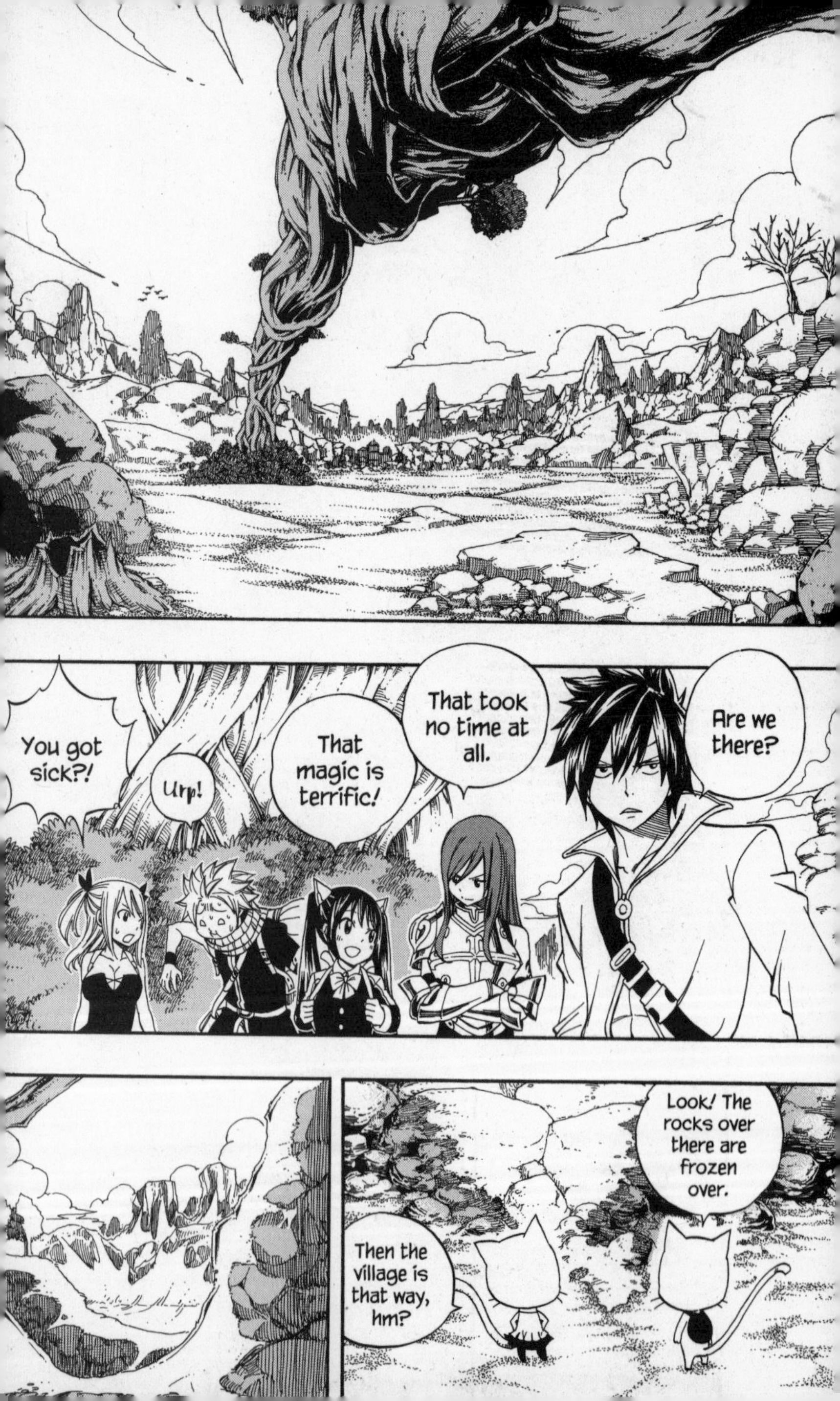
Are we there?
That took no time at all.
That magic is terrific!
Urp!
You got sick?!
Look! The rocks over there are frozen over.
Then the village is that way, hm?

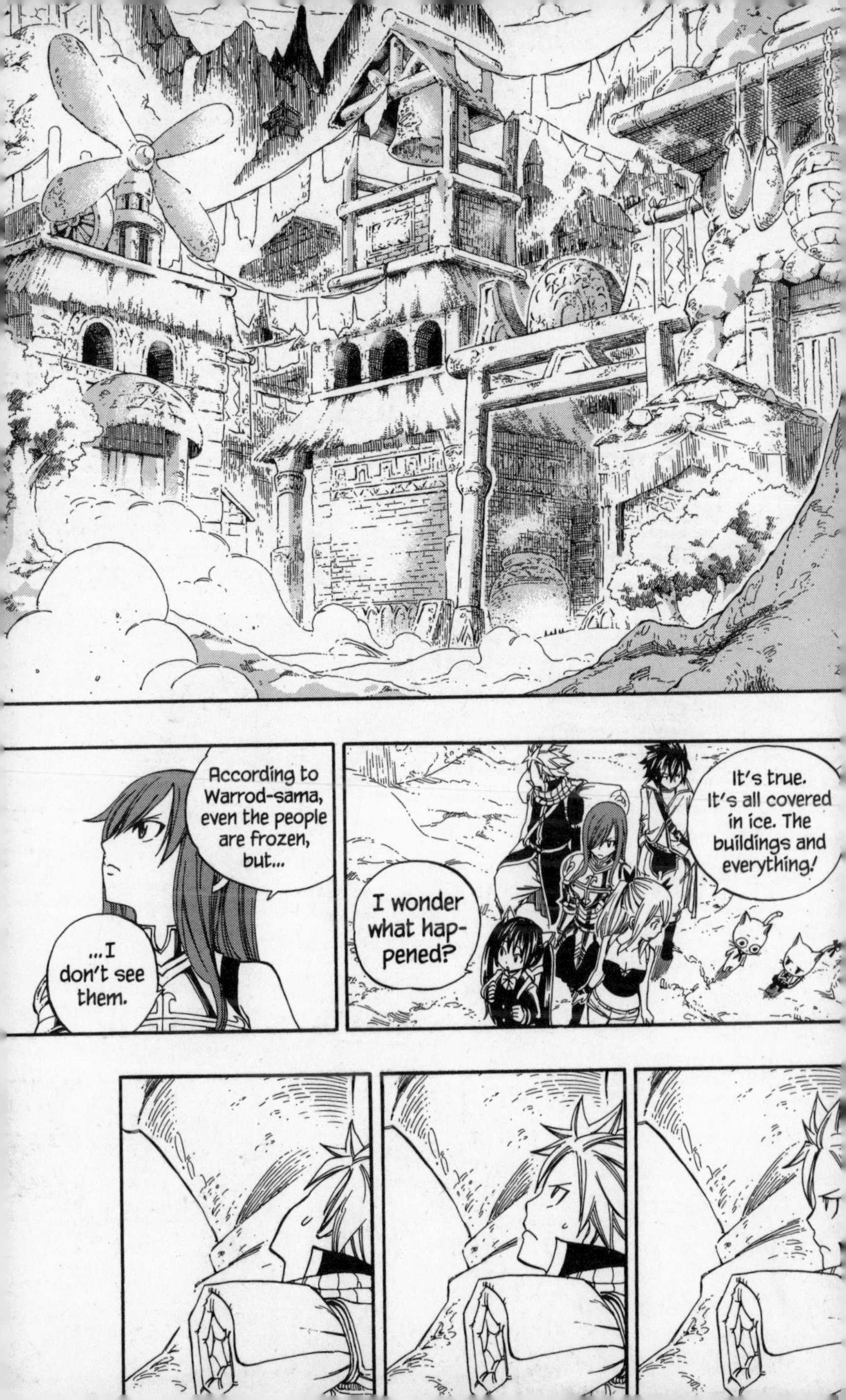
It's true. It's all covered in ice. The buildings and everything!
I wonder what hap-pened?
According to Warrod-sama, even the people are frozen, but...
...I don't see them.

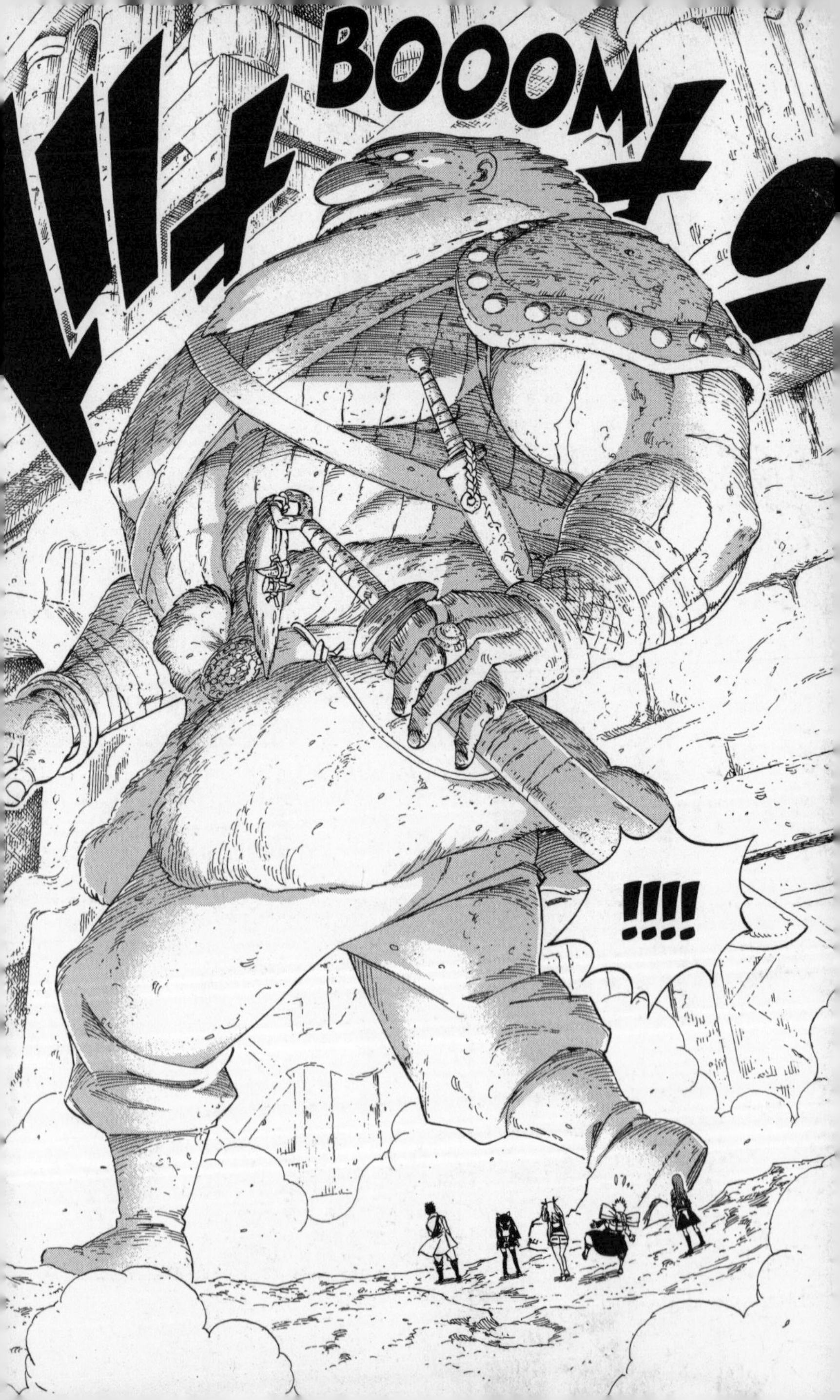
BOOOM
!!!!

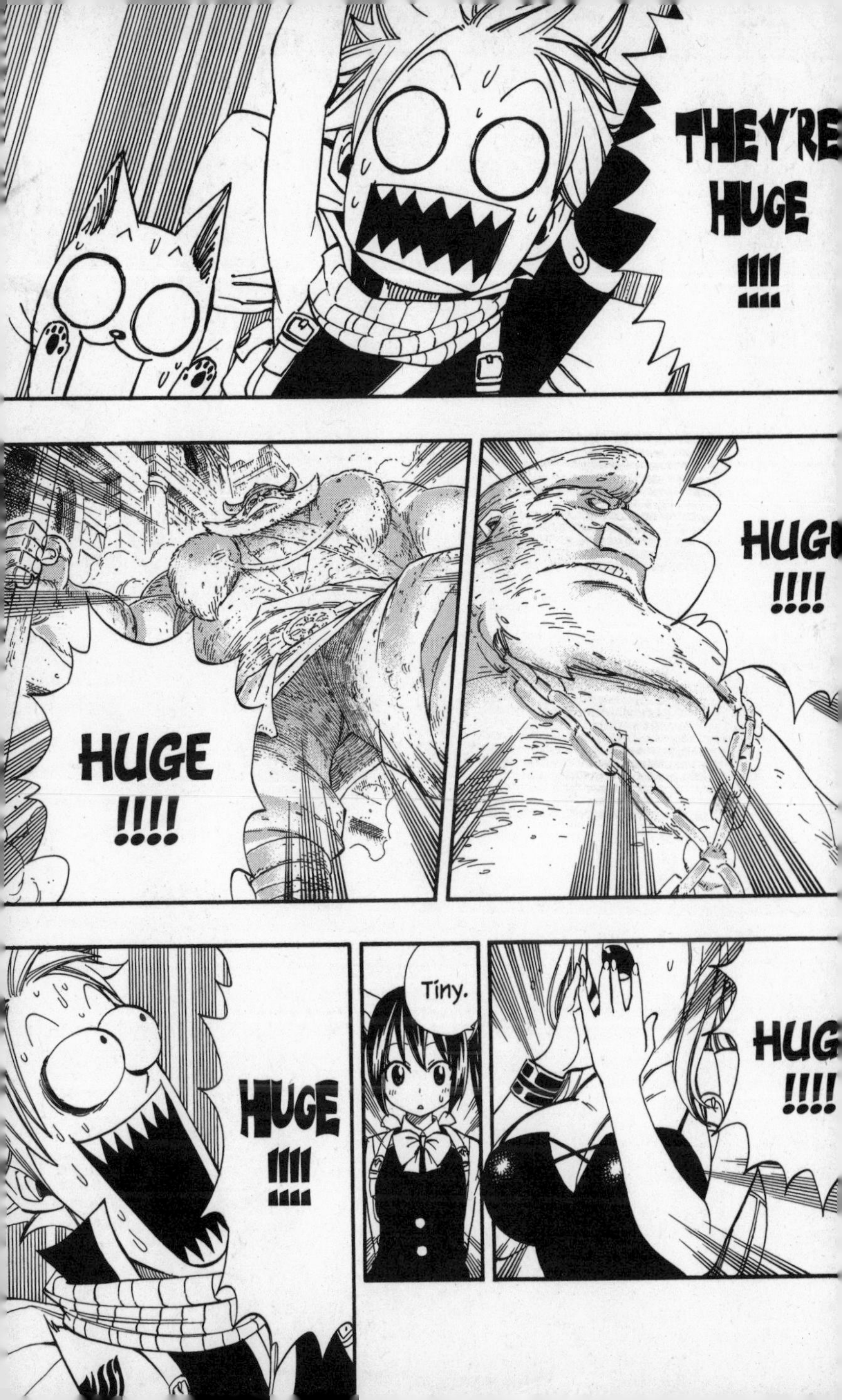
THEY'RE HUGE !!!!
HUG !!!!
HUGE !!!!
HUG !!!!
Tiny.
HUGE !!!!

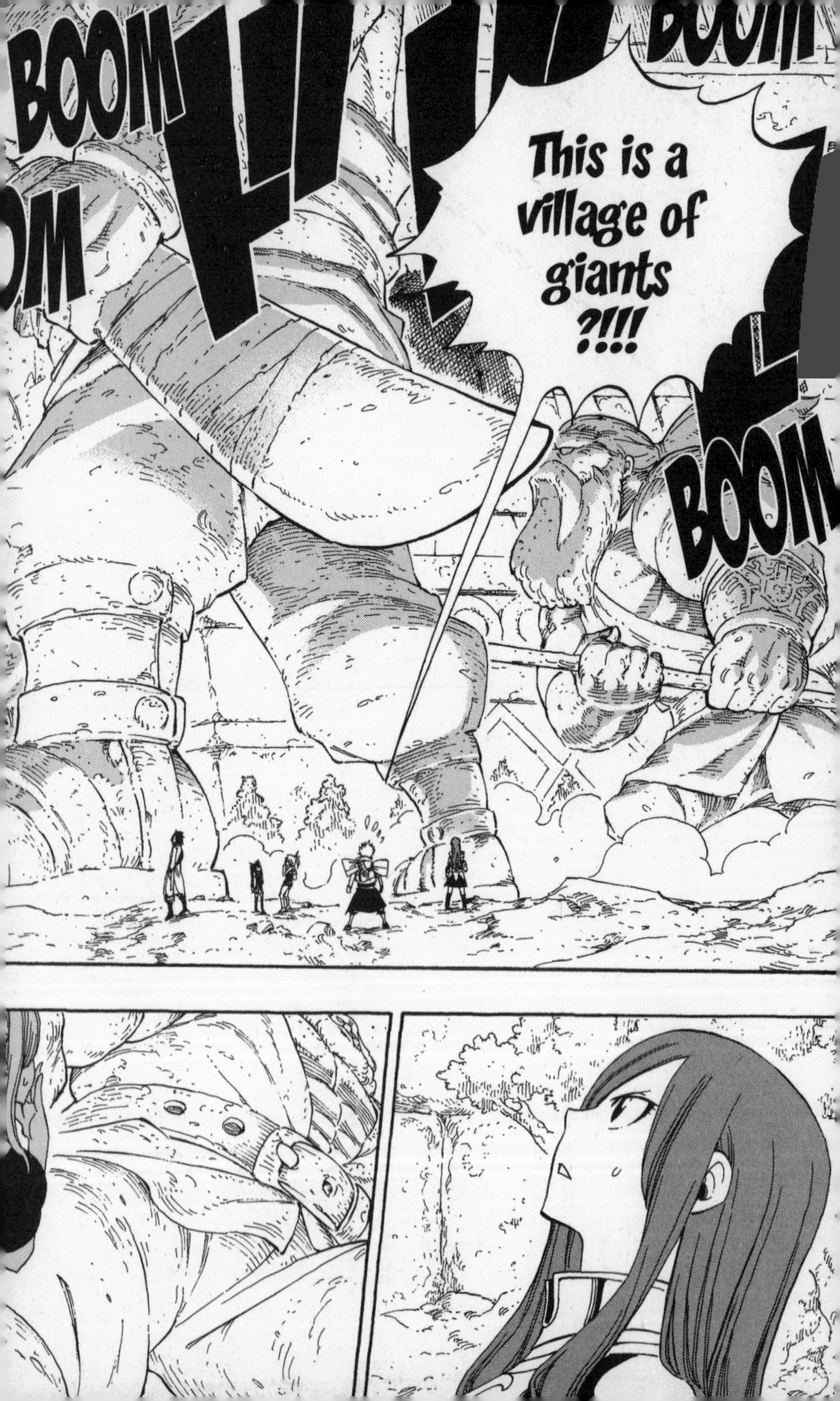
BOOM
This is a village of giants ?!!!
BOOM
BOOM
BOOM

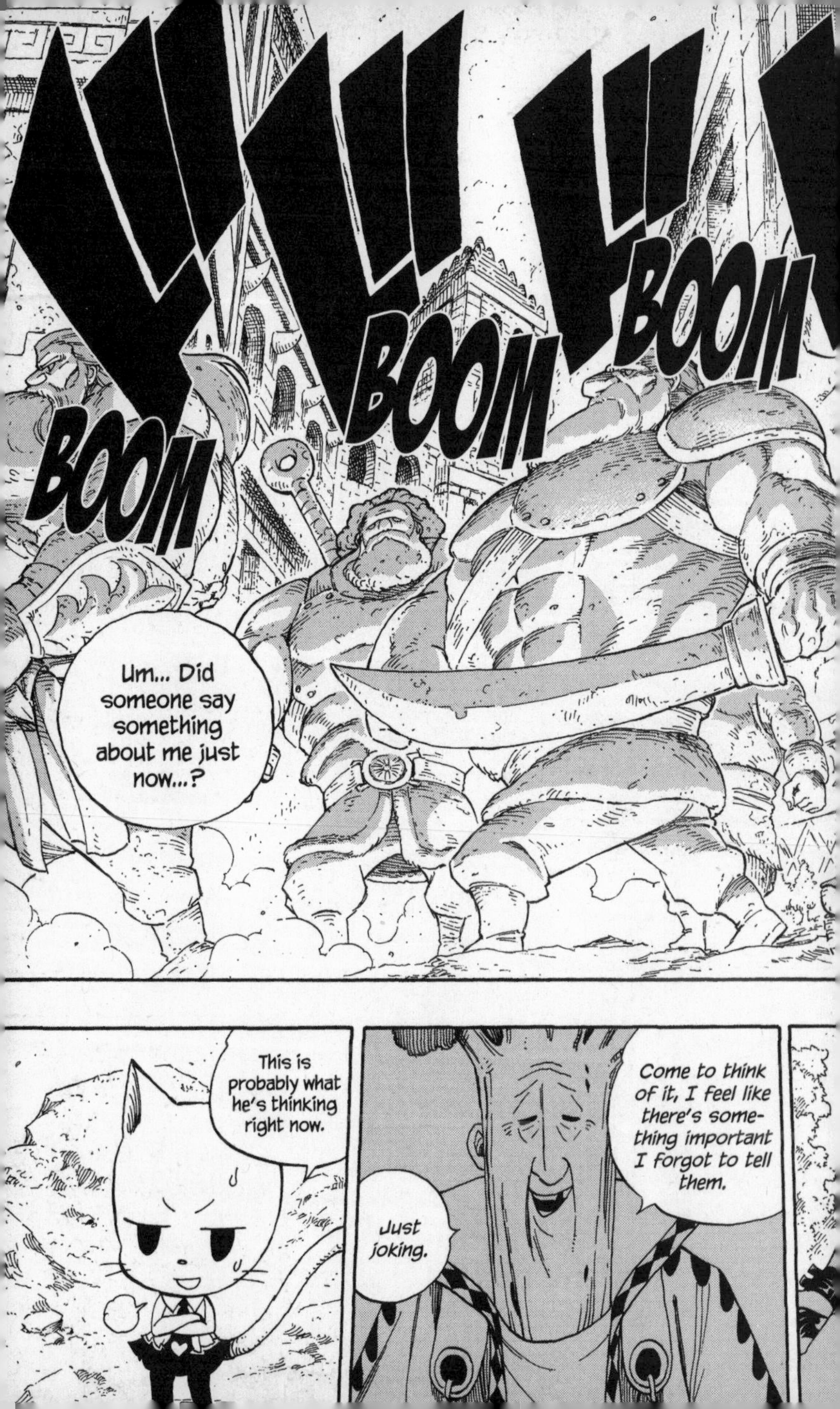
BOOM
BOOM
BOOM
Um... Did someone say something about me just now...?
Come to think of it, I feel like there's something important I forgot to tell them.
Just joking.
This is probably what he's thinking right now.

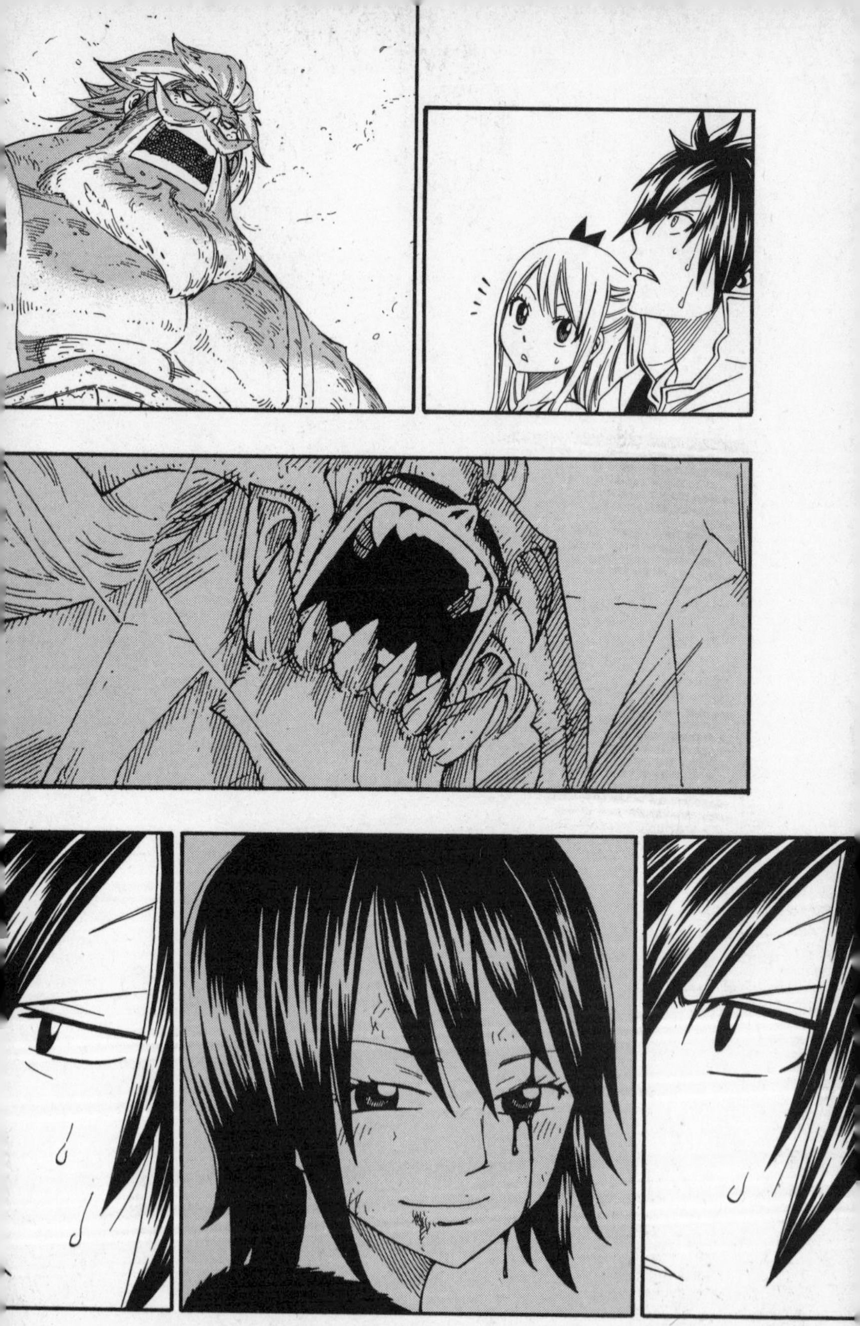

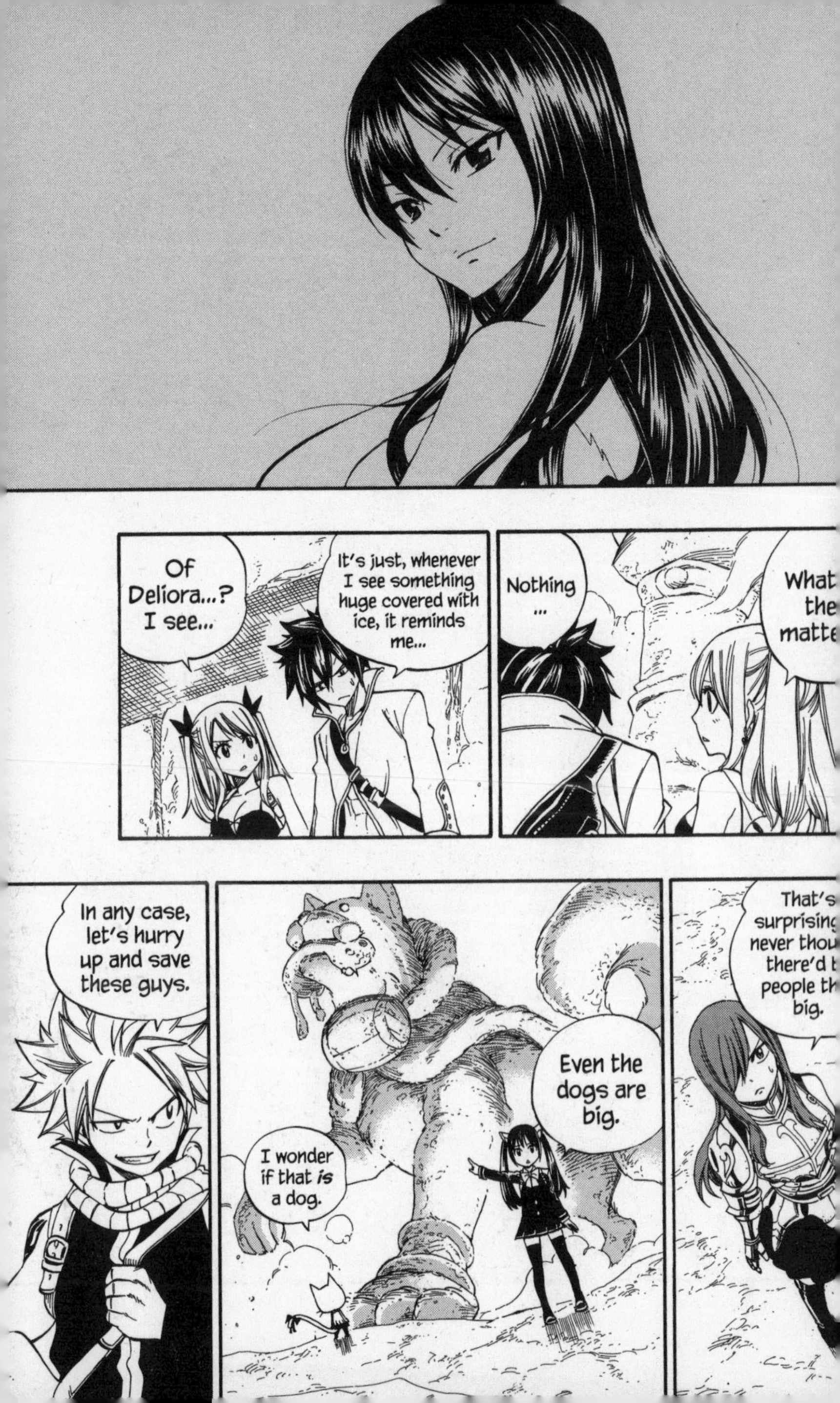

What the matte
Nothing...
It's just, whenever I see something huge covered with ice, it reminds me...
Of Deliora...? I see...
That's surprising never thou there'd people th big.
Even the dogs are big.
I wonder if that *is* a dog.
In any case, let's hurry up and save these guys.

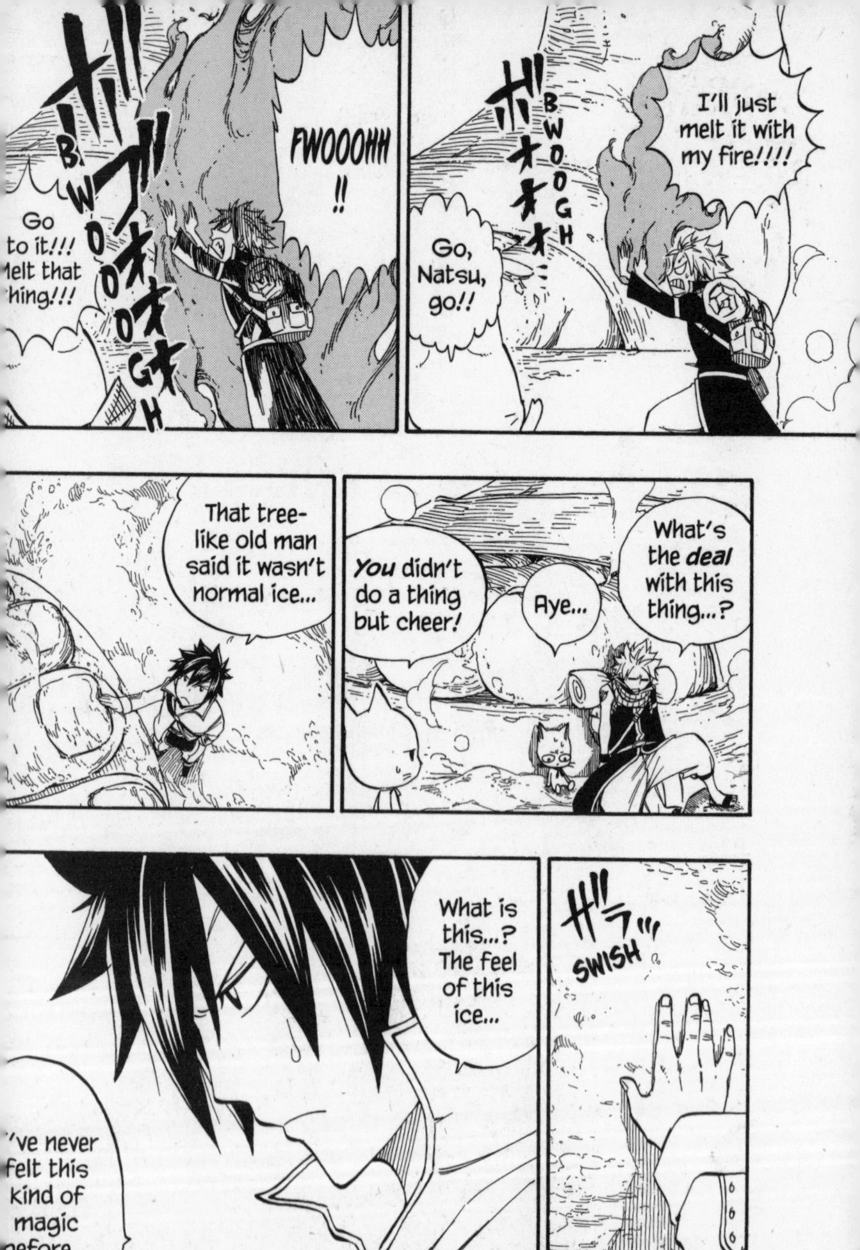
I'll just melt it with my fire!!!!
BWOOGH
Go, Natsu, go!!
FWOOOHH!!
BWOOOOGH
Go to it!!! elt that hing!!!
What's the *deal* with this thing...?
Aye...
You didn't do a thing but cheer!
That tree-like old man said it wasn't normal ice...
SWISH
What is this...? The feel of this ice...
've never felt this kind of magic efore...

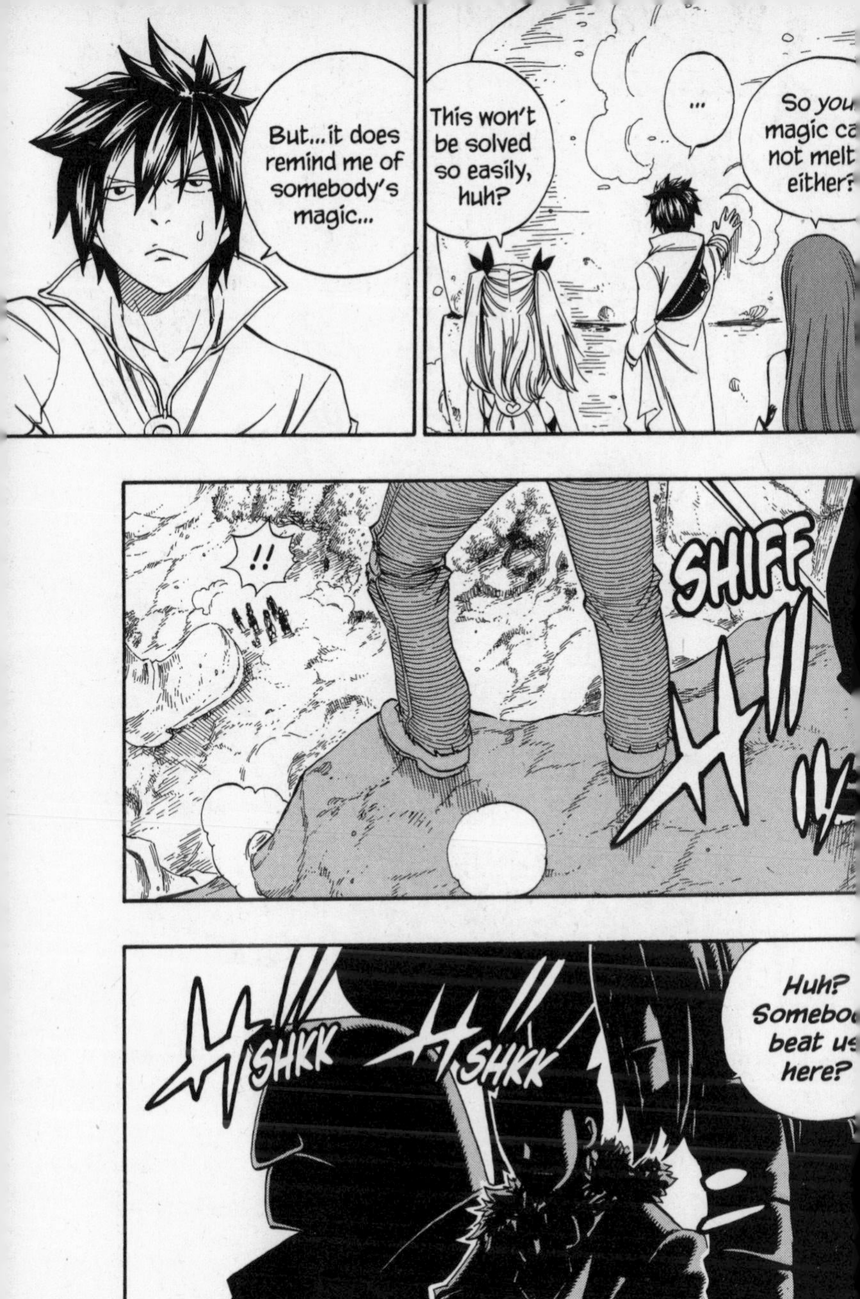
So you magic ca not melt either?
...
This won't be solved so easily, huh?
But...it does remind me of somebody's magic...
SHIFF
!!
Huh? Somebo beat us here?
SHKK
SHKK

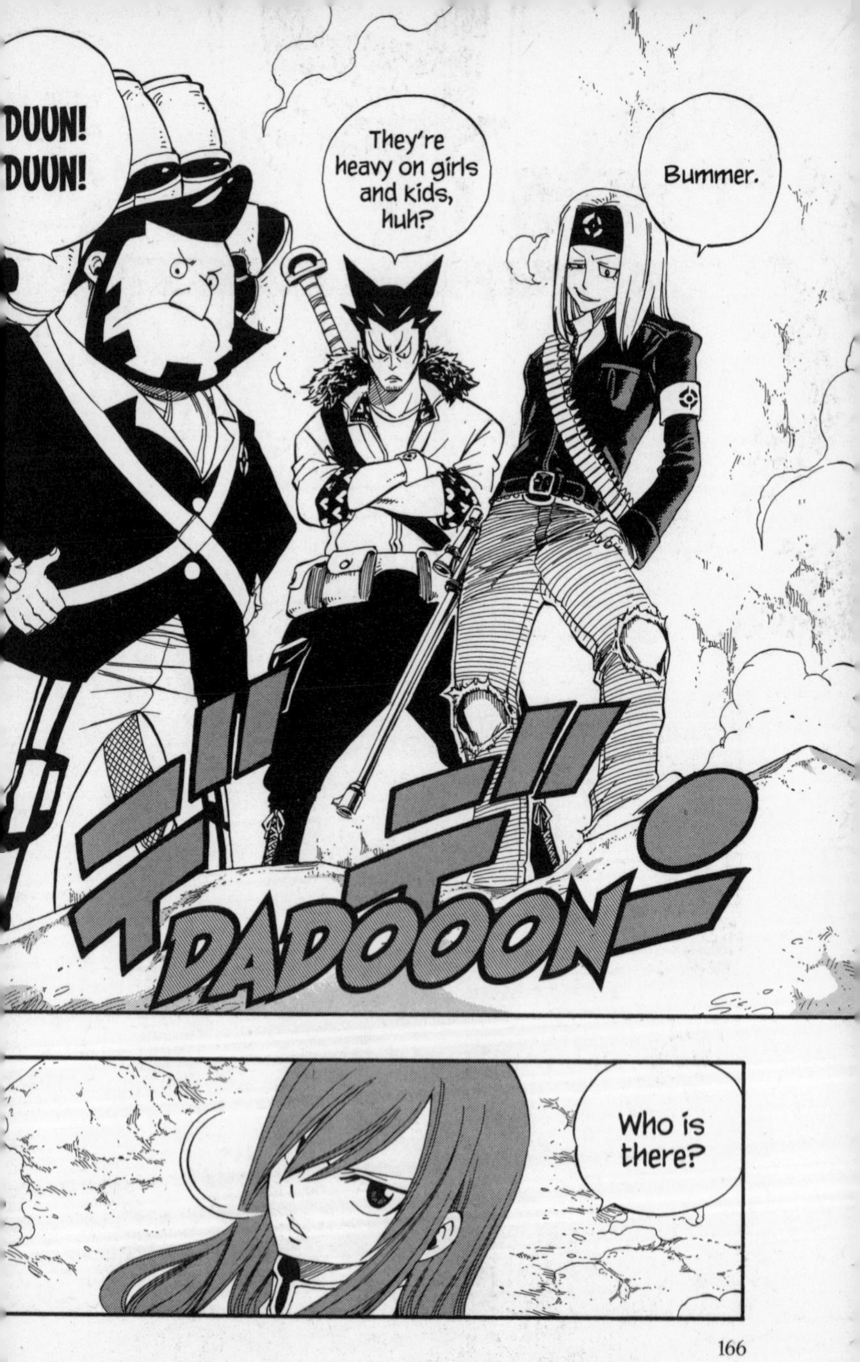
Bummer.
They're heavy on girls and kids, huh?
DUUN! DUUN!
DADOOON
Who is there?

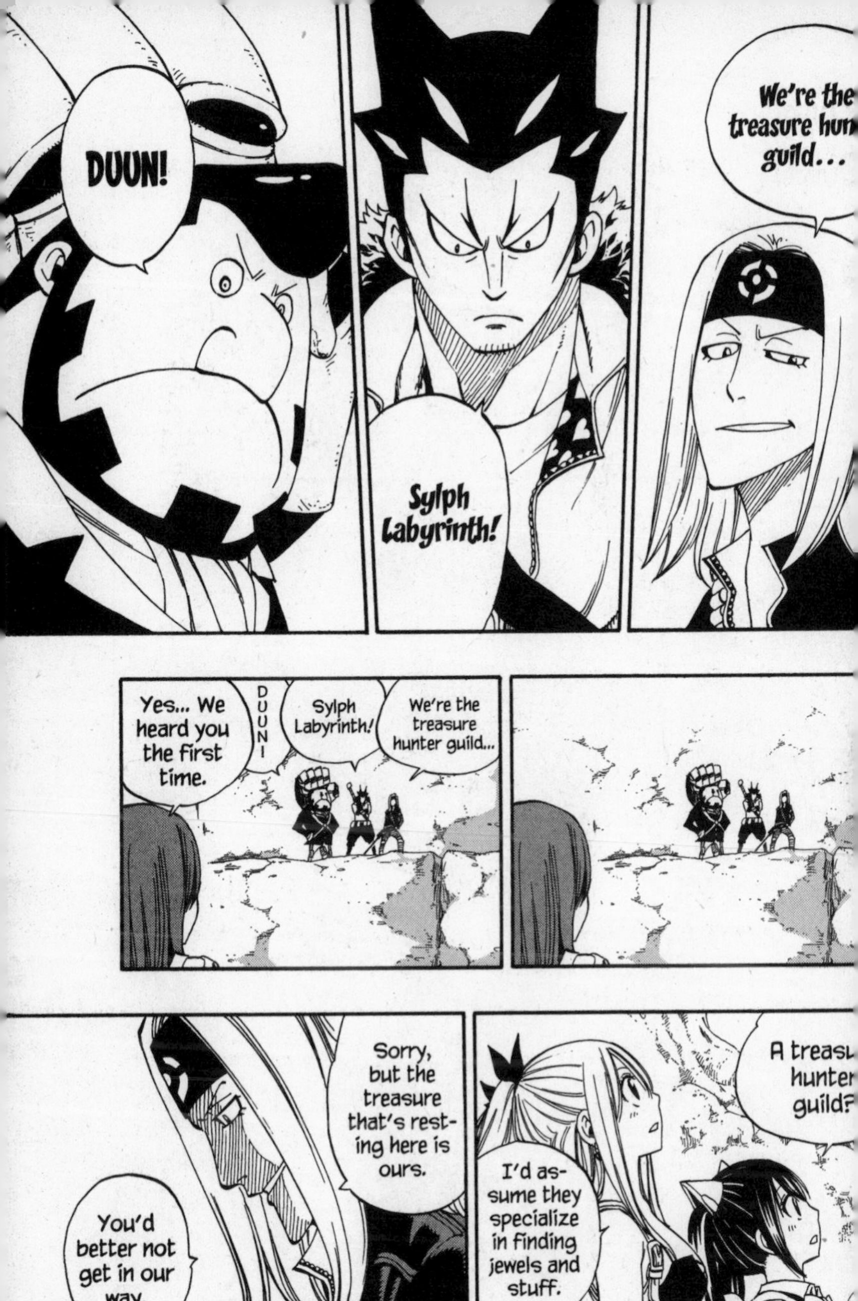
We're the treasure hun guild...
Sylph Labyrinth!
DUUN!
We're the treasure hunter guild...
Sylph Labyrinth!
DUUN!
Yes... We heard you the first time.
A treasu hunter guild?
I'd assume they specialize in finding jewels and stuff.
Sorry, but the treasure that's resting here is ours.
You'd better not get in our way.

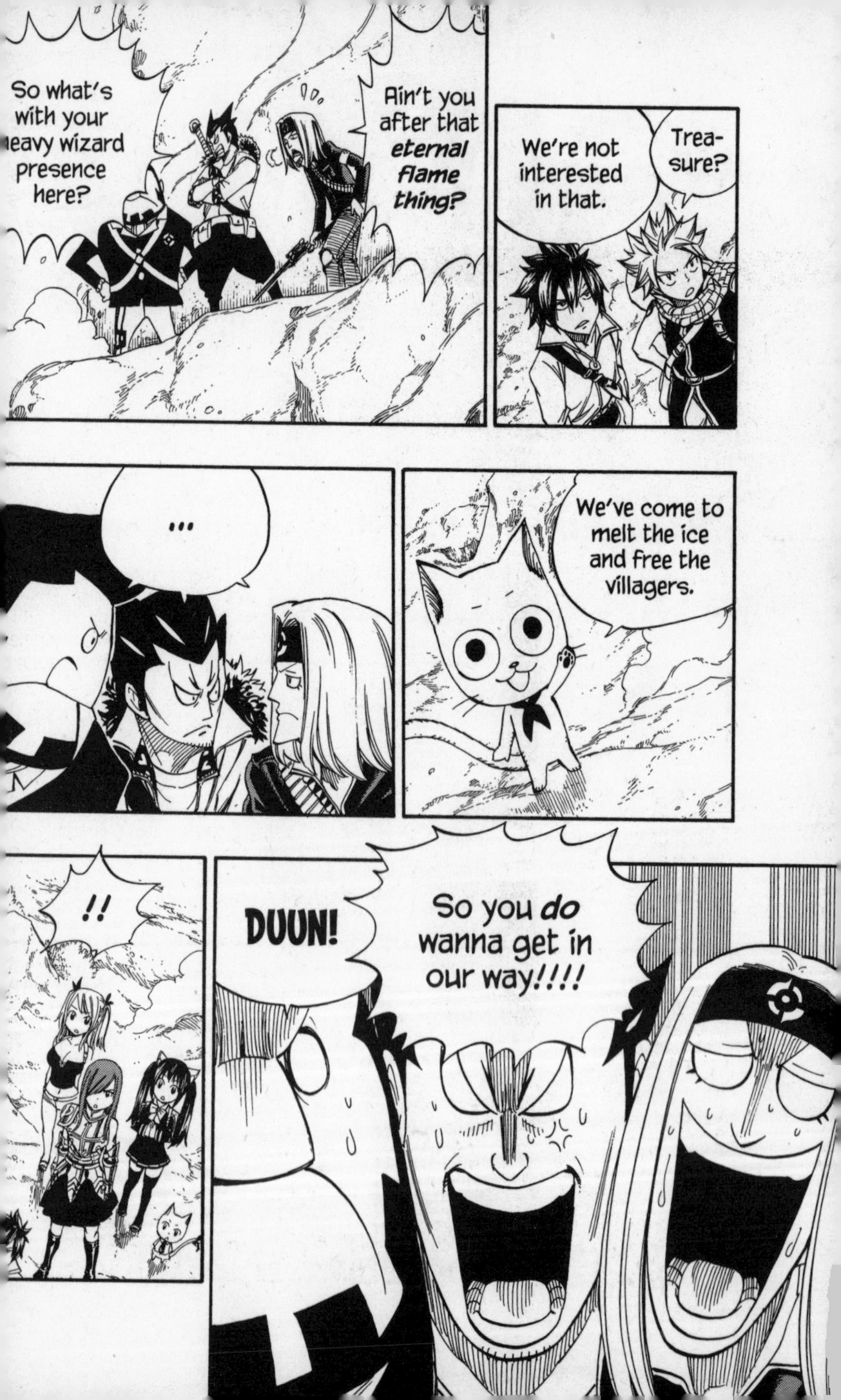

Trea-sure?
We're not interested in that.
Ain't you after that *eternal flame thing?*
So what's with your eavy wizard presence here?
We've come to melt the ice and free the villagers.
...
So you *do* wanna get in our way!!!!
DUUN!
!!

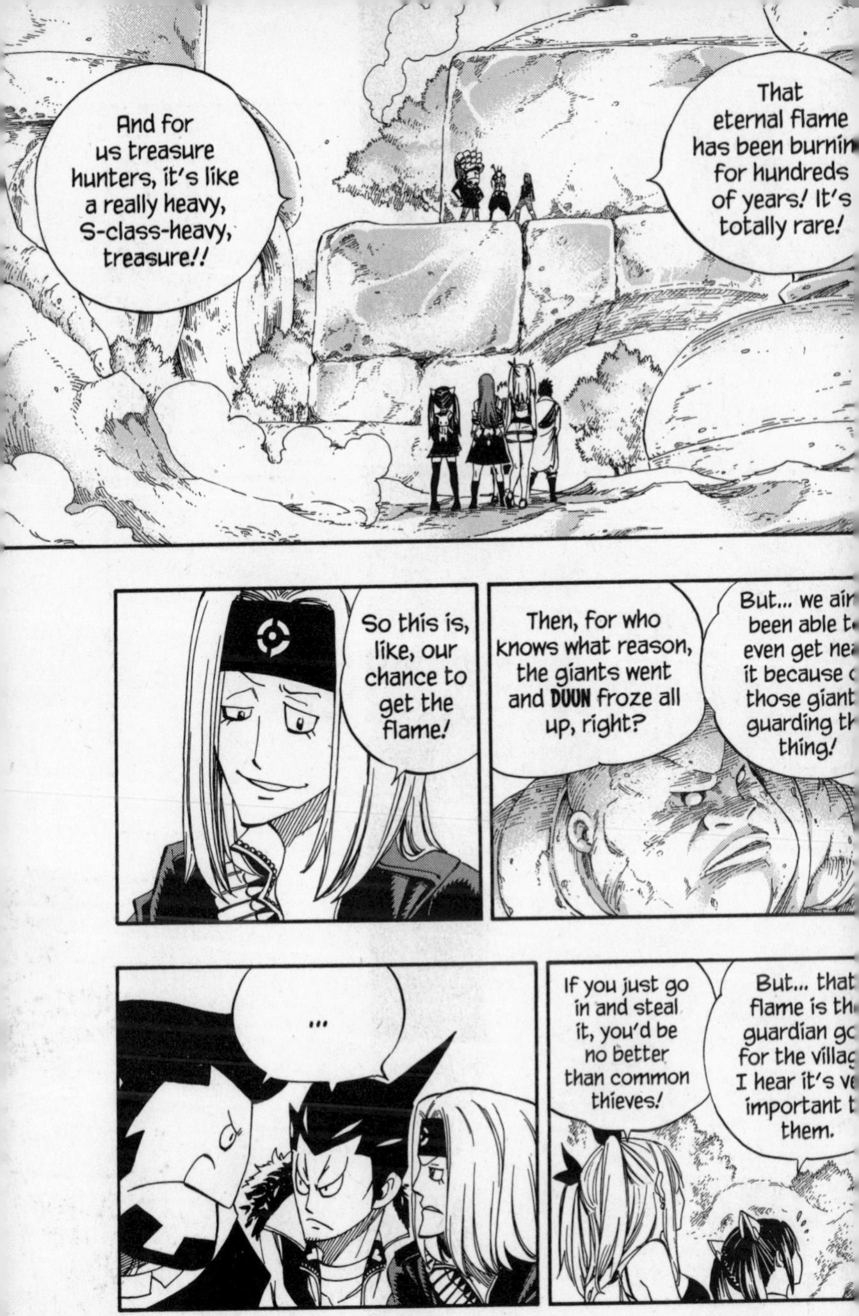
That eternal flame has been burnin for hundreds of years! It's totally rare!
And for us treasure hunters, it's like a really heavy, S-class-heavy, treasure!!
But... we ain been able t even get ne it because o those giant guarding th thing!
Then, for who knows what reason, the giants went and DUUN froze all up, right?
So this is, like, our chance to get the flame!
But... that flame is th guardian g for the villag I hear it's ve important t them.
If you just go in and steal it, you'd be no better than common thieves!
...

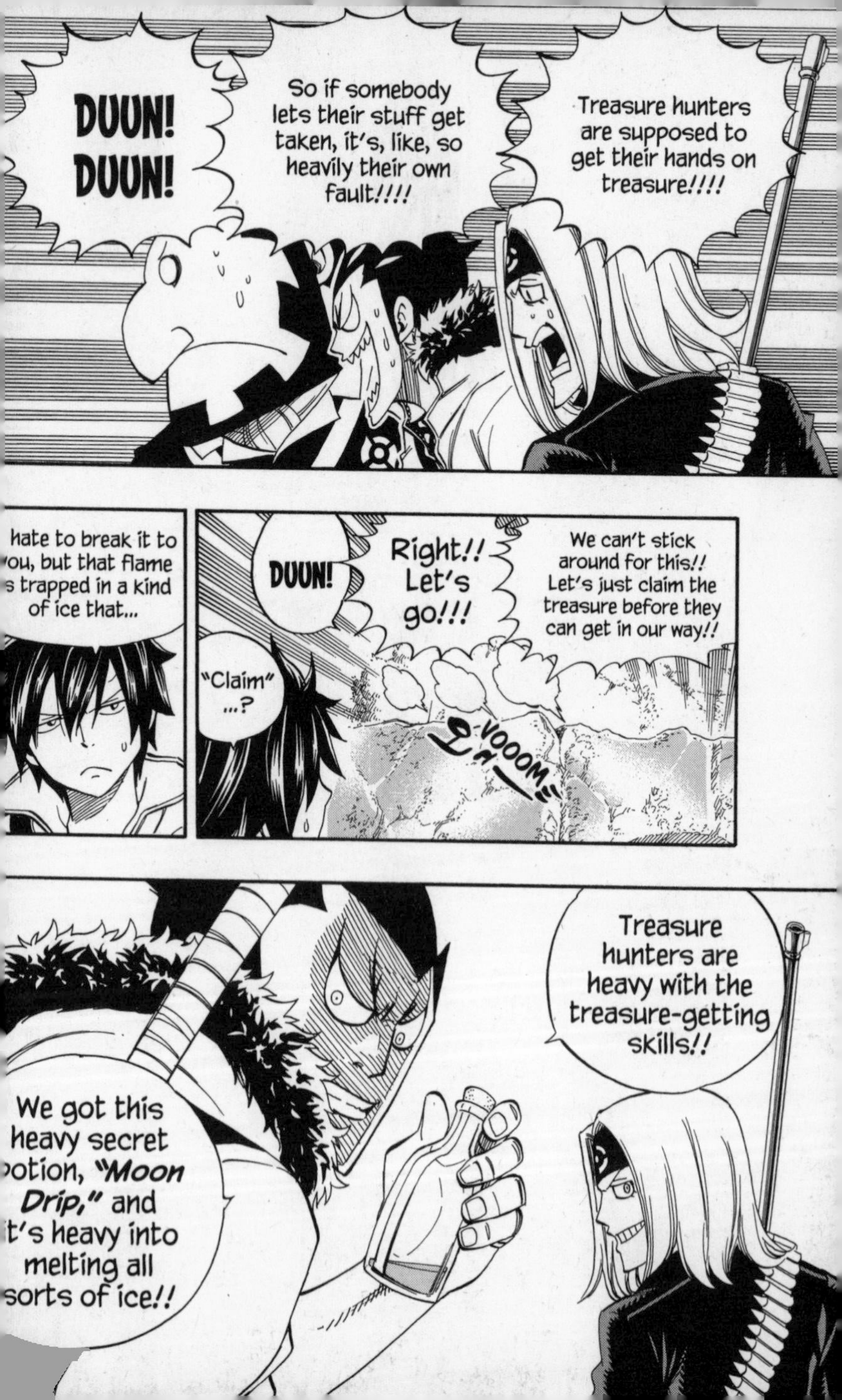

Treasure hunters are supposed to get their hands on treasure!!!!
So if somebody lets their stuff get taken, it's, like, so heavily their own fault!!!!
DUUN! DUUN!
We can't stick around for this!! Let's just claim the treasure before they can get in our way!!
Right!! Let's go!!!
DUUN!
VOOOM
"Claim" ...?
hate to break it to ou, but that flame s trapped in a kind of ice that...
Treasure hunters are heavy with the treasure-getting skills!!
We got this heavy secret otion, "Moon Drip," and t's heavy into melting all sorts of ice!!

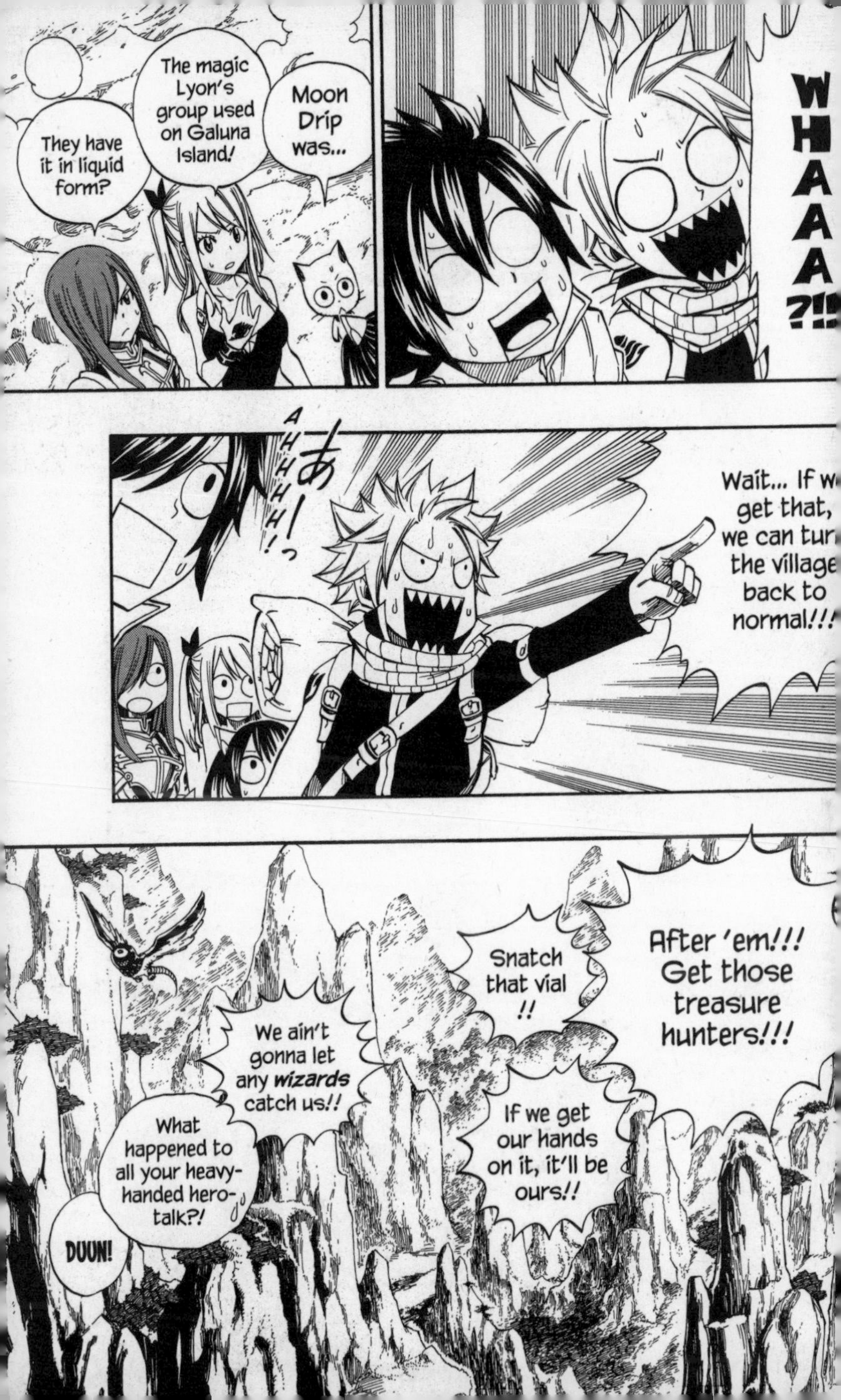
WHAAAA?!!
Moon Drip was...
The magic Lyon's group used on Galuna Island!
They have it in liquid form?
Wait... If w get that, we can tur the village back to normal!!!
AHHHHH!!
あ!
After 'em!!! Get those treasure hunters!!!
Snatch that vial!!
If we get our hands on it, it'll be ours!!
We ain't gonna let any ***wizards*** catch us!!
What happened to all your heavy-handed hero-talk?!
DUUN!

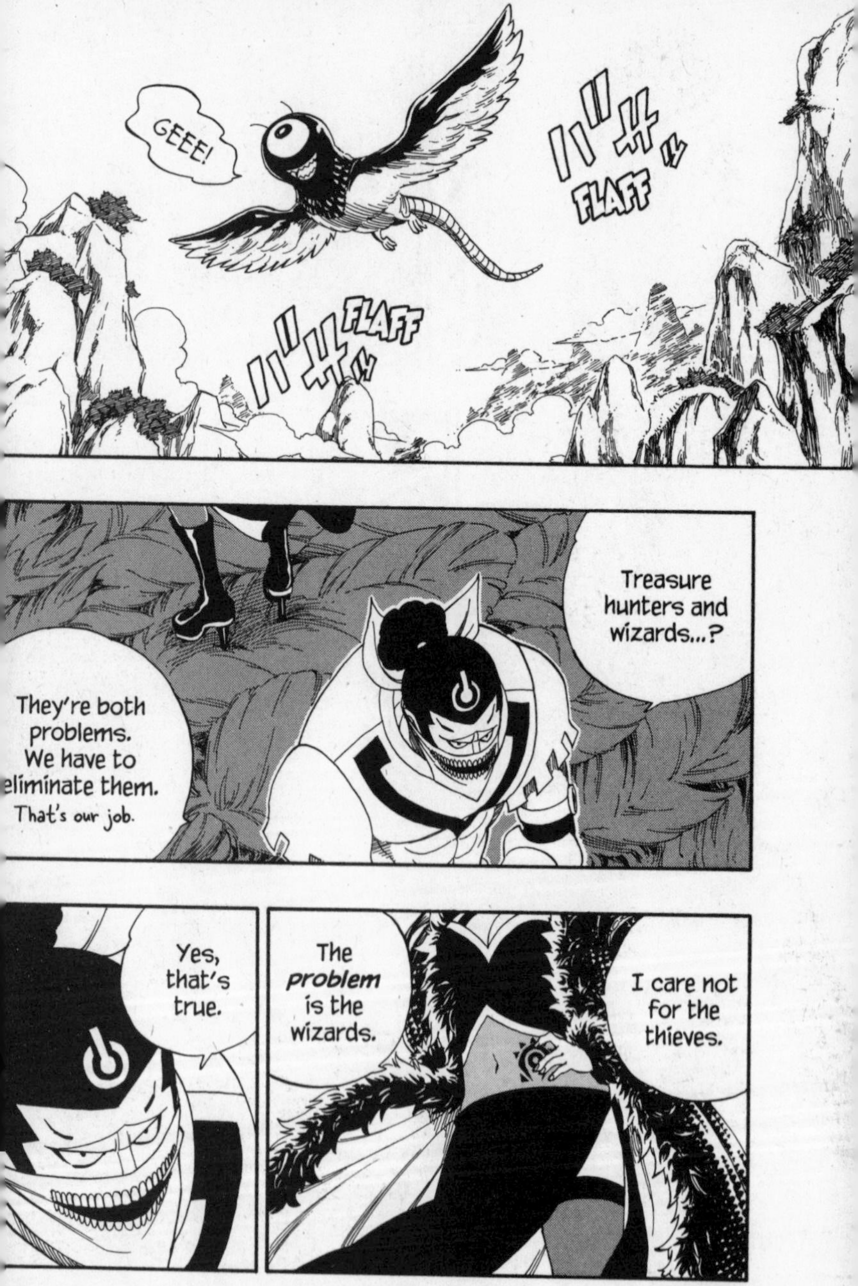
FLAFF
GEEE!
FLAFF
Treasure hunters and wizards...?
They're both problems. We have to eliminate them. That's our job.
I care not for the thieves.
The *problem* is the wizards.
Yes, that's true.

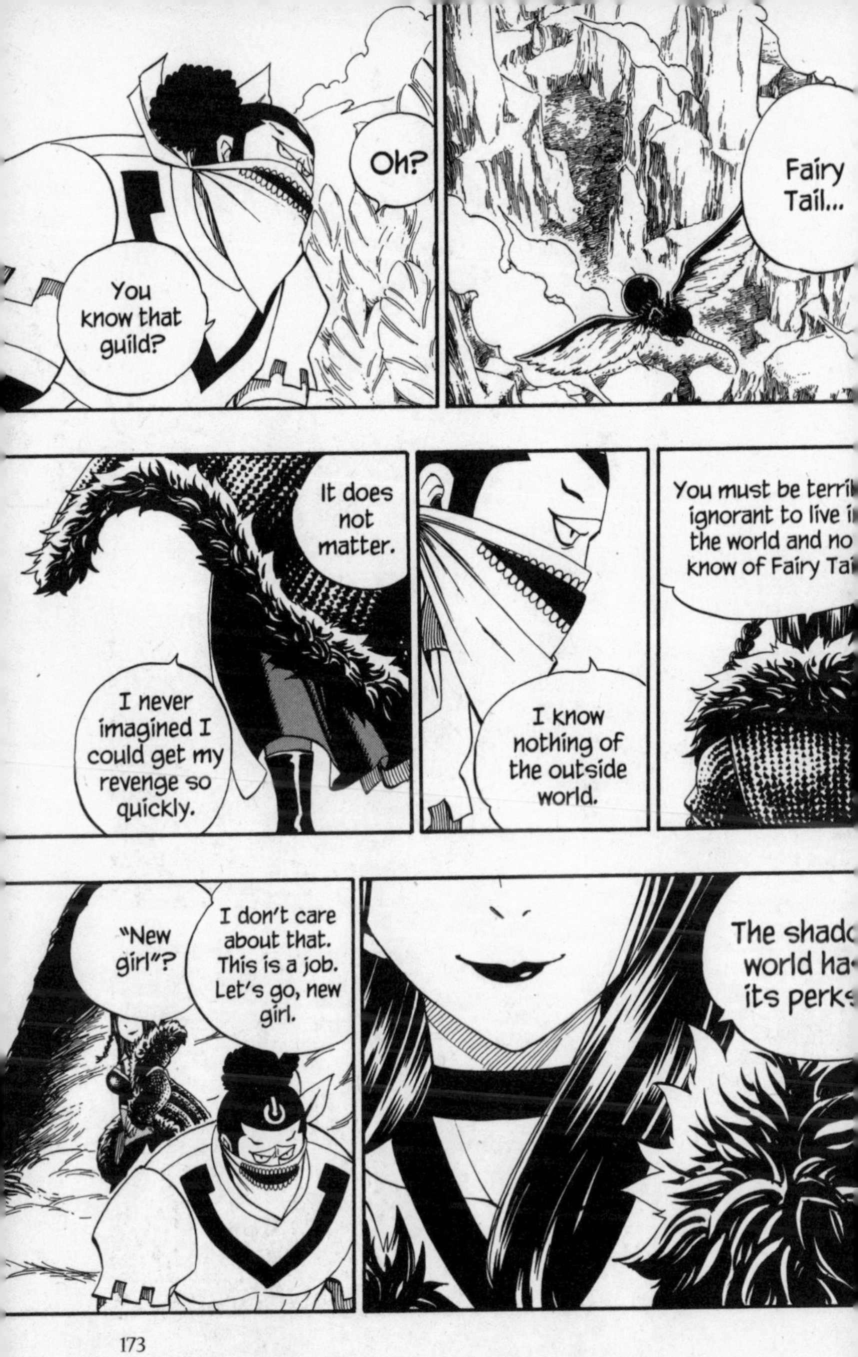

Fairy Tail...
Oh?
You know that guild?
You must be terri ignorant to live i the world and no know of Fairy Ta
I know nothing of the outside world.
It does not matter.
I never imagined I could get my revenge so quickly.
The shad world ha its perk
I don't care about that. This is a job. Let's go, new girl.
"New girl"?

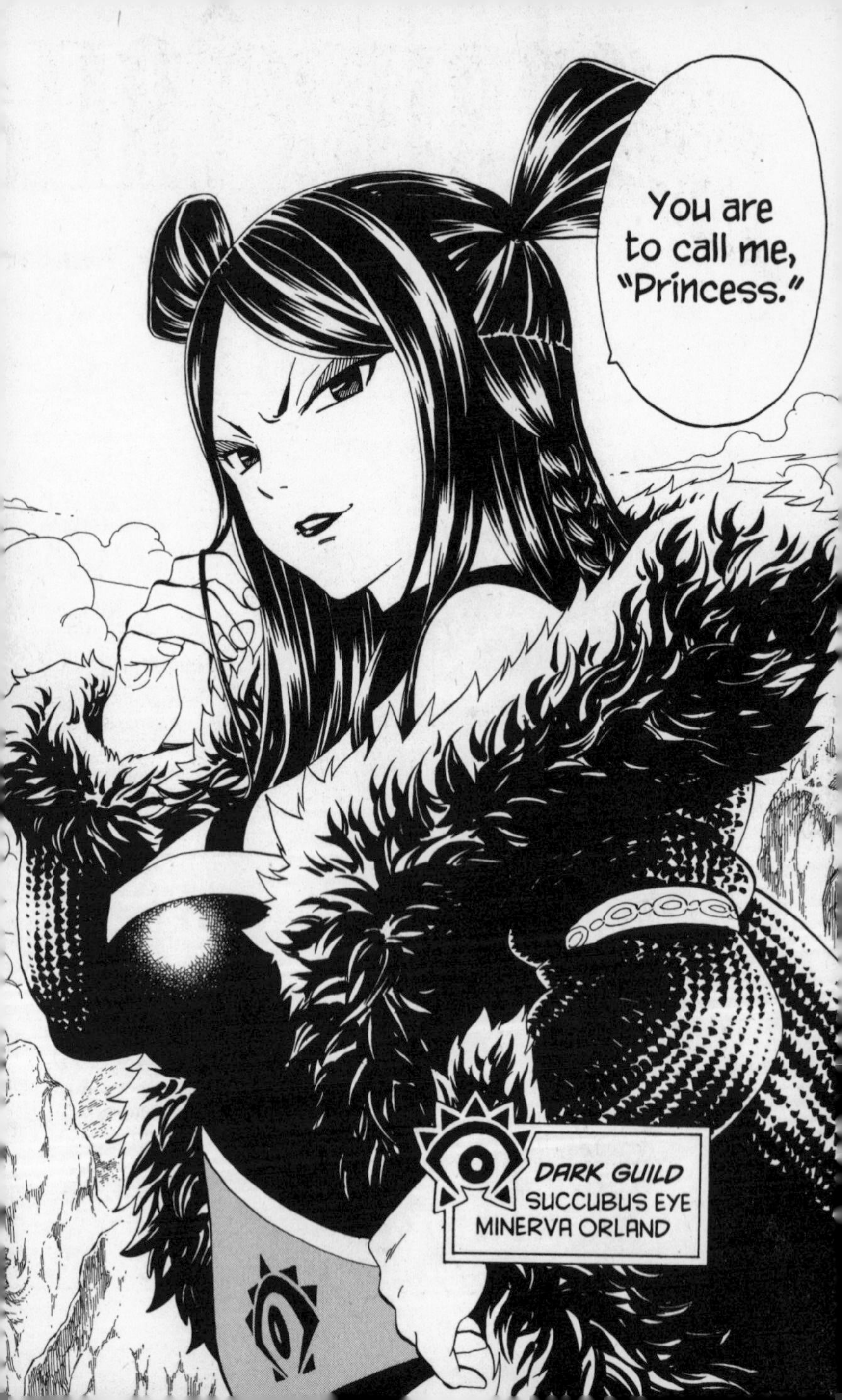
You are to call me, "Princess."
DARK GUILD
SUCCUBUS EYE
MINERVA ORLAND

FAIRY TAIL

Chapter 344: Wizards Vs. Hunte

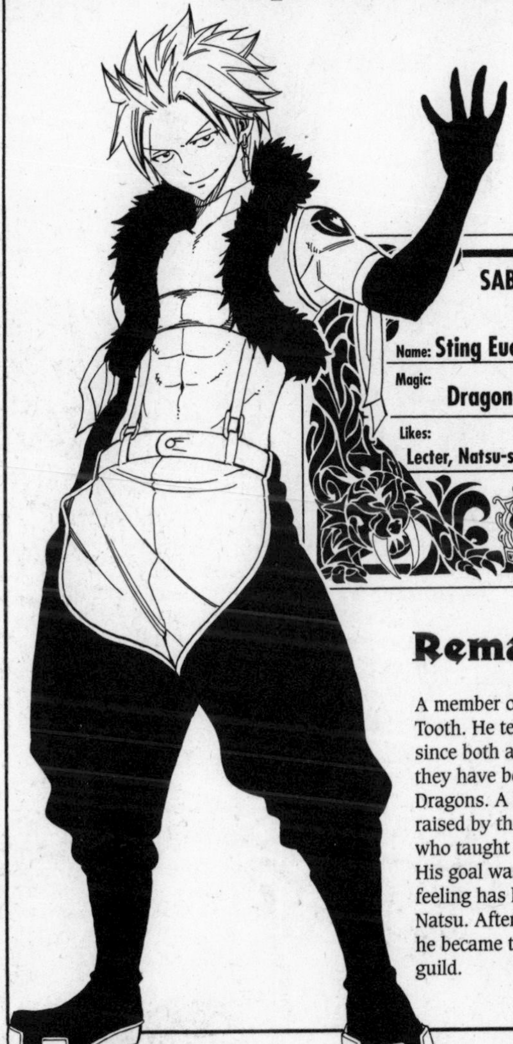

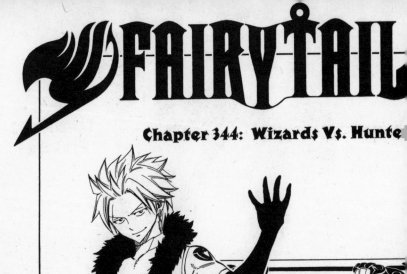

SABER TOOTH

Name: Sting Eucliffe Age: 19 yrs.

Magic: Dragon Slayer Magic

Likes: Lecter, Natsu-san

Dislikes: The old guild

WIZARD GUILD

Remarks

A member of the strongest guild, Sabe Tooth. He teamed up with Rogue, and since both are dragon slayer wizards, they have become famous as the Twin Dragons. A long time ago, he was raised by the White Dragon, Weisslogi who taught him dragon slayer magic. His goal was to defeat Natsu, and that feeling has led to his looking up to Natsu. After the Grand Magic Games, he became the leader of the Saber Toot guild.

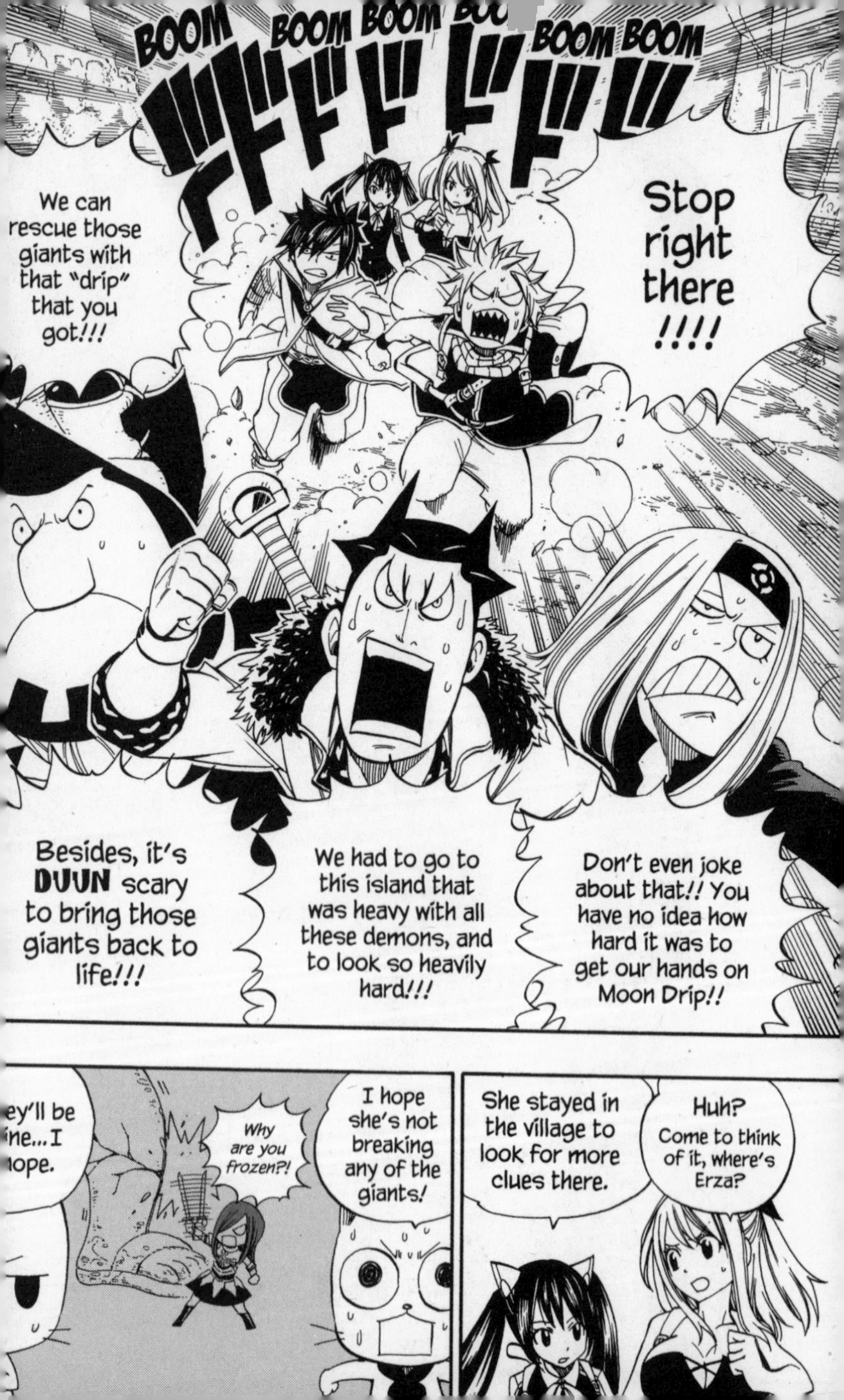
BOOM BOOM BOOM BOO BOOM BOOM
Stop right there!!!!
We can rescue those giants with that "drip" that you got!!!
Don't even joke about that!! You have no idea how hard it was to get our hands on Moon Drip!!
We had to go to this island that was heavy with all these demons, and to look so heavily hard!!!
Besides, it's **DUUN** scary to bring those giants back to life!!!
Huh? Come to think of it, where's Erza?
She stayed in the village to look for more clues there.
I hope she's not breaking any of the giants!
Why are you frozen?!
ey'll be ine... I ope.

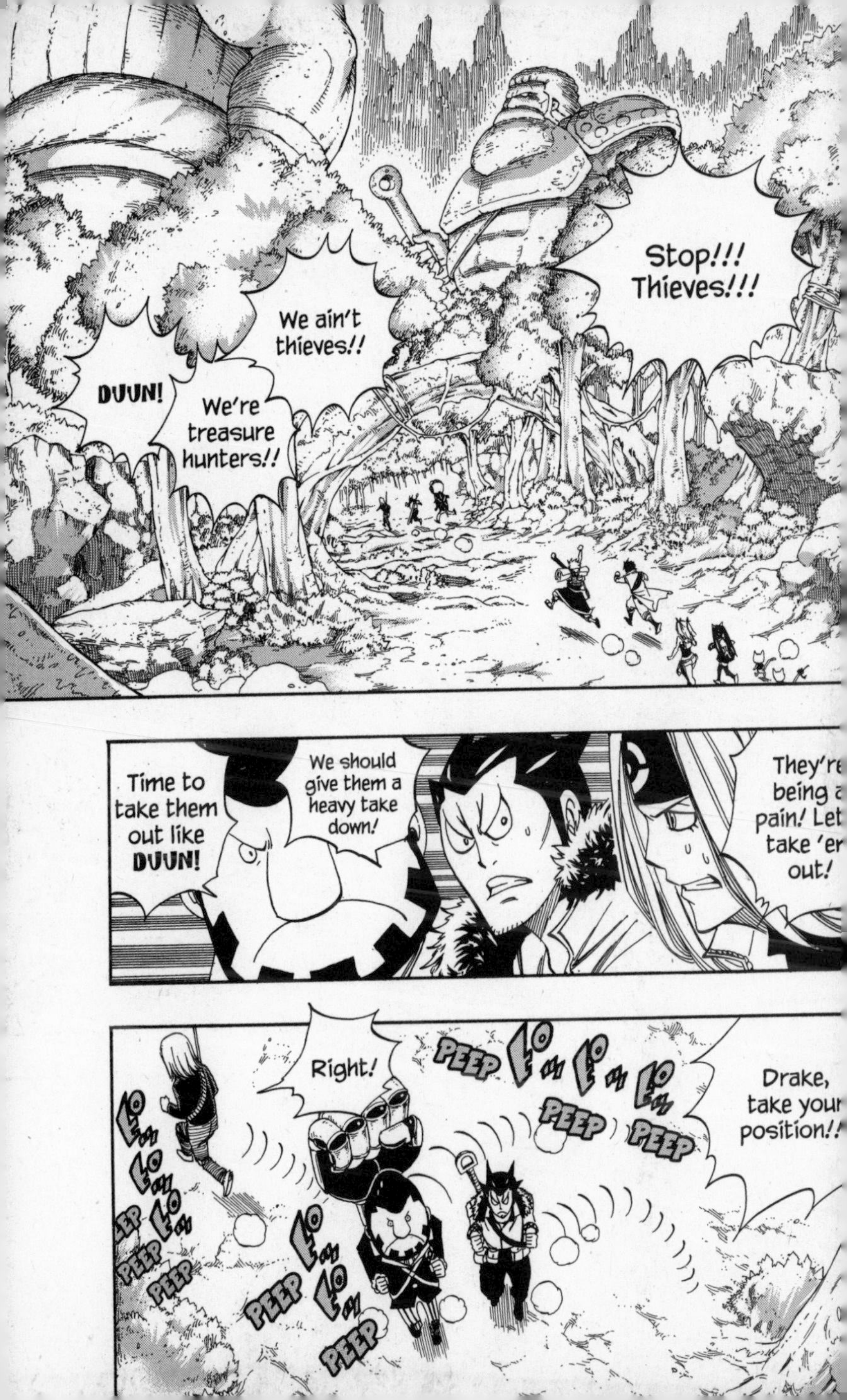
Stop!!! Thieves!!!
We ain't thieves!!
We're treasure hunters!!
DUUN!
They'r being a pain! Let take 'er out!
We should give them a heavy take down!
Time to take them out like DUUN!
Drake, take your position!!
PEEP
PEEP
PEEP
Right!
PEEP
PEEP
PEEP
PEEP
PEEP

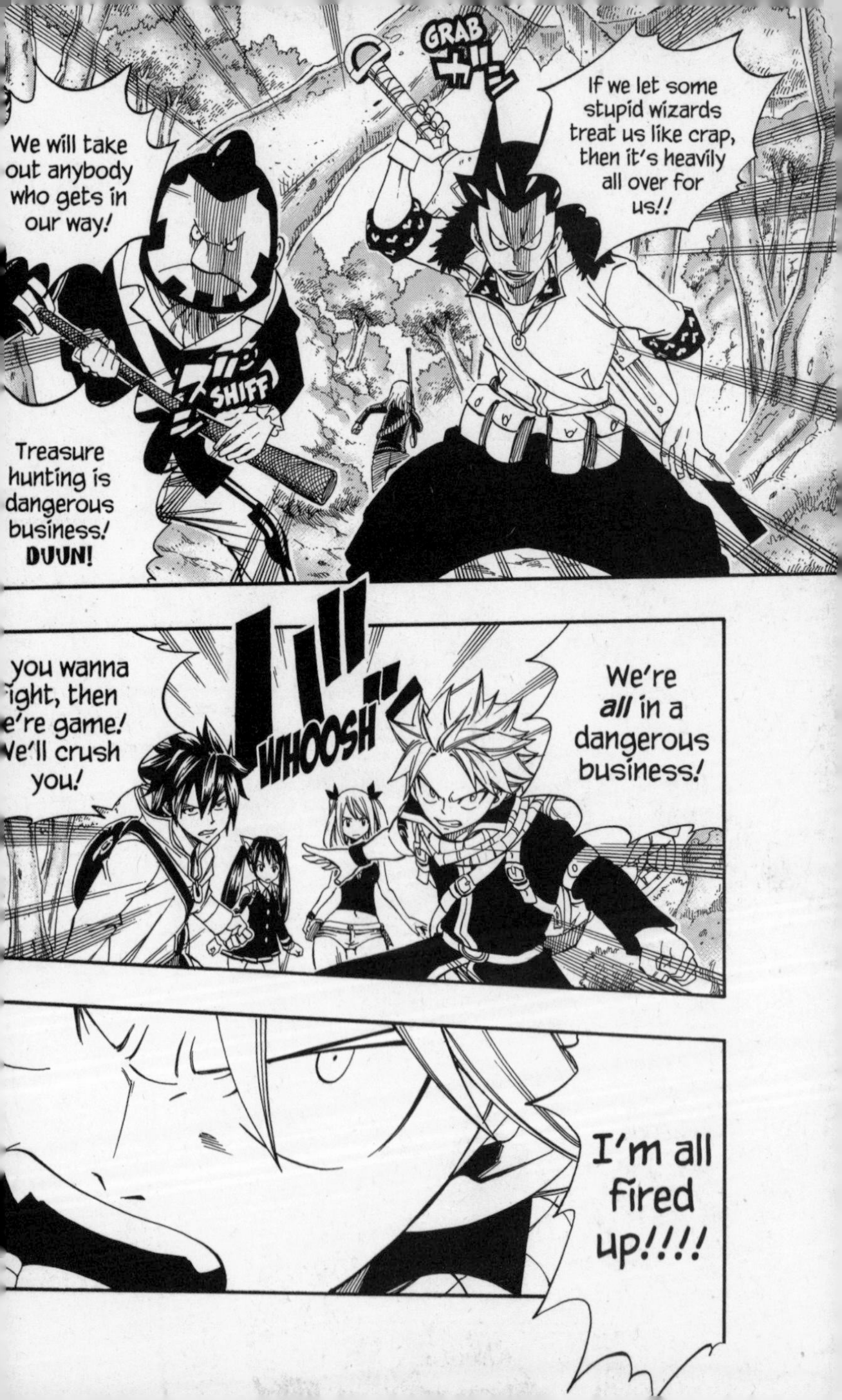
GRAB
If we let some stupid wizards treat us like crap, then it's heavily all over for us!!
We will take out anybody who gets in our way!
SHIFF
Treasure hunting is dangerous business! **DUUN!**
We're *all* in a dangerous business!
WHOOSH
you wanna ight, then e're game! Ve'll crush you!
I'm all fired up!!!!

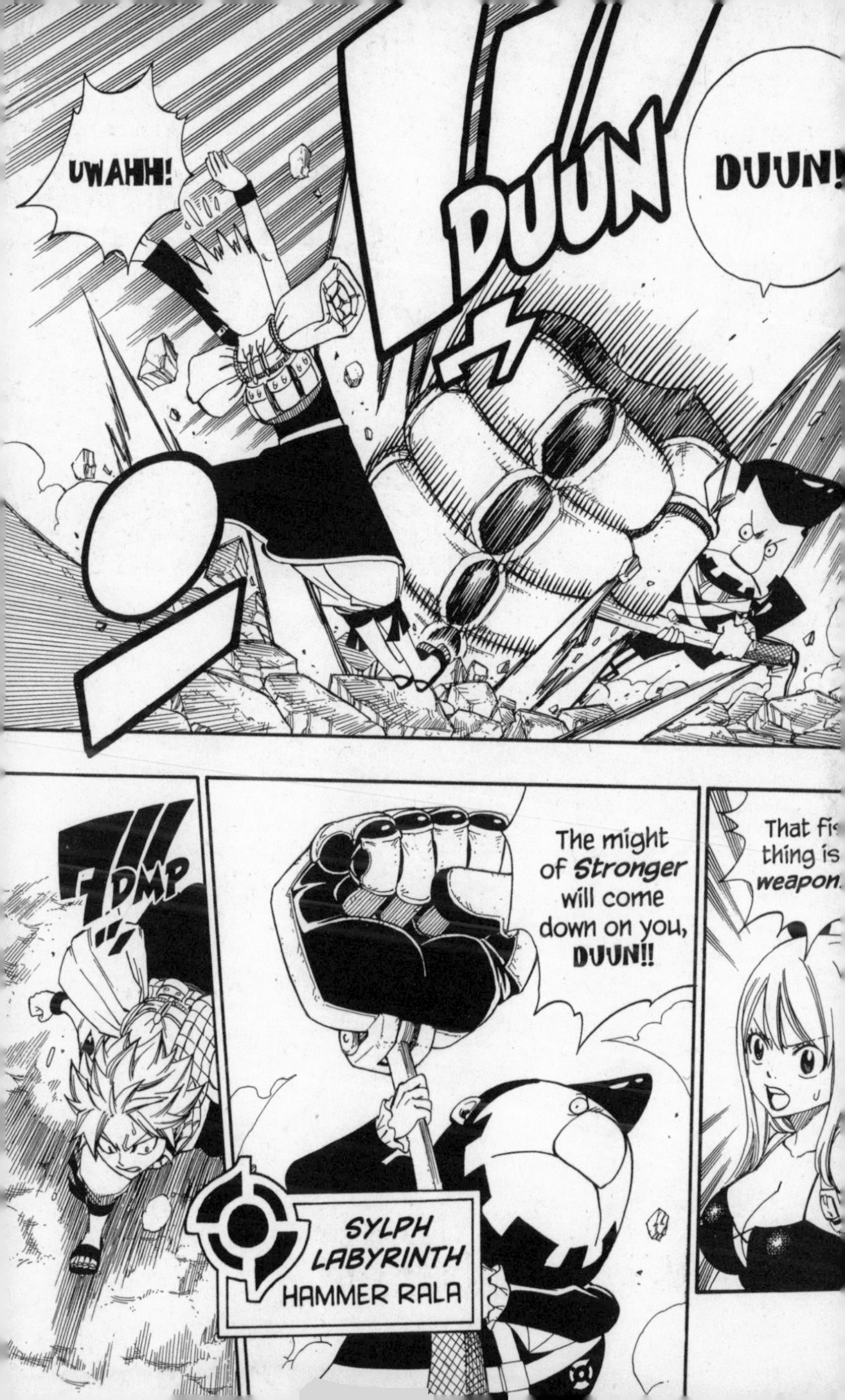
DUUN!
DUUN
UWAHH!
That fi
thing is
weapon
The might of Stronger will come down on you, DUUN!!
SYLPH LABYRINTH
HAMMER RALA
DMP

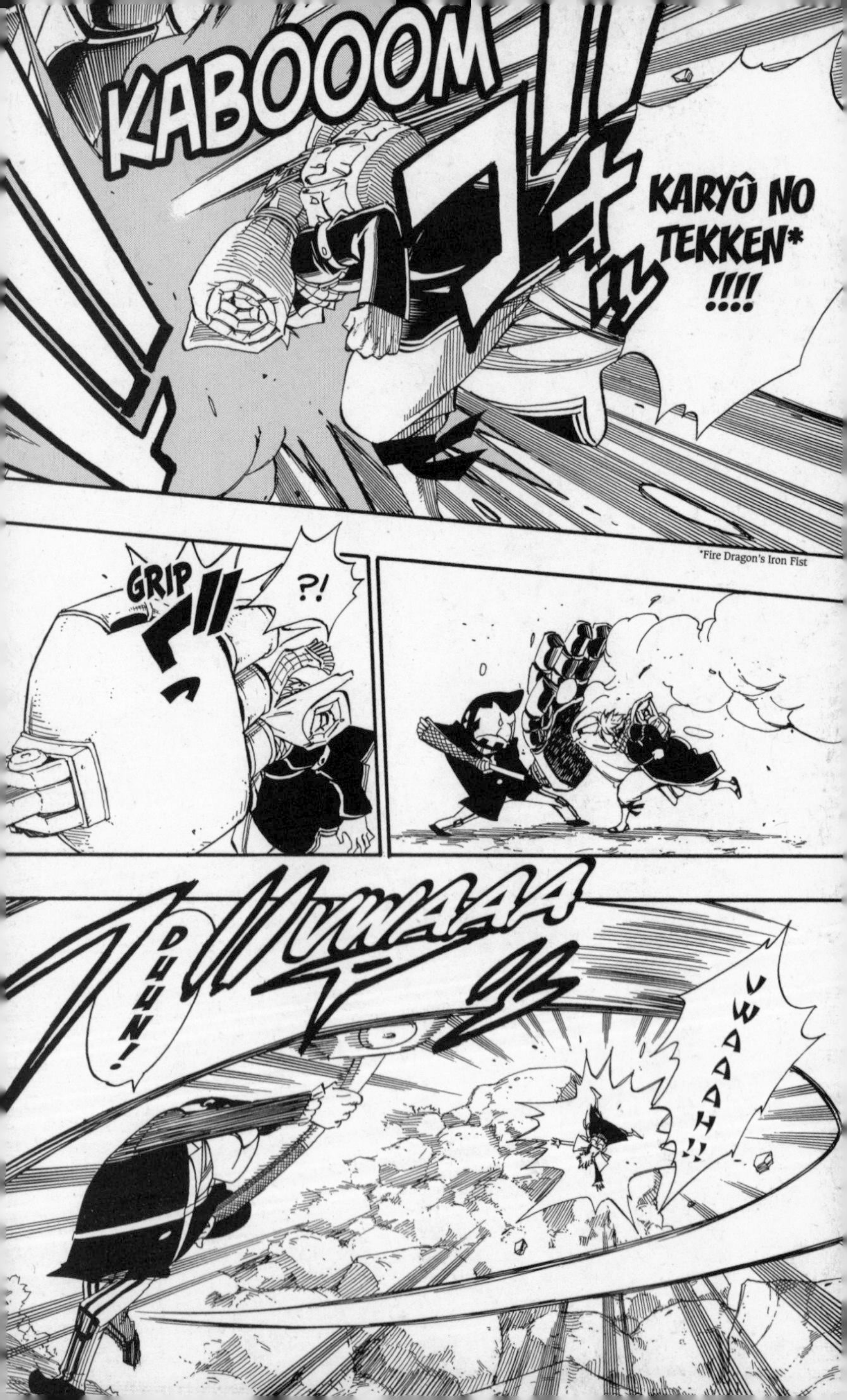
KARYÛ NO TEKKEN* !!!!
KABOOOM
*Fire Dragon's Iron Fist
?!
GRIP
HUWAAA
UWAAAAH!!!
DUHUN!

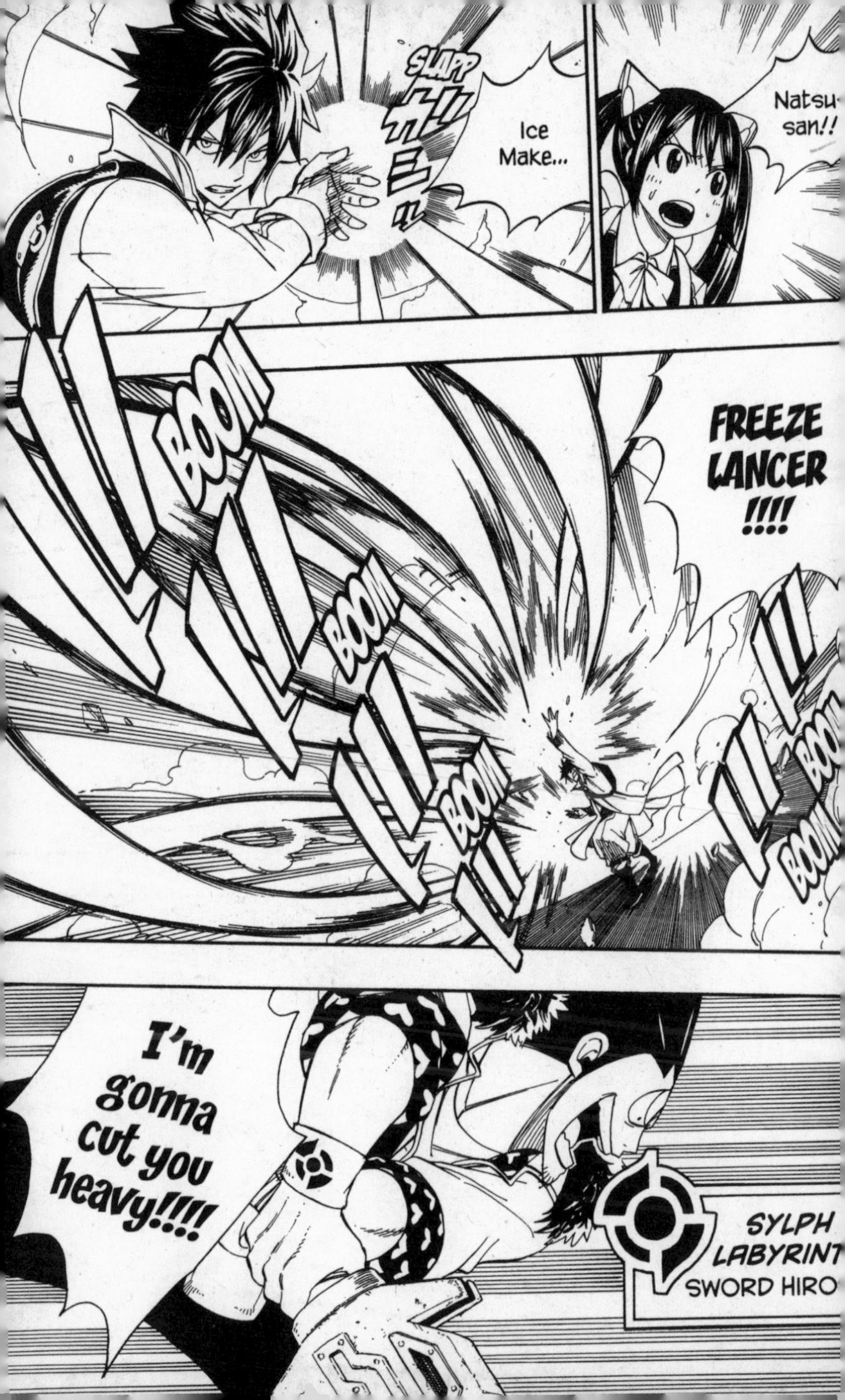

Natsu-san!!
SLAPP
Ice Make...
FREEZE LANCER !!!!
BOOM
BOOM
BOOM
BOOM
BOOM
I'm gonna cut you heavy!!!!
SYLPH LABYRINT
SWORD HIRO

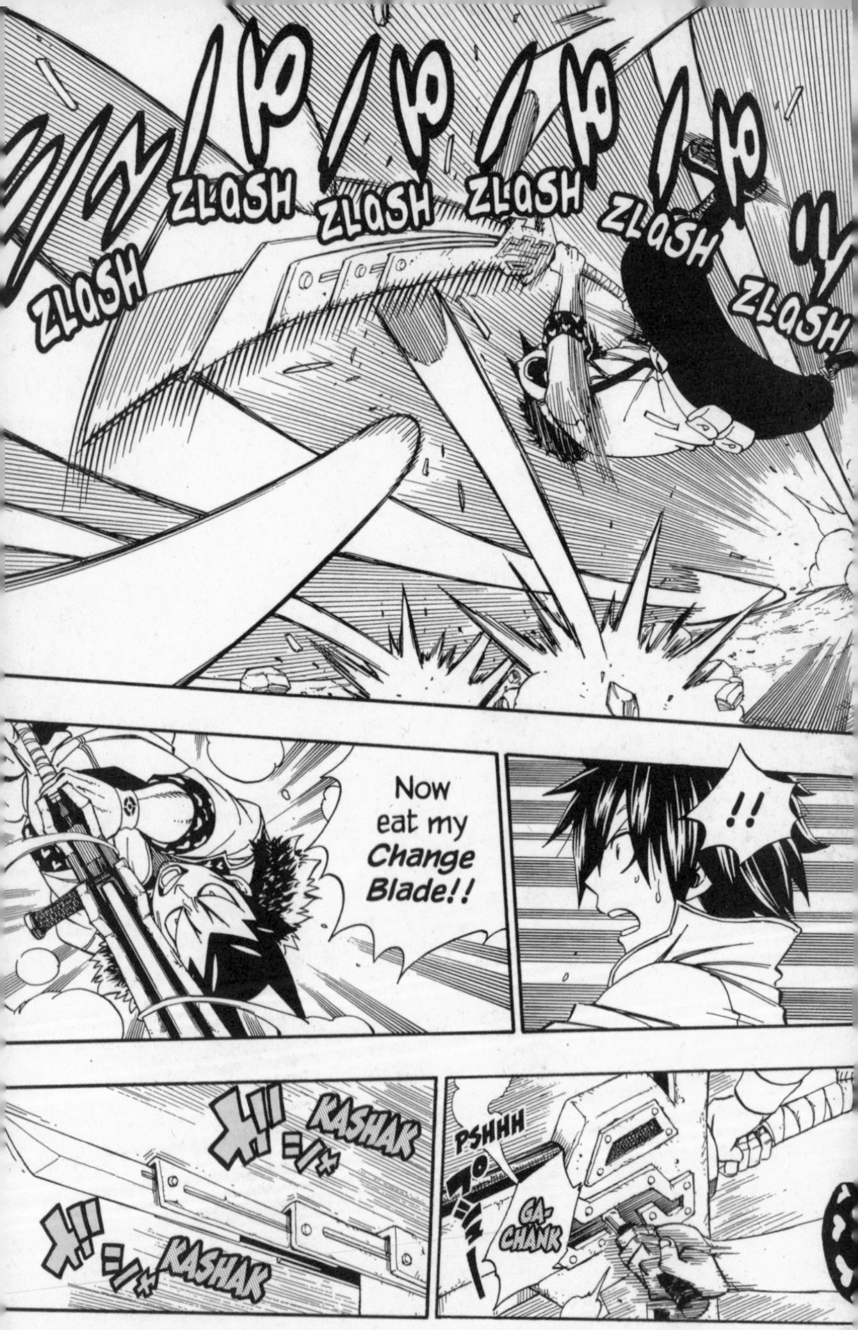
ZLASH
ZLASH
ZLASH
ZLASH
ZLASH
ZLASH
!!
Now eat my *Change Blade!!*
PSHHH
GA-CHANK
KASHAK
KASHAK

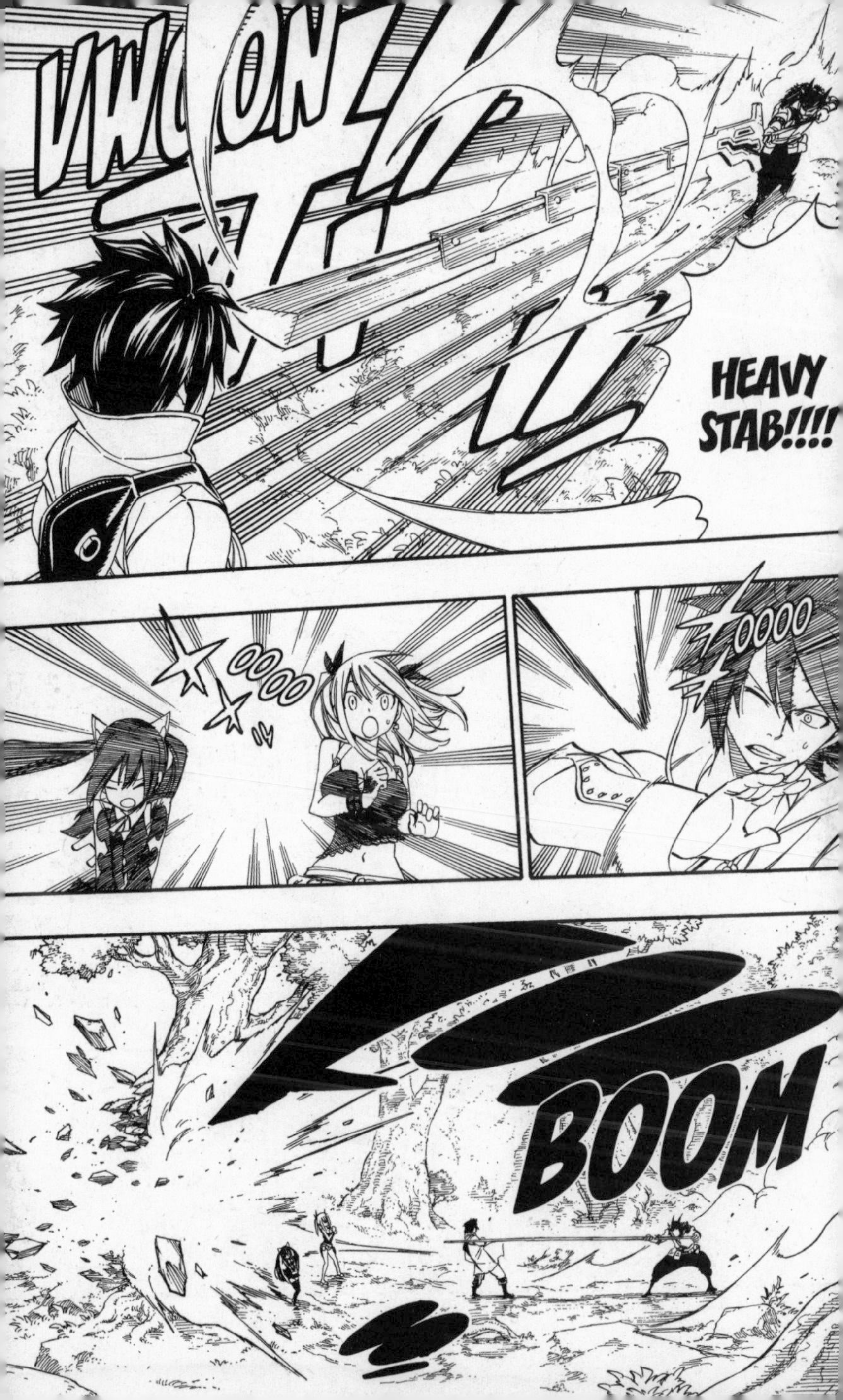
HEAVY STAB!!!!
BOOM

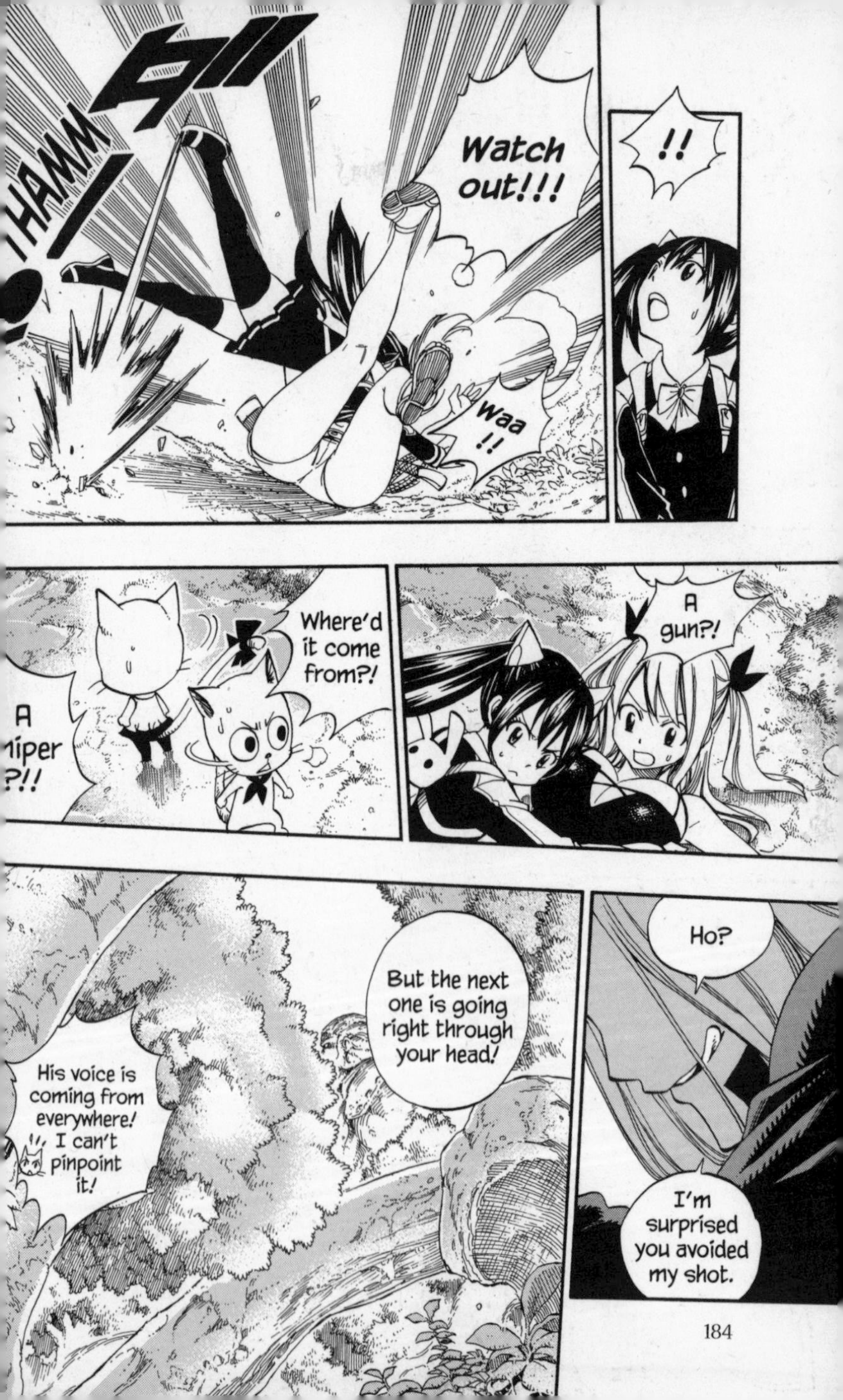
!!
Watch out!!!
Waa !!
HAMM
A gun?!
Where'd it come from?!
A iper ?!!
Ho?
I'm surprised you avoided my shot.
But the next one is going right through your head!
His voice is coming from everywhere! I can't pinpoint it!

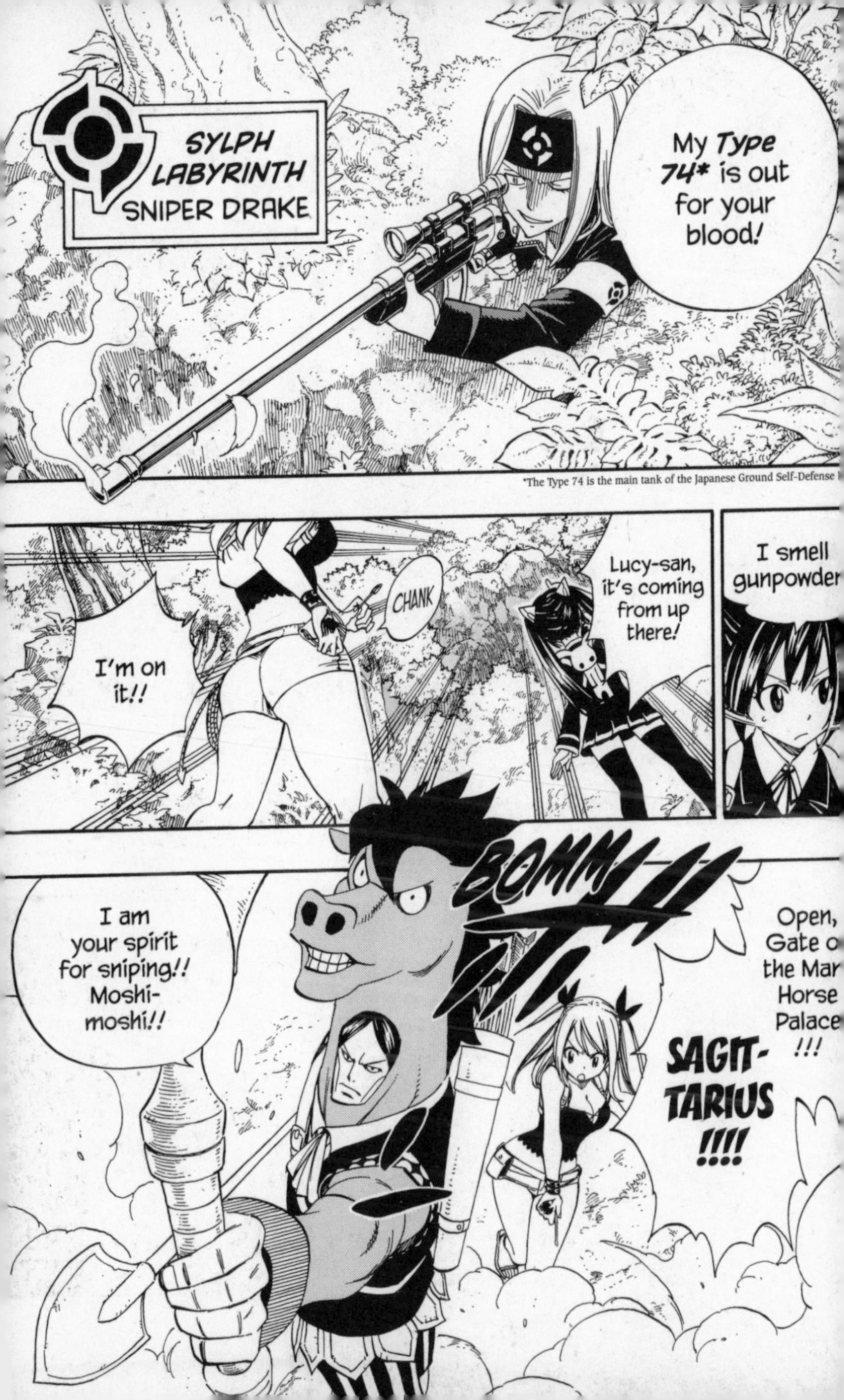
My *Type 74** is out for your blood!
SYLPH LABYRINTH SNIPER DRAKE
I smell gunpowder
Lucy-san, it's coming from up there!
CHANK
I'm on it!!
Open, Gate o the Mar Horse Palace !!!
SAGIT-TARIUS !!!!
I am your spirit for sniping!! Moshi-moshi!!

*The Type 74 is the main tank of the Japanese Ground Self-Defense

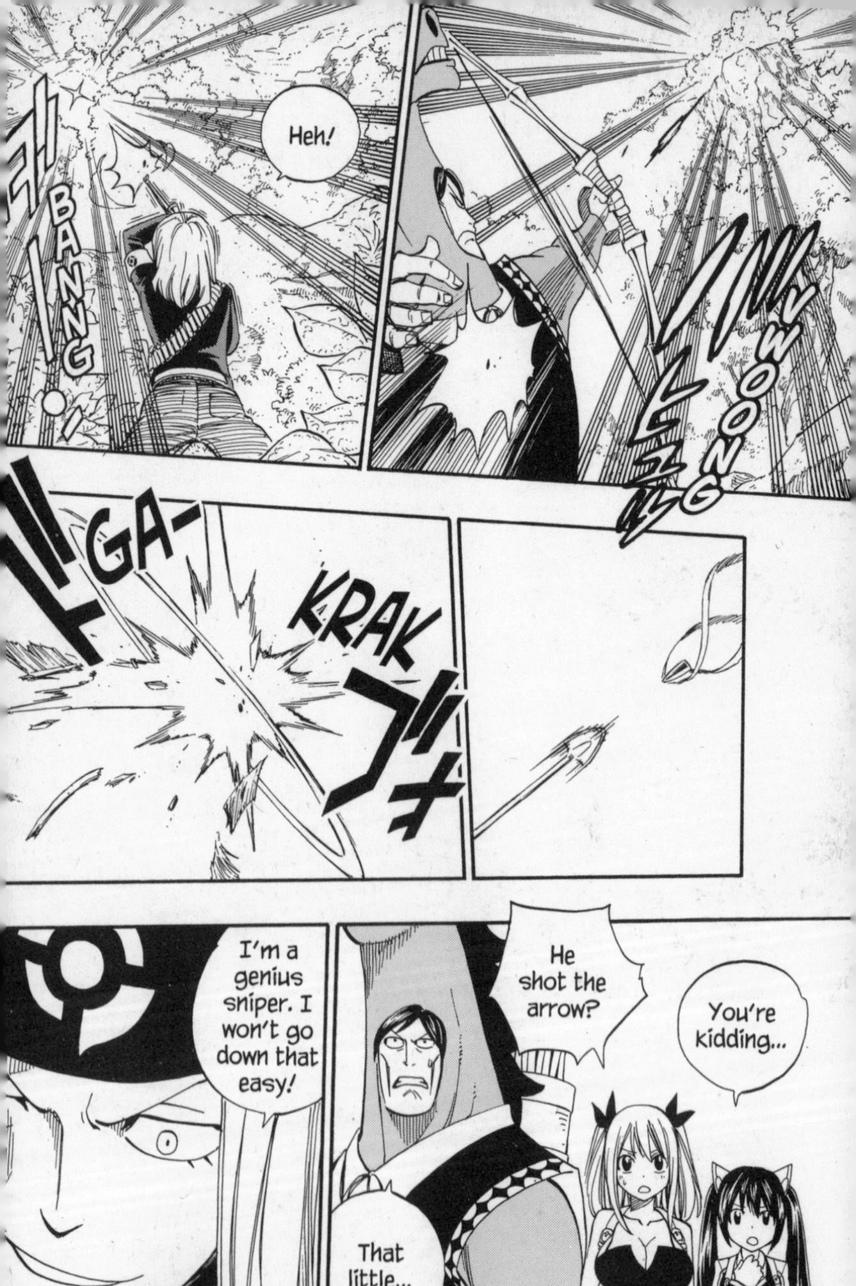
WOONG
Heh!
BANNG!
KRAK
GA-
You're kidding...
He shot the arrow?
That little...
I'm a genius sniper. I won't go down that easy!

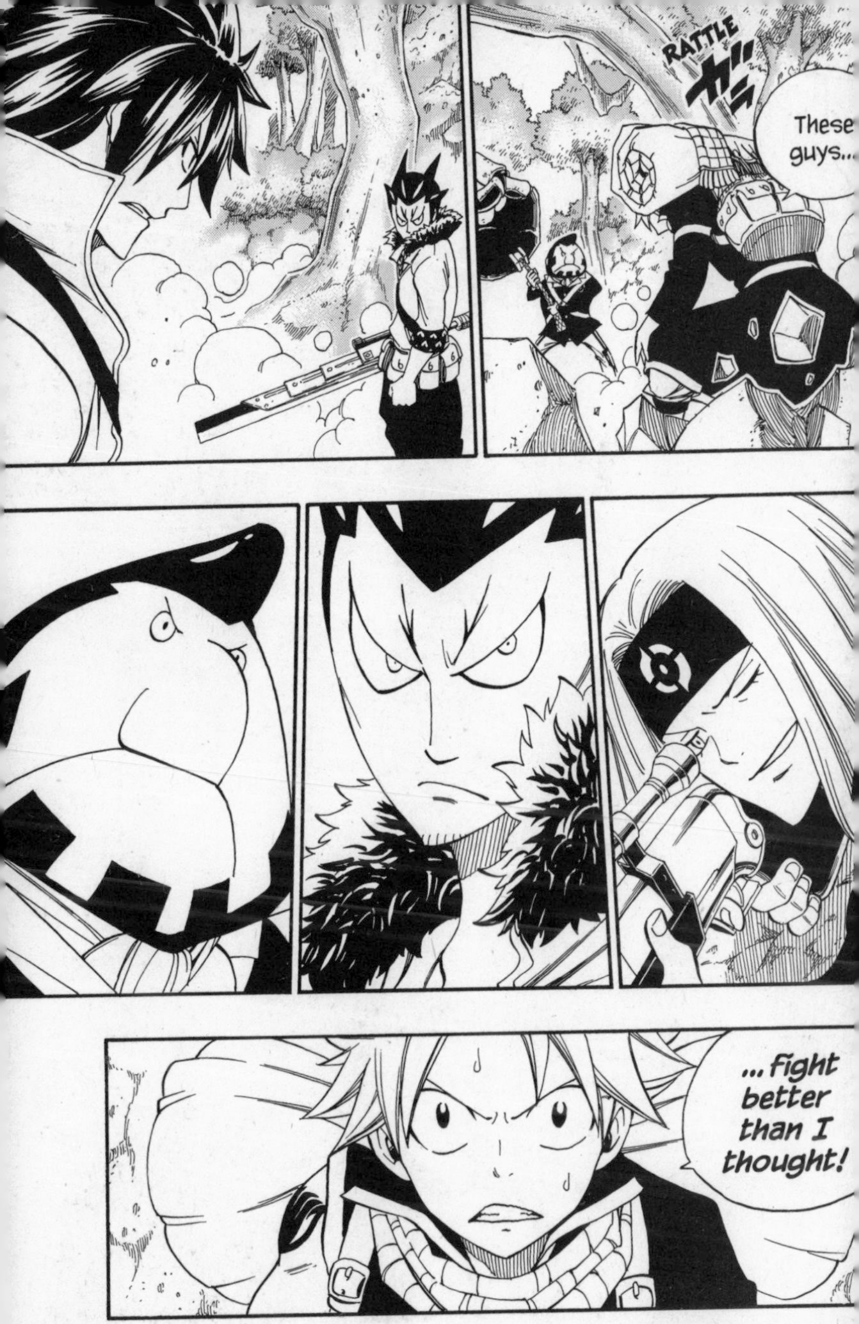
RATTLE
These guys...
...fight better than I thought!

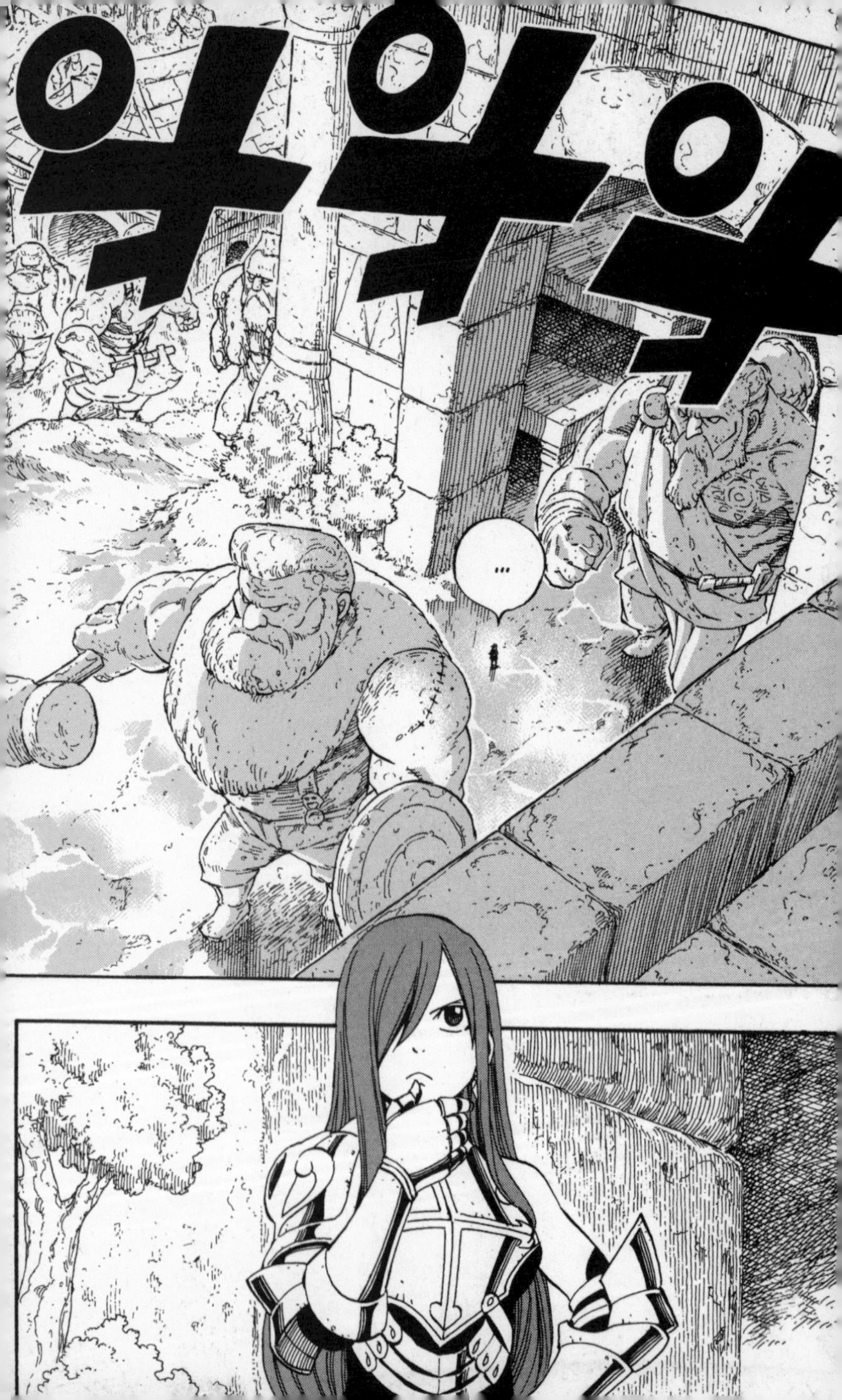

와와와
...

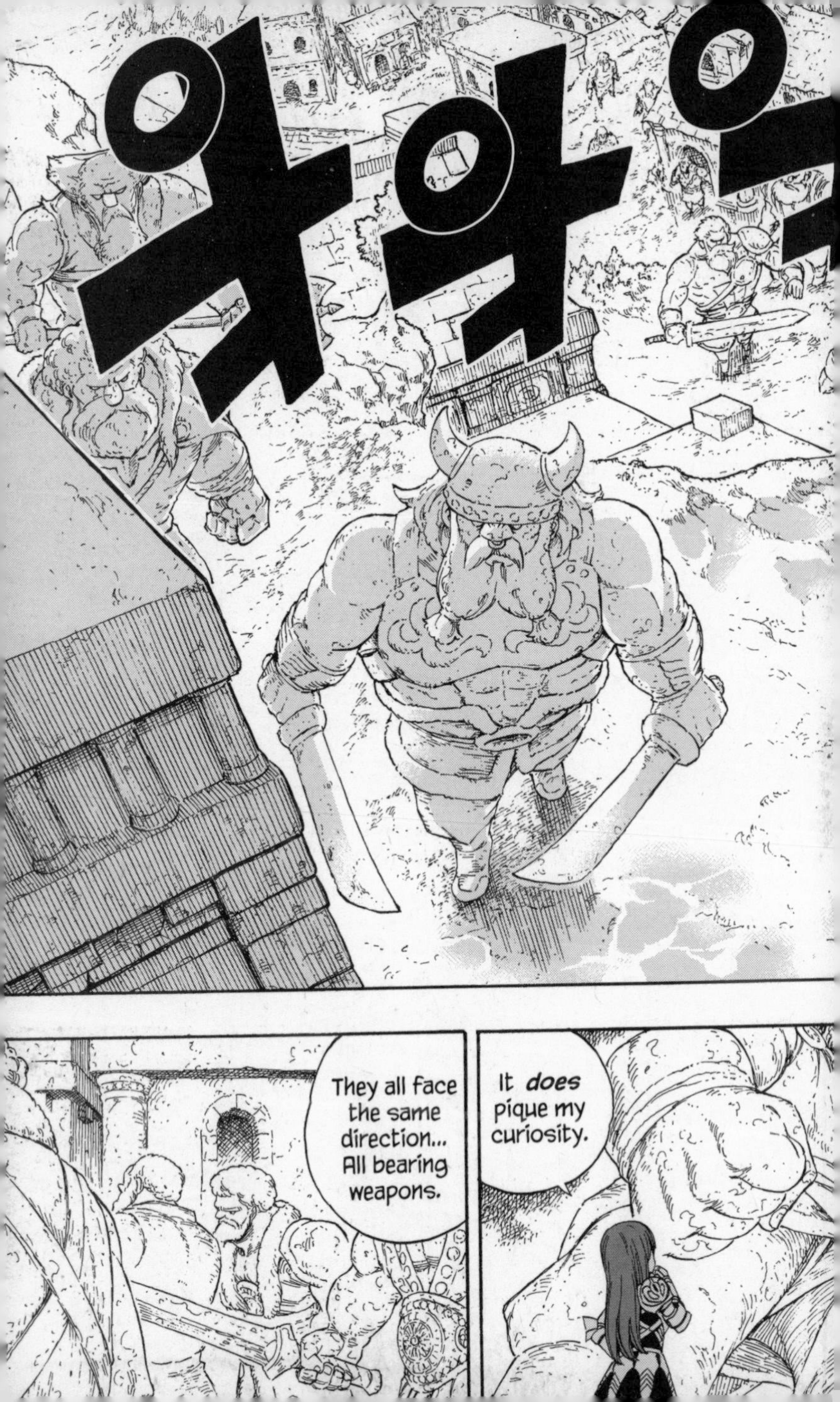
It *does* pique my curiosity.
They all face the same direction... All bearing weapons.

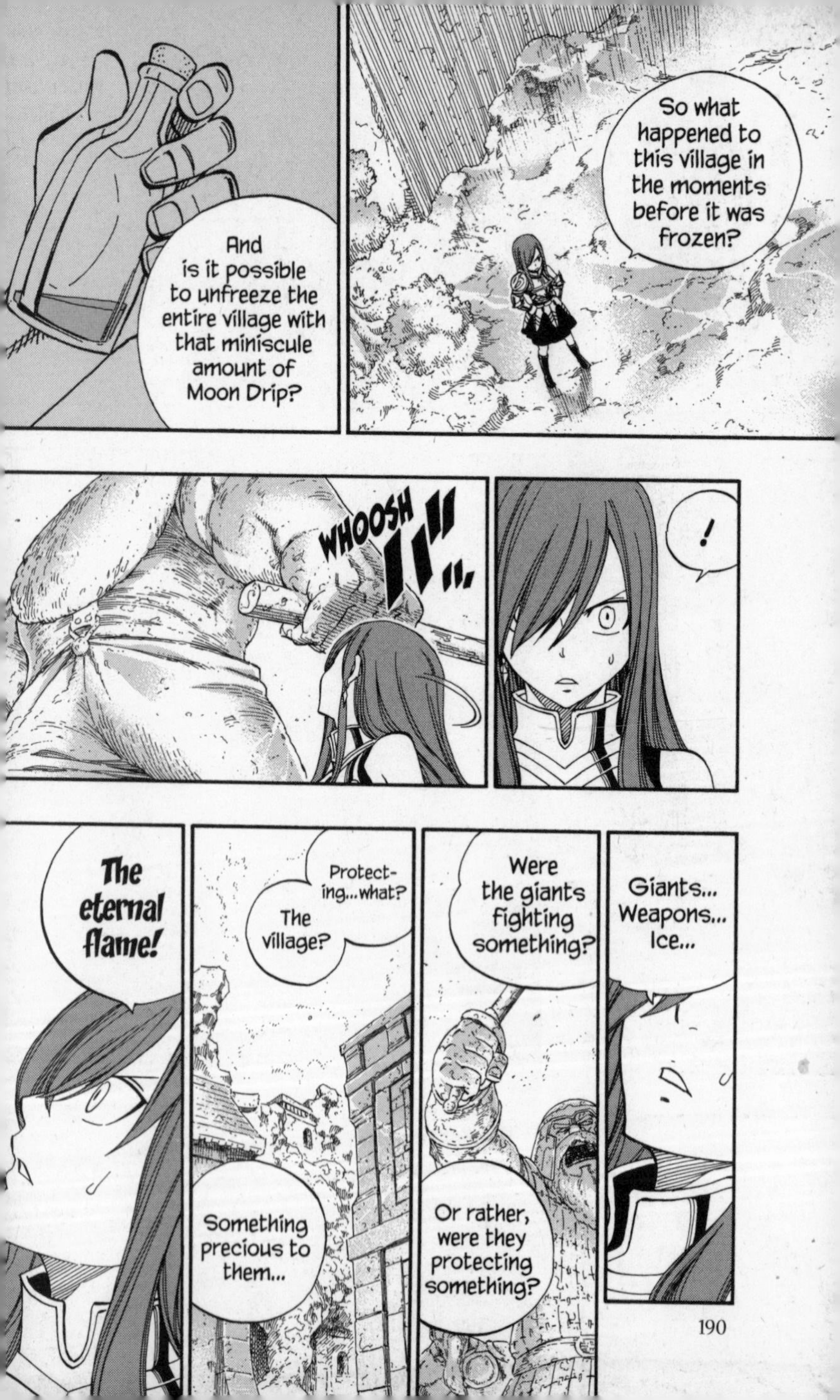
So what happened to this village in the moments before it was frozen?
And is it possible to unfreeze the entire village with that miniscule amount of Moon Drip?
!
WHOOSH
Giants... Weapons... Ice...
Were the giants fighting something?
Or rather, were they protecting something?
Protecting...what?
The village?
Something precious to them...
The eternal flame!

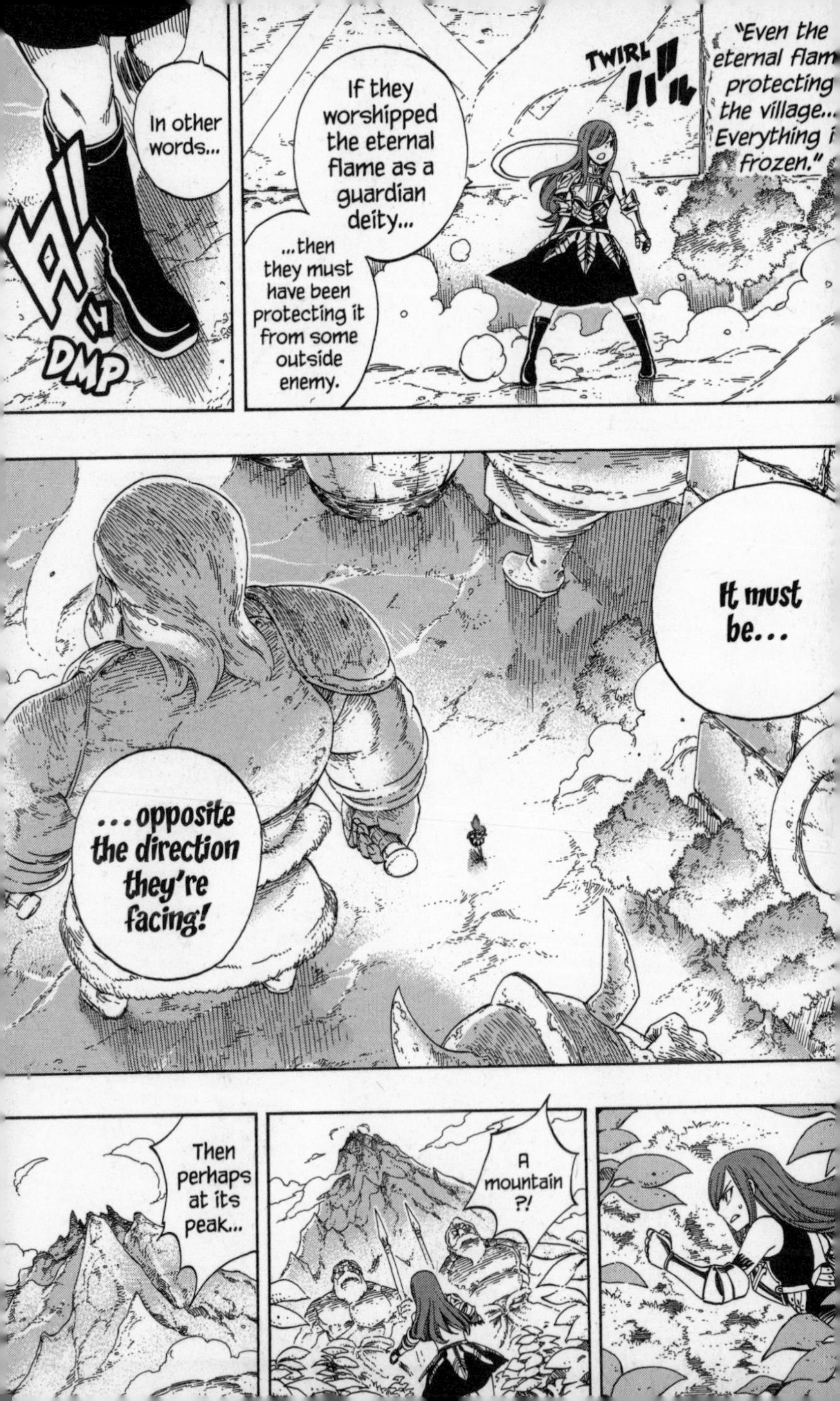
"Even the eternal flam protecting the village... Everything i frozen."
TWIRL
If they worshipped the eternal flame as a guardian deity...
...then they must have been protecting it from some outside enemy.
In other words...
DMP
It must be...
...opposite the direction they're facing!
A mountain?!
Then perhaps at its peak...

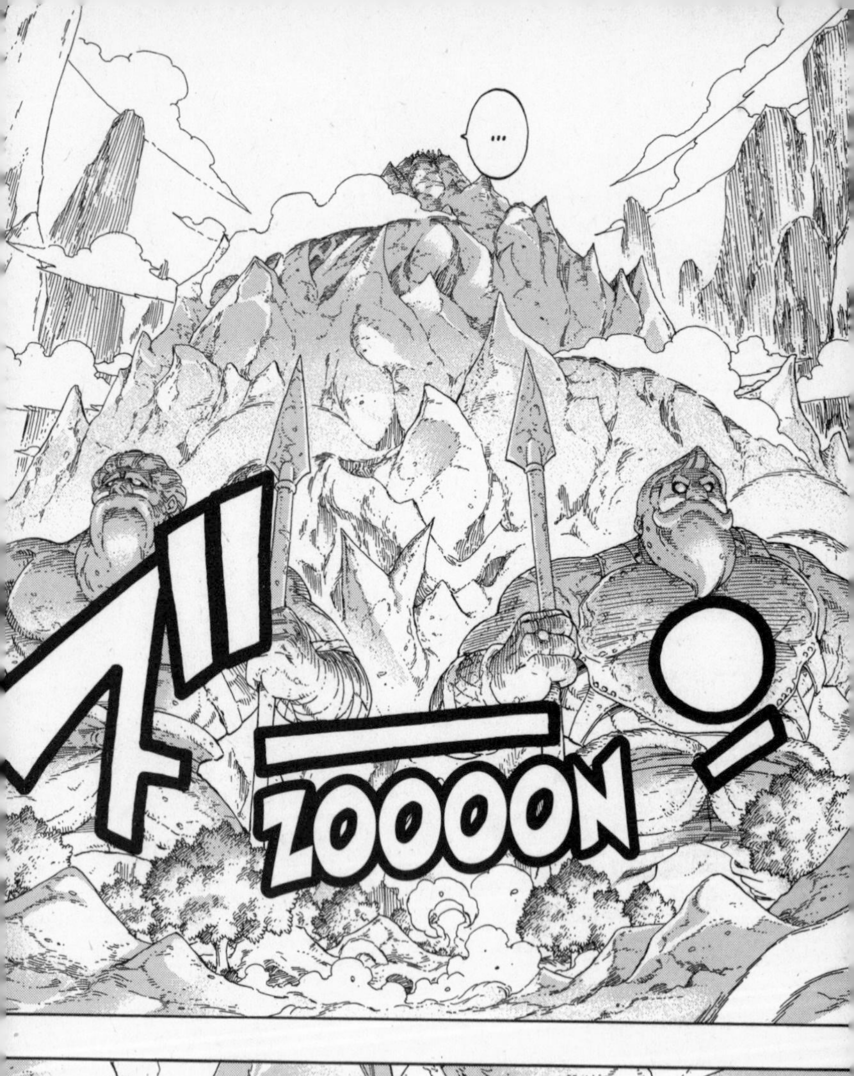
...
ZOOOON

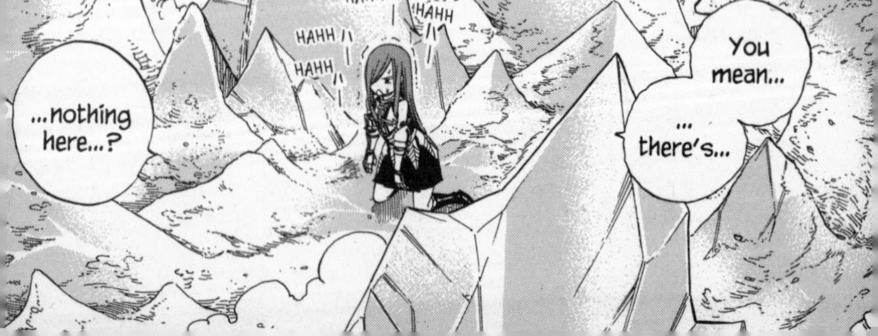
You mean...
... there's...
HAHH
HAHH
HAHH
HAHH
...nothing here...?

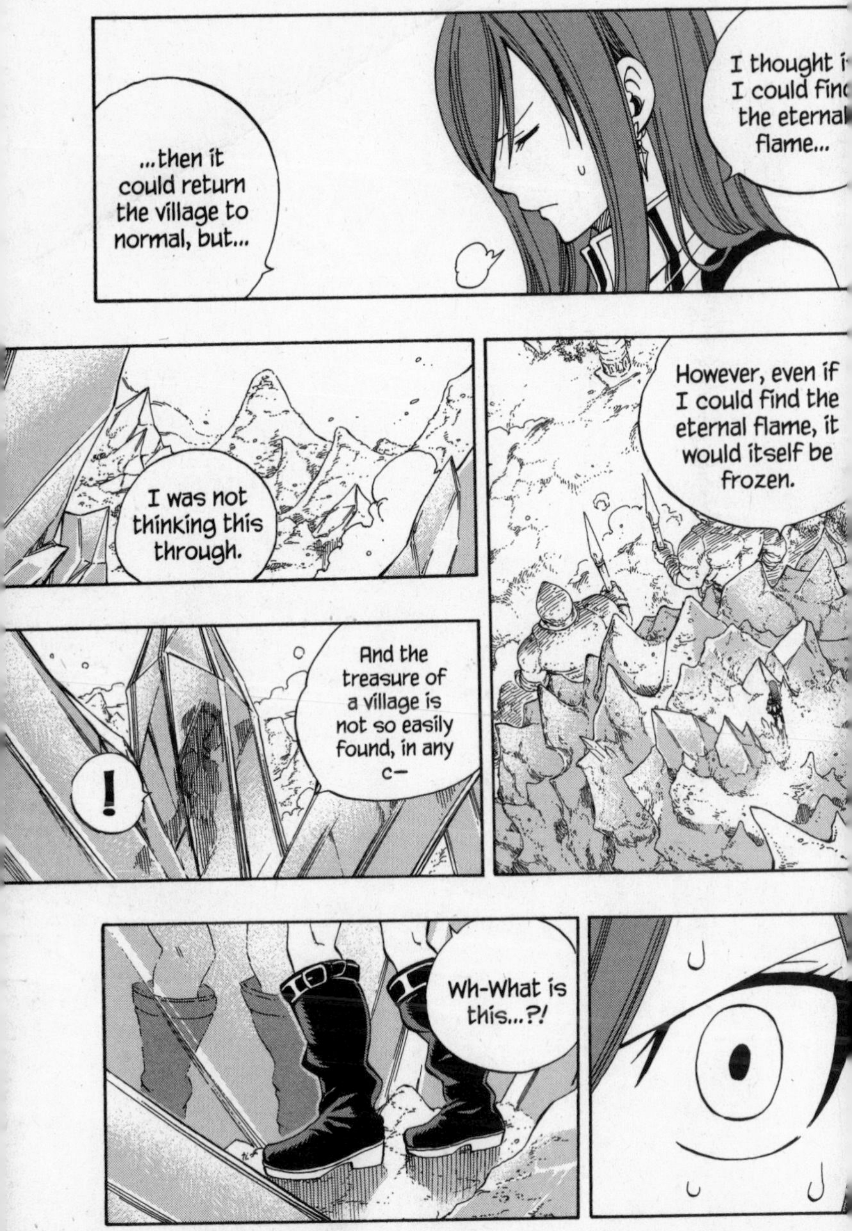
I thought i I could fin the eternal flame...
...then it could return the village to normal, but...
However, even if I could find the eternal flame, it would itself be frozen.
I was not thinking this through.
And the treasure of a village is not so easily found, in any c—
!
Wh-What is this...?!

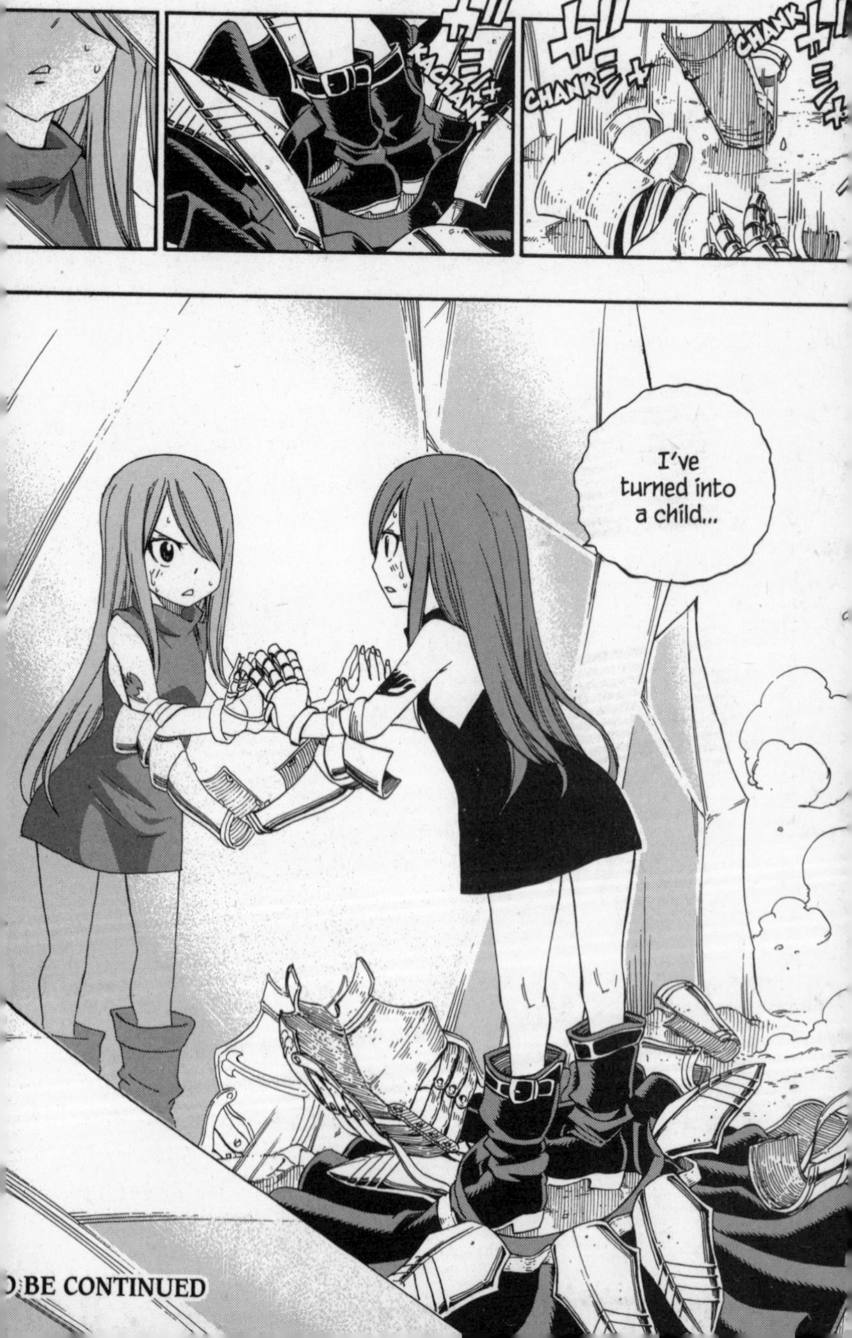

CHANK
CHANK
KACHANK
I've turned into a child...
BE CONTINUED

Afterword

The Grand Magic Games arc is over! And it was long! So long! I wonder how many characters made an appearance? I counted up to eighty, but afterwards, I just stopped counting. I'd like to explain it a little if you don't mind.

When we were planning chapter 337, "The Golden Grasslands," there was a disagreement. It was between "hard to understand" and "the feeling you get when something is hard to understand." In other words, it isn't an easy chapter to figure out. Normally a rule for shonen manga is that it should be easy to understand. And I'm always keeping that rule in mind when I make my stories. For just about every chapter, I'm always trying to twist ideas around in my mind to find ways to make difficult concepts easier to get. So what it came down to is the decision to make chapter 337 a "difficult to understand" chapter. Of the two opinions I mentioned above, we chose the latter. Well, we've been at this a long time, so it's not a bad idea to mix things up with a little of this kind of thing. So we're back to normal time, and where was that place that Future Lucy went to? I have an answer, but I've decided not to talk about it. Pick your own answer, and that'll be the correct one. Also chapters 338-343, six chapters, were all done in the magazine over the course of only two weeks. Now that was an undertaking, but the reaction was big and overwhelmingly positive, so I was really happy with that. If I get the chance, I'd like to do some more fun, special projects like that! By the way, in 338, there were Numbermen! (people who are numbered 1 – 8) hidden in there. Did you find them all?

ntinued from the
ft-hand page.

Mira: Such a thing may come up in the future, so look forward to hearing about it!

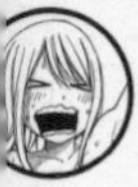

: And I'm going to get that key!! Count on it!

Mira: I'll never give it to you.

Lucy: But you ***just*** said that you didn't have it!

Mira: Next question!

I was really moved by that one minute that Ultear made. But wouldn't Future Rogue and the dragons have seen what happens in the minute too?

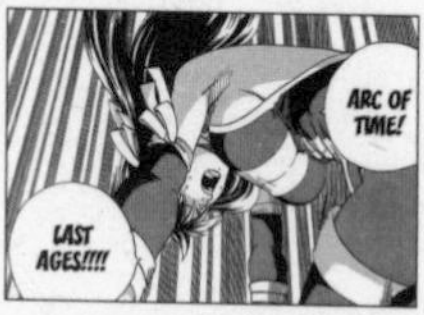
ARC OF TIME!
LAST AGES!!!!

Lucy: I was running for my life at the time, so I didn't even notice it.

Mira: Okay, this wasn't explained well enough in the course of the story, but Future Rogue and the dragons had all passed through time into a different era, right?

Lucy: Yes, that's right.

Mira: And since they're people for whom time is already a bit warped, they didn't even feel the extra minute that Ultear had created.

Lucy: So it was a minute that only people who were from our particular timeline could feel.

Mira: Yes. It's only a minute... But in that minute there were a lot of lives that got saved.

Lucy: I think...she was really heroic there.

Mira: And now the last question for this column.

Was that scene where Lucy got nude really necessary?

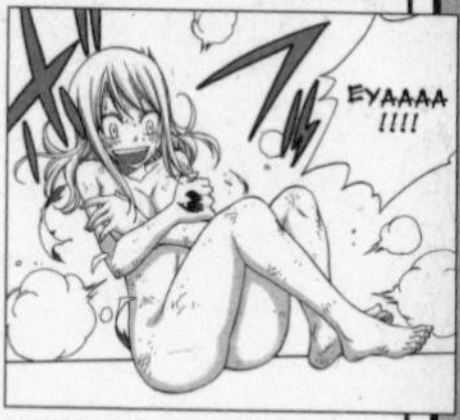
EYAAAA
!!!!

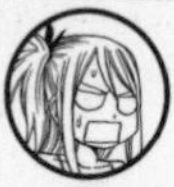

: It certainly was ***not*** necessary!!

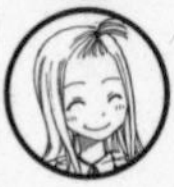

: Still, I predicted it in Volume 37, and it turned out just like I said!

Lucy: Come on!! It's because you say those stupid things that the author is then forced to draw the darned thing!

"Those stupid things" from Vol. 37, page 196.

Mira: Yep! ♥ Actually, Lucy, Carla had a dream about you suddenly becoming nude in front of a huge number of people.

Mira: About that... Many of our readers may not know this, but the magazine installments (in Weekly Shonen Magazine) are published far in advance of the graphic novel volumes.

Lucy: I think I kinda knew that.

Mira: So when 37 was published, Lucy's nude scene had already appeared in the magazine. Or at least it had already been drawn.

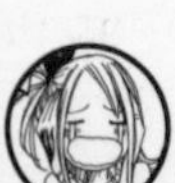

: So it ***wasn't*** Carla's prediction after all!!

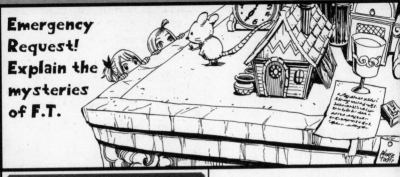

Emergency Request! Explain the mysteries of F.T.

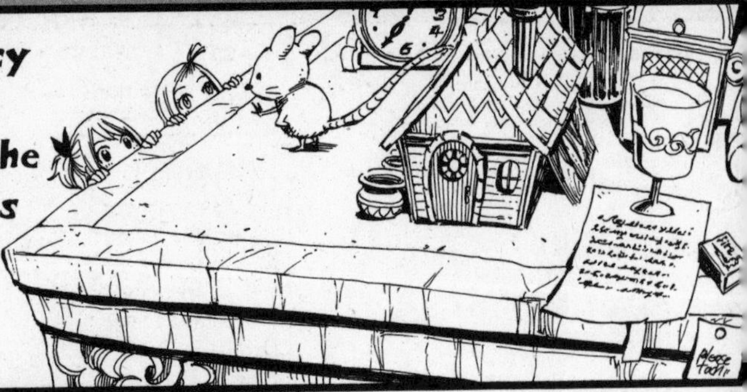

Somewhere in Magnolia...

Lucy: Hi, everybody!

Mira: When our corner was missing from the last volume, I thought it was all over for us!

Lucy: Didn't we have a conversation like this before?

Mira: Here's the first question of the column!

After seeing Makarov's and Ivan's ***HAIR*** *I fear for Laxus's future.*

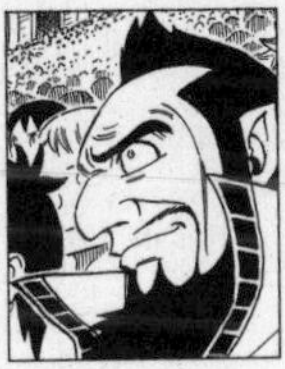

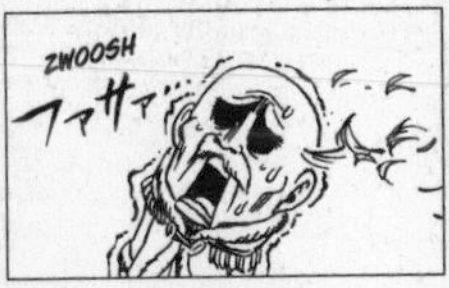
ZWOOSH
ファサァ

Lucy: Awww...

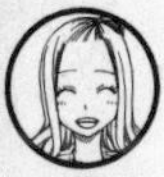
: I think he should just accept it as lost.

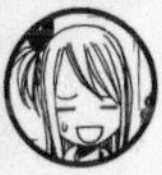
: Hey! That's awful!

Mira: I don't see much help for it.

Lucy: But isn't this something you really can't predict?

Mira: I suppose. Come to think of it, there's me and Lisanna and Elfman. None of our hair matches the others.

Lucy: I get the feeling that your case is a little different from this, though.

Mira: Now the next question.

Is there a key that calls the king of the Celestial Spirits?

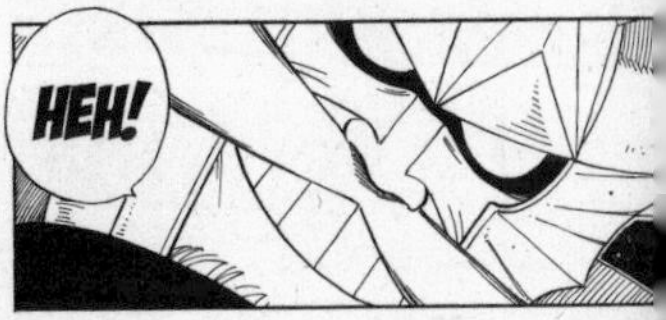
HEH!

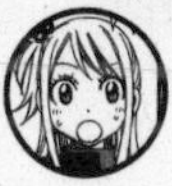
: Oh, yeah!! I want to know!!

Mira: Even if there is, we can't talk about it here.

Lucy: Huh? Why is that?

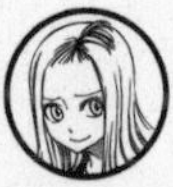
: Heh heh heh... Actually, I own

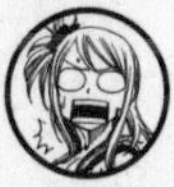
: Whaaa...?!!

Mira: I'm kidding, of course. What did you expect?

Lucy: Can we stop with the disjointe lies, please?

Continued on t right-hand pa

TAIL
d'ART

The Fairy Tail Guild is looking for illustrations! Please send in your art on a postcard or at postcard size, and do it in black pen, okay? Those chosen to be published will get a signed mini poster! ♪ Make sure you write your real name and address on the back of your illustration!

Chiba Prefecture, Kōki Itsukida

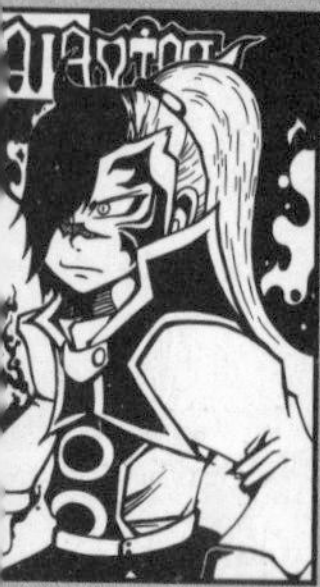

is person did a great epresenting the ks and whites in the ei-ryû (White Shadow on).

Okinawa Prefecture, Ryôma

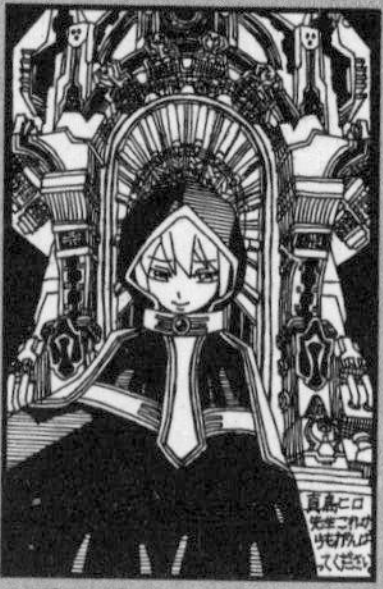

▲ That Eclipse Door is incredibly hard to draw, and he drew it... Gotta hand it to you.

Aichi Prefecture, Minori Fukui

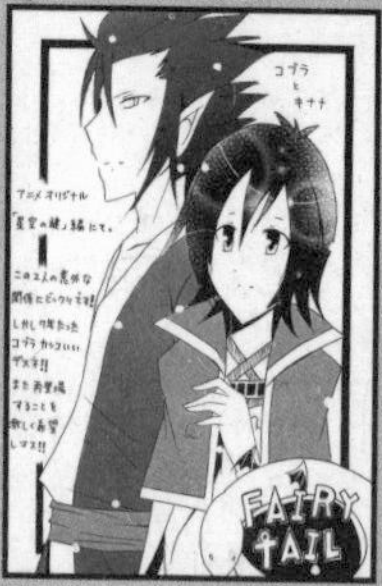
FAIRY TAIL

▲ Two of the main characters that influence an original story for the anime. Cobra and Kinana. Kind of nice, huh?

Hiroshima Prefecture, Taichi Kobayashi

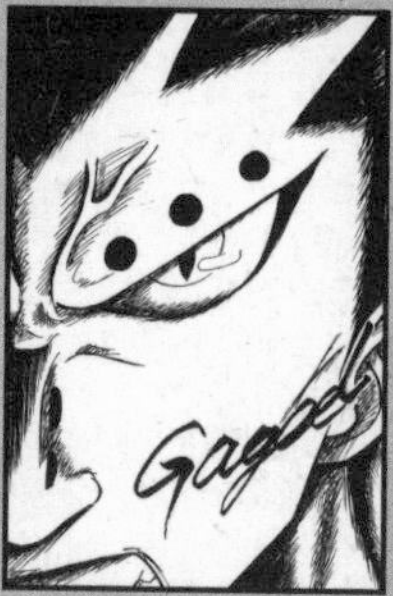

▲ Whoa!! This one's cool!! It's hard to draw large eyes well!

le Prefecture, Yûha Yamamoto

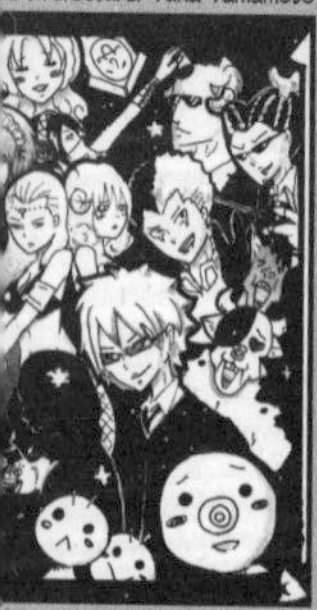

lestial Spirits mble!! It must have a lot of work drawing those spirits!

Osaka, Queen

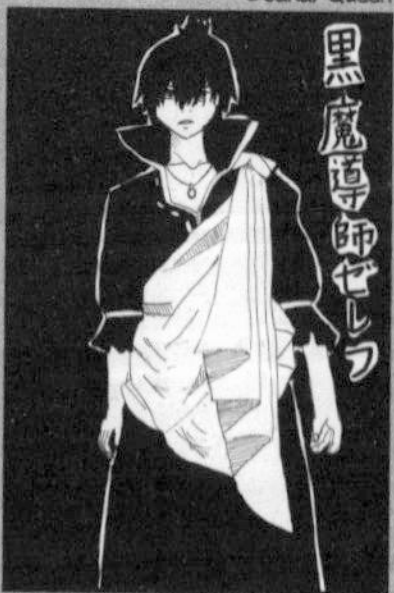
黒魔導師ゼレフ

▲ Is Zeref finally a part of the story again? Keep your eyes open after this!

Hokkaido, Hai-chan

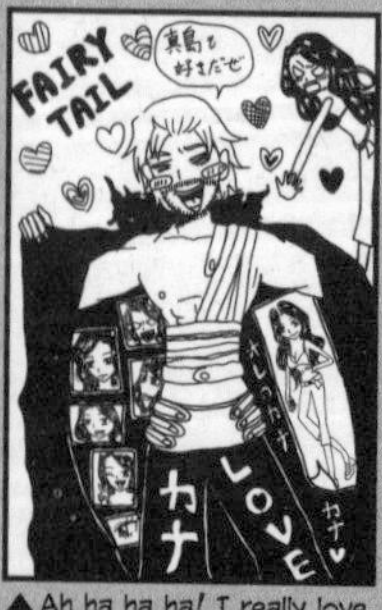
FAIRY TAIL
カナ
LOVE

▲ Ah ha ha ha! I really love this drawing! Gildarts's character really comes out in it!

Okayama Prefecture, Kagura-love

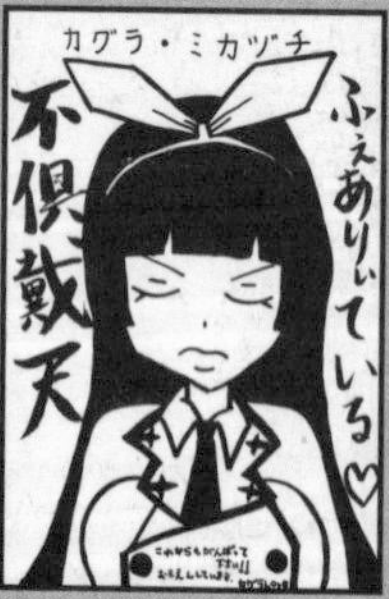
カグラ・ミカヅチ
不倶戴天
ふぇありぃている

▲ Kagura is so popular!! Someday I want her to come back!

Send to Hiro Mashima, Kodansha Comics
451 Park Ave. South, 7th Floor New York, NY 10016

FAIRY
GUILD

Aichi Prefecture, Miran

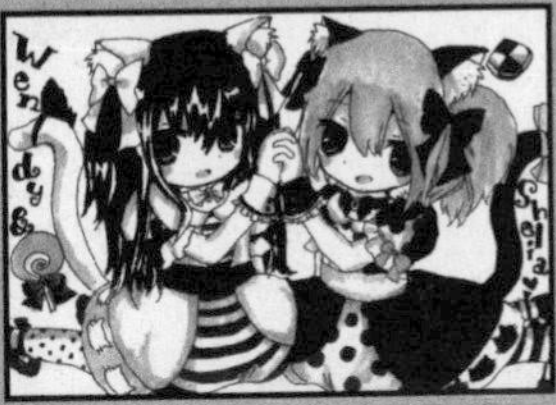

How cute! And they're both wearing animal ears!! It looks good on them!

Aichi Prefecture, Misaki Sugawara

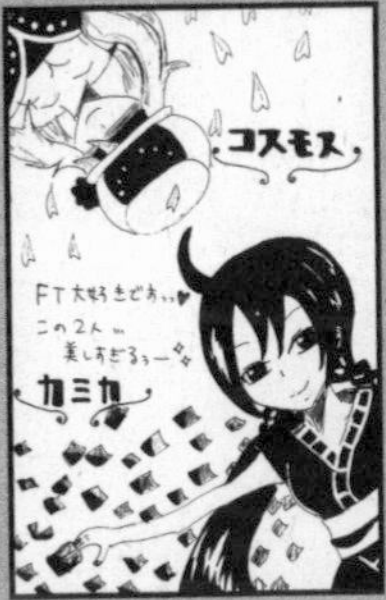

コスモス
カミカ

▲These two have a quiet popularity. They don't seem like executioners, huh?

Nara Prefecture, Kaito

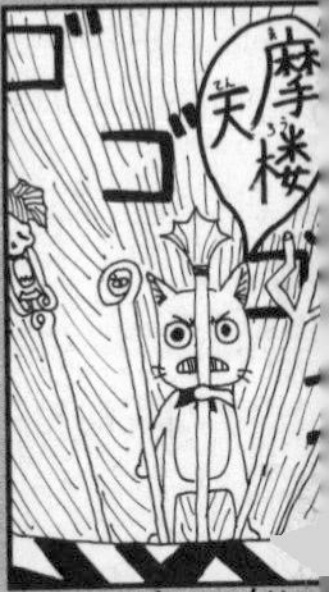

▲This one's cute! Hap
what do you think you'
doing?!

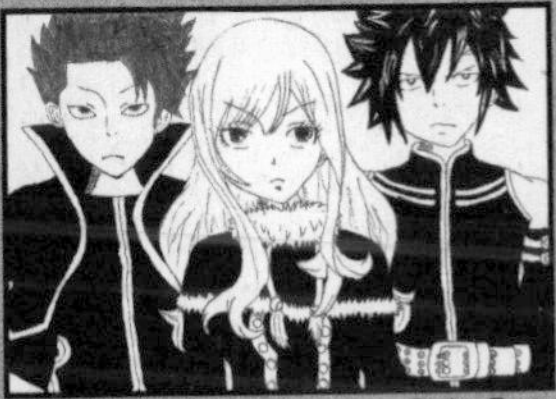

For a while, these three characters have made peace with their relationships. But what happens from here on out?

Osaka, Roruru

REJECTION CORNER

Aichi Prefecture, Ayumu Yamashita

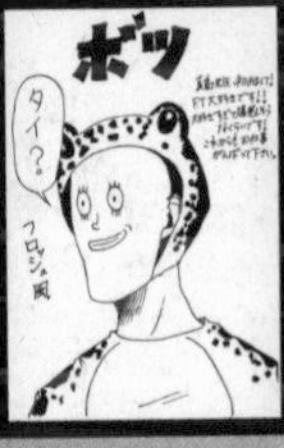

ボツ

Hey! What do you, think you're wearing?! Tai-tai!!

Kanagawa Prefecture, Kōta Takahashi

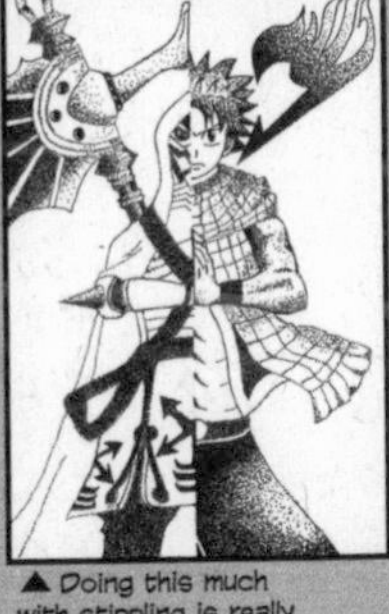

▲Doing this much with stippling is really impressive! That is cool ink work!

Niigata Prefecture, Pikapo

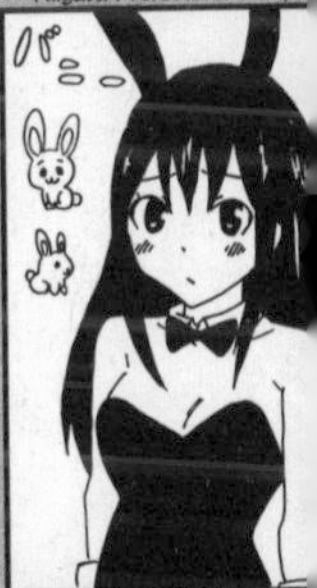

▲Wendy with a little b
sexiness is a good thir
The bunnies are cute t

By sending in letters or postcards, you give us permission to give your name, address, postal code, and any other information you include to the artist as-is. Please keep that in mind.

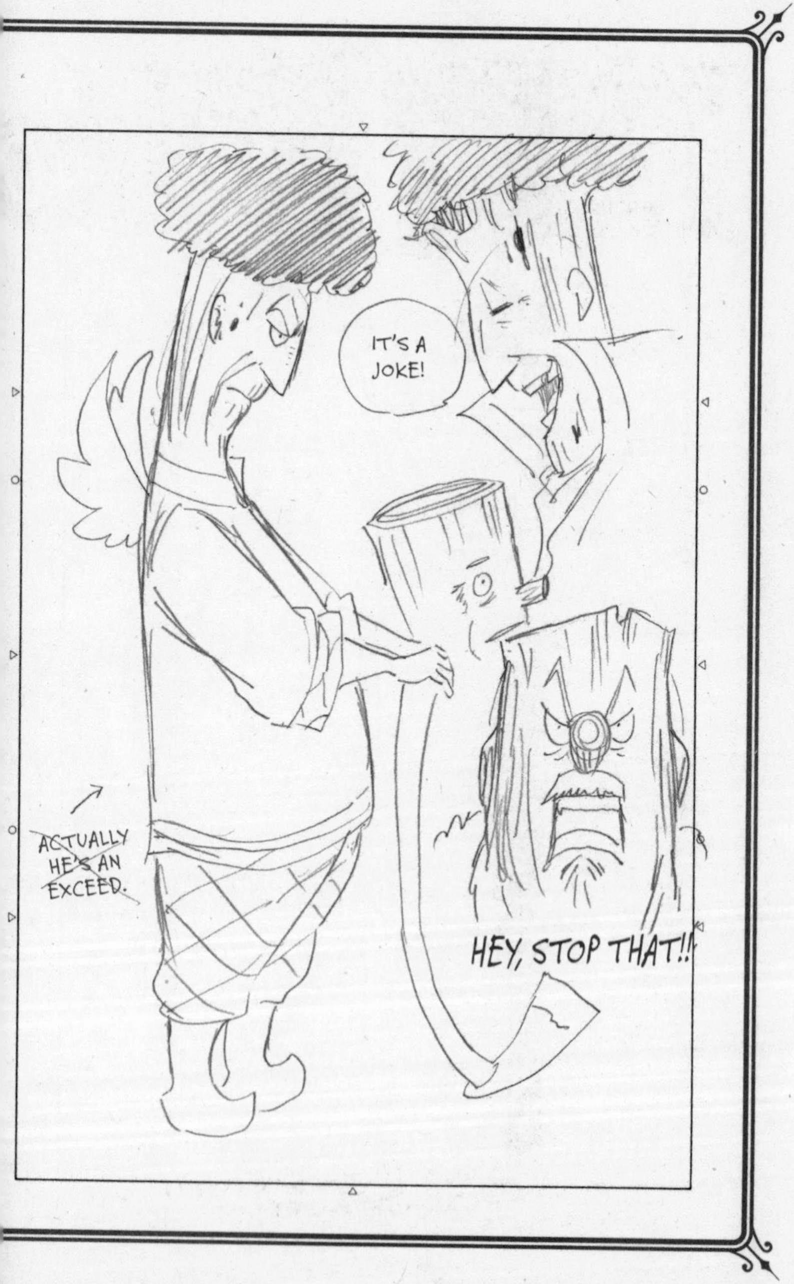

IT'S A JOKE!
HEY, STOP THAT!!
ACTUALLY HE'S AN EXCEED.

FAIRY TAIL フェアリーテイル 40

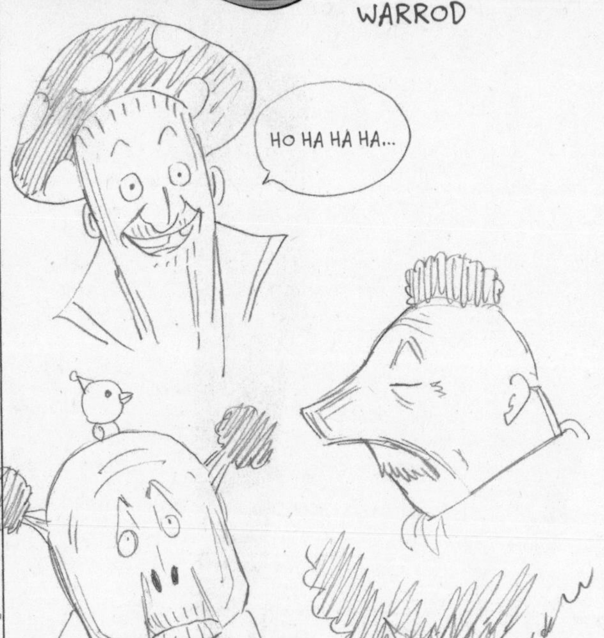

HIRO 真島ヒロ MASHIMA

FROM HIRO MASHIMA

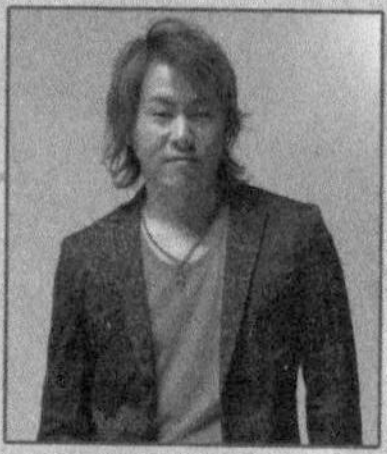

This has become a really long series!
But it's still going on.
With this volume, the extremely long Grand Magic Games comes to an end, and we're already into a new story! I plan to introduce a lot of new characters too. Look for them!

Original Jacket Design: Hisao Ogawa

Translation Notes:

Japanese is a tricky language for most Westerners, and translation is often more art than science. For your edification and reading pleasure, here are notes on some of the places where we could have gone in a different direction with our translation of the work, or where a Japanese cultural reference is used.

Page 23, Festival

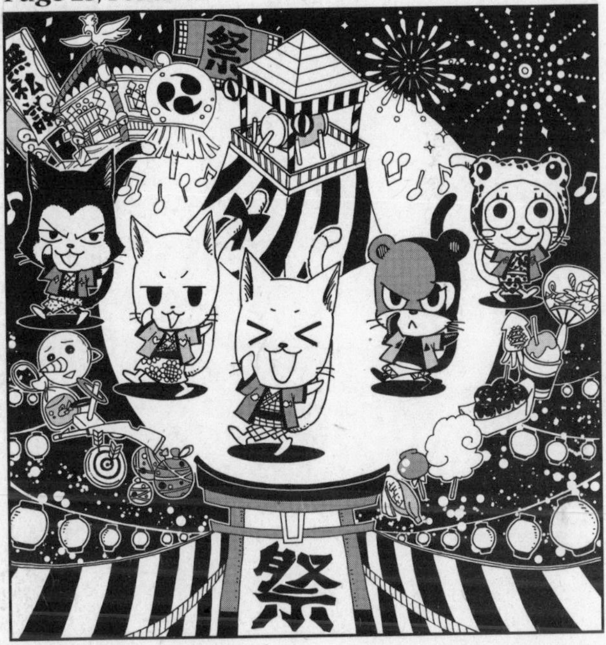
祭
祭

All the elements on this page, except Plue and the cats, are commonly found in summertime festivals *(matsuri)* in Japan.

· All the cats are wearing the light cotton kimono called *yukata* while doing a dance around a pavilion at the center of the festival grounds that commonly hold the festival's organizers and the musical entertainment.

Going clockwise from the top…

· The festival of Obon, held in mid-August, often has fireworks.

· The round fan called an *uchiwa* is used to keep oneself cool.

· Some festival edible treats are fried squid on a stick, shaved ice, takoyaki (octopus balls), cotton candy, candied apples, and corn on the cob.

· The red painted *torii* archway is festooned with paper lanterns and a large banner with the *kanji* for *matsuri*, which means festival.

· Games at a festival include water-balloon yoyos, archery, target shooting, ring-toss, and goldfish catching.

· In the upper left hand corner are common decorations found at festivals.

ge 169, Like, Heavy and Duun

h of these three characters have certain speech patterns that identify them. To rt with, the character codenamed Hammer Rala says, "Duun." He says that in Japa- se too. The character codenamed Sniper Drake (the blonde) speaks like a standard slightly dim high-school guy. The one codenamed Sword Hiroshi always uses the anese word *chô,* which means "very" in certain *kanji* compounds. I've replaced the rd with "heavy," and used it in pretty much the same way he uses *chô*.

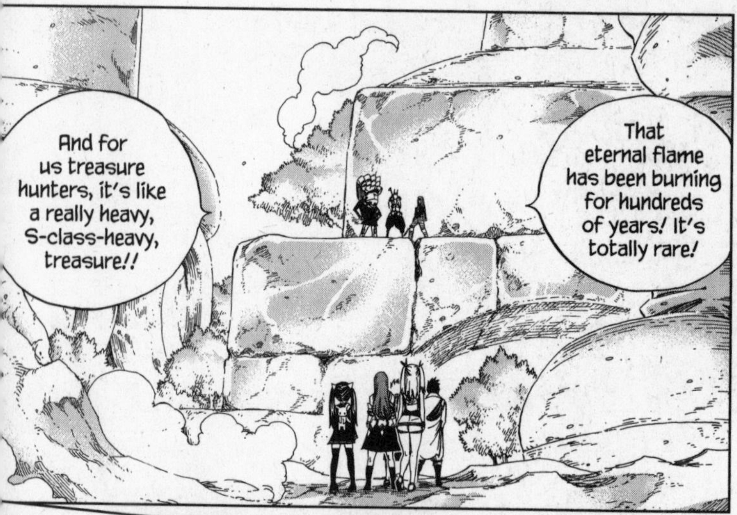
That eternal flame has been burning for hundreds of years! It's totally rare!
And for us treasure hunters, it's like a really heavy, S-class-heavy, treasure!!

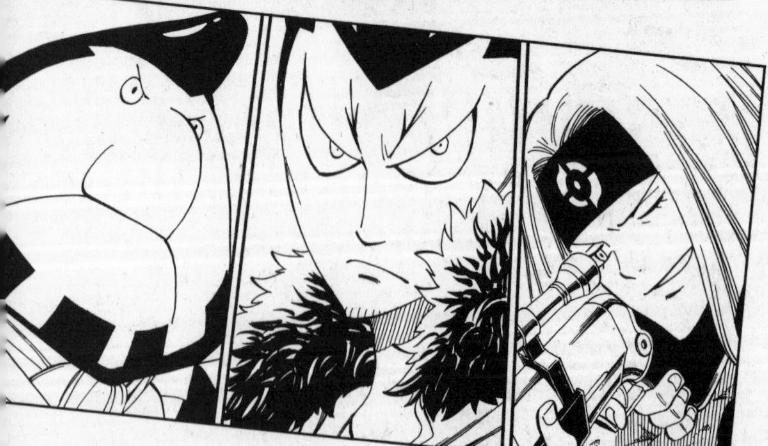

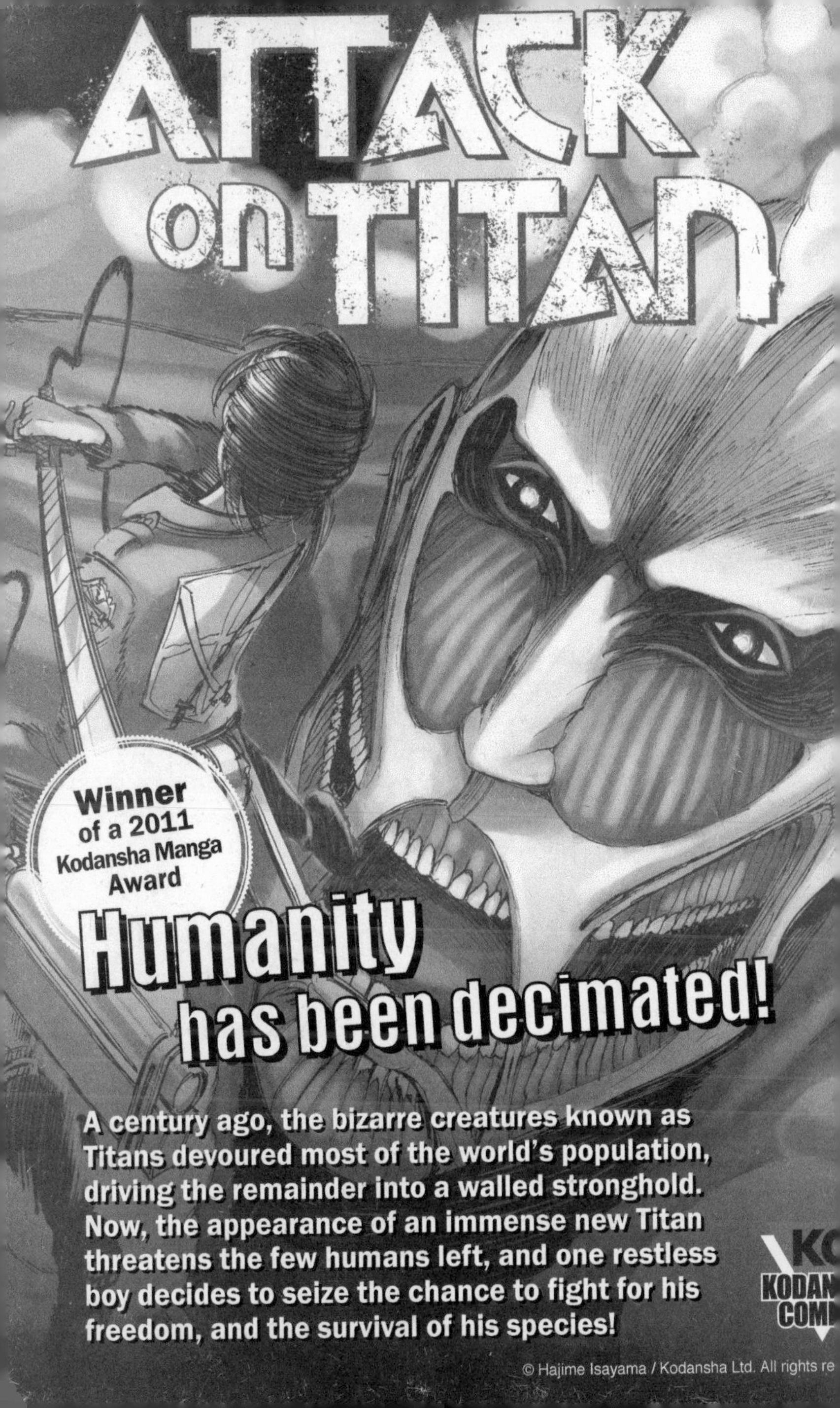
ATTACK ON TITAN
Winner of a 2011 Kodansha Manga Award
Humanity has been decimated!
A century ago, the bizarre creatures known as Titans devoured most of the world's population, driving the remainder into a walled stronghold. Now, the appearance of an immense new Titan threatens the few humans left, and one restless boy decides to seize the chance to fight for his freedom, and the survival of his species!
KODAN
COM
© Hajime Isayama / Kodansha Ltd. All rights re

SANKAREA
undying love

"I ONLY LIKE ZOMBIE GIRLS."

hiro has an unusual connection to zombie movies. He doesn't feel bad for survivors – he wants to comfort the undead girls they slaughter! When pet passes away, he brews a resurrection potion. He's discovered by al heiress Sanka Rea. d she serves as his first test subject!

Fairy Tail volume 40 is a work of fiction. Names, characters, places, and incider are the products of the author's imagination or are used fictitiously. Any resemblance to actual events, locales, or persons, living or dead, is entirely coincidental.

A Kodansha Comics Trade Paperback Original.

Published in the United States by Kodansha Comics, an imprint of Kodansha USA Publishing, LLC, New York.

Publication rights for this English edition arranged through Kodansha Ltd., Tokyo.

First published in Japan in 2013 by Kodansha Ltd., Tokyo
ISBN 978-1-61262-417-4

Printed in the United States of America.

www.kodanshacomics.com

9 8 7 6 5 4 3 2 1

Translation: William Flanagan
Lettering: AndWorld Design
Editing: Ben Applegate

TOMARE!

[STOP!]

You're going the wrong way!

Manga is a completely different type of reading experience.

To start at the *beginning*, go to the *end*!

's right! Authentic manga is read the traditional Japanese way—
right to left, exactly the *opposite* of how American books are
. It's easy to follow: Just go to the other end of the book and read
page—and each panel—from right side to left side, starting at
top right. Now you're experiencing manga as it was meant to be!